HEAVEN:
GOD'S CHALLENGES

JAMES R. FIELDING

ARCHWAY
PUBLISHING

Archway Publishing books may be ordered through booksellers or by contacting:

Archway Publishing
1663 Liberty Drive
Bloomington, IN 47403
www.archwaypublishing.com
844-669-3957

Scripture quotations are from the Holy Bible, King James Version (Authorized Version). First published in 1611. Quoted from the KJV Classic Reference Bible, Copyright © 1983 by The Zondervan Corporation.

ISBN: 978-1-6657-4633-5 (sc)
ISBN: 978-1-6657-4634-2 (e)

Library of Congress Control Number: 2023911676

Print information available on the last page.

Archway Publishing rev. date: 08/23/2023

CONTENTS

ACKNOWLEDGMENTS

Special thanks to my wife for all her support and for providing answers to my questions about the Bible. She once taught a class in Bible as Literature and has helped me enormously with finding, interpreting, and deciding whether or not to include various verses. Many thanks to the local public library staff for helping with word processing and editing. Finally, I thank my colleagues in the local free thought organization for friendship and encouragement while the book took shape.

The biblical references are from *The Holy Bible*, Red Letter Edition, King James Version.

PREFACE

More people in the world believe in an afterlife, a Heaven, than do not. In the USA 70% of adults believe in Heaven. Based on popularity there are five main religions in the world, each having somewhat different views as to how to be saved, get to Heaven, and have everlasting life. Worldwide somewhat over five billion people believe in Heaven. A reassuring belief is that the deceased go to Heaven to meet God face-to-face and be together with family and friends. Religious books, like the King James Bible, refer to Heaven many times. But is Heaven just wishful thinking? Is Heaven a reasonable concept?

In the following chapters, the challenges to God presented by Heaven are discussed. The world holds eight billion people with ages ranging from newborn to over 120. Over fifty-six million deaths occur each year and 300 different ways to die are seen. Heaven is complicated because the deceased come from 195 countries with 7,139 spoken languages. Over 100 billion people have already died but only four people besides Jesus are known to have risen to Heaven, two were deceased. The other two went to Heaven and then returned to earth. How many more of the deceased are in Heaven and in what form?

If bodies are decomposed in the ground, mummified, cremated, frozen, disintegrated in a plane crash or lost at sea, what/who goes to Heaven? The soul? Can the soul communicate? Does the soul carry a person's memories and history? Topics that are discussed include salvation, Jesus, the soul, causes of death, burials and cemeteries, mummies and cryonics, embryos and fetuses that miscarry, still births, the brain, disabilities, illnesses, pain, prodigies and geniuses, Heaven's language, human evolution, Heaven and the universe, age of Heaven's residents, and much more.

Emphasis is on the challenges God faces to establish and maintain a Heaven as depicted by religious people and the Bible. Numerous verses from the Bible and many books, magazines, and newspapers are cited in the discussions.

1

DIRECT REFERENCES
TO HEAVEN

MOST PEOPLE THINK about Heaven quite often and in a positive
manner. Many feel that deceased friends and family are in Heaven and
they will meet them there. Here are some examples of how people refer to
Heaven:

- Preston (not his real name) was the president of his high school
  class. He was an athlete and a long-distance runner. At the start
  of his senior year, he broke his neck in an accident and became a
  quadriplegic. But the paralysis did not hold him back as he grad-
  uated from high school and then from college. He worked many
  years doing things to aid the disabled. When he died, a high school
  buddy said, "One of the things Preston talked about was that once
  he got to Heaven he wanted to run all the way across Heaven
  because running was one of the things he really missed." Preston
  believed that not only was he going to Heaven but that he would
  no longer be paralyzed and that Heaven was a physical place that
  would allow him to run from one side to the other.
- A comedian in an interview with Time magazine, was asked if
  when he got to meet his maker, what he would say to him or her?
  He answered, "I've had some thoughts about this. I'd start slowly,

with 'Could I have a little cushion at the bottom of my chair?' Then, 'A place to put my feet would be wonderful.' And then I might end up saying, 'Uh, where did you put Hedy Lamarr? Is she in an apartment near my place?'"

- The murder of a young girl was solved twenty-two years after the murder. The detective who worked the case said, "I know she is in Heaven because she could not have done anything bad in her short lifetime."

- A sixteen-year-old kidnap victim was back home after the terrible ordeal. She said, "God needed two perfect angels up there with him to get me home." Undoubtedly, she was referring to her parents.

- A basketball player in a Big Ten school had a virus that weakened him considerably and kept him from playing that season. After recovering his health and back to playing, he said, "I'll ask God when I meet him what it was and how he fixed it. But he did something and fixed it for me."

- A fun-loving guy died. His wife said, "He is in Heaven now and having a good time, as always."

- One of the judges on *Dancing with The Stars*, after watching one of the stars dance with his partner said, "My dad is up there watching me. I'm sure your dad is up there watching you and was proud of your performance."

- An eighty-four-year-old felt his heart giving out and, realizing he was going to die, said out loud, "Here I come Lord." He was looking forward to Heaven and seeing God and was confident he would be with God very shortly. But he had to wait because his family got him to the hospital emergency room, he survived that episode, and the next day was fitted with a pacemaker, which kept him alive until he was ninety-four.

- When a country singer Ray was near death, at eighty-seven, he said, "I am at peace. I love Jesus. I'm going to be just fine. Don't worry about me. I'll see you again someday."

- A preacher and author, when interviewed by Time magazine, was asked at what age he would like to die. He answered, "I could die right now and be a happy man. If my son could talk to me from

Heaven – which I don't believe is possible – he'd say, 'Dad, Heaven is a much cooler place than you imagined and I can't wait for you to get here.'" His son had earlier committed suicide.

- A comedian, who died two years short of eighty, just before his death asked to have $100 in small bills put into his sock in his coffin, "just in case there is tipping recommended where I'm going."

- A Big East school vs a Big Ten school, with the latter favored in a non-league basketball game for each, still was predicted to be a competitive game given the two teams were in strong basketball conferences. The Big East school won in what was considered an upset. The coach of the losing team explained the loss by saying, "Players play, tough players win. When I die, I hope they put that on my tombstone, because it'll be the same up in Heaven. Tough angels are going to be better than those other ones (meaning the ones down below). But it hasn't changed since day one."

- In an article in AARP Magazine, a neurologist, upon turning eighty, said, "Some of my patients in their nineties or hundreds say 'I have had a full life and now I am ready to go.' For some of them this means going to Heaven – it is always Heaven rather than hell. I have no belief in (or desire for) any postmortem existence, other than memories of friends and the hope that some of my books may "speak" to people after my death."

- Referring to the death of his wife, Bev, the husband said, "If there is a God I'm gonna see my honey again." And at 5:32 AM in Hawaii, "This is the time she would wake up and climb Koko Head Mountain. Only today, she hiked the stairway to Heaven. We all love you Bev. See you on the other side."

- Two women, best friends from high school days, died of the coronavirus within a week of each other, having gotten ill in their nursing home, transferred to the same hospital and, unknown to either, were only two floors apart. After their death, a friend to both said, "They are up there together, I know that."

- On the light side, the writer of the Calvin and Hobbes comic strip occasionally referred to the afterlife and Heaven. In one strip, Calvin asked his stuffed tiger friend Hobbes, "I wonder where we go when we die."

- After a pause, Hobbes offered, "Pittsburgh?"
- Calvin responds, "you mean if we are good or if we are bad?"
- In another strip, Calvin asks Hobbes, "Hobbes, what do you think happens to us when we die?"
- Hobbes thinks for a moment and then answers, "I think we play saxophone for an all-girl cabaret in New Orleans."
- Calvin asks, "So you believe in Heaven?" Hobbes responds, "Call it what you like."
- A fiction writer described a character in his book finding out that the missionary he was looking for in the jungles of Brazil had died of malaria. Standing at her grave he thought to himself, "She was the bravest person he'd ever known because she had absolutely no fear of death. She welcomed it. She was at peace, her soul finally with the Lord, her body forever lying among the people she loved. And her young friend Lako, handicapped since birth with cerebral palsy, was with her, his Heavenly body cured of defects and afflictions."

The references to Heaven above emphasize that thoughts of Heaven and the afterlife are common. The main view is that the deceased are in Heaven, are alive and well there, and aware of happenings on earth. In the pages that follow, the point is stressed that if there is a Heaven, the challenges to God are formidable.

2

SALVATION AND
HEAVEN

SALVATION MEANS PEOPLE being rescued by God from the consequences of sin (wrongdoing) and thus obtaining eternal life after death in Heaven with God. Who will acquire salvation will be decided on the day of judgment. [1a] Most people probably believe that some form of judgment occurs when a person dies and involves a decision of Heaven or hell. Beliefs about salvation and Heaven differ considerably between atheists and theists.

A renowned physicist who was an expert on black holes and other aspects of theoretical physics, died in 2018 after many decades of struggling with a disease (as an admitted Atheist.) He said belief in a God and Heaven is wishful thinking. [1b] A car salesman, a theist, once did some preaching to a potential buyer and said believing in God and Heaven was the "safe" thing to do. The buyer's reply was that doing the "safe" thing with regard to God and Heaven was not a good reason for believing. The salesman had no comment to that reply. So these are the two extreme beliefs – in one, atheism, there is no Heaven and belief in Heaven is merely wishful thinking and in two, theism, there is a God and belief in him will assure life after death in Heaven. In between these two would be agnosticism, not fully accepting either of the first two views and being non-judgmental of either, due to lack of proof.

A nephew, while visiting his ninety-two-year-old uncle, asked him if he believed in Heaven. The uncle's answer was, "I don't think there is anything up there." Yet the uncle willed money to his church. Was he exhibiting wishful thinking and being safe or just contributing to the church to support its good deeds in the community? Maybe both.

A Christian was asked where Heaven is and promptly answered, "I don't know where it is but I know there is one and I am confident I will get there." A young boy asked the priest, "My dad died as an atheist, but he made sure me and my three brothers were baptized. Is our dad in Heaven?" The pope told the boy his dad had a good heart and then he asked the children in the parish if they thought the father was in Heaven. They all said yes, and the pope told the boy, "that is your answer."[2] Was the father being "safe" by having the boys baptized?

When will life on earth end and life in Heaven begin? Who will get to Heaven? If one does not get to Heaven, then what happens? These and many other questions with alternative answers are discussed and developed historically by Bart D. Ehrman.[3]

Enoch and Elijah ascended to Heaven without dying (Genesis 5:24; 2 Kings 2:1-11) but for most everyone else death seems to be a requirement to get to Heaven. Will there be a resurrection and when will it occur? Does the entire body go to Heaven or just the soul? Are the body and soul combined at some time? Is the soul immortal from the get-go or does God give it immortality upon death of the body? Does the ascent to Heaven occur immediately upon death or at some later time, perhaps not until the day of resurrection. Do only the righteous, the strong believers in God, have the opportunity to go to Heaven? Can the soul without the body enjoy the pleasures of Heaven or the torment of hell? Are the pleasures of Heaven meted out depending on the degree of righteousness of a person on earth? Likewise, is the torment in hell meted out according to what the sinner deserves? Are good deeds essential to get to Heaven? What about the rich vs the poor? Do they both get to Heaven? Opinions and answers with regard to all these questions came about centuries before Christ (Jesus), during Christ's life, and after Christ died. Many individuals expressed views about these issues, including philosophers (Plato), authors (Homer), apostles (Peter and John), Abraham, Jesus, Paul, and others. The views were not science-based but were more individual expressions, most of which were highly imaginative, and they came about while the earth had only millions of people whereas now the earth has 8 billion. The ideas of Heaven and hell evolved through time, sort of like ideas about the evolution of the human species. But evolution is science-based, and studies are still ongoing (see Chapter 31; Human Evolution).

In 2020, during the coronavirus pandemic (COVID-19), in the USA alone there were as many as 4,000 deaths attributed to the virus every day. In the first seven months of 2020, 1.9 million deaths occurred, 215,000 more deaths than the usual 1.7 million deaths in these seven months, the increase attributed to COVID-19.[4] From Nov. 2019 to Mar. 2022, over 6,000,000 people died from COVID-19.[5] Add the worldwide COVID-19 deaths to the usual daily deaths and that is a lot of deceased individuals for God to evaluate and to make decisions about the fates of their souls and bodies.

In Matthew 24, verses 29-51, the reader is reminded that God as Jesus will return immediately after the tribulation. But no one knows when that day will be. Matthew warns us that like in the day of Noah, everyone was happy and enjoying life until the day Noah entered the ark with his family, two of every animal species, and abandoned the rest. Ouch! Matthew continues, "and there may be two in the field and only one is taken," also "and two women are grinding grain and one is taken and the other remains." Then an analogy is to a house owner who does not prepare for burglary and does not prevent his goods from being taken by a thief. Such views from the pulpit try to insure (and scare?) parishioners to continue to come to church and prepare for the return of Jesus.

Given that someone wants to believe in God and get to Heaven, what can he or she do to firm up that belief and to convince God of their belief? According to Richard Wagner,[6] there are different views depending on the religion. First a look at Christianity, the largest religion in the world. According to Wagner, Christianity says that one is saved by "accepting God's grace." The King James version of the Holy Bible gives some more specific views.

The following verses say what is required for salvation and life everlasting:

- John 3:16 states, "For God so loved the world that he gave his only begotten son, that whosoever believeth in him should not perish but have everlasting life."

- John 14:6 states what Jesus is saying, "...I am the way, the truth, and the life: no man cometh unto the Father, but by me."
- Romans 8:10 states, "And if Christ be in you, the body is dead because of sin but the spirit is alive because of righteousness."
- Romans 10:9 states, "That if thy shall confess with thy mouth the Lord Jesus and shall believe in thine heart that God has raised him from the dead, thou shalt be saved."
- John 10:27-28 states, "And I give unto my sheep (my followers) eternal life and they shall never perish."
- I Thessalonians 4:14 states, "For if we believe that Jesus died and rose again, even so them also which sleep in Jesus (the deceased) will God bring with him."
- Matthew 19:24 states: "And again I say unto you, it is easier for a camel to go through the eye of a needle than for a rich man to enter into the kingdom of God."
- Matthew 19:29 states: "And everyone that has forsaken houses, and brethren, or sisters, or father, or mother, or wife, or children, or lands, for my name's sake, shall receive a hundredfold, and shall inherit everlasting life."
- II Chronicles 7:14 states, "...if my people shall humble themselves, and pray, and seek my face, and turn from their wicked ways, then will I hear from Heaven, and will forgive their sins...."
- Matthew 10:32-33 states, "Whosoever therefore shall confess me before men, him will I confess also before my Father which is in Heaven."...But whosoever shall deny me before men, him will I also deny before my Father which is in Heaven."
- Matthew 25:14-30, say that every person on the day of death shall meet God and have to give an accounting of their life on earth. Verse 46 states: "The righteous shall enter everlasting life."
- Revelation 22:14 states, "Blessed are they that do his commandments, that they may have right to the tree of life and may enter in through the gates of the city." (Meaning entering into Heaven).

The above verses may be summarized as follows: Believe in Jesus; be born again; keep God's sayings; keep Christ within you; confess the Lord

Jesus out loud and in your heart know that he died and was resurrected; walk the faith and be present with the Lord; follow Jesus; forsake everything except Jesus; hear the word of God and believe and be righteous.

But is believing in Jesus sufficient to get to Heaven or does one need to do good works? Many would like to think that all the kind things one does will count at the gates of Heaven. Billionaire investor Warren Buffett, in 2008, on offering to help troubled bond insurers by offering a second level of insurance on municipal bonds, said, "When I go to St Peter I will not present this as some act that will entitle me to get in (to Heaven). I am doing this to make money." Another interesting view was expressed by the boxer, Mohamed Ali, as remembered by LeBron James. When Ali went to Iraq and came back with all 15 hostages held there by Saddam Hussein, each of the hostages "joyously thanked him" but Ali felt he was just performing his duty and said, "they don't owe me nothin. I believe that when you die and go to Heaven, God won't ask what you've done but what you could have done."[7]

The following verses suggest that doing good works can, in fact, get one into Heaven:

- John 5:28-29, state, "Marvel not at this: For the hour is coming, in which all that are in the graves shall hear his voice...and shall come forth: they that have done good, onto the resurrection of life; and they that have done evil unto the resurrection of damnation."
- Daniel 12:1-2, state, "...thy people shall be delivered, every one that shall be found written in the book...and many of them that sleep in the dust of the earth shall awake, some to everlasting life and some to shame and everlasting contempt."
- Revelation 20:12 states, "And I saw the dead, small and great, stand before God; and the books were opened...and the dead were judged out of those things which were written in the books, according to their works."
- Revelation 20:13 states, "and the sea gave up the dead which were in it; and death and hell delivered up the dead which were in them: and they were judged every man according to their works." Verse 15 states, "And whosoever was not found written in the book of life was cast into the lake of fire."

Those who are resurrected will have bodily changes. The new body will be fashioned like the body of Jesus. See the following verses:

- I Corinthians 15:42 states, "So also is the resurrection of the dead. It is sown in corruption; it is raised in incorruption." Verse 43 states, "It is sown in dishonour; it is raised in glory." Verse 44 states, "It is sown a natural body; it is raised a spiritual body."
- Philippians 3:21 states, "Who shall change our vial body, that it may be fashioned like unto his glorious body…"
- I Corinthians 15:52-57, state, "In a moment, in the twinkling of an eye, …. for the last trumpet shall sound, and the dead shall be raised incorruptible, and we shall be changed….so when this corruptible shall be put on incorruptible, and this mortal shall have put on immortality…. Then death shall be swallowed up in victory…oh death, where is thy sting? O grave where is thy victory? But the sting of death is sin…but thanks be to God, which giveth us the victory through our Lord Jesus Christ."
- Matthew 19:21 states, "And Jesus said unto him, 'If thou wilt be perfect, go and sell that thou hast, and give to the poor, and thou shalt have treasure in Heaven."

One can be confused by this latter suggestion of giving to the poor when reading the following verses:

- Matthew 19:23 states: "Verily I say onto you, that a rich man shall hardly enter into the kingdom of Heaven."
- Matthew 19:24 states: "It is easier for a camel to go through the eye of a needle than for a rich man to enter into the kingdom of God."
- Matthew 25:34-36 state, "Then Jesus said onto them, come thee blessed of my father, inherit the kingdom prepared for you, for I was hungered and ye gave me meat; I was thirsty and ye gave me drink; I was a stranger and ye took me in; naked and ye clothed me; I was sick and ye visited me; I was in prison and ye visited me." This is the parable of the sheep and the goats in which case the sheep did good works; they fed the hungry, gave water to the thirsty, clothed the naked, and visited the sick and those in prison.

The sheep were welcomed into Heaven. But the goats did none of these good works and had to bear the eternal fire of hell.

Jesus himself, before he was crucified, is credited with making these statements but many statements attributed to Jesus were likely not his words.[8] Doing good for others and being kind to others is called "empathy" and one can wonder if after the idea that good works can gain admission to Heaven caused people to be kinder and empathetic. What were people like before Jesus encouraged kindness to others?

After Jesus died, Paul the apostle gets credit for espousing the idea that Jesus, a criminal who was crucified, is the answer to salvation. Paul became a fervent fan of Christianity after he claimed to have seen Jesus in the flesh. The emphasis on Jesus for salvation is inconsistent with the view expressed in Chap. 3 that Jesus was not born as God but became God via reports of his resurrection and idolization by his disciples.[3] In other words, all the emphasis on Jesus is for naught as he was just a man and not a savior.

Much verse variation is seen. Some talk about good works and getting your name in the "book of life," to give to the poor; don't be rich, help those who need help – give food, drink, clothing, encouragement, and just be a good person. Don't be rich? Who is the Bible kidding? How many people does this include? Some preachers (see below), past presidents, authors, professional athletes, movie and TV actors, business owners, and on and on. The rich would be the 1% of USA citizens who get tax breaks! Yes, many names come to mind!

An ad in a mechanics magazine says, "All you need to know about the Bible for Salvation" and has both web and postal addresses. The very next ad states, "MEET LOCAL WOMEN; listen to ads and reply FREE!" and gives a phone number. Shouldn't these two ads be reversed in order?

Does everyone on earth have the opportunity to get to Heaven? The next few verses answer this question in the affirmative.

- John 3:16 states, "That whosoever believeth in him shall not perish but have eternal life."
- 2 Peter 3:9 states, "The Lord is not willing that any should perish, but that all should come to repentance.

- Acts 13: 1-28 and Acts 17:16-22 state that God sent Paul to teach in Asia and Greece and other countries.
- Rev. 21:24 states: And the nations of them which are saved shall walk in God's light.
- Romans 10:12 states, "For there is no difference between the Jew and the Greek; for the same Lord over all is rich unto all that call upon him."
- Romans 10:13 states, "For whosoever shall call upon the name of the Lord shall be saved."
- Romans 14:10 states: "…for we shall all stand before the judgment seat of Christ."
- Romans 14:12 states: So then every one of us shall give account of himself to God."

Yes, everyone has the opportunity to get to Heaven. But can the word of God be made available to all people? God instructed the people of Babel to spread out into the world, but he did not say they should teach about God or worship God, he just wanted their language confounded so they could not connive against him (Genesis 11:7). Jesus sent his disciples out saying to them in Matthew 10:7, "As ye go, preach, saying the kingdom of Heaven is at hand" and also gave them power to heal the sick and raise the dead (Matthew 10: 8).

Most churches have missionary programs and church members travel far to preach the gospel and to do good works such as digging wells and constructing churches and schools. Most get only room and board for their efforts and of course much personal satisfaction and praise from their church. God must have a special place in Heaven for these missionaries. But then there is the other extreme, the rich church leaders (see below).

Revelation 20:13-15 says that on "judgment day" graves, the seas, and hell will give up their dead so they can be judged according to their works. The problem with this idea is that there will be nothing remaining as a recording of these works because the brain will have decomposed. Note in the chapter on the brain (Chap. 20) that the chemical elements of the brain, where recordings (memories) of works would be found, would be lost as decomposition occurs or, in the case of cremation, be burned and gone up the smokestack. And cremations are increasing in number in the USA; in

2007 the percent of the deceased that were cremated was 35%; in 2020 it was predicted that soon almost half of all deceased will be cremated.[9] These ashes are spread hither and yon. All the organic compounds, like proteins and DNA, are burned up. There is no chance of restoring these bodies! What is God going to do?

Bible verses say that the gospel must be preached all over the earth so that all can hear it and have the opportunity to be saved. Clearly millions of people have died in the distant past and even more recently who have not been exposed to Jesus and salvation. For example, research has shown that over a million people lived in a portion of the Amazon rain forest that was thought to have never been inhabited.[10] Did these people have religion? Did they believe in an afterlife? Did they have souls? Where are those millions of souls today? Are they in "limbo" awaiting the Rapture and then for the first time will become cognizant of God? The same questions can be asked about the indigenous peoples of the Americas. Individuals have different views as to how to get to Heaven. One newspaper columnist wrote about her highly opinionated Uncle Clyde's view on getting to Heaven. Uncle Clyde said, "before a man can die he must do at least one of the following: father a child; work the earth, and be loved by man and beast. Should he achieve them all he will glory forever in the kingdom of Heaven."[11] So a man born sterile, living in an inner-city apartment that does not allow pets, would have no chance to get to Heaven? Okay! And LGBTQ people? No chance! Presumably Uncle Clyde had a list for women too. The world has many different churches/religious beliefs and, not surprisingly, their views as to how one can get to Heaven differ considerably. In other words, "perhaps many pathways can lead to God...the spirit of Christ is larger than Christianity."[12]

What does Christianity, the largest religion in the world, say about how people can get to Heaven? We can thank Ahlquist[13] for her conciseness in answering this question. Christianity is monotheistic, with belief in only one God who is "triune" and consists of the father, son, and holy ghost. By dying on the cross Jesus saved us from damnation. The soul is judged at the moment of death. The body and soul are reunited on the day of judgment. Jesus physically rose from the dead and he will return to judge everyone, those living and those who have died. Sinners can repent and ask for forgiveness and will be given an opportunity to go to Heaven.

Alcorn[14] suggests that souls go to an intermediate Heaven and that maybe God gives everyone a "temporary" body there, until he unites these souls with their "original" bodies. In the first few centuries of the common era (CE), some believed that some souls might have to undergo some punishments or torments to clean them of their sins in order to be saved on the day of judgment, a concept that became known as purgatory.[3]

How are the people in other religions saved and thereby get to Heaven? Wagner[6] and Ahlquist[13] summarize how the world's main religions answer this question:

> Judaism – Observance of the law; awareness of a person's total pattern of behavior. Follow the traditions, rituals, and ceremonies.

> Islam – Follow the five pillars of Islam; surrender and submit to Allah (God). Follow the word of Allah given to Mohammad, the prophet. The soul goes to an intermediate state, a partition, before judgment. Torment occurs here if the life was not a good one. Different levels of torment depending on behavior in life.

> Hinduism – Goal isn't Heaven but to be absorbed into Brahman, the supreme spirit. Hindus believe in karma and reincarnation.

> Mormonism – good works and merit get one to Heaven.

> Jehovah's Witnesses – 144,000 Jehovah's Witnesses are specially anointed to be in Heaven, the remainder of Jehovah's Witnesses earn eternal life on a perfect earth with no belief in hell.

> Christian Science – everyone will be saved with no final judgment.

> Buddhism – the soul is recycled over and over (reincarnated) until it reaches the highest level of enlightenment (bliss, liberation), called Nirvana. Buddhists believe in "karma,"

those conditions of previous lifetimes that influence the present life. The Dalai Lama, the head Buddhist, says to be prepared for death at all times but there are no Gods or deities. Personal spiritual development is important and reflected in compassion, wisdom, morality, and meditation.

Shinto - is common to Japan and is a religion with no common founder or sacred scripture. When a person dies, he or she becomes a "kami" or divine being. Kamis take the form of rain, wind, moon, stars, trees, rivers, or animals and are revered by family.

Taoism - founded by Laozi, a person's conduct is formulated by instinct and conscience. After death the soul ultimately goes to Tao and is perfect and immortal, like nirvana. The soul can migrate to other lives until Tao is reached by proper living.

Aborigines - the first people of Australia, believe in reincarnation and transmigration of the soul, most commonly into a dolphin but into other life forms as well. If a person is good then the soul becomes another good life form.

Eckankar - sort of a science of soul travel established in 1965 by Paul Twitchell, you become a co-worker with God.

Kabbalah - is based on the Hebrew Bible but with deeper meaning and proposes reincarnation over and over until the soul progresses to a high level of spirituality and then dwells with God.

Scientology - believes in a supreme being but does not worship this being and Heaven is not accepted as a concept. Reincarnation occurs after death, but only into other humans, and continues until everything is "right" and then there is no more reincarnation.

<u>Native Americans</u> - have a diverse set of beliefs, depending on the tribe. Some of these beliefs are: the soul goes to another world where there is dancing and rituals and relationships continue. The soul stays close to the dead body. The soul is reincarnated. The soul becomes a ghost. The Navajo believe the ghost resents the living and is bad to have around so they burn the body and the house of the deceased and stand in smoke to purify themselves from the ghost. What is the likelihood of any of the above getting to Heaven?

<u>Egyptians</u> - who built the pyramids with stairs going to the apex and aligned with the stars and planets so the soul could get to Heaven straight forward, were the most interesting. The dead bodies of the well-to-do were mummified, and along with the mummies were placed food, tools, and jewelry in the tomb or grave to aid the deceased to achieve immortality. Sometimes servants were sacrificed to help the deceased in the afterlife. Mummification, drying the body to preserve it, was done to make resurrection of the body easier. All organs, including the brain, were removed except the heart and after mummification the heart had to weigh no more than a feather or the afterlife would be denied. Egyptians believed the afterlife included agriculture, livestock, fish, music, and dancing and was a pleasant and happy place. The Book of the Dead has advice to get through the perils of the underworld or the person would be really dead. (One is reminded of the scene in the Wizard of Oz where the coroner pronounces the wicked witch was "really, really, sincerely dead.") Some of the pyramids had mazes at the entrance to prevent ghosts from entering.

<u>Zoroastrianism</u> - begun in ancient Persia (now Iran), is perhaps the oldest monotheistic religion, and still has 200,000 members. Here, the dead person is lain naked in

the open and vultures are allowed to clean off the flesh. After four days, when the bones are dried, the soul then leaves for the next world. Writings of Zoroastrianism date back to 600 BCE (Before Common Era.) Zoroastrianists believe humans and all animals have a soul. The fate of the soul depends on its store of thoughts, words, and deeds.[15]

Reading about the afterlife and how important being good is to get there, one can think about Santa Clause and the Christmas song, "Oh, you better not pout, you better not shout, you better not cry I'm telling you why....", and..."He knows when you've been sleeping, he knows when you're awake, he knows when you've been bad or good so be good for goodness sake." The movie, *Arthur Christmas* depicts Santa in our present world of computers and supersonic travel and the hundreds of elf nerds and computers needed to keep track of all the world's kids and their desires. NORAD (North American Aerospace Defense) takes calls from all parts of the world from kids asking about Santa. About 1500 volunteers answer the phones on Christmas Eve. In 2016 on Christmas Eve NORAD received 154,000 phone calls and had over ten million visitors to its web site. Kids want to know when Santa will arrive at their house and what food they should leave for him.[16] What is fascinating is that kids as young as six years of age, certainly by age nine, figure out that Santa could not possibly get toys to all the kids in their neighborhood in one night much less to the entire world and that realization begins to give doubts about Santa. But amazingly, theists, yes, adults and often highly educated, have no problems accepting the idea of God keeping track of each and every person on earth, the living and the dead. Chapter 11 considers what information God must accumulate for each and every person.

A local pastor of a Bible Church stated in the local paper that the believer in Christ trusts Christ alone for salvation, and no good deeds, community service, baptism, philanthropy, communion, or church attendance, can be added to Christ's sacrifice on the cross.

A nationally known pastor, after delivering a sermon emphasizing that being good is not enough to get to Heaven, says one has to be perfect, show humility, and trust in Jesus. He adds that when he gets to the Gates of Heaven he won't be alone but that Jesus will be there with him.

Here is a poem reminding us that we are born into sin.

"I prayed to be good and strong and wise, for my daily bread and deliverance,

from the sins I was told were mine from birth, and the guilt of an old inheritance."[17]

Now, a look at baptism, which is mentioned often in the Bible. The question can be raised as to whether baptism is essential for salvation. If we consider the verse John 3:16, which states: "For God so loved the world that he gave his only begotten son that whosoever believeth in him shall not perish but have everlasting life" and Acts 10:43 which states: "To him all the prophets witness, that through his name whosoever believeth in him shall receive remission of sins," these verses and John 3: 5 and others, emphasize faith alone as essential for salvation and do not mention baptism. But Mark 16:16 states: "He that believeth and is baptized shall be saved but he that believeth not shall be damned." Baptism was certainly popular as noted from Galatians 3:27-28: "For as many of you as have been baptized into Christ there is neither Jew nor Greek nor bonded nor free, male or female, all in Christ." I Corinthians adds "Gentiles" to that verse. Also consider Acts 2:41: "Then they that gladly received his word were baptized and the same day there were added about 3000 souls." And Acts 2:38: Peter said, "repent in the name of Jesus and be baptized for the remission of sins and receive the gift of the Holy Ghost."

The view seems to be that baptism identifies Christians with the death and resurrection of Jesus and obedience to that acceptance for salvation.[18] This view is fine for those churches wherein baptism is carried out in the teen years or older by whole body immersion, when the individual can possibly understand the significance of the event. When John came upon bodies of water, he performed many baptisms as noted in John 3:23, which states; "And John also was baptizing in Aenon near to Salim because there was much water there..." and Acts 8:36 which states; "And as they went on their way they came upon a certain water and the eunuch said, See, here is water, what doth hinder me from being baptized?"

The many baptisms of the Bible were presumably mostly adults. What about present day baptisms, such as with the Lutheran church, which baptizes infants, too young to understand the implications. Here the view is that God imparts his grace through the sacrament of baptism. Conservative

Lutherans say that baptism results in the person being born again and brought to saving grace. Moderate Lutherans believe baptism initiates new members of the church into the family of God. The pastor sprinkles water onto the head of the infant/child and says, "I baptize you in the name of the father, son, and the holy ghost." The parents and two Godparents promise to raise the child in the faith. Lutherans believe baptism imparts faith in an infant's heart. Lutherans believe salvation is by faith alone, but faith can come from baptism and baptism can lead one to the written and spoken word of God.[19]

Some members of the Mormon Church believe that it is possible to perform baptisms on people who have died. These are proxy-baptisms and are part of the Mormon teachings that families spend eternity together and give the deceased a choice in the afterlife to accept or reject the baptism offer. Proxy-baptisms have been performed on holocaust victims, deceased celebrities, and deceased grandparents of celebrities. An associate professor of sociology who studies Mormonism says that Mormons are striving to baptize everyone who has ever lived to help get non-Mormons out of "spirit prison" in the afterlife and thus receive exaltation. The baptisms are approved by the Mormon church but only when the person being baptized is a relative. The attempts by some Mormons to baptize non-relatives is raising controversy.[20]

Instead of deciding which religion or belief is best for getting one to Heaven, it makes more sense to think that since God created man and woman "in his image" then he should consider EVERYONE for Heaven. Romans 10:12 states "For there is no difference between the Jew and the Greek for the same Lord over all is rich unto all that call upon him" and verse 13 states, "For whosoever shall call upon the name of the Lord shall be saved." But Revelation 20:13-15, says everyone will be judged according to their works.

Pastor Rob Bell wrote a book that stirred up Christians throughout the USA. The book says that Christians should spend more time on improving conditions here on earth than being concerned about the afterlife and emphasize the positive side of God, for God is a loving God. He says all people should work on removing the "hells" here on earth including rape, genocide, abuse, and scams. The book has been called "heresy," "heartbreaking," "a massive tragedy," by other pastors. Bell thinks people might be able to accept Jesus even after they die and still get to Heaven.[21]

One of the bad things God has allowed to happen is the murdering of women in Mexico (see Chap. 8). In 2019, 3,825 Mexican women were killed.[22] Can we hope that all these murdered women are in Heaven? That would be a reasonable hope but for the fact that many of these women themselves could have been murderers or committed other sins. And what of the murderers? Should they go straight to hell? Murder would seem to be one sin that is not forgivable. But the Bible says that one can obtain entrance to Heaven if one accepts Jesus as his/her personal savior.

The Bible lists the Ten Commandments as spoken to Moses by God (Exodus 20:3-17). Verse thirteen says "thou shall not kill" and is the sixth commandment; one can ask if killing someone will prevent the murderer from gaining access to Heaven regardless of whether or not all the other requirements are met (see above). Going to hell would be the most severe penalty for murder. Exodus 21:12 says, "He that smiteth a man so that he die, shall be surely put to death." But the penalty for murder in the USA is not so straightforward. We have murder in the first degree, second degree, manslaughter, and variations of each, all of which garner different prison sentences, and these differ by state as well. Only first-degree murder warrants prison without parole and execution.[23]

Executions in the USA numbered almost one every other day from the late 1800s to the 1950s. Executions were initially by hanging, often in public, but that changed in the 1920s after an epidemic of lynchings blurred the distinction between legal hangings and vigilantism. Electrocution became the method of choice within walls of prisons with only a limited audience; friends/family of the accused and friends/family of the victim, the prison warden, prison chaplain, the guards directing the prisoner, and a member of the press to witness and report. Hundreds were electrocuted, even as gruesome a sight as it was.[24] A Huntsville, TX, reporter described a 1938 electrocution of Albert, a "tall, powerfully, built man" who was only twenty-three years old. When Albert was led into the death chamber, with witnesses assembled just outside of a metal rail, he knelt and in a booming baritone voice sang "Just a Closer Walk with Thee." Albert was then strapped to the chair, a guard laid a Bible in his lap, and the switch was thrown. Albert's body slammed against the straps and the Bible fell to the floor. Another jolt was given and the odor of burning flesh was detected by everyone. Finally, Albert died. Usually, several minutes elapsed before the prisoner was pronounced dead.

When the moratorium on executions was lifted in 1977, lethal injection became the method of choice, which involved a three-drug cocktail that included a sedative, a muscle relaxant, and a heart-stopping chemical. The first lethal injection execution was in 1982. The prisoner was pronounced dead seven minutes after the injection. Executions followed in many states and became rather routine, with only the prisoner (having been brought in on a gurney by guards who then left), warden, chaplain, and executioner present in the execution chamber. Family members of the prisoner and of the victim as well as reporters were in rooms on each side and able to see the execution through glass panes. The first person to be executed in Texas in the year 2000 was that of Earl, the 200th since executions resumed in 1982. His last words were, "Love y'all – see you on the other side." Did Earl and Albert (see above) sincerely believe that they would go to Heaven or were they just hopeful?

Donna (not her real name) works as a volunteer chaplain for a woman's prison in Midwest USA. Some of the inmates she visits with, and loves are serving life sentences without parole. She says God has called her to that role and God gives her love for the prisoners. She has never felt closer to Jesus and refers to Hebrews 13:3 which states, "Remember them that are in bonds, as bound with them, and them which suffer adversity, as being yourselves also in the body." She says there is nothing she would rather do than her duties as a chaplain. She receives much satisfaction from her work and the prisoners value her visits very much.[25] But does her work result in at least some of prisoners being "saved?"

A reporter for the Texas Department of Criminal Justice for over ten years observed 278 inmates put to death by lethal injection. The reporter described those years and the prisoners that were executed.[24] The Chaplain was there to reassure the prisoner during his/her final moments and usually laid a comforting hand on the prisoner. This gesture by the chaplain, the offer of a pillow by the warden to the prisoner, and other civilities like giving them cigarettes, were noted as somewhat incongruous. In 2000, the reporter's first year, Texas executed forty inmates, the most by any state. George W. Bush, governor of Texas, was also making a run at the presidency. Florida, with Jeb Bush the governor, had only two executions. The reporter noted two kinds of people on death row. There were true sociopaths who had no reservations about killing and planned them. The other group had run into the wrong situation, wrong crowd, been drinking or on drugs, made a wrong choice and ended up killing someone, like a store clerk, without intending to. Noted also was that some death row inmates, including one woman, chose to become Christians while incarcerated. One murderer just before being executed said, "may God pass me over to the Kingdom's shore softly and gently." The reporter thought that some death row inmates could definitely be rehabilitated.[24] But are some innocent? Estimates are that over 4% are innocent yet only 1.6 % are exonerated (freed of prison). From 1973-2004 of 7,482 prisoners on death row, 117 were exonerated and 65% were executed.[26]

But death row inmates are seldom executed today (2020) and even the list of federal prisoners under sentence for execution (death row), including the Boston marathon bomber, is over sixty individuals. Every state has prisoners on death row. After a brief moratorium from 1972-1976, the US Supreme Court approved executions in 1976; Texas became the state with the highest number per year with a peak of forty in 2000. But since then, even Texas has executed few death row inmates, with only 10 in 2014, and has joined Nebraska, Delaware, and Pennsylvania in a complete moratorium on the death penalty. California had ten executions from 2005-2015 and had 750 death row inmates in 2015.[27]

Can a prisoner be admitted to Heaven if he/she accepts Jesus, lives a clean life in prison, reads the Bible, and meets all the above criteria for salvation? Will those death row inmates that become Christians, or accept religion of some other faith, have a chance at Heaven if they die in prison? If they are executed? Does God take into account the nature of the murder (violence, ax, gun, knife), the number of victims murdered by one inmate, the age of the victim(s), whether or not the victim is a relative (parent, brother, daughter, son, cousin)? If a person accepts Jesus, i.e., is saved on the day of execution, and thus cannot demonstrate his faith and love for God and Jesus for any length of time, will that person get to Heaven? (see Philippians 1:6, "he that hath begun a good work shall perform it until the day Jesus comes;" Matthew 10:22, "for he that endureth to the end shall be saved;" Psalm 37:29, "The righteous themselves will possess the earth and they will reside forever upon it."

An execution is itself a killing of a person and it is premeditated and intentional. Does it go against the sixth commandment? Who should be penalized for that killing? Officials of the state or federal government? The person's defense attorney? The prosecuting attorney? The executioner (the person who pulls the switch or delivers the injection? Does God go along with the justification, as stated in Exodus 21:12, "He that smiteth a man, so that he die, shall be surely put to death?"

Now a look at suicide. Is suicide a sin in God's view? In the Old Testament six suicides are mentioned in the books of Judges and Samuel. Perhaps Samson is most justified because he brought down the walls of the temple in order to kill Philistines. For the other five, the reasons for the suicides are: Avoiding shame; avoiding dishonor; despair; avoiding capture. In the Bible none of these six are condemned. In the New Testament there is one suicide, that of Judas Iscariot, who betrayed Jesus. The Bible did not condemn him but did not approve either. The Bible says "greater love has no man than he who lay down his life for his friends." We can raise the issue of assisted suicide here. The laws of people differ in different countries. What God's personal view is we don't know, but the Bible says suicide is OK.

There are some famous unsolved murders, five of which Reader's Digest describes.[28] Perhaps the worst case is the Atlanta Child Murders in which twenty-four black children and teens vanished from the streets between 1979 and 1981. One child could be identified only by her teeth when the remains were found. When the family has a funeral and buries the limited remains will God be able to restore the entire body, brain, and personality? In 2017 there were 15,657 murders and 61% were "cleared" while 39% were unsolved.[29] Does God know who the murderers are and the circumstances of the murders? If some have become Christians will they go to Heaven? If murderers confess, will they get to Heaven? Will they meet their victims in Heaven? Will the victims meet their murderers?

Are there individuals who should definitely, sincerely, not have a chance to get to Heaven? A reverend or priest or other man of God is present at the execution of a prisoner. Is that to pray for the murderer's soul so that it might go to Heaven? Is that a reasonable possibility given that the person committed premeditated, intentional murder? A particularly heinous crime would be for a father to be in a state of drunkenness and to sexually molest his own child and then beat the child to death. Is that a crime that is unforgivable? But, if after many years of regretting and apologizing for his crime and being the best inmate possible, can that man accept Jesus as his personal savior and thus gain access to Heaven? And will the murderer meet the victim in Heaven? Are there other crimes that are unforgivable?

We see many terrible crimes in news articles. Examples are:

- A mother kills six of her newborns and stores them in her garage.
- A son kills his grandparents.
- A son kills his mother.
- A boyfriend kills the baby he is caring for while the mother is at work.
- A father does not lock up his loaded rifle/gun, his son is playing with it and shoots a friend, killing her.
- A ten-month-old boy was shot by his seven-year-old brother with his grandfather's gun while playing with it.
- A mother gave birth in her garage and the baby girl, wrapped in an old shirt, was found in a trash bin by sanitation workers.
- A mother tortured two of her children, then killed both and kept them in a freezer.
- Doctors removed life support from a comatose boy who is brain-dead, and the family is upset, thinking the boy would ultimately regain consciousness.
- A woman with terminal cancer moved from her state to Oregon to be able to end her life with dignity because Oregon allows physicians to prescribe life-ending medications in cases of terminally ill patients.
- Doctors want to take a pregnant brain-dead woman off life-support to end her life and the life of her eighteen-week-old fetus because of no hope for either. The woman's blood was becoming toxic.

Yet the decision to end life-support could not be made because the country had a law preventing abortions and ending life-support would abort (end) the pregnancy; so each year thousands of women travel to a neighboring country for abortions. Because of laws restricting abortion clinics in Texas, women travel to New Mexico for abortions. How does God look at abortions? As sins? Who is committing the sin? The pregnant woman? The person performing the abortion? Certainly, someone in real life like the physician at an orphanage, acted by Michael Caine and by his successor, Toby McGuire, in the book/movie, *Cider House Rules*, as they performed countless abortions, might not get to Heaven.

A televangelist who heads a megachurch spends his parishioners' money on a private jet plane that cost millions, and now has a carbon footprint greater than all of his parishioners put together. He claims God spoke to him and told him to buy the plane. Huh? God only spoke to a few men by name in the entire Old Testament! This preacher claims the jet is important to spread the gospel around the world. He is rich and lives in an extravagant mansion, on money from his flock! And they keep filling the pews in his megachurch! Another preacher says God gave the OK for him to purchase a jet! Ouch![30] Also note Matthew 19:23; "Verily I say onto you, that a rich man shall hardly enter into the kingdom of Heaven." Will these preachers get to Heaven?

At this writing, the year 2021, about 15% of the people in the USA do not believe in God.[31] Will these atheists have a chance to get to Heaven. Apparently Pope Francis thinks so. Bill Maher, an atheist and host of *Real Time with Bill Maher* on HBO, remarked, "We atheists do not believe in Heaven but there was a generosity of spirit in the pope's statement that signaled a new kind of pope."[32]

NOTES

1a Christian Enquiry Agency website, "What is salvation?," accessed January 2019, Christianity.org.uk/article/what-is-salvation.

1b *Detroit Free Press*, March 15, 2018, 9A.

2 Kelsey McShane, "Boy Asks Pope if Atheist Father's in Heaven," *Detroit Free Press*, Friday, April 27, 2018, 2A.

3 Bart D. Ehrman, *Heaven and Hell, A History of the Afterlife* (New York: Simon and Schuster, 2020.)

4 Alex Fitzpatrick and Elijah Wolfson, "The American Nightmare," *Time*, September 21/28, 2020, 42-47; *NBC Nightly News*, January/February 2021.

5 Wikipedia website, "Covid-19 pandemic deaths," last edited on March 8, 2023, https://en.wikipedia.org/wiki/COVID-19_pandemic_deaths.

6 Richard Wagner, *Christianity for Dummies* (New Jersey: Wiley, 2004). 25.

7 *Sports Illustrated*, September 2020, 59.

8　Bart D. Ehrman, *Heaven and Hell*, 147-167.

9　*The Philadelphia Inquirer*, November 4, 2014.

10　*Time*, April 9, 2018.

11　*Detroit Free Press*, January 18, 2008.

12　*Northern Express*, March 9, 2015.

13　Diane Ahlquist, *The Complete Idiots Guide to Life After Death* (Indianapolis: Penguin Random House. 2007.)

14　Randy Alcorn, *Heaven: A Comprehensive Guide to Everything the Bible Says About Our Eternal Home* (Illinois: Tyndale Momentum, 2004.)

15　K.E. Eduljee, "Zoroastrian Heritage," *Heritage Institute* (website), 2005-23, www.heritageinstitute.com/zoroastrianism.

16　*The Arizona Republic*, December 25, 2017.

17　Louise Penny, *Glass Houses* (New York: Minotaur. 2017), 274.

18　Got Questions website, "Is baptism necessary," accessed on December 2018, gotquestions.org/baptism-salvation.html.

19　Zion Lutheran Church website, "Lutheran Beliefs on Baptism," accessed on January 2019, https://zionhc.org/lutheran-beliefs-on-baptism/.

20　*The Arizona Republic*, December 3, 2017, 4A; Internet sources- proxibaptisms.

21　Rob Bell, 2011, *Love Wins: A Book About Heaven, Hell and the Fate of Every Person Who Ever Lived* (San Francisco: HarperOne, 2011.)

22　*Detroit Free Press*, March 10, 2020, 13A.

23　Geoffrey Nathan, Esq., "2nd Degree Murder Laws & Charges," FederalCharges.com (website), accessed January 2020, https://www.federalcharges.com/2nd-degree-murder-laws.

24　Pamela Colloff, *The Witness* (New York: Penguin Random House, 2014), 111-115; 188-204.

25　*Detroit Free Press*, April 20, 2014.

26　Michael McLaughlin, "Shocking Number of Innocent People Sentenced to Death, Study Finds," *HuffPost*, December 6, 2017, www.huffpost.com/entry/innocent-death-penalty-study_n_5228854.

27　David Von Drehle, "Execution in America," *Time*, June 8, 2015, 28-33.

28　Bill Hangley, Jr., Andy Simmons, and Marc Peyser, "They Got Away With Murder," *Reader's Digest*, April 2020, 56-68.

29　Max Jaeger, "A shocking number of US murders went unsolved last year," *NYPost*, September 25, 2018, https://nypost.com/2018/09/25/a-shocking-number-of-us-murders-went-unsolved-last-year/.

30　Internet source- megachurch pastors and jet planes.

31　Wikipedia website, "Demographics of atheism," accessed on January 2019, https://en.wikipedia.org/wiki/Demographics_of_atheism.

32　*Parade Magazine*, Sunday, April 20, 2014, 10.

3

JESUS

HOW DID JESUS become so relevant to the lives of people? How did he become the center of Christianity? Largely, it has to do with Heaven. Heaven became important because it provided a place to go after death and satisfied the strong survival instinct of humans, going back to the earliest hominids. Death, therefore, was not the end of life. Heaven was where we could believe our deceased grandparents, parents, siblings, children, relatives, friends, and heroes were now residing, happily ever after. We would be together again and interact and speak to each other. Because of Jesus, these are all possible.

Starting small, Christianity is now the world's largest and most diverse religion, with 2 billion followers. Yes, these are Christians, followers of Jesus.[1] Belief in Jesus is paramount for Christians to gain entrance to Heaven and have everlasting life. Of many Bible verses which state this importance, perhaps John 3:16 is most recognized which says: "For God so loved the world that he gave his only begotten son that whosoever believeth in him should not perish but have everlasting life." Other verses emphasizing the importance of accepting Jesus include:

- John 3:3 – Jesus answered and said unto him, "Verily, verily I say unto thee, except a man be born again, he cannot see the kingdom of God."

- Acts 4:12 – Neither is there salvation in any other: for there is none other name under Heaven given among men, whereby we must be saved.
- I John 1:7 – ...and the blood of Jesus Christ his Son cleanseth us from all sin.
- I John 5:11 – ...God hath given to us eternal life and this life is in his Son.
- I John 5:12 – He that hath the son hath life; and he that hath not the son of God hath no life.
- I John 4:14 –...The father sent the son to be the Saviour of the world.
- I John 4:15 – Whosoever shall confess that Jesus is the Son of God, God dwelleth in him.
- Colossians 2:6 – As ye have therefore received Christ Jesus the lord, so walk ye in him.
- Galatians 3:26 – For ye are all the children of God by faith in Christ Jesus.
- Romans 10:9 – That if they shalt confess with thy mouth the Lord Jesus, and shalt believe in thine heart that God hath raised him from the dead, thou shalt be saved.
- Romans 10:10 – For with the heart man believeth unto righteousness; and with thy mouth confession is made unto salvation.
- Romans 10:12 – For there is no difference between the Jew and the Greek: for the same lord overall is rich unto all that call upon him.

Note that Jesus is also referred to as Jesus Christ or just Christ. Christ means "the anointed one" and even though Jesus did not have a last name, he is often referred to as Jesus Christ.[2] The words Christians and Christianity then followed naturally.

Some churches require that members, most often at a very young age but at any time in their life, come forth at a church service publicly in front of the congregation, and acknowledge acceptance of Jesus as their personal savior. Some churches insist that only if they accept Jesus *in their specific church* will their acceptance gain them entry into Heaven. Baptism by immersion is often connected with this public acceptance of Jesus. In other churches, baptism occurs during infancy, just splashing holy water on the infant's head, again in front of the church and congregation, and is believed to be essential to entrance into Heaven upon death.[2]

Because accepting Jesus as one's savior is necessary to get to Heaven and have everlasting life, it is important to look at the evidence for Jesus as the son of God, his crucifixion, his being raised from the dead, and how he became God. Here I borrow much from Bart Ehrman's book, *How Jesus became God*, which thoroughly and critically discusses these subjects.[3] A relevant statement made by Wagner is: "the faith of Christians hinges on Jesus actually being raised from the dead. If the resurrection is make believe, then Christianity is just a huge waste of time and energy."[2] In I Corinthians 15:12-19, Paul, the apostle, preaches to his brethren the story of Jesus' resurrection and says, "if Christ be not risen then is our preaching vain, and your faith is also vain." In other words, believe it, says Paul.

The life of Jesus had 5 parts: The Virgin Mary giving birth to him; his three and a-half years of ministry; his crucifixion/death; his resurrection into Heaven; and his acceptance as Lord and Savior (his becoming God).

Let's start with the description of the birth of Jesus in Luke 1. The angel Gabriel came to Mary whom God chose to conceive in her womb and bring forth a son. Mary asked how this can come about as she was a virgin, not even married and with no spouse. The angel said to her that the holy ghost, through God's power, will come upon her and impregnate her and she would give birth to a son who will therefore be "the son of God." The gospels differ somewhat in their writings about the birth of Jesus. For example, the book of Matthew says that the birth of Jesus is fulfilling prophecy from the book of Isaiah (Isaiah 7:14), a book difficult to read and make sense of, written in the eighth century BCE, which said that "A virgin shall conceive and bear a son," suggesting that a sperm was involved to provide a Y chromosome and thus a male child. (see Chapter 5). Ehrman points out that in the original word "alma" of Isaiah, written in Hebrew, a "young woman" in the Greek translation meant "parthenos," and that took on the meaning of a "young woman who had never had sex." Matthew 1 lists the fourteen generations leading up to Joseph, but Joseph was not the father of Jesus genetically. The generations of Mary are not given in the Bible. When Joseph realized Mary was pregnant he was troubled but an angel of the Lord came to him in a dream and said it was OK to take her as his wife and that she was conceived by the Holy Ghost and that she would have a son. (Matthew 1:18-25). Joseph awoke, accepted the angel's suggestion, and became Mary's husband. Both the Holy Ghost and the angel were able to communicate with Mary, apparently in her language!

If the Holy Ghost in fact impregnated Mary, it seems that a haploid set of chromosomes was provided, housed in some kind of sperm cell. Since Jesus was a man, then the Holy Ghost, a spirit, must have provided a Y chromosome. Thus, if not, Jesus would have developed as a haploid female. Without a Y chromosome the sex of a human would be female.[4]

The virgin Mary was told by an angel that she was chosen by God to give birth to a child (Luke 1:28) but this troubled her, and she asked in Luke 1:34, "how shall this be, seeing I know not a man?" In verse 35, "And the angel answered and said the Holy Ghost shall come upon thee and the power of the highest shall overshadow thee...and a holy thing shall be born of thee." If the Holy Ghost did not provide a set of chromosomes, Jesus would have developed as a virgin birth, with the chromosome set only from the mother.

Virgin births are fairly common in the insects and other invertebrates, worker bees being one example, but uncommon in the vertebrate world, with some fish, amphibians, and reptiles as examples, and no virgin births are found amongst mammals (humans are mammals). Development with only one set of chromosomes is called parthenogenesis (from the Greek word parthenos, see above) in biology and results in a haploid organism. Another set of chromosomes and their genes are essential, to make a diploid, and thus to provide normal genes on one set of chromosomes to counterbalance any mutant genes on the other set. The sperm gives the egg a stimulus to divide. The genes of the egg and of the sperm are both imprinted in different ways and to different degrees. Alone, neither set of genes is adequate for normal development. Considering the above history and biology, the "virgin" birth of Jesus can be questioned historically and biologically.[5]

In the story of the birth of Jesus in Bethlehem, mentioned are God the father in Heaven, the Holy Ghost, and Jesus. Jesus becomes to be known as God the son. How is it that there are three Gods? (see discussion in Ehrman[3]). This question has been dealt with by historians, three of whom are Hippolytus, Tertullian, and Origen. Hippolytus put forth that God is a three-in-one God, the Triad. Tertullian called it the Trinity. Origen advanced the idea that Jesus was one of many souls created by God, but Jesus was the most divine, most righteous, and closest to God. Other souls were ordinary imperfect humans and still others were demons. Origen tried to explain how Jesus could be both human and divine. Ultimately, through decades and much arguing and discussion, the Nicene Creed came about (the concept of a triune God; father, son, and holy ghost) which was supposed to satisfy various differing views of Jesus as man and/or God. Ehrman admits to believing only the part of the creed stating that Jesus was crucified under Pontius Pilate, died, and was buried.[3]

Here are some of the views bantered about. Novatian (210-278 CE), active in the church, proposed that Christ was divine, fully God, but subordinate to God the father. Christ had to be "born" not always existing like God. Thus, Christ was distinct from, but in perfect unity with, God the father. Dionysius (Bishop of Rome, 260 CE) proposed three beings that made up the "Divine Triad" and are so harmonious as seen to be a "unity" and this unity is the God of the universe. Arius of Alexandria (312 CE), a priest, proposed that God had no beginning whereas all else, including Christ, had a beginning. Christ is a second tier God. Alexander of Alexandria (313-328) proposed that Christ is immutable and unchangeable, like God the father, and exactly resembles God the father. But God the father is unbegotten, always existed, whereas Christ was begotten from God the father (came out of the father).[3]

The differing views of dealing with Christ vs God became known as the Arian Controversy. Emperor Constantine, who committed to the Christian God in 312 CE made Christianity a "favored" religion and ended the centuries-long persecution of Christians, thus helping to launch Christianity into the world. The number of Christians increased from five percent of the roughly sixty million people in the Roman empire to fifty percent during these years and Emperor Theodosius made Christianity the official religion of the Roman Empire. But back to Constantine, who wanted to clear up the God, Jesus, Holy Ghost controversy; he wanted "oneness" and keep in mind that at one time pagans worshiped dozens of Gods. To accomplish his goal, Constantine organized the Council of Nicaea (in Turkey) with 318 bishops present, representing Egypt, Palestine, Syria, Asia Minor, and other countries. At issue were the teachings of Arius and his supporters.

After much debate the council came up with an agreement (298 yes,

twenty no, and seventeen acquiesced). This agreement became the Nicene
Creed, which was close to how it is recited today. Most of the discussion
was about Jesus, not much about God, and very little about the Holy Ghost.
The idea put forth was that Christ was begotten from the substance of the
Father God and therefore always existed, and was equal to God, in unity
with the Holy Ghost. Thus, Christianity was going to be the worship
of only one God, the Triune God. According to Ehrman[3] Jesus became
"recontextualized" through history to become truly God some 300+ years
after his death; discussions continued through many years. The point is
that Jesus becoming God was a concept that evolved through history with
considerable disagreement and with no proof one way or the other.

Only three and a-half years of the life of Jesus are documented. These
are the years he traveled and taught, gathered followers which were mainly
his disciples, and carried out his miracles, prior to his crucifixion.

The crucifixion of Jesus was viewed by early Christians as being for
the saving of sinners. In the Nicene Creed is stated: "For our sake he was
crucified under Pontius Pilate, he suffered death and was buried." The event
that led to the view that Jesus was divine was his resurrection from the dead.
His disciples probably left the scene of crucifixion, afraid for themselves, but
later, one or a few had visions of Jesus not only being alive but having a meal
with them. Ehrman[3] raises the question as to whether Jesus was buried in a
tomb and suggests that it was more likely that he was buried in an earthen
grave, with other common people, as he too was a commoner. The views
that Jesus escaped the tomb, ascended into Heaven, and returned to visit
with his disciples, are not strongly supported.

Consider the death and crucifixion of Jesus. What we know is that
Jesus was crucified but we don't know when he actually died. Most often
in Roman crucifixions, the body was left on the cross to be scavenged by
animals and then to decompose, thus leaving no trace of a wicked man. The
process was open to be seen by the public to dissuade others from commit-
ting crimes. It was humiliating for the family, who was ultimately allowed
to bury the remains. But Jesus had no family there and the disciples had
fled. Being a common criminal, most likely Jesus was not buried in a tomb.
Pontius Pilate, Governor of Judea (26-36 CE), has been described as a less
than kind person and likely had no mercy or respect for Jewish traditions
and thus would probably not have allowed a decent burial for Jesus.

A person brought back to life is said to be resurrected. The Old Testament of the Bible says three people were resurrected and the New Testament says five. Elijah brought a boy back to life. Elisha brought a boy back to life. Jesus brought two women and Lazarus back to life. Peter and Paul each resurrected one person. These are people brought back to life after death but did not ascend to Heaven. A few others were apparently brought back to life at the time of the resurrection of Jesus.[6a] Note that 117 billion people have died in the past 200,000 years and very few, other than Jesus, have been resurrected.[6b] Why is that?

Arguments can be presented for the resurrection of Jesus[6b] but an important observation is that Jesus is the only person who was resurrected and then ascended into Heaven. What is the evidence? What about eyewitnesses to the death of Jesus? Perhaps they were superstitious and saw what they wanted to see. Maybe they were reporting only Jesus "in spirit" and over many decades their reports were altered to suggest they saw Jesus in the flesh. Many accounts of the resurrection were not in the original gospels and were added in subsequent centuries. The gospel of Mark says nothing about an empty tomb. Nor does Paul in his writings. But the tomb burial idea is nevertheless pretty much accepted. In the Gospels, women visited the tomb and saw that the body of Jesus was not there; but the number of women visiting is not clear. Here are some non-supernatural explanations for the body of Jesus not being in the tomb:

1. Jesus was not buried in the tomb. Jesus was a commoner and commoners were buried in graves, not in tombs.
2. The Romans moved the body.
3. The women went to the wrong tomb.
4. Jesus never really died but maybe was in a coma and revived.

If Jesus really died and was resurrected three days later, his brain would have been dead (true for other resurrections as well). Also, at that time in history resurrection was of the spirit, not the body. Even today, most churches believe the spirit goes to Heaven and the body turns to dust.[7] Jesus was observed in the flesh by his disciples but these may have been visions which were "wishful thinking" and the visions were not real.[3] Thousands of people have had visions of loved ones. One said her grandfather's face appeared on her TV screen. The virgin Mary and the Virgin of Guadalupe have been seen in visions by thousands.

Another interesting set of visions is that of the three shepherd girls of Fatima, Portugal, in 1917. That vision, now called Our Lady of Fatima, passed on three secrets to the girls. Secret one was a vision of hell, two was instructions for saving souls from the torment of hell, and three was forecasting the death of the pope and other religious leaders. One of the girls, Sister Lucia, had another vision three years later of Mary and the baby Jesus on a luminous cloud.[8] Jesus was present for forty days among his disciples who then saw his body go up to Heaven (Luke 24:51). The belief that Jesus was resurrected became firmly entrenched in Christianity and the view that Jesus was "divine" took hold. But the Gospels are not consistent on most of these points.[3]

A further complication is that Jesus had a brother who perhaps people saw after the crucifixion. Matthew 12:50 states: "For whosoever shall do the will of my Father which is in Heaven, the same is my brother, and sister, and mother." Mark 6:3 states: "Is not this the carpenter, the son of Mary, the brother of James, and Joseph, and of Juda, and Simon? And are not his sisters here with us? And they were offended at him." As with his becoming God, his genealogy is not clear.[9]

It can be disturbing and revealing to read these lost scriptures, the books that did not make it into the New Testament. Two examples might be sufficient. In The Coptic Gospel of Thomas, verse 114, Simon Peter said to the disciples, "let Mary leave us, for women are not worthy of life." Jesus answered, "I myself shall lead her in order to make her male, so that she too can become a living spirit resembling you males. For every woman who will make herself male will enter the kingdom of Heaven."[9] Perhaps it was a good thing that these books did not get accepted into the New Testament. When the descriptions of Heaven and hell are viewed, the latter point is further emphasized. A soul is taken on a visit to Heaven, seeing rivers of milk and honey, of wine, and of oil, and told how to reach each one. Then the soul is taken to hell and shown what one faces there depending on his "level" of sin; the visualization of hell for a sinner is awful.[10]

The library of St. Catherine's Monastery in Egypt holds and preserves hundreds of manuscripts going back to medieval times and earlier. Some of these ancient writings on parchment were "erased" and used over again.

The erased portions can now be recovered using multispectral imaging. Almost 7000 hidden pages have now been revealed from some 163 recycled parchments, called palimpsests, in ten languages. Many more hidden texts revealing more religious history are still likely to come.[11]

But when did Jesus become divine? Was he divine at birth; not until his baptism; at his crucifixion; or at his resurrection? Here again the Gospels differ.

Further complicating Jesus's resurrection and his being the savior of sinners, are reports of other saviors. One such case is that of Apollonius[3], from the town of Tiana, a remote part of the Roman empire. Before his birth, his mother had a visit from Heaven telling her that he would be divine. As an adult he was a preacher telling people from town to town that they should be concerned with the spiritual and eternal, not the materialistic things. His followers believed him to be the son of God. He performed miracles, healed the sick, cast out demons, and raised the dead. But he aroused opposition to the ruling party of Rome, was put on trial and killed. His soul ascended into Heaven and appeared as a vision to at least one of his followers. A devotee, Philastratus, wrote a book in eight volumes about Apollonius, 220-230 CE, some years after Jesus. Followers of Jesus (monotheists) and followers of Apollonius (polytheists) argued and called each other frauds and charlatans. Ehrman[3] raises the question as to which story is true and which is embellished and also gives examples of other "divine" beings, of humans becoming divine and of Gods becoming human.

In the year 380 CE, Theodosius, the Roman emperor, declared Christianity to be the only acceptable religion of the Roman empire. He also declared that the people who followed the Nicene Trinitarian were the only people who were entitled to call themselves Catholic. A year later he called together an ecumenical council which defined Nicene orthodoxy and healed the schism between the Western and Eastern empires, including accepting the Holy Spirit as the third person of the Trinity and to be equal to the Father. The council condemned Apollonarian and Macedonian heresies (polytheisms).[12]

Additional "crucified saviors" have been reported.[13] Records of these saviors go back to 6000 yrs. BCE. Comparison of one of these, Chrishna (Krishna), is most interesting. Dozens of similarities are seen between Chrishna and Jesus:

- Both were foretold by prophets
- Both were here to atone for sins
- Both were God's sons sent down from Heaven in the form of a man
- Both were born of virgins
- Their fathers were carpenters
- The Holy Ghost was the source of conception
- Both were born near the 25th of December
- Both healed the sick and performed other miracles
- Both proclaimed "I am the resurrection."
- Both were between 30-36 years old at death
- Both were crucified
- Both descended into hell
- Both were resurrected and ascended into Heaven but returned to earth briefly. There were witnesses to both resurrections
- Their doctrines were similar
- On and on the similarities continue and can be applied to Jesus and other saviors, such as Apollonius (see above), Osiris, Magus, Horus, and more

Now compare Jesus and Horus of Egypt.[14] Note that stories of Horus had been circulating for hundreds of years in Egyptian writings.

- Horus was born of a virgin, Isis-Meri, as was Jesus born to Mary
- Horus was the only begotten son of the God Osiris; Jesus the only begotten son of the God of Israel
- Horus was born in a cave, Jesus in a manger
- Birth of Horus was heralded by the star Sirius, birth of Jesus by an unidentified star
- Shepherds witnessed both births
- Both were outspoken and bright children
- No life history of either is available between twelve and thirty years old
- Horus was baptized by Anup the baptizer in the river Eridanus; Jesus was baptized by John the Baptist in the river Jordan
- Both walked on water, healed the sick, cast out demons and performed other miracles.

- Both had close followers; each had about twelve disciples
- Horus died by crucifixion (or sting of a scorpion – sources differ), Jesus by crucifixion
- Horus raised his dead father, Osiris, from the grave; Jesus raised Lazarus from the grave
- Both were buried in tombs, both descended into hell, and both were resurrected after three days
- Both resurrections were announced by women

What was going on in these early times? Did God provide many saviors, perhaps so that most countries could have their own savior? Could the story of Jesus have been copied from the stories of one or more earlier documented saviors, such as Krishna or Horus? Could the stories of saviors other than Jesus have been written <u>after</u> the story of Jesus was written, and copied from the story of Jesus, but dated before Jesus? Copying might be a reasonable explanation for the story of Apollonius, who lived after Jesus, but what about those saviors that lived hundreds of years <u>before</u> Jesus? Was there one early story that all the others were copied from? How will we ever know the answers?

One way to obtain answers is to study the archeological history of Jesus and determine what that history says about Jesus as a man and his birth, travels, and life. Is the biblical story of Jesus consistent with the archeological history? Such studies are described and discussed by Ariel Sabar in Smithsonian Magazine.[15] Two findings seem most relevant: A city unearthed near Golan where the Jordan River enters the Sea of Galilee is apparently Bethesda, where some of Jesus' apostles lived and where Jesus healed a blind man and multiplied the loaves of bread and fishes to feed many. One of the ruins resembles more a place of pagan worship and not a synagogue, suggesting a place for Jesus to preach to his followers. Another city being studied is Magdala, believed to have been visited often by Jesus and where Mary Magdalene joined his disciples and became a devoted follower. During these "digs" a heel was found in an ancient tomb with a nail protruding through it. This suggests that a common person, such as Jesus, could in fact be buried in a tomb after being crucified.

Another article of the search for Jesus appeared in Natl. Geographic magazine by K. Romey.[16] Romey presents sixty-two pictures/faces of Jesus, from around the world including Israel, Germany, Italy, USA, Russia, Britain, Spain, and others. Most of these are on public display in museums or churches. All are Caucasian, seven have beards, all have long hair, eleven have halos, one is an infant, one is a child. The last face is a computer reconstruction of the face from a skull of a first century Jewish man and, with the black, thick beard, looks quite ordinary. Obviously exactly what Jesus looked like is not known and does not really matter to believers. People in every culture portray him as "one of their own" looking like people they know but mostly white given that by the 1500s most Christians were European.[17]

Here are some of the archeological findings discussed by Romey in Natl. Geographic.[16] The best-known archeologist in Jerusalem is Father Alliata, who admits that evidence for proof of the life of one man, like Jesus, who lived 2000 years ago, is unlikely to be obtained. But still, the findings may be consistent with Jesus's life, traces of which are found in the gospels of Matthew, Mark, Luke, and John. Remnants of tombs were discovered in a shrine in Jerusalem's Church of the Holy Sepulchre. Two kinds of tombs were utilized back then: tombs with niches for the body and tombs with benches for the body. The stones used to close the tomb entrance (sort of cave-like, thus the idea that Jesus was buried in a cave) could be rounded or rectangular. Remnants of a ritual pool were discovered in Bethesda where Jesus healed a paralyzed man. People are still being baptized in the Jordan River, where Jesus was baptized by John the Baptist.

Only two of the gospels mention the birth of Jesus, with Luke describing the birth occurring in a manger (stable) with shepherds present. Matthew mentions the wise men, the massacre of children and flight of Jesus to Egypt. Maybe the gospel writers located the birth of Jesus to be Bethlehem to tie him to the Judean city prophesied in the Old Testament. Excavations at the Church of the Nativity revealed no artifacts or signs dating back to the time of Jesus and thus no indication that early Christians considered the site sacred. The theologian Origen of Alexandria visited Palestine and noted "in Bethlehem there is the cave where Jesus was born." Most scholars according to Romey[16] agree that there is no solid evidence of the birthplace of Jesus. Even so, the Christmas story of Jesus being born in Bethlehem is entrenched in the minds of Christians.

Jesus grew up in Nazareth as a social reformer while the Roman Empire ruled Palestine.

The Jews were unhappy with the Roman taxes and idolatrous religion and likely accepted Jesus because he denounced the rich and blessed the poor. Jesus lived just three miles from Sepphoris, the Roman provincial capital and some theorize he may have worked there. A detailed map provided by Romey[16] shows the travels of Jesus and where he performed miracles; he raised a widow's son from the dead; raised Lazarus from the dead; walked on water; changed water into wine; and healed the sick. Leprosy and tuberculosis were prominent back then, especially among the youth, so there were many opportunities for healing. Half of the uncovered graves from the time of Jesus contained bodies of children. A young Russian woman pictured at what is the possible tomb of Jesus is praying for the healing of her son who has cancer.

A synagogue was unearthed in Magdala, which is possibly where Jesus preached and recruited disciples. The heel with the spike found in an unearthed tomb is shown in graphic picture, again indicating that common people, such as Jesus, may have sometimes been buried in tombs.[16]

The four gospels are more in agreement on Jesus' death than on his birth.

Jesus' life as a preacher was only three and a-half years. What was his life like before then? What happened to his mother Mary? And Joseph? What about his brothers and/or sisters?

Romey[16] finishes her article with the following statement: "At this moment I realize that to sincere believers, the scholar's quest for the historical, non-supernatural Jesus is of little consequence. That quest will be endless, full of shifting theories, unanswered questions, irreconcilable facts. But for true believers, their faith in the life, death and Resurrection of the Son of God will be evidence enough."

No official New Testament existed in the first few centuries after Christ. Early religious people followed early scriptures that are not in the present New Testament. Those "lost scriptures" led to the beliefs that there were a dozen or even up to thirty gods, that Christ's resurrection meant nothing about people being saved, and that Christ did not die on the cross.[18]

Religious scholars, archeologists, scientists, and collectors are all looking for ancient texts. Why? Because none of the original New Testament books have been found. Most of what is available are copies and their authenticity is in question. There may have been additions or subtractions many years after the original writings. Seven Dead Sea Scrolls were found in 1947 in a cave in an ancient Jewish settlement by Bedouin goat herders. Since then, 100s more have been found dating to 300 BCE. These are the oldest biblical texts ever found, are written mostly on papyrus, and represent links to God's messengers – Muhammad, Moses, and Jesus – an early fragment of the book of Genesis is one component. Many manuscripts that would be useful in understanding the New Testament are not yet published. Because of centuries of copying, we may never know what the original texts said.[18, 19]

Elsewhere in this book is discussion of Santa Claus and many other fictitious individuals that people dreamed up centuries ago. The legend of Santa persists, but only for youngsters. The same is true for the Easter Bunny and Tooth Fairy. By age nine, most kids no longer believe in these three characters. Other fictitious characters are SpongeBob SquarePants, Superman, Batman, Cinderella, Robin Hood, Tarzan, Sherlock Holmes, Frankenstein, Popeye, Mary Poppins, Indiana Jones, Zorro, Tom Sawyer, and many more. The popularity of these legends was enhanced by comic books, novels for kids and adults, movies, and television. By adult age, everyone pretty much knows these are fictitious characters. Their persistence in the minds of children varies depending on how strongly they were imprinted and helped along by parents.

But there are more persistent characters. One is Yeti, also known as the Abominable Snowman, which is believed to roam the Himalayan mountains, the legend having begun in the 19th century. There is no conclusive evidence of the existence of Yeti but there are many believers and reports of sightings.[20] Another persistent fictitious character is Big Foot (also called Sasquatch), an ape-like hairy fellow supposedly seen by 1000s in N. America, mainly in the NW USA. Big Foot is believed to be folklore, a hoax, or a case of miss identification. Big Foot has been suggested to be the missing link between humans and apes. The European Wild Man is the equivalent of Big Foot. According to an Assoc. Press poll, more Americans believe in Big Foot than in the Big Bang! Ouch! Again, there is no scientific evidence for Big Foot's existence.[20]

We would be remiss to not mention a non-human legend, which is the

Loch Ness Monster (known also as Nessie), first reported in 1933, so it is not that old a legend. One of the most cited photos, of a dragon-like creature swimming in the Loch Ness, was exposed as a hoax in 1994. Again, 1,000s of people claim to have seen Nessie but the evidence is all anecdotal. (wikipedia.org/wiki/loch_ness_monster, n.d.)

The fictitious characters extend to the religious world. At one time at least ten greatly loved saints were popular but, having no evidence to support their existence, are now considered fictitious. St. Philomena came about from the name Filumena inscribed on some earthenware at a grave site. St. Christopher carried a very heavy child across a river; heavy because the child, who was Jesus, had the weight of the world on his shoulders. (Christ pher = Christ carrier). With no evidence supporting the existence of St. Christopher, he was removed from the church's liturgical calendar. St. Veronica supposedly wiped the face of Jesus with a cloth (vera icon = true image). There are seven more in the list of ten.[21] Can we add fairies to the list? Someone, way back in time, added wings to fairies without thinking about what muscles (pectorals) might power them and that for wings to work there must be air.

A mythical character of Japan, called Amabie, has been receiving much attention due to the coronal virus pandemic of 2020. This female "mermaid-like being," with three legs, goes back to 1846 when Amabie first appeared in Japanese folklore. But in 2020 Amabie re-appeared to a government official and predicted a pandemic but said the pandemic could be held in check if her likeness was drawn and shared around the world. The Japanese Minister of Health, Labor and Welfare has tweeted her image encouraging people to use her image to thwart the pandemic. Her image appeared on five continents and was seen on face masks, hand sanitizer containers, and truck doors. Images of Amabie are more varied than those of the faces of Jesus (see above) but the most often seen one is a character with long hair, a beak-like nose, scales, and fins or paddles on the feet. Amabie is one of many yokai, common mythological prophetic creatures of Japan, many having begun at times of diseases, like cholera, being rampant.[22] Proof of a negative or positive effect of Amabie would be difficult to obtain.

God has sometimes been depicted as mythical[23] but what about Jesus? Evidence is rather strong for Jesus being a real person[1] thus that part of his life is not mythical and he escaped being listed as a fictitious, mythical individual. But Jesus as someone who fed the hungry, healed the sick and resurrected the dead is perhaps more likely to be mythical as there is no proof of any of these feats and they are limited to a few cases. Jesus is sometimes referred to as the Messiah but that is erroneous because the Jewish messiah is prophesied to be a strong, king-like figure whereas Jesus was a commoner. Yet billions of Christians throughout the world view Jesus as God and their personal savior. Much of that view comes from the Bible.

Jesus presents challenges for God. God could have Jesus help to sort and evaluate new residents to Heaven. These would be aborted embryos, miscarriages, still births, infants, children, teens, and adults. God would have to instruct Jesus in these evaluations, millions every day, throughout the world, with many different languages involved. Both God and Jesus would be challenged.

But questions abound about the validity of what the Bible says. Most readers of the Bible take the "devotional" approach, what the Bible says relevant to their personal life and to society. Religious scholars take a historical and critical approach and attempt to understand what the Bible is and is not.[24] The latter studies lead to views such as; Jesus, Paul, Matthew, and John are associated with fundamentally different religions; the gospels were not written by Matthew, Mark, Luke and John but instead were forged in their names by Christian writers who lived many years later. Furthermore, scribes who copied the original Hebrew and Greek old and new testaments may very well have altered the texts to say what they wanted them to say. Some Christian doctrines, such as the divinity of Jesus, the trinity, and the suffering messiah, were ideas of later theologians.[24] What should readers of the Bible believe?

NOTES

1   Kristin Romey, "The Search for the Real Jesus," *National Geographic*, December 2017, 34-69.
2   Richard Wagner, *Christianity for Dummies* (New Jersey: Wiley Publ. Co., 2004.)
3   Bart D. Ehrman, *How Jesus Became God* (New York: Harper Collins, 2014.)

4 W.S. Klug and M.R. Cummings, *Concepts in Genetics* (New Jersey: Prentice Hall, 2003.)

5 Daniel Engber, "FYI: Could A Virgin Birth Ever Happen?," *Popular Science Magazine*, December 2013, 95.

6a Shermer, M., *"What is Truth, Anyway?,"* *Scientific American*, April 2017, 78.

6b Reasons for hope* Jesus website, "How Many Other People in the Bible Were Resurrected from Death?," accessed December 2019, https://reasonsforhopeje-sus.com/other-people-resurrected/; Got Questions website, "How many people were raised from the dead in the Bible?," accessed January 2020, https://www.gotquestions.org/raised-from-the-dead.html;

7 Genesis 2:7, Ecclesiastes 12:7 (King James Red Letter Version).

8 *Cheboygan Tribune*, May 8, 2020, A5; Wikipedia website, "Our Lady of Fatima, last edited March 15, 2023, https://en.wikipedia.org/wiki/Our_Lady_of_Fátima.

9 Bart D. Ehrman, *Lost Scriptures; Books that Did Not Make It into the New Testament* (Oxford: Oxford University Press, 2003.); Bart Ehrman, "The History & Literature of Early Christianity," *The Bart Ehrman Blog*, accessed January 2019, https://ehrmanblog.org.

10 Bart D. Ehrman, *Lost Scriptures*, 288-296.

11 A.R. Williams, "Recovering Erased Wisdom." *National Geographic*, March 2017.

12 *Cheboygan Daily Tribune*, February 28, 2020, A5.

13 Wikipedia website, "The World's Sixteen Crucified Saviors," last edited March 31, 2023, https://en.wikipedia.org/wiki/the_world's_sixteen_cruci-fied_saviors.

14 Wikipedia website, "Ontario Consultants on Religious Tolerance," last up-dated May 11, 2021, https://en.wikipedia.org/wiki/Ontario_Consultants_on_Religious_Tolerance.

15 Ariel Sabar, "Unearthing the World of Jesus," *Smithsonian Magazine*, January/February 2016.

16 Kristin Romey, "The Search for the Real Jesus," *National Geographic*, December 2017.

17 Wikipedia website, "The Race of Jesus," *Cheboygan Daily Tribune*, December 26, 2013; Wikipedia website, "Race and appearance of Jesus," last edited March 20, 2023, https://en.wikipedia.org/wiki/Race_and_appearance_of_Jesus.

18 Bart D. Ehrman, *Lost Christianities: Christian Scriptures and the Battles over Authentication* (Chantilly, VA: The Teaching Company, 2002); Ehrman, *Lost Scriptures: Books that Did Not Make It into the New Testament.*

19 R. Draper, "The Bible Hunters," *National Geographic*, December 2018, 40-75.

20 Wikipedia website, "Yeti," last edited February 17, 2023, https://en.wikipedia.org/wiki/Yeti.

21 Larry Jimenez, "10 Beloved Saints The Church Just Made Up," May 17, 2014, Listverse (website), listverse.com/2014/05/17/10-beloved-saints-with-fictitious-biographies.

22 Yokai website, "Yokai.com, the online database of Japanese folklore," accessed February 2021, yokai.com/amabie; *Northern Express*, June 1, 2020, 9.

23 Karen Armstrong, *A History of God: The 4,000-year quest of Judaism, Christianity and Islam*, (New York: Balantine Books, 1993.)

24 Bart D. Ehrman, *Jesus, Interrupted, Revealing the Hidden Contradictions in the Bible* (New York: Harper Collins, 2009.)

4

THE SOUL AND
HEAVEN

MOST RELIGIOUS PEOPLE believe that upon death the soul leaves the body and goes to Heaven. Then at the second coming the soul is recombined with the body that God restores. The soul must remember the body it came from; God must remember both and combine them correctly. A common view is that you save your soul by accepting Christ as your personal savior. The concept is that the soul maintains its unique "personness" and provides everlasting life after death. A plethora of differing views of the soul and Heaven exists going back to 100s of years BCE. [1a]

Our understanding of Heaven and the soul would be much greater if we could learn from those who have gone to Heaven. But things are not so clear! The four people who have gone to Heaven are Enoch, Elijah, Moses, and Jesus. The Bible says, "Enoch walked with God, and he was not, for God took him" (Genesis 5:24). Enoch did not die so God must have just "lifted" him into Heaven. "...Elijah was swept up to Heaven in a whirlwind" (II Kings 2:11). Michael, the archangel, chose to lift Moses to Heaven (Jude 1:9) and Moses and Elias appeared briefly and talked with Jesus on the mountain after Jesus was transfigured (Matthew 17:2-4). John 3:13 says, "No man hath ascended up to Heaven but he that came down from Heaven, even the son of man which is in Heaven." Did Jesus come down from Heaven? Jesus was born in Bethlehem and came from Mary's womb.

Jesus presumably ascended to Heaven after his crucifixion, then came down to earth to visit with his disciples, and again went back up to Heaven where he is to this day. Ascending to Heaven is different from being raised from the dead, i.e. resurrected. For example, Jesus raised Lazarus from the grave but not to Heaven. (John 11:43-44). We can learn very little about the soul and Heaven from these four Heaven residents.

Perhaps the most commonly held view of what happens after death is that the soul goes to Heaven and there it can interact with God and Jesus and also recognize and interact with (see and hear) previously deceased family, relatives, and friends who are in Heaven. The soul can presumably look down on earth and see the living. This view of the soul leaving the dead body comes mainly from Genesis 2:7 "…and the Lord God formed man of the dust of the ground and breathed into his nostrils the breath of life; and man became a living soul." From that statement writers and believers have come to accept the view that man has a soul, in addition to life and body, and therefore has three parts. But the early translations of the Hebrew and Greek writings use the word nephesh when referring to the soul. Nephesh means life. Thus, man is really only two parts: body and life (soul). And God made grass, herbs, and fruit trees (Gen 1:11-12) and cattle and all beasts (Gen. 1:24-25) and gave every living thing life. Thus, plants and animals have life and thus are also living souls but do not have souls as a separate entity. In this view the soul is not a separate entity that leaves the body. Life (soul) ends at death. When God made Eve of one of Adam's ribs in Genesis 2:21-23, no mention is made of breathing life into Eve but presumably he did so. The main point here is that in the earliest translations of Genesis 2:7 the word nephesh was translated to life not to soul. Somewhere along the next centuries "life" was switched to "soul" and ever since, the accepted idea is that man has a soul, distinguishable from life. Furthermore, the soul is now believed to be a physical or spiritual thing that can leave the body and maintain its identity; attempts have even been made to weigh the soul (see below).

At the funeral for a catholic bishop in one mid-western city the following prayer was stated: "Eternal rest grant onto him O Lord and let perpetual light shine upon him. May his soul and all the souls of the faithful departed rest in peace. Amen." The Sunday newspaper of a major midwestern city, following the listing of forty-seven death notices/obituaries, had this statement: "May eternal rest be granted upon them."[1b] The question is whether the soul, which is a spirit, can feel, see, and sense its surroundings; on earth or in Heaven? But who would want to be resting eternally and under perpetual light? And what is the source of that light? In *The Catcher in the Rye*,[2a] Holden Caulfield is talking about visiting his brother's grave with his parents and admitting it was not his favorite thing to do. He says, "I couldn't stand it. I know it's only his body and all that is in the cemetery and his soul's in Heaven and all that crap, but I couldn't stand it anyway. I just wish he wasn't there." Holden doesn't take religion very seriously.

Many questions can be asked about the soul. What is the history of the concept of the soul? What does the Bible say about the soul? Where does the soul reside in the body? When is the soul put into the body by God? When after death does the soul leave the body? Does the soul have a physical basis, i.e. can it see, hear, feel, smell, taste, and communicate? Can the soul be seen, heard, felt, interacted with, or weighed? Can the concept of the soul hold up to scientific scrutiny or is it a concept based only on faith? The First Law of Thermodynamics is used by Eli, the leader of a cult in the book by Jeffery Deaver, *The Goodbye Man*,[2b] to explain how immortality is achieved. Eli says, "When your body ceases to exist, the energy that is your True Core remains. This is because of the First Law of Thermodynamics, which says that energy cannot be created or destroyed. So after you die your True Core can end up in another body." So, are the True Cores, these bundles of energy, of the billions of people who have died, being cared for by God until the resurrection, at which time they will be reunited with their original bodies? Or with new bodies?

In *The Mermaid Chair*, Sue Monk Kidd's main character, Jessie Sullivan,[3] after a visit with the monk, Thomas, wondered what the soul was and offered the following. "Did anyone actually know? Sometimes I pictured it like a pilot light burning inside a person – a drop of fire from the invisible inferno people called God. Or a squashy substance, like a piece of clay or dental mold, which collected the sum of a person's experiences – a million indentations of happiness, desperation, fear, all the small piercings of beauty we've ever known." She was about to ask Thomas about the soul but was distracted by the church bell.

Someone said that true love is the soul's recognition of its counterpart in another person. In *The Painted Veil*, the head nun, upon her sister's death, said, "her good and simple soul has flown straight to Heaven."[4] A Jeopardy contestant describing the response when an audience was told how good a present contestant was said, "the gasp from the audience was like the sound of the soul escaping from the body." In a book written by a famous mystery writer, the detective said, "I don't want to lose what is left of my soul from birth." Clearly different people view the soul similarly yet differently but references to the soul are abundant enough to warrant their individual beliefs that the soul exists.

B.D. Ehrman has some vivid descriptions of the soul in his book Lost Scriptures.[5] Saint Paul, who had been snatched up to Heaven, said to the angel, "I wish to see the souls of the *just* and of *sinners*, and to see in what manner they go out of the body." The angel had him look upon the earth where he saw people growing weak and one man in particular who had done everything God expected and he was a just man. Both the impious (not holy; irreverent) and holy angels attended the man's death. The holy angels took possession of his soul, guiding it till it went out of his body, and they roused the soul saying, "soul, know the body you leave, for it is necessary that you should return to the same body on the day of resurrection, that you may receive the things promised to all the just." Receiving therefore the soul from the body, they immediately kissed it as if it were familiar to them, saying to it, "Be of good courage, for you have done the will of God while placed on the earth." There came to meet it the angel who watched it every day, and said to it, "Be of good courage soul; I rejoice in you because you have done the will of God on earth; for I related to God all your works just as they were." The spirit, the soul's helper, was also welcoming. And God and even Michael, the angel of the Covenant, welcomed the soul. And the voices of a thousand angels and archangels and cherubim and twenty-four elders were singing hymns and glorifying the Lord and respecting the decision to accept the soul into Heaven. In Chapter 5 the angel has Paul down on the earth but this time to watch the soul of an impious (irreverent) man. And Paul saw all the scorn of the sinner and all that he did. There came the holy angels and the evil angels, but the holy angels did not take interest. The evil angels cursed it and after drawing it out of the body admonished it saying, "O wretched soul, look upon your flesh so you can return to it on the day of resurrection and receive what is due for your sins and impieties." And the soul's guardian angel said, "I am the angel belonging to you, relating daily to the Lord your evil works and were it in my power not one day would I minister to you but was forced to until you repented but you have lost the time of repentance." And the angel and spirit led the soul into Heaven and presented the soul to the Lord. The Lord admonished the soul and it was led to the Angel Tartaruchus for punishment. And in verse 17 another soul was admonished for lying to the Lord, the Lord telling the soul that he can lie on earth to people, but the Lord knows when a lie is being told. Additional chapters describe how Paul was shown that the good and the pure souls were living among rivers of milk and honey, honey alone, wine, and oil, each environment with different souls with different holy backgrounds.

From this account of souls in The Apocalypse of Paul,[5] here is what can be said about the soul. The soul can be seen. The soul can see and speak. The soul is composed of flesh. The soul has at least one angel assigned to it on earth, keeping notes on what the soul and the person the soul occupies does or does not do, whether or not the angel approves. When a person dies, the soul is guided out of the body. The angel talks to the soul. The soul can talk to angels and to God. There is a spirit of some kind involved with each soul. Both good and bad souls are initially led to Heaven where God judges them as to where they should reside and be rewarded or punished until the resurrection. The soul is instructed to remember the body which it had inhabited so as to reunite with the correct body at the resurrection. Is it any wonder that some scriptures were left out of the Bible?

Ehrman[6] recounts from the Odyssey the story of Odysseus who visits Hades and sees his mother there as a shade (soul). He rushes to her to hug her but grasps nothingness. She flutters through his fingers like a shadow. She is an immaterial shade, but she can see her son and she can speak.

According to Alcorn[7] the Bible sees the disembodied soul as unnatural and undesirable and he therefore suggests that the body must be resurrected so that the soul can be reunited with the body. This reunification occurs on the New Earth. The soul at death goes to the intermediate Heaven and awaits the resurrection of the body so that reunification can occur. A problem is immediately posed when thinking about this reunification because dead bodies deteriorate, decompose, are lost at sea, are burned in part or completely (cremated) or are lost at early stages (zygotes, embryos, fetuses). Also, if the soul is "unnatural and undesirable," what is to be said of the view that the deceased is already in Heaven and viewing family members from above?

More history of the concept of the soul. Here is the biblical definition of the soul: the word soul is a translation of the Hebrew word "nephesh" and the Greek word "psykhe". The Hebrew word literally means a creature that breathes, and the Greek word means a living being. The soul then is the entire creature, not something that survives the death of the body."[8] A soul is a living being, a body that breathes.[8]

Given those definitions, nevertheless the view persists that the soul is separate from the body and leaves the body at death. Thus, various places in the body have been historically suggested as the place or seat of the soul. One of those places was the heart but only until it was realized that the heart is a muscle, and its role is to pump blood through the body. The pineal gland, a small structure at the base of the brain, was another suggested residence for the soul, as was the brain and even the lungs. An early view was that the soul leaves the body when the person sleeps and then returns when awaking. It would seem that a problem would be posed in cases where the body sleeps fitfully, awaking often throughout the night, or is awakened suddenly. Consider that these early views preceded knowledge of anatomy and physiology and thus may have seemed reasonable at the time. Note also that the concept of the soul was forthcoming prior to any knowledge of science, particularly the science of the body and how it functions.

Does the soul have weight? Considering the view that at death the soul leaves the body and is resurrected, then to early thinkers the soul could have some physical basis, perhaps even weight. In this early view the soul was made up of a "refined" material, much finer than that of the human body or trees and rocks. Being of some kind of material would explain how the soul could hear, see, smell and exhibit senses of pain and pleasure.[6] The seventeenth century philosopher Descartes contributed to Western civilization the idea that the body was matter but the soul was not matter. In 1907, Duncan MacDougall, a physician (we will call him Dr. Mac), published results from his tests to determine if the soul has weight.[9] The idea of the study was of course interesting and Dr. Mac was serious in his effort. Presumably the journal's reviewers of the article thought the results were worthy of publication.

Being a physician, Dr. Mac had patients suffering from diseases and/ or old age and were on the verge of death. Thus, he had these patients individually placed on a platform that was really a scale that measured to a sensitivity of 0.2 ounces (5.6 grams). Note that 1 ounce = 28 grams. While on the scale the patient's weight was continuously being measured so that at the time of death, if the soul had weight, the scale would show a loss of weight as the soul departed from the body. This loss in weight is referred to as "mortuary degravitation" by B. Evans.[10] Dr. Mac could have theoretically answered three questions: When does the soul leave the body in relation to the time of death? Does the soul have weight? How much does the soul weigh? Dr. Mac did the measurements on dying patients.

At this point, the reader might feel the whole idea is crazy because everyone knows the soul is a spirit and could not have weight. But based on curiosity alone, perhaps some readers will want to know the results of these rather macabre tests. Dr. Mac provided the results for six patients. Patient #1 lost ¾ ounce; patient #2 lost ½ ounce; patient #3 lost ½ ounce; patient # 4 results were inconclusive due to interference; patient #5 lost 3/8 ounce; patient #6 died before the scale could be adjusted. Dr. Mac could not account for the weight losses of patients 1, 2, 3 and 5 by urine loss, feces loss, sweat loss, or air loss). Of these four patients, one showed an immediate loss and no more with time, two showed an immediate loss and more later, and results of two patients were inconclusive and thus discarded. Dr. Mac concluded that the soul weighs between 14 and 21 grams and that the soul leaves the body upon death (not before death and not long after death). Dr. Mac's explanation for the fifteen-minute delay in one patient was that the person's "sluggish temperament" was responsible for the soul remaining in the body for a time. Dr. Mac had plans to take pictures of the soul using x-rays but apparently nothing came of that venture. The movie 21 Grams with Sean Penn was based in part on the study of Dr. Mac.

It was accepted at the time of Dr. Mac's measurements that dogs and other animals did not have souls. Thus, in fifteen cases Dr. Mac tested whether the weight of dogs changed upon death. Dr. Mac does not say how the demise of these dogs came about. As predicted, when a dog died, there was no weight loss, consistent with the view that only humans possessed souls. Interestingly enough, Alcorn[7] says there will be dogs and other animals in Heaven, on the new earth. Presumably God will resurrect select pets and other animals. Note that some religions believe all animals and even rivers and other physical things possess souls.

No repeat of Dr. Mac's tests has been reported. Perhaps no one has been interested or, having done the tests, didn't report the results for whatever reason. In any case, Dr. Mac's results are generally not considered believable because the methodology was suspect, the sample size was small, no statistical tests were carried out, and the results were variable.

Dr. Mac presumably had some definition of the time of death and believed that the soul leaves the body at that time. But the time of death is not so clear. Consider that stories in the news describe individuals that are on life support due to disease, strokes, or accidents, and families are unwilling to discontinue the life support in the hope that the person is still alive and will eventually "recover consciousness." This unwillingness is seen even when medical experts agree that the person is dead, as shown by complete lack of electrical activity in the brain or brain stem as determined by a CAT scan or EEG (electroencephalograph). But in some states in the USA the definition is based on the lack of a pulse and heartbeat. Now with CPR, a person's heart can be resuscitated and thus a person can be dead in one state but alive in another. Life support can maintain "life" of the body, such as respiration and metabolism, or function of organs even if the person is by definition dead! In such a case, the soul has presumably left the body and is already in God's hands!

The legal definition of death is important with regard to agreeing to organ donation. An interesting case is of the man in prison who was in the eighteenth year of a life sentence and had a medical emergency in that he suffered several heart attacks. After each he was resuscitated, and his heartbeat was restored. The man claimed therefore that he had died and thus had served his life sentence and should be released. The Appeals court did not agree and he remains in prison.[14] Ahh shucks! Why can't dying be straight forward?

Can the soul be seen? In this regard, a passing motorist stopped at the site of a motorcycle accident and took a still picture of the soul of the individual that died in that accident and the camera operator said it was the soul leaving the body and going to Heaven (Natl. Inquirer, Aug. 8, 2016). Does this mean the soul can be seen? The problem with this view is that the man did not die until later in the hospital. Also, the picture was likely just a tree in the background and the photographer should have come back a day later and taken another picture. Also, in primitive Christian art the soul was depicted "as sort of a gremlin" leaving the dying person's mouth, a depiction much like the balloon used to enclose words in comics.[10] When people report seeing the Virgin Mary or Lady of Guadalupe what are they seeing? Their souls? If so, then in the case of certain individuals the soul can in fact be seen and recognized.

Instead of weight loss, another school of thought was that the body "gains" weight upon death but, according to Evans,[10] that is only because the body stiffens after death and becomes more ungainly and only seems to be heavier.

Animals were often studied not to understand them in terms of zoology, anatomy, physiology, and genetics but to find "moral examples" to apply to humans. One curious example is the story of the beaver which, when hunted for its testicles, chewed them off and threw them to the hunters, the lesson being that men must give up wealth to save their souls. The story was no doubt derived because the beaver's testicles were highly valued for curing tooth aches, aiding abortions, and adding flavor to coffee.

The reader must be reminded that many of these ideas are from the 17th century or earlier, prior to much knowledge about science. The old belief that "you cannot change human nature" likely contributed to the view of the "immortality of the soul."[10] But, although immutable, the soul was thought to be amenable to discipline. The soul, for all its divine nature, was thought to be controlled by malignant spirits which could compel its owner to commit terrible acts, even its own damnation.

As with many aspects of Heaven, the soul is mentioned in novels. In one such novel, wherein the subjects were discussing the frequency of homicides and the perpetrators who commit those homicides, a grandmother said, "they have cracked souls…I think some people are born with souls that are not all there or maybe their souls got cracked somewhere along the line, like a broken leg." Here the view is that the soul has physical substance.[11]

UNANSWERED QUESTIONS ABOUT THE SOUL

Does God put the soul into the body? When does God put the soul into the body? Does God create a new soul for everybody? Where does the soul reside in the body? What is the soul doing before the body dies? Is the soul aware of the physical and mental processes of the body? When after death does the soul leave the body? In considering the past deaths of the billions of people through the ages, where are their souls and what are they doing?[1a] Are they in the empyrean (highest Heaven) or in some earthly paradise or some "lesser Heaven"[1a] or intermediate Heaven?[7] If the body has decomposed, been cremated, lost, or torn apart, does the soul have a blueprint so God can restore the body?

If a ship sinks into the depths of the ocean and people die after the ship sinks, can the souls escape the weight, pressure, of the water? If people die after being buried by tons of cement blocks when a building collapses, can the souls escape from under the crushing weight?

If the soul has no weight, what is its nature? Does it have physical strength? Does it have a mind? Can it think? Does it have memory? Can it communicate and if so, how? Can it see, hear, and smell? Does it interact with other souls? Can it talk? Can it shout? Can it sing? What would hold the soul in Heaven or on earth; without weight, gravity could not influence the soul.

Where does a person's soul come from? Does everyone initially get a soul from God? Does the soul enter the individual at the time of fertilization of the egg, even before the first cleavage division, or later in embryonic life or maybe at birth? According to Dr. Mac (see above) the soul weighs twenty-one grams; that is much more weight than the human zygote. Even at nine weeks gestation the human embryo only weighs nine grams. Does the soul grow as the body grows? If a person's body is abused physically or injured in an accident, or by drugs, alcohol, or other chemicals, or is burned, is the soul adversely affected as well? If an embryo is in some way deformed is the soul likewise deformed?[12] If the body at birth or sometime later is abnormal due to genetic or chromosomal defects is the soul similarly abnormal? Does it matter with regard to whether or not the soul is saved as to when an abortion is performed, first, second, or third trimester?

Consider the soul in the case of identical twins. Identical twins form after a considerable number of cleavage divisions, in which case two inner cell masses form instead of one. Each inner cell mass then develops into an embryo which goes on to become a fetus and finally a baby. The two babies are genetically identical. Are their souls identical as well? What happens to the souls of each if one twin leads a clean life as a God-believer but the other a sinful life as a non-believer?

More questions can be raised about what would happen to the soul if a person was cloned once? Or twice? Or three times? Would each have a soul and would they be identical to the original soul?

What about the soul in cryogenics? When a body (or just the head) is frozen immediately after death what happens to the soul? Has it already gone to Heaven? If that individual is thawed and restored to life some decades later, will a soul be present?

When a baby, teen or adult is baptized, does the soul get added at that time? If the soul is already present, does the soul get changed somehow by the baptism? When a person accepts Christ as their personal savior, does their soul somehow change at that time, perhaps breathing a sigh of relief?

What happens to the soul in cases of near-death? Is it the soul which sees things, like a bright light and family members, and hovers above and looks down at the body? When the person comes "back to life" does the soul immediately reenter the body? How does it reenter the body and through what orifice?

Consider the case of a teen who suffered a serious medical situation causing brain injury, loss of consciousness, and was hospitalized and put on life support. The hospital personnel concluded after three weeks on life support that the teen's brain was dead (brain dead).[16] The definition of death as "the complete cessation of all functions of the entire brain, including the brain stem" was approved by the Amer. Med. Assoc. and Amer. Bar Assoc., 1980 and 1981. The life support technology allowed the teen's perfused body to be warm and have a beating heart and thus the family was optimistic that the brain-dead teen was alive and might possibly regain consciousness. However, the life support was discontinued after the hospital personnel concluded that the teen was in fact dead. A priest was appropriately called in to give last rites, but the teen had presumably already died three weeks earlier.[17]

How does God handle these situations? When does God take the teen's and baby's souls? After three weeks of being dead, the teen's brain must have deteriorated considerably and lost most if not all of its memories, experiences, and knowledge gained from school and life. The premature baby's brain had few if any memories of experiences or knowledge.

Lee M. Silver, in his book *Challenging Nature,* discusses the possibility of the soul being coded in a person's DNA and apparently the Riken Institute in Japan is investigating that possibility.[15] If the gene(s) that code(s) for the soul can be isolated then that gene could be transferred into a non-human primate and therein give that primate a human soul. Maybe one difference in the genes of a human and a Neanderthal are the genes for the soul. But note that data from DNA sequencing indicates that early *Homo sapiens* bred with Neanderthals and may have bred with *Homo erectus* even earlier.[13]

When God made Eve of one of Adam's ribs in Genesis 2:21-23, no mention is made of breathing life into Eve but presumably he did so. As an aside, genetically, the XY male chromosome karyotype of those rib cells of Adam must have been changed by God into XX chromosome female cells of Eve. From where did God get that extra X chromosome? The main point here is that in the earliest translations of Genesis 2:7 the word nephesh was translated to life not to soul. Somewhere along the next centuries "life" was switched to "soul" and ever since, the accepted idea is that man has a soul, distinguished from life. The idea that the soul is a physical or spiritual thing that can leave the body and maintain its identity and communicate seems to be wishful thinking.

NOTES

1a   J.B. Russell, *The History of Heaven* (New Jersey: Princeton University Press, 1997.)

1b   *Detroit Free Press*, November 3, 2019, 26A.

2a   J. D. Salinger, *The Catcher in the Rye* (Boston: Little, Brown, and Co., 1952.)

2b   Jeffery Deaver, *The Goodbye Man*, (New York: Penguin Random House LLC, 2020.).

3   Sue Monk Kidd, *The Mermaid Chair* (New York: Penguin Books, 2005.)

4   *The Painted Veil*, directed by John Curran (2006, Universal City, CA: Studio Distribution Services), DVD.

5   Bart D. Ehrman, *Lost Scriptures; Books that Did Not Make It into the New Testament* (Oxford: Oxford University Press, 2003.)

6   Bart D. Ehrman, *Heaven and Hell, A History of the Afterlife* (New York: Simon and Schuster, 2020.)

7   Randy Alcorn, *Heaven: A Comprehensive Guide to Everything the Bible Says About Our Eternal Home* (Illinois: Tyndale Momentum, 2004.)

8   Bible Ask website, "What does the word soul in the Bible mean?," accessed February 2020, https://Bibleask.org/what-does-the-word-soul-in-the-Bible-mean.

9   Duncan MacDougall, "Hypothesis concerning soul substance together with experimental evidence of the existence of such substance," *American Society of Psychical Research,* Volume 1, 1907: 237-244.

10   Bergen Evans, *The Natural History of Nonsense* (New York: Vintage Books, 1958.)

11   Janet Evanovich, *Twisted Twenty-Six,* (New York: GP Putnam's Sons, 2019.) 171.

12   Michael Barresi and Scott Gilbert, *Developmental Biology,* 12th Edition (British Columbia: AbeBooks, 2018.); Bruce Carlson, *Human Embryology and Developmental Biology,* 6th Edition (Amsterdam: Elsevier, 2018).

13   Science and Technology Section, *Science,* Volume 314, October 2006.

14   Healthguidance.org website, "When Are You Dead?," updated on January 6, 2020, https://www.healthguidance.org/entry/14200/1/when-are-you-dead.html; News of the Weird, "Fine Points of the Law," *Northern Express,* November 25, 2019, 9.

15   Lee M. Silver, *Challenging Nature: The Clash of Science and Spirituality at the New Frontiers of Life* (New York: Ecco, 2002)

16   Wikipedia website, "Uniform Determination of Death Act," last edited April 8, 2023, https://en.wikipedia.org/wiki/Uniform_Determination_of_Death_Act.

17   John Wisely, "Boy at center of brain death case officially dies after life support is stopped," *Detroit Free Press,* October 16, 2019, 4A, October 17, 2019 1A.

5

EMBRYOLOGY, BIRTH DEFECTS, TWINS, AND TRANSPLANTS

GOD WILL HAVE major challenges with the subjects of this chapter, and to begin, a brief description of the initiation of embryonic development is in order.[1] The human egg, the oocyte, is fertilized in the upper reaches of the female reproductive system, within the fallopian tube, by a sperm cell that is haploid in that it contains only half of the chromosomes, one of each of the twenty-three pairs. Upon entry of the sperm nucleus, the egg nucleus continues in meiosis and a polar body is released. The egg nucleus remaining is then also haploid. When the sperm and egg nucleus combine, the diploid condition is restored and the first cleavage division soon occurs. Proteins and nucleic acid signaling molecules, maternal gene products, were already added to the egg while it was in the ovary. These maternal gene products initiate and control early development. After several cleavage divisions a round ball of cells, the blastocyst, forms. The blastocyst, now having an inner cell mass, continues down the fallopian tube to the uterus where it implants. Now, after the maternal gene products have done their job, cell to cell interactions (inductions) occur and embryo gene products, produced by the cells of the embryo, begin controlling development. The inner cell mass flattens and the embryo forms from the flattened cell mass.

Soon the brain and spinal cord become noticeable and meanwhile the internal organs begin to form. As cell to cell and tissue to tissue interactions occur, more genes are differentially expressed, and an embryo with a defined head, neural tube, eyes, heart, arms, and legs, takes shape. The genes that are expressed are those of the diploid genome, the two chromosomes of each of the twenty-three pairs, forty-six total. Whether the embryo develops in the female or male direction is dependent upon the Y chromosome. A gene on the Y chromosome initiates development of the testis which then produces the male hormone (testosterone) resulting in the male phenotype (a boy baby). If the Y chromosome is not present, the default pathway is seen, the ovaries develop and the subsequent female hormones (progesterone and estrogen) are produced resulting in the female phenotype (a girl baby). After nine months of gestation, a girl or boy baby is born.[1] Whether the phenotype is boy or girl, the child may grow up to be anywhere on the spectrum of LGBTQ (lesbian, gay, bisexual, transsexual, and queer).

To many, a baby is God's miracle and from fertilization to birth the process is controlled by God. After all, Psalms 139:13-14, says, "for you formed my inward parts, you wove me together in my mother's womb. I praise you for I am fearfully and wonderfully made." Referring to this biblical passage, a guest columnist in a local newspaper reminded readers that God plans every birth in every detail. But the columnist admits to enduring three miscarriages and a stillborn child before finally having three healthy births and thus three grown children, for which she offers much praise to God. But she directs no criticism toward God for the miscarriages nor for the still birth and makes no suggestions as to the fate of the respective souls. If God controls the development and birth of babies, why do we see miscarriages and still births and various abnormalities in babies? (see Chapter 6).

Your genes determine that you will be a vertebrate, a mammal, and a human being and not a lizard, a fox, or a monkey.[1] Genes influence not only how you look but also how tall you are, how intelligent you are, what abilities you have, your eye color, and your many other characteristics. Now we know that your genetic make-up also influences your tastes in foods, your politics, and even your love life. In fact, every human behavior is controlled in part by a person's genes- addiction, attraction, and anxiety. But even identical twins are not exactly alike due to the environment affecting gene expression by a process called epigenetics. These epigenetic influences are due to chemical changes to genes, like methylation, influencing how they are expressed, an area of great interest in the field of genetics.[2] God will have quite a time sorting out epigenetic from direct gene influences.

Twins represent interesting challenges for God. There are two kinds of twins, fraternal and identical. Fraternal twins are the result of two eggs (oocytes) being fertilized by two different sperm cells and thus can be both female, both male, or one female and one male. They can be as similar or different as any pair of siblings. Identical twins are derived from the fertilization of one egg by one sperm cell but as development progresses two inner cell masses form and each one develops into an embryo, fetus, and a child. Identical twins are the same sex, either two boys or two girls, and are genetically identical. Worldwide from ten to twenty sets of twins are born for every 1,000 births; this range is due to differences from country to country. Identical twins are seen in three of every 1,000 births worldwide. Fraternal twins can be as similar or different as any two sisters or brothers and are not identical genetically. Differences between two identical twins can result from epigenetic factors (environmental). Note that 140 million births occur each year worldwide (census data).

Presumably God gives each fraternal twin a unique soul, just as he would with any siblings. Similarly, triplets or quadruplets or more multiples would each have a unique soul. The question can be raised as to when the soul enters the developing individual. Does God put the soul into the egg and when does he do that? What about identical twins? If the soul enters at the time of fertilization and then twinning occurs (two inner cell masses), how does the soul get partitioned? Is the soul split into two identical souls? Does only one embryo get the soul? Does God add another soul when he sees that two inner cell masses are forming? If this early stage is miscarried, does God recognize that there are two inner cell masses, and does he direct their development in Heaven into identical twins? Maybe the soul is not added to the embryo until later, given that many embryos are miscarried or aborted, and thus God does not have to monitor these early stages. Or perhaps God gives each child a separate and unique soul at the time of birth or baptism.

A greater challenge to God will be Siamese (conjoined) twins, which can be connected in various ways. And what about Siamese twins which are then surgically separated after birth? Or Siamese twins that live their lives connected to each other? Twinning is a challenge in terms of the soul and Heaven. If the inner cell masses do not separate completely, Siamese or conjoined twins are the result. They can be conjoined at the head, the back, the side, or the front and can even share an organ or two. If God puts the soul in the egg, does it split in two when identical twinning occurs, or does it duplicate itself when the inner cell mass splits? In conjoined twins are the souls also conjoined? What is the fate of souls in conjoined twins when they are surgically separated? Does each have an identical soul? If the surgery results in loss of a leg or an arm from each twin or from one of the twins, does God give that twin a new leg or arm in Heaven? If Siamese twins die, does God separate them in Heaven and give each a complete functional body? Or do they live in Heaven as Siamese twins? Will he give these twins a choice? If they have lived for decades as conjoined twins maybe they don't want to be separated.

Many factors are known to adversely affect the normal course of development and can cause birth defects, some having more profound effects than others. One of these factors is genetic. Genes are expressed to make (transcribe) RNA which makes (translates) proteins. Many proteins are necessary at the right time and place to control development of the embryo's tissues and organs. The combinations of the two sets of haploid chromosomes results in genes being paired. Thus, if one gene that is normally expressed during development is mutated, the paired chromosome gene is most often normal (wildtype) and development proceeds fine. But if the mutated gene is on both chromosomes of the pair, abnormal development can occur and the result is referred to as a genetic abnormality; genetic abnormalities can be external, such as influencing the eyes, face, or limbs, or internal, influencing the brain, heart, or other organs. Many, many people die of causes other than the genetic abnormality they exhibit. God will have to diagnose each deceased person as to the cause of death but also whether they might have a genetic abnormality which causes day to day problems even though not the cause of death.[4] Genetic diseases are discussed in detail in Chapter 14.

German measles, called rubella, is a disease caused by a virus that can cause abnormalities in the developing embryo carried by a mother exposed to the virus. German measles has been in the news because of the fear that

the measles vaccine causes autism. That is an unfounded fear but neverthe-
less, almost 15 % of pregnant women do not have their children vaccinated
and thus measles is now becoming prevalent in certain parts of the coun-
try leading to fear of a widespread measles epidemic. German measles is
spread via a virus. Apparently, there was a case of rubella at the USA auto
show in Detroit in 2019, a finding that is scary because the rubella virus
is easily spread (contagious). After exposure to the virus, symptoms of ru-
bella include a rash that usually begins on the face and then spreads to the
body followed by a low-grade fever, sore throat, headache, and tiredness.
In 1964-65 a rubella epidemic resulted in 12.5 million Americans getting
rubella, including 11,000 pregnant women who miscarried, 2,100 infant
deaths, and 20,000 babies born with birth defects caused by rubella virus. A
vaccine was developed in 1969 which immunized against mumps, measles,
and rubella (MMR vaccine); vaccination became a requirement 10 years
later in Michigan and other states. If a woman who is not immunized to
rubella is exposed to the rubella virus while pregnant, she can miscarry,
have a still birth, or have a baby with defects. The most common defects are
cataracts, heart abnormalities, deafness, mental disabilities, liver and spleen
damage, low birth weight, and a skin rash at birth. There are additional
birth defects as well.[5]

Diagnosing must have been a challenge for God. Correcting the ab-
normalities would have been the second challenge. God must be dreading
a new rubella-caused set of challenges. Such a challenge may not be far
away because more and more mothers are neglecting to have their children
vaccinated. The center for disease control (CDC) personnel have predicted
where measles numbers will increase and that prediction is being shown to
be true in 2019; dense populations with low vaccination rates are showing
the highest rates of rubella, including the cities of Seattle, Spokane, Salt
Lake City, Fort Worth, Detroit, and Phoenix. Interestingly, centers with
high populations of Orthodox Jewish and also of Amish, are showing higher
levels of rubella because these people are not vaccinating; they receive reli-
gious exemptions.[6] It seems incongruous for religious people to not immu-
nize their children against MMR and allow rubella to occur, and to risk the
adverse effects of rubella in pregnant women. Is God going to destroy every
trace of the rubella/measles/mumps viruses in Heaven? Several states are no
longer accepting religious or philosophical reasons for their children to not

be immunized before beginning school. 2020-2022 coronavirus pandemic should further encourage immunizations.

Mothers who took thalidomide as an antidepressant in the 1950s often gave birth to babies born with arm and leg abnormalities. These so-called flipper limbs, the most common result, were arms without the long bones (humerus, radius, and ulna) but the hands and digits formed. In other cases the arms and legs did not develop at all with no hand or foot or long bones. Will God correct these abnormalities in the deceased? Thalidomide apparently adversely affects the expression of the genes necessary for normal limb development. The sequence of differential gene expression required for limb development has been studied in model organisms, such as the chick embryo and mouse embryo, and is still being elucidated.[1] Does God know this gene expression sequence?

What about direct human-caused abnormalities? For a millennium, Chinese women had their feet bound up as an effort to be more attractive and sexual. This foot-binding is perhaps best illustrated by examining the tomb of Lady Huang Sheng, the wife of an imperial clansman. Lady Huang Sheng died in 1243. In her tomb, archeologists found tiny misshapen feet, wrapped in gauze inside specially shaped "lotus shoes." These are not toy shoes but in fact were actually worn by Chinese women. A three-inch foot was the most desirable and considered a golden lotus. A four-inch foot was a silver lotus, and anything above that was not desirable and the woman likely did not marry. At age five-six years, girls had their toes fractured and bent down and back against the bottom of the foot, followed by straining of the arch to bend it double. Estimates are that 40-50% of all Chinese women had their feet bound and 100% of the upper class. This cruel and painful process has been largely banned.[7] When these women go to Heaven will they ask God to give them "normal" feet? Will God automatically correct their feet to normalcy? Or, since they lived many decades with the "lotus" feet, as cerebral palsy people lived with their handicapped body parts, will God have them live in Heaven the same way? Sexual mutilation of young girls involving cutting off the clitoris is required in some societies. Will God correct this horrible mutilation in these women?

People can be born with facial abnormalities, or they can be the result of injury (gun shot, dog bite, burns or other), cancer, or mutant genes. Various parts of the face can be mildly or severely affected. Eyesight, speech, breathing, eating/swallowing can all be affected. In some cases, bones or other tissue can be taken from another part of the body and grafted to the face.[8] To correct a severely abnormal face, medical researchers have begun doing partial and even complete face transplants. Only about 50 face transplants have been carried out around the world (through 2019); the first partial transplant was done in France in 2005; the first full transplant was performed in Spain in 2010. The first face transplant in the USA was performed in 2011. The first African American to receive a facial transplant had the surgery in 2019.[9] Facial transplants have been done in Canada and Turkey as well. The Johns Hopkins School of Medicine has a transplant center that advertises facial transplants. The Cleveland Clinic performed its 3rd facial transplant from a medically declared dead thirty-one-year-old woman to a twenty-one-year-old woman in need of a new face, the 40th facial transplant in the world. The face expresses the emotions of joy, fear, anger, disgust, sadness, and surprise. The face enables a person to converse, kiss, bite, chew, sing, and sigh. The face is like any organ and an immunological match is necessary to keep rejection possibilities low. Immunosuppressant drugs are taken by the patient.[10] The donor by necessity must have died. When the donor reaches Heaven, will God provide the exact face he/she had before? Will the donor have the same face as the recipient still on earth? When the recipient person dies, will God restore his/her original face to what it was before any disfiguring occurred (accident, burn, cancer etc.)?

In Chapter 11 are listed the kinds of information God needs at the time of death of a person. Some of these include: facial features, disabilities, genetic defects, history of surgeries, history of diseases, organ and tissue transplants/donations. One important facial feature is the teeth. Most adults have had one or more cavities which have been repaired by a dentist. Fifteen million people in the USA have had a crown or bridge work done by a dentist. Thirty-five million people have all the teeth missing in one or both jaws. Three million people have had dental implants and 500,000 more are done each year. Consider that the first dental implant was done by a Swedish orthopedic surgeon in 1952. Many millions before that and since then have died with one or more missing teeth. (www.Dental_implants_F&Q.html). Does God replace these missing teeth? If a person has one or more implants, will God replace these with the person's own teeth or leave the implant(s) in place forever? Like an artificial lens, dental implants are more stable through the years than the person's own teeth. After the body decomposes, dental implants, the metal in joint replacements, and artificial lenses will be the only things remaining in the coffin/grave.

Breast implants have become rather commonplace. There are 400,000 breast implants done in the USA each year, roughly ¼ for medical reasons such as cancer surgery and ¾ for cosmetic reasons. If a woman has one or both breasts removed or augmented due to a medical condition such as cancer, she could have reconstructive surgery using tissues from her own body or she could have implants of foreign material (silicone; or fluid). One of every five women who get implants need to have them removed and replaced after 8-10 years. Possible side effects of implants include scarring, pain, rupture, arthritis, fatigue, and even a rare form of cancer.[3] Will God remove the implants in Heaven?

Various organs can be transplanted. Heart transplants can add many years to a person's life, an average of twelve years and in a few cases over thirty years.[11] But not enough donor hearts are available to meet the need for transplants. Nearly 4,000 people in the USA are on the national waiting list of a heart transplant; twenty Americans die every day waiting for a transplant. The average number of days a person in need of a new heart spends on the waiting list is 312, almost a year. In 2016 there was an estimated six million Americans living with a failing heart. In 2016, a total of 3,191 heart transplants were performed; 3,408 in 2018.[12] A well-known person in football who was a player, coach and executive, 60 years of age, was in need of a new heart due to having amyloidosis, a build-up of amyloid protein in the heart which interferes with the heart's pumping capacity and strength. He received a new heart in 2019. The donor was 26 years old. The age is not as important to match as are the immunological and size comparisons. In this case the donor heart was "perfect" in both conditions.

More donor hearts are becoming available for two reasons: First, diseased organs can be utilized because some of the diseases, for example hepatitis C, can be cured; second, many young, healthy individuals are dying of drug overdoses and their hearts are perfectly healthy and are being donated more and more.[13] Rarer is to have heart and double lung transplants, with only thirty-two done in all of 2018, usually with patients that have pulmonary hypertension, a condition found at all ages but more so after seventy-five years of age, and more often in women and non-Hispanic blacks.[14]

The same questions raised above for facial transplants can be raised for heart transplants. Will God replace the donor's heart in the recipient patient with his/her own heart? What will become of the donor's heart? Will the deceased donor, now in Heaven, already have received a new heart from God? What happens to the malfunctioning old heart of the patient? Most are apparently tossed away but one hospital keeps them; each is in a jug of formaldehyde and can be viewed by the patient.[15] The transplanted heart may not continue to function, and the patient may die. Or the patient may die of other causes with the transplant heart functioning fine. In either case, God must diagnose that the deceased heart is a transplant. Will God make a new heart from the patient's own cells or make sure the transplant is doing fine, perhaps with some overhauling, and keep it?

There is a great need for organs. In the USA in 2021 there are 108,000 people on the list of waiting for a transplant. Twenty people die every day waiting for a transplant.[16] Other organs that have been transplanted are the liver, kidneys, lungs, cornea, hand, pancreas, small intestine, uterus, and more. In each case there are far more people waiting for a transplant than there are donors available.[17] The lens of the eye is worth looking at more closely. When the lens becomes opaque or develops cataracts, ophthalmologists can replace the diseased lens with an artificial lens, made of plastic, which functions beautifully. The patient's original cataract containing lenses are discarded. A patient asked his ophthalmologist how long the new lens would last; the answer was, "forever." That answer makes for an interesting situation in Heaven. Will God replace the plastic lens with the patient's own lens and if so, won't it age as it has on earth? Perhaps God will give all residents of Heaven plastic lenses since the Bible says no one will age in Heaven. How else will aging of the lens be prevented in Heaven, especially with all that bright light bombarding the eyes?[18]

Livers and kidneys are the most common internal organs transplanted.[19] They are often diseased and can lead to the patient's death. The most common liver disease is cirrhosis, which is scarring of the liver, and is associated with heavy alcohol consumption. Other liver ailments are hepatitis B and C, fatty liver disease, autoimmune disease, metabolic disease, and newborn liver disease. Livers are in short supply. Each year 8,000 liver transplants are performed in the USA. About 13,900 people are on the waiting list for a new liver. Each year 1,500 people in the USA die while waiting for a new liver. God has to diagnose that their deaths were due to liver disease and then diagnose which liver disease was the cause of the liver malfunction. After a liver transplant the one-year survival is 89% and the five year survival is 75%.[19] When people with a liver transplant die, God has to decide whether to give them a new liver made from their own tissues or to keep the transplant. Presumably by this time God would have given the donor person a new liver, yes?

More than 100,000 people are on the waiting list for a kidney and thirteen people die each day while waiting for a kidney. Since 1988, 430,000 kidney transplants have been performed. Thirty-five thousand kidney transplants were performed in 2018. The three-year survival is 92%. Donated kidneys come mostly from people who die due to stroke, anoxia, head trauma, cancer, and drug overdoses.[20]

Of all African American patients awaiting organ transplants in 2015, only 17% received a transplant, compared with 30% of white patients. Donors of all organs are in shorter supply among African Americans. Face transplants would necessarily be done from black to black and white to white to maintain identity, but internal organs could be any combination.[9, 16]

The first uterus transplant in which a baby subsequently developed was of a sixty-year-old woman donor uterus into a thirty-two-year-old woman recipient. The donor uterus had sustained a life three decades earlier. The thirty-two-year-old had been born without a uterus.[21] In another case a uterus from a deceased woman was transplanted into a woman born without a uterus. The recipient woman subsequently got pregnant and gave birth to a healthy baby. In Heaven, having children by sex is maybe not going to occur. But menstruation is a normal process and will seemingly occur in Heaven as it does on earth. Will God provide a new uterus for women in Heaven who do not have one? Or will the new body God provides for that deceased woman not have a uterus? Perhaps all the aborted and miscarried embryos will be carried to term by women in Heaven and thus in these cases a uterus will be necessary. If there is no sex in Heaven and no childbirths, a uterus would not be necessary. Would women accept not having menstrual periods?

In the news is the question of whether health insurance should cover preexisting conditions such as asthma, diabetes, or cancer and should the rates be higher for those people? Well, God will see very few people in Heaven without some kind of pre-existing condition. God will have a considerable amount of diagnosing every minute of every day as the population of Heaven grows.

NOTES

1   Bruce Carlson, *Human Embryology and Developmental Biology*, 6th Edition (Amsterdam: Elsevier, 2018); Michael Barresi and Scott Gilbert, *Developmental Biology*, 12th Edition (British Columbia: AbeBooks, 2018.)

2   Bill Sullivan, "Why You Like What You Like," *National Geographic*, September, 2019, 17-20.

3   *Detroit Free Press*, October 24, 2019, 3B.

4   *Detroit Free Press*, January 18, 2015, 1A, 8A.

5   "Rubella," *Detroit Free Press*, February 5, 2019.

6   *Popular Science*, February 5, 2019.

7   Amanda Foreman "Why Footbinding Persisted in China for a Millennium," *Smithsonian Magazine*, February 2015, https://www.smithsonianmag.com/history/why-footbinding-persisted-china-millennium-180953971/; Wikipedia website, "Foot binding," accessed March 10, 2020, https://en.wikipedia.org/wiki/Foot_binding.

8   *Detroit Free Press*, July 16, 2017, 10A.

9   Jamie Ducharme, "A face-transplant first," *Time*, November 4, 2019, 62-67.

10   Joanna Connors, "Transplanting A New Face," *National Geographic*, September 2018, 40-50.

11   *Detroit Free Press*, April 1, 2015, 1A, 7A.

12   *Time*, November 6, 2017, 20; statista website, "Number of heart transplantations in the U.S. from 1975 to 2020," accessed March 20, 2020, https://www.statista.com/statistics/671451/heart-transplants-number-us/

13   *Time*, November 6, 2017, 20; *Detroit Free Press*, June 4, 2018, 1A.

14   *Northern Express*, October 28, 2018.

15   Lauren Young, "I Held My Own Heart," *Reader's Digest*, September 2017, 50.

16   Susan Bromley, "Gift of Life Keeps Giving Amid Covid," *Cheboygan News*, April 28, 2021.

17   S. Rudavsky, "Doctors Fear New Policy May Mean Longer Wait to Receive Transplants," *Indianapolis Star*, March 1, 2018, 3A; Maggie Steber and Joanna

Connors, "What it means to have a new face," *National Geographic*, September 2018, 90-95.

18 Revelation 22:5 (King James Red Letter Version).

19 Donate Life America website, accessed April 9, 2020, https://www.donatelife.net/statistics/.

20 Shari Rudavsky, Health Editor, *IndyStar*, accessed April 28, 2020, https://www.indystar.com/search/?q=kidney+transplants; National Kidney Foundation website, accessed April 28, 2020, https://www.kidney.org/

21 Erin Biba, "Something Borrowed," *Popular Science*, Summer, 2018, 36-43.

6

MISCARRIAGES
AND ABORTIONS

THERE HAS BEEN considerable fervor in the USA concerning induced abortions. Consider the numbers. Planned Parenthood performed 4,068,749 abortions between 1977 and 2005. In 2005 alone 264,943 abortions were performed. In 2016 there were 623,471 abortions performed. From 1990 to 2016 there were 46,413,319 abortions performed.[1] A local pastor reminds us of Psalm 139:13-14, which states "For you formed my inner parts; you knitted me together in my mother's womb...I am fearfully and wonderfully made." Well, apparently God does not do a perfect job, given all the spontaneous abortions (miscarriages) and the malformations and genetic diseases seen in the newborn.

Abortion remains a controversial topic. Proponents believe it is the woman's right to decide to terminate her pregnancy, especially if her life is in danger or the fetus is malformed and making abortion illegal will result in "backroom abortions" under non-sanitary conditions. Those against abortion, mainly the religious right, believe abortions of any kind or any stage should be made illegal, and twenty-nine states have banned abortions at some stage, such as after a heartbeat has been detected. From 1969 to 2019 one Midwestern State's legislature has introduced fourteen separate laws concerning abortion.[2]

Since 1973, the year Roe vs Wade was passed, legalizing abortion throughout the USA, 58,586,256 legal (induced) abortions have taken place. In 2015, there were 996,000 induced abortions in the USA.[3] In 2011, there were 1,060,000 induced abortions.

Each year in the US there are 4,400,000 pregnancies. Of these, between 900,000-1 mil are lost; 500,000 miscarry in the first 20 weeks, and 26,000 end in still birth (lost after twenty weeks of pregnancy). Thus, a total of 1.5 million embryos/fetuses die before birth each year, or over 4,000 each day. Many of the pregnancies are estimated to be unintended and many of those pregnancies are aborted. Furthermore, an estimated large but unknown number of early cleavage stage embryos are lost spontaneously.[4] Abortion rates have fallen in many states, partly because of increased awareness of the humanity of the unborn fetus but also because of a decrease in teen pregnancies. Some states have closed many abortion clinics, such as Texas and Indiana, causing women to seek abortions in neighboring states, Louisiana, and Michigan, respectively.[5] Also, laws have been passed ruling that induced abortions after a certain pregnancy time are not allowed, such as after a heartbeat is detected.

Legislation put together by republicans in some states, if signed by the respective governors in 2021, will ban all abortions and doctors who perform abortions will be charged with murder. A federal judge blocked similar legislation in Alabama in Oct. 2019. More common is to have states ban abortions when the fetus has a heartbeat. Aborted embryos and fetuses are sometimes referred to as "babies."[6] Some religions have defined the fertilized egg as having life, and thus presumably a soul. The fertilized egg, called the zygote, is therefore sacred and must not be destroyed by abortion. No matter how early the stage of development it is referred to as a "baby." What then should be considered about spontaneous miscarriages? Some women have experienced several miscarriages, as many as five in some cases. Miscarriages occur primarily before the fetus reaches 500 g in weight, before twenty weeks of gestation, as counted from the first day of the last menstrual period. The causes of these spontaneous abortions are many and include chromosomal abnormalities, uterine abnormalities, chemotherapy taken by the expectant mother, use of drugs, alcohol and/or tobacco by the expectant mother, exposure to pesticides, bacterial and viral infections, hypothyroidism or diabetes, and heavy lifting.[6]

Estimates are that at least ¼ of all pregnancies end in miscarriages.

This estimate is based on the assumption that many pregnancies abort spontaneously without clinical recognition. In the USA in each year there are 900,000 pregnancy losses during the first trimester. Of clinically diagnosed pregnancies, up to 20% are spontaneously aborted.[7] Why does God allow all these embryo losses to occur?

RU486 (MifeprexR), often called the abortion pill, if taken early in pregnancy, aborts the pregnancy. In the USA, in 2009, there were 1.2 million RU486 caused abortions. RU486 is mifepristone, which blocks the role of progesterone in establishing the early pregnancy. Then, 48 hrs. after taking RU486, misoprostol is taken which empties the uterus by causing cramping and bleeding. RU486 is 90-98 % effective when taken before 10 weeks of pregnancy. A relatively new "morning after pill" (which is levonorgestrel or ulipristal acetate) came on the market in 2013 and has received favorable press because it prevents or delays fertilization of the egg and thus prevents pregnancy in cases of unprotected sex or rape. Yet some view this pill as possibly working by preventing the fertilized egg from implanting into the wall of the uterus and thus aborting a pregnancy and killing a human life. If an abortion pill is not available or not effective, then other chemicals can be taken or an "in clinic" abortion can be done.[8]

Without a fertilized egg there is no "life" and no soul to account for. If the egg is fertilized, i.e., conception occurs, the two-part question we can raise is: when does life begin and when is the soul added to that life? In any case, when an abortion takes place, God must deal with the aborted zygote, early blastocyst, early, mid-, or late-stage embryo, or fetus. God must evaluate each with regard to developmental potential and correct for any physiological or genetic problems and correct any such problems. Then God must decide what age body to resurrect in Heaven and when to unite the soul with that body. Decisions about parentage would be difficult. To identify the father, would God do a DNA sequence test?

"The soul is a theological abstraction that cannot be measured or detected."[9] Even so, different religions have different beliefs as to when the soul is added to the developing embryo; at the time of conception, at the time of the first heartbeat, at four months, or when the first breath is taken. Note the argument was presented earlier (Chapter 4) for a total lack of a soul separate from the body and that the "body becomes the soul" (Genesis 2). Thus, there is the view that once the body has a soul, abortion is no longer acceptable. Another view is that when the embryo exhibits a heartbeat then abortion is not acceptable thereafter. But a heartbeat is not proof of life. Brain activity and consciousness is proof of life. A person can be declared dead when brain activity stops, even if the heart is still beating. In fact, the heart of a brain-dead person can be transplanted to another person and continue beating.[9]

Aborted embryos and even children can die without being baptized, raising the question of whether they can get to Heaven. All are born with original sin, going back to Adam and Eve. Martin Luther in a sermon in 1533 said Jesus descended into hell (called Harrowing of Hell) after he was entombed and there conquered the devil and took away his power. Christian theology developed the view that Jesus thus brought salvation to the righteous who had died previous to his crucifixion. One view is that he took all these non-baptized individuals with him to Heaven. Prior to 2007 the catholic church believed that embryos, fetuses, and babies who died without being baptized would go to "Limbo" and be in Heaven in a state of happiness but not be in communion with God. Pope Benedict agreed with the reversal of this view and that the view of the church is that baptism is not essential to gain acceptance to Heaven but does initiate an individual into the church.[10] The New Testament in accounts of the crucifixion of Jesus (books Matthew, Mark, Luke and John) does not mention Jesus descending into hell nor is it mentioned in the book of Revelation. Yet the Apostles Creed and Athanasian Creed, while mentioning that Jesus descended into hell, say nothing about liberating the dead who are there in Limbo due to their original sin, not having been baptized, and who died before Jesus died on the cross and saved sinners.

Genetic testing is now possible for adults and newborns. Finding out if a predisposition to diabetes or breast cancer exists could be useful as preventative steps might then be taken. But for some genetic diseases, such as Huntington's disease, muscular dystrophy, or sickle cell disease, there are no preventative steps, but might still influence family planning or career choice. The genetic results will not account for environmental/epigenetic influences nor interactions of other genes and thus the severity of a disorder or its progression cannot be accurately predicted. What about genetic tests for newborns? Yes, they are recommended except for diseases the phenotype of which will not show until adulthood. Kits for these tests are now available and involve taking a sample of saliva or a swab from inside the cheek to obtain cells. The samples are sent to a laboratory and within several weeks the family receives the genetic information. Of the 30,000 genes in the human genome, only a small fraction, those known by earlier studies, are tested for. Chapter 14, Genetic Diseases, includes a discussion of genetic testing.

God would have to do some form of genetic testing on aborted embryos but presumably he would examine the entire genetic code of an individual (including the genome of the nucleus of the newly fertilized egg), not only the structural genes that code for proteins, but the regulatory sequences in between. Epigenetic changes to the DNA, such as the addition of methyl groups, which can cause identical twins to differ from each other and may cause disorders such as autism, will have to undergo God's purview as well. These would be tasks that are formidable to say the least when one considers the sheer numbers of embryos to be sampled.

There is much risk associated with pregnancy and childbirth in the USA, wherein the maternal mortality rate is the highest among the developed countries and is especially high among women of color. By outlawing abortions, women are forced to continue pregnancy, to undergo childbirth, and to become mothers before they are ready. Women who sought an abortion but were denied, were more likely to live in poverty, to stay with abusive partners, and to suffer life-endangering complications during pregnancy and childbirth. Instead of telling women what they can or cannot do with their bodies, our government could pass legislation to pay women equally, give women equal opportunities in the work force, and provide childcare.[11] God should recognize that an abortion would ensure that a woman can wait to get pregnant and then have a child when she is healthy, mature, and ready for that responsibility. Aborted embryos and fetuses could be raised by angels. But their life in Heaven would be devoid of a normal childhood and they would miss out on their teen years.

NOTES

1   Wikipedia website, "Abortion statistics in the United States," last edited January 23, 2023, www.wikipediaabortionstatisticsinUSA.
2   *Detroit Free Press*, August 15, 2019, 1A, 6A.

3   *NBC News*, January 17, 2017.
4   "Birth Defects or Congenital Anomalies," CDC, last reviewed January 18, 2023, https://www.cdc.gov/nchs/fastats/birth-defects.htm; HopeXchange website, "Miscarriage Statistics," accessed January 2020, http://www.hopex-change.com/Statistics.htm.
5   *Detroit Free Press*, June 8, 2015, 2A.
6   *Detroit Free Press*, November 16, 2019, 13A.
7   Guttmacher Institute website, *Fact Sheet*, February 20, 2022, https://www.guttmacher.org/.
8   Planned Parenthood Website, "Abortion," accessed May 10, 2020, https://www.plannedparenthoodaction.org/.
9   Letter to the Editor, "Restricting Abortions Doesn't Protect Anyone," *Detroit Free Press*, June 16, 2019, 27A.
10 N. Winfield, "Pope Revises Limbo, Gives Babies a Chance," *Detroit Free Press*, April 21, 2007, A18; T. Marshall, "The Doctrine of Limbo," *Catholic Tradition*, 2015.
11 Lyz Lenz, "America is Failing Moms," *Time*, August 17, 24, 28-29, 2020.

7

DIAGNOSING DISEASES, ABNORMALITIES IN EMBRYOS AND FETUSES

A VARIETY OF tests have been developed to diagnose real or potential problems during pregnancy. Every woman progresses through pregnancy with different concerns and preferences as to how much she desires to know about her developing embryo/fetus. Some tests are recommended for every pregnant woman, some for women at advance ages, and some for women with certain risk factors. The most common tests are as follows:

> Pregnancy stick test: This is a test for human chorionic gonadotrophin (HCG) in the urine. This is the so-called blue line test. If the home pregnancy test is positive, a first prenatal test at the doctor's office involves a blood draw. This test will confirm the pregnancy, see if the woman has enough iron and folate, determine blood type and Rh factor, screen for cystic fibrosis, sickle cell disease, Tay-Sachs, hepatitis B, syphilis and HIV. Blood pressure and previous infections of rubella and chicken pox will be tested. All of these are important to know about to help insure a healthy baby.

First-trimester screening: This test is offered to pregnant women usually between 11 and 14 weeks of the pregnancy to determine the risk of chromosomal abnormalities and birth defects. An ultrasound will measure the thickness at the back of the developing fetus's neck. These results, combined with the blood protein results, will help determine the odds of the baby having Down's syndrome or other abnormalities. This test can be given at 15-20 weeks if missed earlier.

Fetal anatomical survey: This test is at 18-20 weeks and involves detailed ultrasound that gives information on the fetal brain, heart, kidneys, bowel and bladder and the sex of the fetus can be revealed.

Glucose tolerance and diabetes: This is a screen for diabetes. If in a previous pregnancy the woman had gestational diabetes or there is a family history of diabetes, her doctor will monitor her condition carefully to insure no adverse effects on the fetus.

Group B strep test: This a test for bacteria infecting the woman's vagina or rectum. Antibiotics may be necessary to avoid passing the infection to the fetus.

Additional tests for older women or those at high risk: Chorionic villus sampling: Between ten- and fourteen-weeks doctors remove a piece of the placenta and cells are taken, grown in the lab, and analyzed for chromosome abnormalities. Amniocentesis: Amniotic fluid is obtained with a long needle. Cells of the fetus in the fluid are analyzed similarly as above. Fetal DNA testing: Fetal DNA is in the woman's blood and is assessed for genetic risks. Distress test: Straps connected to a monitor are wrapped around the woman's belly and can indicate if the fetus is in any kind of distress.

Would God be aware if a pregnant woman chooses one or more of these tests and would God then have the results in his memory? If the pregnancy was terminated, by abortion or miscarriage, or if a stillbirth occurred, would this information be helpful to God in deciding what to do with the fetus or infant?

The US Department of Health and Human Services recommends that all states screen all newborns for thirty-four different conditions. These include cystic fibrosis, hearing loss, immuno-deficiencies, and sickle cell anemia. Companies such as "23andMe" and "Ancestry" that will sequence a genome will alert the person, whatever the person's age, of disease genes or genes that make a person susceptible to a disease or condition, such as heart disease, depression, and alcoholism. Such screenings can give parents and doctors the chance to detect a possible problem and address it in a new born baby before it leaves the hospital, and in children, teens, or adult persons of any age.[1] It would make sense that God would do such a screening for anyone who dies, of whatever cause, including embryos, fetuses, newborns, children, teens and all adults, and correct any of these conditions so that anyone entering Heaven would be in perfect health and not come to realize some medical condition at some later time. The coronavirus flu is detected preliminarily by measuring increased body temperature with an infrared thermal detector.[2] Skin color and texture due to illness/disease will soon be part of facial recognition camera capability.[3] God would need to do such a screening immediately upon death, before any lowering of body temperature, or decomposition of DNA, cells, or tissues takes place as even minimal decomposition could mask any of these thirty-four conditions. Decomposition begins within 4 minutes of death, probably before death is even conclusive.[4] God would also have to restore the brains of those deceased, determine their sex (male, female, or LGBTQ), and their religious history, in order to decide if the deceased is going to be accepted into Heaven.

NOTES

1   Kids Health Section, "What to Know About Newborn Screenings," *Cheboygan Tribune*, October 2, 2017.
2   *NBC News*, March 13, 2020.
3   *Detroit Free Press*, March 13, 2020, 15A.
4   Richard Beliveau and Denis Gingras, *Death, the Scientific Facts to Help Us Understand It Better* (Canada: Firefly Books, 2012.)

8

BURIALS AND CEMETERIES

BELIEF IN AN afterlife goes far back, possibly to the earliest homi-
nids[1] including the Mousterians and associated Neanderthals in Europe,
W. Asia, and N. Africa more than 160,000 years BCE (before the common
era). Evidence from archeological studies indicates that the deceased were
often buried along with flowers, food, goods, tools, money, and weapons,
with many bodies buried together and placed in certain positions, such
as the fetal position, suggesting that these items/practices would help the
deceased get to the afterlife and survive in the afterlife. Bodies were often
stained with dyes such as hematite (iron ore) or ochre.[2] If the Neanderthals
prayed, it did no good for the living, since they went extinct as a branch
of humans. Perhaps there is a Neanderthal Heaven. Some of their DNA
is still alive and is being carried by us "modern" humans. (see Chapter 31,
Human Evolution).

Belief in an afterlife was also demonstrated by evidence of mummifi-
cation as far back as 3500 BCE, particularly in ancient Egypt. Egypt had
very little rain and bodies buried in sand were seen to not decompose very
much. The view evolved that the deceased would do better in the afterlife
if their body was less decomposed. Much effort went into preserving the
body by drying it. Bodies of well-known pharaohs such as Tutankhamen
(King Tut) but also princesses have been uncovered and found to be very

well-preserved. The entire mummification process for one body took 70 days and was carried out by special priests who carried out rituals and recited prayers to further enhance passage to the afterlife.

The process involved removing the internal organs except the heart, which was believed to be the center of a person's being and intelligence. The brain was liquified and then sucked out through the nostrils using a straw-like tube. The internal organs and brain mishmash were placed into a "canopic," a jar containing the mummification preservative, and buried with the body, to be available for the soul when it leaves for the afterlife. The body was treated over and over with a salt to remove most of the water; the eyes were known to deteriorate and thus were replaced with artificial eyes. Any hollow or sunken areas were filled in with linen or grasses. The body was then wrapped over and over many times with hundreds of yards of linen and resins; amulets and prayers and magical words were written on the linen as the wrapping occurred to protect the body on its journey to the afterlife. Food was commonly added to the tomb for the deceased. The process was expensive and thus mainly pharaohs, priests, and other dignitaries were mummified.

Due largely to the high cost, a common person it seems was less likely to be mummified and thus was provided less help to gain the afterlife. Animals which had religious significance, such as sacred bulls, baboons, cats, birds, and even crocodiles, were often mummified.[3] These mummified bodies are not yet in the afterlife. What will be their fate? Is their soul in the afterlife? In Heaven? Are the Gods going to combine the souls with these somewhat preserved bodies to live happily ever after?

Mummification and other means of body preservation, sometimes by nature alone such as the cold of permafrost or the acid conditions of bogs, were seen in various cultures around the world. Most interesting is the examination of mummy princesses.[4] A few are described here. Princess of Xiaohe died some 3,500 years ago; her body was found in a tomb in W. China along with 100s of other bodies. The mummified body of Lady Dai, from the Han Dynasty in China of the second century BCE, was autopsied by medical archeologists who concluded that she was about 50 years old at death, had high cholesterol, high blood pressure, diabetes and had schistosomiasis (a parasitic infection). The Ice Maiden, who died 2,000 years ago in Siberia, was a member of the Pazyryk people. She was about

30 yrs. old and had elaborate tattoos. Buried with her was a horse with a gold-trimmed harness, a man who had died from a fatal blow to the head, a teen believed to have been a sacrifice, and a pouch of cannabis, all provided to help her to reach the afterlife. The Beauty of Xiaohe, who lived about 2,000 years ago in W. China, was found in a tomb with 300 other burials. She was part of an ancient, isolated society of farmers and herders which prized fertility and thus sexual symbolism adorned graves. And there were more. A mummification workshop dating back 2,500 years was uncovered in 2018 giving clues to the process and which contained more mummies and the equipment and supplies utilized in the process. A gilded silver mask was on the face of a mummy believed to be that of a priest.[5] Otzi man was found in 1991, under ice for 5,000 years, and very well preserved. Tollund Man was found in a peat bog, dated to 400 years BCE. The acidic, cold and oxygen deprived bog preserved the body quite well. Finally, Japanese monks sometimes underwent a change of diet to lead to self-mummification after death, eating grains and nuts followed by bark and roots, to rid the body of fats which is a big part of the decomposition process.[6] Where are the souls of these deceased? Are they in God's care?

In May 2015, archeologists digging near the ancient Palace of Nestor on a hilltop near Pylos in Greece, unearthed a tomb of incredible interest.[7] For 6 months the archeologists uncovered bronze basins, armor and weapons, cups of gold and silver, beads of carnelian, amethyst, amber, and gold, gold rings, and dozens of beautifully carved stones depicting goddesses, lions, and bulls. At the bottom of the grave was an almost intact skeleton with the skull from which a digital face reconstruction was made. The skeleton was believed to be that of a famous, highly esteemed warrior of the Mycenaean culture, from which originated the world's common traditions of language, literature, philosophy, democracy, and religion. The Mycenaean culture exploded between 3500 and 1600 BCE but disappeared a few hundred years later. Many other graves of men, women and children were found in the late 1800s by other archeologists, graves containing gold and other riches, dating back to 3500 BCE. These individuals, buried with so many riches, certainly must have reached the afterlife! In Greece, the lost city of Tenea was located by archeologists and a jar was found containing the remains of two human fetuses. At a cemetery, evidence was uncovered of many human burials with gold, jewelry, pottery, and coins. These bodies are still apparently waiting for resurrection and the Gods have not yet taken the gold and other valuables. Are their souls in Heaven?

A discovery in a royal Maya tomb at Takalik Abaj in Guatemala in 2012 revealed how important additions to the corpse were in early times, here being 500 BCE. Six ceramic figures, all women, were in the tomb, each unique from the others. One theoretical role for the women was to accompany the king to the afterlife. Four were positioned at the cardinal points, the corners of the Maya universe. Two others, positioned east and west, perhaps represented the rising and setting sun.[8]

Considering that over 140 million people die each year and over 350,000 die on any single day in the world today, mummification is not reasonable, thus embalming with subsequent burial in a coffin is a common procedure. In Brazil, in late May 2020, over 1,000 people were being killed each day by COVID-19. In the world, during COVID-19 in 2020, 12,000 people died from the virus each day; in Dec. 2020, over 3,000 people were dying from COVID-19 each day in the USA. Over 150 countries have had COVID-19 deaths. Worldwide, the funeral/embalming/burial services were being overwhelmed and graveyards were overflowing with bodies.[9] God has been busy.

Embalming fluid contains formaldehyde and glutaraldehyde, both liquids noxious to living organisms, very carcinogenic, and which can seep into the environment from cemeteries. Enough embalming fluid is used each year in the USA to fill eight Olympic-size swimming pools (Sarah J. Marsden's writings about the death industry). Both kill bacteria and delay decomposition effectively. Methanol, phenol, and other chemicals are also used depending on how long decomposition needs to be delayed – perhaps just until the funeral, while the body is transported home from a war zone, or as long as possible. Without embalming, a body will decompose at a rate dependent upon temperature, moisture, and the immediate environment. Bodies of union soldiers killed in the south were embalmed for transportation to the north in make-shift coffins until the family decided on a permanent coffin.

Coffins have been used for at least 100,000 years. The coffin allows visualization of the dead before burial, hides odors from decomposition and prevents animal scavenging. A coffin protects the body from floods and thus does not allow spreading of germs from the deceased.[10] Most present-day coffins are not environmentally friendly in that huge amounts of steel, wood, and concrete are generally used to build them and this material is buried forever. Thus, green burials are becoming more accepted. They are less expensive, a non-hazardous embalming solution is used to delay decomposition only temporarily, or there is no embalming fluid used at all. The decomposed body contributes to the natural environment. There is no coffin, so no wood or metal is utilized. A step even further toward a greener grave is the idea of composting the body, known officially as "natural organic reduction" and a company in Washington state called Recompose is specializing in this process. Washington, Colorado, and Oregon allow these organic burials with several other states likely to follow. The body is placed in a container with wood chips, alfalfa, straw and bacteria. The temperature and moisture content are regulated to enhance composting. The cost is $5500, the process uses less than 1/8 the energy of cremation or burial, and the end result is one cubic yard of compost which the family is free to distribute into nature.[11] How will God restore these composted bodies on Judgment Day so they may be combined with their souls?

The Nenet reindeer herders of the Arctic region of Russia do not use coffins and do not bury their dead. The body of the deceased is placed under an overturned sled. It is considered sacrilegious to place a body in the ground. A ritual for the deceased involves cutting a reindeer in half, leaving one half for the Gods and the other half to be eaten by the family. A spiritual leader, a shaman, conducts a service using the power of wooden idols and unusual shaped stones. Here one sees belief in an afterlife, even if not the Heaven of the Christian Bible.[12]

The body of a baby boy, an early American, who died at twelve to eighteen months of age and was buried in Montana 12,500 years ago, revealed much information about the beliefs of America's early peoples. (see Chapter 31, Human Evolution). Of interest for this chapter is that the body was buried with 125 artifacts, including spear points, elk antler tools, ritual objects, and heirlooms, all covered with red ochre, a natural pigment, which archeologists believe indicates a burial ceremony. Early Americans prepared their dead for an afterlife by including weapons and tools with the deceased body. But would a boy, not even a year old, find tools and weapons useful? The boy was believed to be of the Clovis culture, thought to be ancestral to many if not all native Americans.[13]

Examination of a decomposing body can provide clues as to when death occurred and sometimes even identify the cause of death. People can donate their bodies for research in forensic anthropology to The Body Farm at the Univ. of Tenn., headed by Wm H. Bass, who has written mystery books with Jon Jefferson using the author's name Jefferson Bass.[14] A study of pigs dropped to the bottom of the ocean showed that the factors influencing decomposition rate were depth of the water, oxygen content at that depth, and water temperature. Pigs could be chewed down to bone by crustaceans in as little as 3 weeks and as long as 90 days (Quora). Time, moisture, temperature, and soil conditions on the land similarly influence decomposition. The decomposition process begins within minutes of death before it is concluded that the person has died and certainly much before mummification or embalming.[6] The idea that a mummified or embalmed body can be restored for life in Heaven is not reasonable. The hope would be that some of the DNA of the deceased would not be degraded. We can be reminded of the quote from Edward Munch (1863-1944), "From my rotting body flowers will grow and I will be part of them and that is eternity."

How the deceased get to the afterlife we have traditionally left very much in the hands of God and Jesus as noted by funerals usually held in churches and carried out by priests or ministers; about 80% of USA residents have a religious affiliation. Even when an urn with cremains (ashes with no organic matter) is buried in a cemetery or emptied over a lake, river or other specific area, prayers are most often part of the event. Decorative, personalized urns are now available, and these can be positioned on the mantle in the home of the family or buried in place of a coffin.[15] An interesting belief is from South Africa. At the funeral of Nelson Mandela the skies were cloudy and it was raining. No problem. In South African culture "if it rains when a person is buried, it means the gods are welcoming the deceased and the gates of Heaven are opening."[16]

The extent of religious involvement in deaths and funerals is indicated by comparison of the states of Oregon and Mississippi. In Oregon, a more secular state, 73% of bodies are cremated; in Mississippi, a more religious state, only 18%. Yet even some members of the Jehovah's Witnesses have their bodies cremated. In the USA about 7% of bodies are donated. Jewish custom is to bury the body within 24 hrs. and definitely no later than 48 hrs. after death with no tampering and no embalming; autopsies are not permitted. Green burials are the modern trend; caskets utilize bio-degradable materials (wood or cloth) and no caustic embalming fluid. Body and casket components will therefore degrade and contribute to nature. The prediction is that by 2030 only 25% of Americans will be buried as whole bodies.[17] How can people believe that God will still be able to restore their original body in Heaven, even after cremation or complete decomposition?

A funeral serves several purposes. It is an acknowledgment that someone we love has died. The funeral allows family and friends to say goodbye but at the same time offers continuity and hope for the living. The funeral provides a chance to express respect and thoughts and feelings about the deceased. It provides an opportunity to review the life of the deceased, his/her beliefs, the good things in that life, contributions to society, and interests.[18] Families believe in the importance of finding the remains of loved ones lost in battles so that a proper funeral and burial service can be arranged. The Defense POW/MIA Accounting Agency said that 7,600 Americans remain unaccounted for from the Korean war. When even one set of these remains is recovered, identified, and given a proper burial, such as in the Arlington Natl. Cemetery, the family is very grateful.[19]

Funerals are a large business, there being 21,680 funeral homes in the USA with 106,000 employees. A total of fifty-five names were listed in the obituaries/death notices section of the metropolitan area of one mid-western major city Sunday newspaper, with thirty-seven funeral homes listed for the arrangements. One funeral home was listed six times, two were listed three times, six were listed twice, and the remainder once. During COVID-19, on a Sunday, in Dec. 2020, that same newspaper listed eighty-seven deaths and fifty-one different funeral homes, one listed twenty-six times, no others more than twice. Why is that one so popular? Most of the names of the funeral homes have no religious significance and appear to be named after family members, such as A.M. Smith and Sons Funeral Home. One is called "Heaven's Gate Funeral Home" and we can wonder if it is popular because of that title. In the paper on the first Sunday in 2021, 103 deaths were listed, consistent with increases in the daily covid-19 deaths in the USA in 2021.[20]

In the spring, summer, and fall of 2020 COVID-19 ravaged the world, not sparing the USA. So many deaths were occurring that funeral homes were barely able to manage all the bodies, with up to 3,000-4,000 deaths in a given day in December 2020 and early 2021, and as many as 1 death every one to two minutes. The resources of hospitals and funeral homes were so stretched that for the first time ever one mid-west state activated its Mortuary Response team, to provide "safe and secure transfer, identification, and storage of human remains until funeral homes can help families make plans." In the Sunday newspaper mentioned above the list of deceased numbered 120 on Sunday, April 19, 2020, 101 the next Sunday, April 26, 2020, and 116 on Sunday, May 3, 2020, more than twice the typical number seen before the pandemic.[20-21] Decomposing bodies were found in the back of a semi-truck, waiting for a funeral or burial.[22] Jewish funerals for persons deceased before the pandemic would typically have family members and many friends gathered in the synagogue/church and home and much food presented and served. A seven-day period of mourning would normally be observed with a stream of visitors. But with COVID-19 and with states restricting people from gathering and requiring six feet of social distance and masks, the funeral services were adversely affected. Even the body had to be embalmed quickly and orifices disinfected so as not to release virus particles. No usual grieving procedures like kissing, hugging or shrouding were allowed. Funeral homes were close to being overwhelmed and some completely overwhelmed. The number of deaths listed in the same paper on Sunday, Sept. 13, was sixty-five, clearly dropping off but the pandemic was still present. The number of funeral homes listed was twenty-six.[23]

Death is a major part of *The Iliad and the Odyssey* going back to Greece at 700-800 years BCE.[24] The soul was recognized as a "life breath" and referred to as a "shade" which leaves the body at death via the mouth never to return. The shade was thought of as sort of a bodiless replica of its human body of origin but unable to experience pleasure, torment, or pain and had no strength; the shade's residence is the underworld. Most important is to have a proper burial without which the shade is in "agony and displaced forever." Funeral rites were essential to gain admission to the underworld, Hades. Religion was significantly influenced by Homer in *The Iliad and the Odyssey* and by Virgil following in his epic, *Aeneid*, and then further by Plato and others. The early view that the dead who fail to make amends for their earthly transgressions go to Hades (hell), a large and gloomy place deep within the earth, not much believed today. Most today believe that we receive our due rewards and go to Heaven or cease to exist. Examining the history of views of death and the afterlife led to the invention of Heaven and Hell.[24]

Death is a big business and costs vary around the world; there are roughly 2.4 million funerals in the USA each year (6,575 each day on the average); the cost of a burial, the service, and interment is $4-$6,000; cremation, service and interment is $3-$4,000. In Ghana, where pall bearers dance the deceased into the grave, total cost is less than $400.[25]

There are 1,700 crematories in the USA; cremation is gaining more and more interest as are "green" burials. In the state of Michigan 60% of the people who die are cremated. For the entire USA that figure is 53% while forty years ago only 8.5% of the deceased were cremated. Cremation gardens are growing in popularity. Instead of cremains being spread into an ocean, lake, river or the air, now they are often buried, and a permanent grave marker is purchased so that visitations and remembrances can occur. Cremains, whether in an urn on the mantle, in a grave, or spread in a lake, are only ashes. Not one organic molecule, certainly not nervous tissue (neurons and axons) which might contain memories, would remain intact. Any carbon, nitrogen, phosphorous, and oxygen containing molecules would be gone, destroyed, and scattered about (see Chapter 21, The Brain). How could God restore these bodies and brains?

There are 115,000 cemeteries in the USA; at least one is in most cities and usually more than one, with some interesting names.[26] Here are some of the most famous cemeteries: Woodlawn in the Bronx, NY, has a monument for the Titanic and includes graves of Duke Ellington, Irving Berlin, and Miles Davis; Hollywood Forever, Calif., has the graves of Judy Garland and Toto, a Greenwood cemetery can be found in more than one city, the first being located in Brooklyn, NY, established in 1838, as one of the first "rural" cemeteries, with flower gardens and trees, and is over 500 acres. A Greenwood cemetery is in N. Michigan and visitors can view Lake Michigan from the cemetery grounds and can participate in various activities on cemetery grounds like scavenger hunts; on-line information and services are available.[27]

The Arlington Natl. Cemetery is one of the largest with 400,000 graves and thirty funerals each day; thousands of new graves are added each year. A guide or computer app is available to find one's way around. The Tomb of the Unknown Soldier has three soldiers, one from each world war and one from the Korean war and graves of 4,641 additional unknown soldiers are in the general cemetery. Burial spaces remaining available number 95,000 but with restrictions for eligibility will be sufficient for 150 years.[28] Evidence has revealed serious mix-ups at Arlington Natl. When a person is seen hugging a tombstone there, perhaps it is not the grave of the loved one they think it is, but the hug is no doubt appreciated just the same. Veterans were disgusted by the mix-up.[29] At the site of the Battle of the Bulge in WWII are rows and rows of thousands of white flags, each marking the grave of a brave, young soldier who died during this, perhaps the greatest battle in American history.[30] It is not easy to visualize each of these bodies being reunited with their souls at the Rapture and undergoing judgment by Jesus. (See John 5:28-29).

As COVID-19 spreads across the world, not yet over its peak of infections with still many deaths in the USA, funeral homes are different. A funeral home director says that typically a funeral transforms loss from pain and grief to offering love, support and remembrance, to acknowledge death but mostly to celebrate life. But COVID-19 has changed things. There are many more funerals, many more bodies to embalm and perhaps store, and more cremations. Many fewer mourners attend the funeral and burial and might have to do so in shifts, must wear masks, must not hug, and must be six feet apart. Religious services are brief, and interments are swift. Employees must wear masks, shields and suits, just like hospital workers. One wonders if funerals will ever return to normalcy or be changed forever. The Detroit Free Press obituary column lists 120 deceased people on April 19, 101 on April 26, and 116 on May 3, double the typical number for a week.[31] Is even God feeling rushed and overwhelmed?

A clever cemetery/burial marketing scheme was begun in China. Gravestones in this cemetery are affixed with names of important and well-known people, even if still alive, such as Yao Ming, a seven-foot basketball player, now retired. The idea is to attract customers by suggesting that they will meet these famous people in the afterlife. Price increases and land scarcity have resulted in intense competition between burial companies.[32] Radboud University, Netherlands, offers students time in a "purification grave" which is a hole the size for a coffin in which the student can lie down for several hours for special meditation without phones or books to really see what is going on in one's mind.[33]

In the gang-plagued South American country of El Salvador there are so many murder victims, mostly young men, that many businesses are making a living making caskets and providing funeral services. At one time there were fourteen murders a day nationwide and now eleven a day after a govt. crackdown of gangs. In the city of Jucuapa, with a population of 18,000, there are thirty coffin factories. A body riddled with bullet holes is not easy to fill with embalming fluid, sew up, and clean up for a funeral. Preparing the body and coffin, providing the twenty-four-hour wake (visitation and prayers), and having the funeral service, costs from $350 - $3200. The top seller of coffins is the economy style for $90 and the top of the line is almost twenty times that. The coffin and funeral businesses will keep going as long as the gangs keep killing. God has some messy diagnosing to do in El Salvador. El Salvador's people are 39% catholic, 28% protestant and 30% atheist.[34]

A proper burial and tombstone are essential as they provide dignity to the deceased and to the family. On D-day of WWII, 160,000 Allied soldiers landed on the beach of France, at Normandy, and ultimately France was liberated but at a cost of 9,000 deaths plus injuries. Many of those deceased are in unmarked graves in cemeteries in France. To give dignity to the soldiers from Michigan, students from Michigan communities carried vials of Michigan sand to France, prayed at the graves, and sprinkled the sand on the graves of the Michigan soldiers as a gesture of commemoration. They carried sand from the Normandy beaches to Michigan for the same gesture.[35] Finland is still recovering bodies from Russia. There were 10,000 bodies of Finnish soldiers that died during the Finland-Russia Winter War and the Continuation War from the early 1940s, most buried in mass graves. Many of these unclaimed and/or unidentified war dead have been returned to Finland to be buried with ceremonies in Lappeenranta, Finland, in the war grave cemetery there. Of 1,300 remains of soldiers brought home from Russia, only 377 have been identified. Intact bodies were rarely found so, after examination, the remains, sometimes only skulls or just a few other bones, were buried in small caskets and given dignity.[36] Thousands of bodies of Finns in mass graves are being investigated in Karelia, believed to be victims of Stalin's persecutions and executions of the 1930s and 1950s.[37] The majority of Finns are Lutherans and probably most of these soldiers were Lutherans and had been baptized. Is there a chance that these decomposed body parts will be joined with their souls in Heaven? Is God caring for their souls?

While most would agree that "death with dignity" should be given to all, what should be done when the dead are not claimed, no one mourns for them, and there is no organized farewell? Such is the situation in one mid-west county medical examiner's office. But wait! There is "human decency" exhibited by government workers, funeral home directors, and cemetery personnel, composed of Jews and Christians, blacks and whites, who together are a model of cooperation, an effort stressed to the limit by COVID-19 deaths, to deal with unclaimed bodies. The medical examiner's office attempts to locate the deceased next of kin using fingerprints, databases, social media, service records, phone calls, letters, and more. Sometimes no next of kin is found. Sometimes the next of kin are not interested, have no money, or don't want to be bothered. The worst cases are the dead infants with no one claiming the tiny bodies. "It's heartbreaking" said one funeral home director. Every year two county funeral homes have about 500 deceased that go unclaimed. Before the bodies can begin to decompose, the group of kind-hearted individuals listed above sees to it that each body is given a proper burial and the dignity each deserves. No, they do not rot in a Potter's Field.[38]

Some cemeteries have been abandoned and have fallen into disrepair. Fortunately, in many of these cases volunteers have cleaned up the tombstones, replaced the broken ones, and generally restored the entire grounds. Such a project, going on now for over twenty-three years, is designed to identify the headstones and reassemble the death records of those buried in this cemetery founded in 1889 by Detroit's Sweetest Heart of Mary Catholic Church. The deceased are mostly of Polish nationality. The cemetery contains a data base of 13,000 names but information is missing on some 5,000 more where the grave sites have fallen deep below the surface soil.[39]

The Cliff Cemetery in Clifton, Michigan, now a ghost town in the Upper Peninsula, holds the remains of copper miners and their families, dating back to 1845 when the Clifton copper mine opened. The cemetery is now overgrown with trees and shrubs but is open to tourists and to people fascinated by old cemeteries. Head stones that once were intricately carved, even one with a scene of Jesus on the cross, have fallen over, are chipped, and are breaking down with words still visible in different languages. Buried in the Cliff cemetery are Catholics, Episcopalians, and Lutherans. The nationalities were mainly Irish, Finnish, Cornish, German and French. Clifton and six other once thriving towns in the Keweenaw Peninsula, some with more than 1,000 residents, became ghost towns as people left when the ore was mined out and/or the demand for copper decreased and the mines closed down. The town of Central has only a single resident.[40,41] Each of these towns no doubt had their own cemetery. At the resurrection God will have quite a challenge sorting out the sinners from the non-sinners from these graves.

Occasionally a funeral home becomes "lax" and does not care for the deceased. In one case, the ownership changed, and the new owners found bodies of fetuses and children and ashes of others totally neglected and abandoned. In some cases, those who recovered ashes of loved ones were not sure they had the correct ashes. In other cases, the several dozen fetuses were so decomposed that identification and assignment to a woman/family was not possible. But some records provided identifications and family notifications to allow proper, dignified burials. Some pet cemeteries are allowing the burial of the pet's cremated remains to lie next to their human owner's remains.[40,41] Will the pet join its owner in Heaven?

In Michigan and other parts of the Midwest, in March 2019, heavy rains and melting snow caused water to accumulate where snowbanks and natural land features prevented run-off. Some cemeteries were flooded and the graves were in water-saturated earth. Coffins no doubt often leaked causing more rapid deterioration of the bodies. The non-bony parts of the body would be the nucleic acids (DNA and RNA), the proteins, lipids, and carbohydrates; these would be decomposed first. The brain and facial features that give each person identity and personality would be gone. Not much will remain for God to "resurrect" at tribulation.

A well-known author included a statement in his 2019 best seller concerning a visit by the main character to a cemetery containing the remains of Civil War union soldiers: "This area smelled of death even though the last burial…had taken place more than 150 years ago. The stench lingered… and would be here forever… If you believed in God, you would trust that their spirits had long gone to a better place. But six feet under…the human remains of those 'spirits' would have an eternal presence in this town.[42]"

A university professor, Dr. M, who specializes in understanding why human relics are falling apart, is studying Chilean mummies from 5000-7000 years ago. The mummies, numbering in the hundreds, are adults, fetuses and children. This Chilean society was at the hunter-gatherer stage of social evolution and was more democratic than the Egyptians, thus common people were mummified, not just those of the top classes. Why this interest? Because due to global warming the mummies are melting and the associated bacteria are going to work, decomposing the tissues. Why fetuses and children? Fetuses presumably because of miscarriages caused by high arsenic levels in the environment; children because of poisoning due to arsenic. Sorrow expressed by adults led to mummification. Along with faculty of the University of Tarapacá, Dr. M will be searching for ways to stop the deterioration and aid the preservation of these mummies.[43] These mummies represent quite a challenge for God to decipher.

Now a problem exists. If there is no soul or spirit that leaves the body and goes to Heaven and the body has decomposed, is buried under the rubble of a collapsed building, cannot be found, or is cremated, what is left for God to resurrect? Here we have a conundrum. The parts of the body, such as brain cells, that give a person thought, memory, intelligence, senses, personality and identity come from the person's organic compounds, mainly nucleic acids (DNA and RNA) and proteins. When a body is cremated or it decomposes, it is these organic compounds that are burned or degraded and lost to the air, water or soil. Thus, whether remains are in an urn or grave there is no information nor molecules to restore the body, only ashes after cremation, or bits and pieces of skeleton and teeth after body burial. God would have to have in his memory the exact body/brain details and the necessary organic and inorganic molecules in order to resurrect the person. Can the soul escape from under tons of rubble or under the immense water pressure at the bottom of the ocean? If there is a soul, which is a spirit, how can the soul carry all the information needed to resurrect a person with the original identification, memories, and personality?

There are frequent cases of body remains being found and not identified easily or not at all. The remains of one identified soldier from WWII were brought home to the USA and laid to rest giving much satisfaction to the family. In another case, human body parts were found encased in concrete, the head and torso separate from the arms and legs. The body was identified by a tattoo and was believed to be that of a man murdered months earlier. The New York Court of Appeals ruled that when a body is autopsied and organs are removed, the family does not have the right to insist that organs be replaced; the body itself is sufficient. Remains dating to the late 1800s of African Americans imprisoned in forced labor camps were uncovered; of ninety-five skeletons, two dozen were relatively intact and are being examined, some as young as fourteen and as old as seventy. Convict leasing across the south was common and more than 3,500 died between 1866 and 1912. Graveyards were segregated, blacks v whites. The remains of an infant boy were discovered in the American West in 1968 and were reburied in 2018 by tribal members in a dignified ceremony. DNA and forensic analysis dated the boy's remains to be 12,500 years old and of American Indian ancestry. The boy's genome is believed to be the oldest ever discovered in the New World and DNA sequence analysis indicates the boy's ancestors came from Asia via a land bridge no longer in existence.[44] There were 2,753 deaths from the 9/11 attacks on the US Trade Center but 1,115 have not been identified. Those unidentified remains were transferred to a repository seventy feet underground in the same building as the 9/11 Memorial Museum. Some family members support this site while others would like the remains buried in a separate, above ground monument. How many of these 9/11 victims, identified and non-identified, are in Heaven with bodies restored?[45]

For three centuries, from the 1500s to the 1800s, Europeans brought Africans as slaves to the Americas to maximize the mining of silver and gold and increase the profitability of crops including cotton, sugar, tobacco, and rice. The slave trade brought nine million men, women, and children to the Americas to be owned as property and forced to do hard labor. President Lincoln said after the Civil War that slavery was America's original sin and that the Civil War was God's judgment on that sin. Slaves were very valuable and the economy depended on their labor. An enterprising landowner decided to make money by importing additional slaves, so he hired a captain and the schooner Clotilda for the job. On July 8, 1860, 108 captives disembarked from the schooner Clotilda to become the last recorded Africans enslaved in the USA. The 108 (minus two who died during the voyage) people on the Clotilda were the last of 307,000 Africans brought to the USA to be slaves. The charred, sunken remains of the Clotilda were discovered in

May 2019, off the shore of Alabama. The captain had lit the ship on fire and towed it out to sea to destroy evidence of slave transport as slavery was then illegal. After the war, the Clotilda descendants established settlements up-river from Mobile, and built a community named Africatown with fishing, hunting, gardening, and livestock farming and with a school, church, and graveyard. Many of the Clotilda descendants still live in Africatown. The Clotilda Africans came from several regions of Benin and Nigeria. Earlier slaves came from Cape Verde going south to what now are Senegambia, Sierra Leone, and continuing past the Congo and also from SE Africa. They had different languages, cultures, and religions but in America they became "Africans" and adjusted as best able to American ways without giving up their African heritage.[46] Are the original slaves, all nine million of them, in Heaven? Are their descendants in Heaven? Are they back together with their families and friends from their original African communities?

An archeology firm using ground penetrating radar discovered what seem to be forty-four graves of a long-forgotten African American cemetery under a Florida parking lot. The firm thinks there may be additional graves in the vicinity. This is the third such discovery in the Tampa Bay region.[47] We can wonder about the lineages of these deceased and forgotten. Are their souls with God?

Learning about our distant ancestors, their origins, and their journeys to different parts of the world, has depended very much on archeological findings of tools, weapons, pottery, footprints, and skeletal components. These archeological types of evidence have led to the view that the Americas, both North and South, were populated by small groups of Stone Age hunters, who walked across a land bridge connecting eastern Siberia with western Alaska, now the water covered Bering Straits, some thirteen thousand years ago, eventually making their way down an ice-free corridor on into North America and established a thriving culture that then spread further into South America. They lived primarily on bison, wooly mammoths, other mammals, and fish. More recently uncovered archeological sites along the West Coast of N. America indicate that early humans arrived in North America at least 15,000, perhaps even 20,000 years ago, by sea and by land, as the massive ice sheets of the glaciers receded. The Bering Straits and the land flanking it, large as a continent and given the name Beringia, was an area believed to be occupied by early peoples and is now part of

British Columbia. Many islands are now present where then was just dry land. Indigenous people live on some of these islands, for example the 600 or so members of the We Wai Kai Nation, some of whom are archeologists searching out the history of the early peoples.

With methods of DNA sequencing becoming more efficient and our understanding of DNA evolution now in the forefront, DNA sequencing is impacting archeology. The first ancient human DNA was sequenced in 2010. These were the remains of a 12,400 yr. old boy from Montana, and the skeletal DNA of a boy whose 24,000 yr. old remains found near Lake Baikal in Russia. Sophisticated analysis of such DNA by evolutionary geneticists can reveal when early human populations merged, split, or were isolated and where they came from. Such continuing analysis will reveal much about early Americans.[48] Many of these early Americans likely died at a rather young age, from disease, injuries, or starvation, and God would have duly noted these deaths and taken the souls of these early peoples into Heaven. But what of their bodies which might be under twenty feet or more of glacial sediment or under hundreds of feet of water? Will God have the ability to extract the DNA of the skeletal components and restore the complete bodies of the individuals? Will he restore the language(s) of these Indigenous peoples in Heaven?

In the southeast corner of the state of Utah, where formations of red rock tower to hundreds of feet, there is an area of cultural and geological significance to native Americans, particularly to the Utes and Navaho. The area is called the Valley of the Gods. Mythology suggests that the towering spires hold the spirits of their warriors. More than 100,000 sites are cherished by Native Americans in this valley, including creation mythologies. The area surrounding the Valley of the Gods, called Bears Ears, is the Native American equivalent of the Garden of Eden, rich in fossils and artifacts, bones of indigenous ancestors, and plants that healed and fed them. One can visit these 32,000 acres without the likelihood of encountering another person; it is a precious place of true wildness. Unfortunately, President Trump's administration in 2017 shrunk the Bears Ears National Monument by 85% and another protected area, the Grand Staircase-Escalante National Monument, was shrunk by nearly 47%.[49] When the earth is made into the "new earth" of Heaven, will these beautiful, cherished national monuments be retained and possibly expanded to be enjoyed by the billions of people in Heaven? Tony Hillerman refers to the beauty of our Western peaks in his books about native Americans, the Hopis. One such peak, Humphreys Peak, at 12,600 feet, was considered the gateway to the spirit world when a Hopi was called there to dance and celebrate eternal rewards.[50]

Columbus discovered America in 1492 and saw only native Americans. But Charles C. Mann, in his book, *1491*, argues that there were millions, perhaps as many as 100 million, people already in N. and S. America. Pre-Columbian and subsequent visitors from Europe brought the diseases smallpox, viral hepatitis, and others to these shores and up to 90% of the native population was killed off. The Mayflower colonists came upon 1,000s of corpses and empty villages along the New England coast. One English trader noted that Native Americans had died in heaps, so many that proper burials were not possible.[51] Is God caring for these souls?

A very sad situation is a cemetery named Potter's Field, such as the one in Sault St. Marie, Michigan. The name Potters Field comes from the Bible and refers to land with soil not suitable for anything but making pottery. Few knew about the cemetery as there were no headstones and the graves had become grown over. A resident historian discovered the grave site a few years ago and decided to provide some information and bring it to the public's attention. Her extensive research of county burial records, newspapers, and other sources led to identification of many of the deceased. With volunteer effort, a headstone is now at each grave. At the edge of the cemetery is a marker listing the 285 names of the deceased buried there who died between 1890 and 1935. Worse, the deceased there were of the lowest, the most destitute, the poorest, the forgotten, people who seemingly had no family or friends to care about them. They died from alcohol abuse, disease, accidents, and suicide; some left only their names while others their individual stories. Twenty-five were not recognized by name and are listed as "Unknowns." One of these unknowns was a strangled baby; another was an adult found floating in the canal. Are these 285 individuals in Heaven and now recognized by God, perhaps having found family and friends?[52] Are they waiting for the return of Jesus and hope to be recognized then?

A reform school for boys in Florida, the Dozier Boys School in Mariana, which ran from 1900 to 2011 has been accused of horrific beatings and mental and sexual abuses. Over 100 bodies in unmarked graves have been discovered, suggesting that boys died at the hands of staff. An anthropologist is leading the effort to exhume, examine and perhaps identify at least some of the remains.[53] A book of fiction but based on facts, *The Nickel Boys*, by Colson Whitehead, provides an inside look of one "hellish" reform school. Historical research suggests that the book documents true events. Does God have a record of these boys and are they in his safekeeping? Are they in Heaven and reunited with parents, family and friends?

A cemetery in a mid-western city, part of a training school, was in the news because the unmarked graves of 60 boys were discovered. An effort is underway to identify as many graves as possible and provide a marker with the name, date of birth and date of death, to give each boy dignity. The boys were assigned there because of shoplifting and other delinquencies, because they were orphans, or the families could not afford to care for them. Historical studies indicate that half the deceased boys were black, and half were white. The boys died from natural causes, afflictions of the times: tuberculosis, pneumonia, typhoid fever and measles. The school ran from 1856-1972. Fund raising is underway to support more studies. Are these boys in God's hands?

Another more gruesome case of dead youth is the discovery of 269 remains of boys and girls along with bodies of alpacas, all killed in what is believed to be some kind of ritual 500 years ago, involving the Chimú people of northern Peru.[54] A copper knife was found within the burial site and is believed to have been used to slice through the breast bones of the children and alpacas. One idea presented was that the chest cavity was opened to gain access to the heart – the hearts were the sacrificed material. Centuries ago, the heart was viewed as the seat of the soul (Chap. 4). The bodies of these children were preserved quite well due to the dryness of the soil at the mass grave site. Children and alpacas were undoubtedly very important to the present and future of the community and thus the killing of both was thought to be sacrificial. It was an offering to the Gods of the very best the community had. Archeologists have found evidence of human sacrifice around the world, but the killing of children is rare. What is the difference between offering children to Gods compared to adults offering themselves to God? In both cases there is an attempt to please God and avoid punishment. In the case of the children of the Chimú people, the sacrifice of children is thought to possibly have been to get the Gods to stop the heavy rains of El Nino and the associated chaos. What were the people thinking? Were the Gods going to somehow make use of the bodies of these dead children? What is the Christian God going to do with the remains of these children?

In 2017, in Ireland, a mass grave was found at a Catholic orphanage; uncovered were the remains of nearly 800 children believed to have died there. The remains were scattered among twenty chambers in an underground structure; DNA analysis and other forensic evidence indicate that the deceased ranged from three to thirty-five years of age. This was only one of many orphanages in Ireland offering shelter to orphans, unwed mothers, and their children. Most of the children who died at the homes were interred in unmarked graves at the orphanage at a time of high child mortality in Ireland in the early 20th century.[55]

There are many unmarked graves of young boys on the grounds of a former reform school in Florida that was open from 1900 to 2010. Ex-inmates from the 1950s and 1960s recounted severe beatings at the school. The Florida governor and cabinet has allowed exhuming to progress into perhaps far more than 100 unmarked graves. An anthropologist of the Univ. of Florida is leading the excavation with the aim of using DNA and other forensic evidence to identify the remains.[56] How can a God allow such deaths to occur? Will these deceased young people be reunited with family and friends in Heaven? Will all the youth in the above "aged" be age thirty-three?

Indigenous survivors in Canada met with Pope Francis in 2022 and called for a papal apology for the role of the Catholic Church in the abuse and deaths of thousands of native children. From the 1800s to the 1970s, more than 150,000 Indigenous children were forced to attend stated-funded Christian boarding schools. The idea was to assimilate these children into Canadian society. But thousands of these children died of disease, abuse, and other causes and many never returned to their families. Presbyterian, Anglican, United Church, and other denominations have apologized for their roles in the abuses. There were over 130 of these schools and in 2021, at the sites of two of the schools, over 800 unmarked graves have been found using ground penetrating radar. How many more graves will be found at the other 128 schools? Some have called for the Catholic church to apologize for the terrible treatment of Indigenous children within their boarding schools, yet propaganda exists in the Holy Childhood history room in some churches depicting Catholic nuns and priests interacting very favorably with Indigenous children.[57] Are the souls of these children in God's care? Will they be united with their parents in Heaven?

Consider the sex abuse cases in the Catholic church, which exploded in the news media after exposure of sex abuse in the Catholic church in Boston in 2002.[58] Research led to the finding that sex abuse of children was exposed more and more after the second Vatican Council in the 1960s and by the many attempts by the Catholic church to cover it all up. Publicity began in earnest in the 1980s but was still sporadic and then increased to a level resulting in apologies from three popes – John Paul II, Benedict XV1, and most recently Francis. The list of countries with reports of clergy sexually abusing children is long and includes Australia, Ireland, and the USA. Clergy of many denominations, perhaps all of them, were guilty, including Catholics, Lutherans, Episcopalians, Church of Christ, and Church of the Nazarene. Mainly boys but also girls were sexually abused, mostly between the ages of 11 and fourteen, but as young as three years old. In 2019, in a mid-Western state, three pastors were arrested for sex trafficking and sexual abuse of teenage girls. Perhaps as high as 15% of all clergy are sex abusers. New findings implicate 286 priests in the Texas Diocese of sexual abuses in the last seventy years.[59, 60] Many of these priests are now deceased. They no doubt had Christian funerals and burials and were praised for their work for the church and for the Lord. How many of us can now attend a wedding, funeral, or church service without wondering if the clergy officiating is/was a sexual abuser? Both the abusers and the abused will carry those experiences to their graves. Which of them will get to Heaven? Will God strike those memories from their minds, or will they live with them in Heaven? Will they be reprimanded in Heaven? Will the abused meet the abusers?

How many religious denominations are there in the world?[60] Let us consider just the Christian religion. There were several hundred Christian denominations in 1800 worldwide and thousands in 2012. Wikipedia does a good job of listing these denominations. Let us hope that not all these denominations have clergy that are sex-abusers. What is going to happen to all these members in Heaven? Will they remain separate with unique beliefs? Will God put them all together as a hodgepodge and give them directions to get along? Will they now all get along given that they are in Heaven, which was their goal from day one?[61]

When God ages deceased infants, children, or teens, one can wonder if he provides a history for each individual. Every child is entitled to grow up, through good and bad times, and those experiences are what we remember and what are so important parts of our lives. Consider too the situation when children die at the hands of their parents. In Jan. 2019, two such reports were in the news. A boyfriend and mother of a two-year-old child who died of exposure having been left outside without adequate clothing in Feb. were sentenced to prison. Also, a mother killed her six-year-old son and eight-year-old daughter to save them from the evils of the world. She was ruled insane by the judge who ordered her to a mental facility. How is God going to handle these youngsters, killed by their parents, when he accepts them to Heaven? Will the parents have any chance to get to Heaven? If not, will these youngsters be aged in Heaven and not have parents at all? Will they have a history? Will they remember dying at the hands of their parents?

Funeral traditions are variable. Protestants have few rules; open or closed caskets, and Bible passages are usually read with the view that those who die in Christ leave the body but are in Heaven with the lord; in other words, the funeral is a home-going celebration wherein the deceased is going home to be with the Lord. Cremains may be scattered or buried. Catholics have similar rules but prefer burial in a Catholic cemetery, no scattering of ashes after cremation. With Hindus the body is burned with no burial. Prayers are for the soul to find peace and rest.[62] A prayer at a funeral for a catholic bishop in a mid-west city stated as follows: "Eternal rest grant unto him, O Lord, and let perpetual light shine upon him. May his soul and all the souls of the faithful departed rest in peace. Amen." But eternal rest in constant light while his soul rests in peace? What? Is this Heaven?

Funerals are becoming more offbeat given that one-fifth of USA residents have no religious affiliation, and that number is growing (Pew Research Center data). Mourners are choosing personalized life-tribute type services. Inspirations come from knowing the deceased interests such as hunting, fishing, crossword puzzles, jigsaw puzzles, and dancing. The music can be polkas and waltzes instead of traditional church music. Iridescent bubbles may be puffed into the air. The ceremony is designed as a celebration of the deceased life and designed toward healthy grieving, healing and remembering.[63] A woman wrote to an advice columnist that her husband died and wondered if he now, being in the afterlife, found out about the affair she had that she had been hiding.

Every country no doubt has various traditions associated with funerals. Finland's are very interesting historically.[64] If a Finn was dying at home, the near-death body was placed on the floor to not contaminate the bed with spirits. An ax was then struck onto the floor (wood floors were the rule back then) to keep the deceased (or its ghost?) from coming back. The deceased, when removed from the home, was taken out feet first so it could not find its way back and the coffin was knocked 3 times on the house threshold to delineate the border the deceased was not allowed to cross anymore. Bells were rung at the church to drive evil spirits away. The clothes of the deceased were sewn with thread with no knots because it was believed knots could turn into fire on the way to the afterlife. The coffin was covered with very loose, light soil to make it easier for the spirit to leave for the afterlife. In the days of horse carriages, they were driven as fast as possible going home so that evil spirits from the graveyard could not tag along.

In contrast were the Ain Mallaha, a Naturian settlement in Northern Israel, who were hunter gatherers and early dog domesticators, that lived 10,000 to 8,000 years ago. These people buried their loved ones in their houses, directly under the areas of the living. This custom led Becky Cooper to the book she recently published.[65]

Clearly many societies had many odd beliefs and superstitions going back thousands of years. Perhaps in thousands of years in the future people will look back on us here in the 21st century and wonder about our strange traditions and beliefs.

We all at times when things are not going well would like to "escape" from our present life. Some people actually do that by faking their own death. E. Greenwood looked into just that idea because of being in debt and then wrote a book exposing the world of faked death.[66] In the Philippines one can rent a corpse and stage a mock funeral. People have faked their deaths in England and in the USA as well.[67] God would undoubtedly not look favorably on people faking their death and especially of a second funeral for the faker when they really, really die.

Here are a few more interesting tidbits about funerals and burials. During the Klondike gold rush many deaths occurred, often from scurvy due to lack of fruits (vit. C) in the diet. It was a challenge and costly to pay for a dog team to transport the casket ($2000), to pay for the casket and nails (nails cost $8/lb.), and to bury a body because the ground was frozen solid; work men took up to a week to dig a grave and were paid $200 each.[68] In a cemetery in N. Michigan Indians built a small house of wood and birch bark above each grave which was to keep loved ones safe from evil spirits. Indians left the area and the little houses became covered by moss and leaves and looked like mounds; tribal members for many years returned to the area to celebrate their ancestors.[69] A plane passenger was transporting his mother's ashes but when he opened his suitcase he found the ashes spread among his clothes.[70] To honor her husband's wishes, a woman tossed his ashes over the Mackinaw Bridge, but in an unopened box. The box floated and was found and returned to her along with an admonishment of the danger of dropping things from the bridge which might hit someone on a boat underneath. It is not known whether she tried again.

Finally, a man in Mexico became incurably ill. His son bought him a new truck to ease his suffering but the father was too ill to drive it so he asked his son to bury him with the truck so he could enjoy the truck in Heaven. The son excavated a large hole and buried the truck along with the coffin containing his father's body in the truck's bed.

NOTES

1   Kate Wong. "Controversy and Excitement Swirl around New Human Species," *Scientific American* 314, no. 3 (2016): 28–37; Michael Shermer, "Murder in the Cave." *Scientific American* 314, No. 1 (January 2016) 75.

2   Lee R. Berger and Brett Hilton-Barber, *In the Footsteps of Eve: The Mystery of Human Origins* (Washington, D.C.: National Geographic Society, 2000.)

3   Anthropology Outreach Office, Smithsonian's National Museum of Natural History "Egyptian Mummies," *Smithsonian Magazine*, accessed December 2019, https://www.si.edu/spotlight/ancient-egypt/mummies.

4   Nathaniel Scharping "The Princesses," *Discover*, March 2017.

5   *Detroit Free Press*, July 15, 2018, 2A.

6   Richard Beliveau and Denis Gingras, *Death, the Scientific Facts to Help Us Understand It Better* (Canada: Firefly Books, 2012.)

7   Jo Marchant, "The Golden Warrior," *Smithsonian Magazine*, January/ February 2017, 38.

8   A.R. Williams, "The King's Maidens," *National Geographic*, July, 2014, 25.

9   *NBC News*, November 12, 2020.

10 Wikipedia website, "Coffin," last edited March 19, 2023, https://en.wikipedia.org/wiki/Coffin.

11 Eileen Finan, "A Greener Grave," *People*, June 29, 2021, 96-99.

12 Facts and Details, "Nenets," last updated May 2016, https://factsanddetails.com/russia/Minorities/sub9_3f/entry-5134.html.

13 *Detroit Free Press*, February 13, 2014.

14 Jefferson Bass, *The Devil's Bones* (New York: Harper Collins, 2008.)

15 *Detroit Free Press*, March 23, 2015.

16 *Detroit Free Press*, December 11, 2013.

17 Funeralwise website, accessed January 2020, https://www.funeralwise.com2018; *Washington Post*, December 2018.

18 Funeral Basics website, accessed December 2019, https://www.funeralbasics.org

19 *Detroit Free Press*, December 31, 2019, 5A.

20 *NBC Nightly News*, January 7, 2021.

21 *Detroit Free Press*, May 3, 2020, 15A.

22 *NBC News*, April 30, 2020.

23 "Virus is Affecting Funerals," *Detroit Free Press*, March 20, 2020, 1A, 5A. *Detroit Free Press*, 2020, 28A, September 23.

24 Bart D. Ehrman, *Heaven and Hell, A History of the Afterlife* (New York: Simon and Schuster, 2020.)

25 *Bloomberg Businessweek*, Summer, 2013; *Detroit Free Press*, September 14, 2019, 1A.

26 Frank Olito, "This extremely detailed map shows where all of America's dead are buried," Insider website, published October 30, 2018, https://www.insider.com/map-us-graveyards-cemeteries-2018-10.

27 *Mackinaw Journal*, October 2014.

28 *AARP Bulletin*, July/Aug 2018; Emily Goodman, "Saluting Arlington Cemetery," *Readers Digest*, May 2021, 40-42.

29 *Time*, April 11, 2011.

30 *Detroit Free Press*, December 14, 2019, 12A.

31 *Detroit Free Press*, April 19, 2020, pp 21-22A; May 3, 2020, 15A.

32 *Northern Express*, August 10, 2015.

33 *Northern Express*, November 25, 2019, 9.

34 M. Bremner, City of Coffins, *Bloomberg Businessweek*, March 11, 2019); Wikipedia website, "Religion in El Salvador, accessed December 2019, https://en.wikipedia.org/wiki/Religion_in_El_Salvador.

35 *Detroit Free Press*, May 26, 2014, 1A, 4A.

36 J. Rauvala (translator), "War Victims Ready Final Resting Place," *Finnish American Reporter*, February 2020, 5.

37 Ilta Sanavat, "Mass Graves from Stalin's Purges Surrounded by Mystery, Misinformation," *Finnish American Reporter*, February 2021, 12-13.

38 *Detroit Free Press*, July 26, 2020, p 21A.

39 J. Carlisle, "For Some Up North, a Ghost Town is Home," *Detroit Free Press*, February 18, 2018, 1A, 6A-8A.

40, 41 *Detroit Free Press*, July 13, 2017; *Detroit Free Press*, December 23, 2018; *Detroit News*, January 7, 2019.

42 David Baldacci, *A Minute to Midnight* (New York: Grand Central Publications, 2019), 187.

43 *Detroit Free Press*, May 11, 2015, p 6A.

44 *Northern Express*, July 2015; *Cheboygan Daily Tribune*, July 19, 2018; *Detroit Free Press* November 22, 2018; June 26, 2014; June 29, 2014.

45 *Detroit Free Press*, May 11, 2014, 10.

46 *National Geographic*, February 2020, 42-67.

47 *Detroit Free Press*, March 1, 2020, 14A.

48 Jo Marchant, "This 3,500-Year-Old Greek Tomb Upended What We thought We Knew About the Roots of Western Civilization, *Smithsonian Magazine* on-line, January 2017, https://www.smithsonianmag.com/history/golden-warrio r-greek-tomb-exposes-roots-western-civilization-180961441/.

49 R. Haile, "Hallowed Ground, The Haunting Beauty of an Ancient Desertscape," *Smithsonian Magazine*, June 2020, 5-7.

50 Tony Hillerman, *The Shape Shifter* (New York: Harper-Collins, 2006), 92.

51 *Northern Express*, November 4-5, 2013, 2.

52 Site Staff, "Potter's Field: No Longer Forgotten," 9 and 10 news, https://www.9and10news.com/2017/05/22/potters-field-no-longer-forgotten/.

53 *Detroit Free Press*, September 1, 2013.

54 *National Geographic*, February 2019, 54.

55 *CBS News*, March 3, 2017.

56 *Detroit Free Press*, September 1, 2013, p 11A.

57 "Pope to Meet with Canada Indigenous," *Rome news as reported in Cheboygan Daily Tribune*, July 2, 2021, 5A; "Catholic leaders should apologize for Indigenous boarding schools," *Detroit Free Press*, November 21, 2021, 29A.

58 Wikipedia website, "Catholic Church sexual abuse cases," accessed January 2020, https://en.wikipedia.org/wiki/Catholic_Church_sexual_abuse_cases.

59 Center for the Prevention of Sexual and Domestic Abuse; Archives of the New York Times.

60 AbuseLawsuit.com website, "Priest Abuse In Texas," accessed February 2020, https://www.abuselawsuit.com/church-sex-abuse/texas/.

61 Wikipedia website, "Gordon-Conwell Theological Seminary," last edited February 23, 2023, https://en.wikipedia.org/wiki/Gordon–Conwell_Theological_Seminary

62 Death Notices, *The Wichita Eagle*, 2018.

63 *Detroit Free Press* August 13, 2013, 9A.

64 Editorial, "Tradition and Superstitions Surrounding Funerals," *Finnish American Reporter*, October 2021, 21-22.

65 Becky Cooper, *We Keep the Dead Close*, published by Grand Central 2020 (Book Page, November 2020, 5).

66 Elizabeth Greenwood, *Playing Dead: A Journey through the World of Death Fraud* (New York: Simon and Schuster, 2017.)

67 Devin Leonard, "A Look at the Weird, Wild World of Death Fraud," *Bloomberg Businessweek*, July 25-31, 2016, 70.

68 Pierre Berton, *The Klondike Fever* (New York: Alfred A. Knopf, Inc., 1958.).

69 *Cheboygan Daily Tribune*, April 18-19, 2015.

70 *Detroit Free Press* October 16, 2016.

9

OBITUARIES AND MEMORIAMS

WHEN SOMEONE DIES, regardless of the cause of death or the age of the deceased, society tries to provide a positive view. That view is most often expressed in the local newspaper in the obituaries. Reference is made to the deceased, to friends and relatives who died previously, to surviving friends and relatives; the person's life on earth is often reviewed in a very positive manner. Often reference is made to God and Jesus, and to Heaven, particularly indicating that the deceased is now in Heaven, even if death occurred within just the past week. The idea is to assure the readers that the deceased is now in the hands of God and/or Jesus and is quite content and happy. As stated earlier, 70% of the USA population believes there is a Heaven. It is thus curious that only a small percentage of obituaries indicate that the deceased has gone to Heaven. Two categories of death notices are included in one midwestern city newspaper: "In Remembrance" and "In Memoriams."[1] In the same Sunday paper there are fifty to sixty Remembrances (there were sometimes over 80 during the COVID-19 pandemic); in the daily paper there are from fifteen to twenty-five. The lengths can be from twenty to over 600 words. Memoriams are fewer in number and shorter.

Examination of over 1,161 "Remembrances," in the newspapers of a large mid-western city show that the majority (65%) of the obituaries make no direct mention of the person's death. That is understandable as an obituary is only written for a deceased person. Nevertheless, many (406 of the 1,161 examined) included "passed away" or "died" as well as other statements indicating death. Some obituaries indicated that the loved one is on his/her way to Heaven or is already there.[1]

Here are the various phrases used: Passed away (37%) and died (31%) are the most commonly used. A smaller number add a descriptive word or phrase to follow passed away or died. These total a little over 15% with passed away peacefully and died peacefully used most frequently: Passed away suddenly; passed away unexpectedly, died peacefully, and died suddenly are in this category as well.

Infrequently used (less than 5%) were the following phrases: Passed away at home; passed away quietly; passed away while sleeping; passed on; passed quietly; paused and passed; and lost battle with or died of (different cancers mentioned; diseases); died of heart failure or heart attack or complications after heart surgery; died after a short illness or long illness; died at home; died unexpectedly and left our arms.

The following phrases indicate that the deceased has left this life and gone to another place or another life. These include: passed from this life... departed this life...and walked on.

The next 5 phrases indicate that the person dying has gone on to a place that is very satisfying, a wonderful place that is full of peace, happiness, and love, and is very beautiful. There is no other place than Heaven that these obituaries could be referring to.

- Now is at peace with happiness and love...
- Went to peace and beauty...
- Went to her/his final resting place...
- Passed from this world to a world free of pain and illness...
- Is in a better place...

This unique obituary must be included: Entered this part of his life on July 5, 1937, and consistent with his meticulous and precise style of editing, he chose to exit on July 5 as well.

The following phrases strongly indicate that the deceased has gone to Heaven:

- Was called to his eternal home...
- Went to her Heavenly home...
- She will always be with us spiritually...
- Was called to his eternal home...
- Went to be with her lord and savior...
- Her homecoming was...
- Delivered home...
- Completed his journey on earth when his Heavenly father called him home...
- Entered into eternal rest...
- She became an angel on...
- God called Jack to his side...
- Unexpectedly went home to Heaven to be with the Lord and her Mom and Dad ...
- Went to be with her Heavenly father...
- Completed his journey on earth when his Heavenly Father called him home...
- Joined the Lord on...
- Met her Savior...

Some obituaries indicate that the loved one has now joined previously deceased family members/loved ones and where else would that be but in Heaven. Consider the following:

- Was called home to be with her husband...
- Left us to be reunited with her mother...
- Returned to the arms of his loving mother...
- Joined his beloved...
- Called into the presence of Jesus and is now reunited with her husband, parents and sibling...

More specifically, some obituaries make it clear that the Lord/God "called" the person to Heaven.

- God called your name...
- God called her/him to his side...

- He/she was taken from us...
- God has you in his keeping...

Sometimes Memoriams (remembering a loved one who died some time ago) indicate that the deceased is in Heaven, that God made the decision to "take" the person, and that the individual is now with family and with God and that other family members will join him/her. References are often to the person's interests on earth. Requests are sometimes made to God and to the deceased. Consider these:

- As I held your hand you passed away. God saw you were getting tired, a cure was not meant to be. So, he wrapped his arms around you and whispered, 'Come home with me.' One day we will be together again forever...
- My sweet twin sister, I miss you very much. Knowing you are with the Lord is comforting. Rejoice in Heaven with the rest of our loved ones. See you later. I love you sis...
- She was called into the presence of her savior, Jesus Christ, and is now reunited with her beloved husband, her precious parents, and all her deceased siblings...
- Ruth's spirit has risen to Heaven to meet her God, her husband, and eldest son. Soon she will be part of a very special and long-awaited Smith reunion with her parents and 6 brothers and sisters...
- Cal completed his journey on earth on Dec. 4 when his Heavenly father called him home...
- As you are surrounded by your family in Heaven, you are lovingly remembered by your nieces, nephews, and family...
- Watch over all of us from Heaven...
- Walt, thank you for being our guardian angel for all these years and watching over us...
- We wait to be united with our beloved Tim, in Jehovah, God's earthly paradise...
- Jerry, on earth you would be 100 yrs. old, but in Heaven only 2 hrs. and 30 minutes old...
- It has been one year since the lord took you from us; tell everyone there hi from me...

- I know you are up there in Heaven watching over me...
- Merry Christmas to you in Heaven; please give baby Jesus a gentle hug from me...
- Jeannie, we miss you and hope there are strawberry margaritas in Heaven...
- Mom and Dad, we pray that you are finally together in Heaven and free of pain and suffering...
- Happy 55th birthday. For reasons known only to God, you were taken from us so early...
- God, she is with you now; please let her know how much she is missed...
- We know you are looking down and looking after us...
- We all hope to go to Heaven to see your beautiful, sparkling eyes again...
- It has been 5 years now, on Valentine's Day, since the Dear Lord took you into his loving arms...
- We trust you are in God's reigning light; we love you Betty...
- I will only be at peace when I am with you again...
- I feel your presence in spirit and in my heart, so I know you are with me constantly...
- Happy Thanksgiving to you in Heaven mom and dad.; may you be showered with blessings...
- Marge has been hiking the trails of Heaven for 5 years now; we love and miss her...
- May you still be cheering for your beloved Tigers baseball team...
- Dear son, may you be resting in peace with all the angels and saints in Heaven...
- Dad left us 10 years ago to go to a better place; mom has joined him now...
- Save a place on the first tee for your mom and dad; we miss you son...
- Rover died and we are sure he is with you in Heaven, giving you comfort...
- Dad, I know you are watching me from above at every game, giving me strength; thank you...
- OK dad, we are sure you are driving mama all over Heaven, as you did on earth...

- He is dancing on streets of gold, singing and whistling with choirs of angels...
- Hugs to you Marvin; perhaps God will convey them to you.
- A life in eternity with you is the last space I want to fill...
- A year has passed since you gently placed your hands in mine and entered the kingdom of Heaven...
- I talk to you every day and I know you hear me...
- Happy 87th birthday dad from your loving daughters; take care of mom and Carl...
- Happy Sweetest Day hon; look down and see the beautiful roses I bought for you...
- Bob you are no doubt fishing the beautiful trout streams of Heaven...
- I know that when my time comes, you will be the first person welcoming me home...
- I am channeling my loving thoughts from earth to Heaven through God to you...
- God please pick a dozen roses from your Heavenly garden and give them to our mother...

Interestingly, these Memoriams indicate that those remembering the deceased person believe he/she is very much able to communicate in Heaven, with God and with other deceased people, and can drink, eat, hike and even drive. Yet the deceased body is in the ground, very much lifeless, or as ashes in an urn on the mantle or in the ground. What is the relationship of these deceased already in Heaven going to be at the end, the judgement day, when God brings forth bodies and unites them with their souls?

One might expect an obituary to be more religious if the person died on Christmas Day, perhaps correlating the person's death with the birth of Jesus. Such was not the case for 2010. Of the ten who died on Dec. 25, 2010, seven of the obituaries had no mention of death while three did as follows:

- Delivered home
- Passed away peacefully
- Passed away

Interspersed among the obituaries in this newspaper[1] are statements about life and death by some famous people. Note that none of these say anything about God or Heaven but instead encourage living a full life here on earth. Consider the following:

- *It is not death that a man should fear, but he should fear never beginning to live.* Marcus Aurelius
- *It is not the length of life but depth of life.* Ralph Waldo Emerson
- *The greatest use of life is to spend it for something that will outlast it.* William James
- *I am beginning to learn that it is the sweet, simple things of life which are the real ones after all.* Laura Ingalls Wilder
- *Relish love in your old age. Aged love is like aged wine; it becomes more satisfying, more refreshing, more valuable, more appreciated, and more intoxicating.* Leo Buscaglia
- *When you were born, you cried and the world rejoiced. Live your life so that when you die, the world cries and you rejoice.* Anonymous
- *The person born with a talent they are meant to use will find their greatest happiness in using it.* Johann Wolfgang von Goethe
- *We all live with the objective of being happy; our lives are all different and yet the same.* Anne Frank
- *Security is mostly a superstition. It does not exist in nature, nor do the children of men as a whole experience it. Avoiding danger is no safer in the long run than outright exposure. Life is either a daring adventure, or nothing.* Helen Keller
- *We are all born for love. It is the principle of existence and its only end.* Benjamin Disraeli

From these obituaries and remembrances, we can list some of the views people have about Heaven.

- People who go to Heaven become angels (guardian angels).
- The deceased in Heaven watches over those on the earth.
- The deceased can look down from Heaven and see loved ones.
- Heaven is eternal.
- Heaven is free of disease and suffering of all kinds.

- Heaven is the ultimate "home."
- There is rejoicing in Heaven.
- There is singing (choirs), whistling, and dancing in Heaven.
- The deceased is reunited with family and friends (loved ones).
- Birthdays are recognized and counted in Heaven.
- Holidays are recognized in Heaven.
- The deceased in Heaven even after many years can receive oral or written messages from earth.
- God can accept messages from earth and relay the messages to those in Heaven.
- Messages from earth can go to God and then be relayed to the deceased in Heaven.
- There are pets (dogs) in Heaven.
- The deceased may be here on earth in the body of a bird.
- The deceased can remain a sports fan and follow their earth team in Heaven.
- The deceased may be watching an athlete perform in a game on earth.
- There is alcohol in Heaven.
- There are sports like golf and fishing in Heaven.
- There is a Heavenly garden and God can pick flowers for the deceased.
- There are automobiles in Heaven.

ANALYSIS

God has major challenges.

> Challenge One. There are over 25,000 obituaries yearly in the USA alone for God to be aware of each day. Worldwide there are many thousands more newspapers printed daily.

> Challenge Two. The world's newspapers may be in thousands of different languages for there are now believed to

be 6,909 different spoken languages and 3,866 written languages in the world. God will need to know all of them.

Challenge Three. Heaven must accommodate the thousands and thousands of people who die every day. God must be paying attention to not only the obituaries of current deaths but also to the memoriams referring to people who died years ago.

Challenge Four. If everyone initially goes to an intermediate Heaven,[2] and may not have their own body, is it reasonable to assume there are cars, sports, singing, and all the other activities as listed above available upon death? God must evaluate all the deaths and provide conditions for all in Heaven.

Heaven is wishful thinking. This wishful thinking is very reassuring to those who knew the deceased.

NOTES

1   Obituaries and Memoriams, *Detroit Free Press,* Sunday issues, 2017 and 2018.
2   Randy Alcorn, *Heaven: A Comprehensive Guide to Everything the Bible Says About Our Eternal Home* (Illinois: Tyndale Momentum, 2004.)

10

CAUSES OF DEATHS AND NUMBER OF DEATHS

A MAJOR CHALLENGE for God will be dealing with the large number of deaths worldwide, the plethora of different causes of death, and the variety of ages at which people die, including before birth. God will have to diagnose the cause of death, do the healing, do repairing and restoring, add age to some of the individuals and remove age from the others.

Worldwide, in 2012, there were fifty-six million deaths or 153,424 deaths each day: 14.1 million from heart disease and other cardiovascular conditions. Worldwide, in 2018, deaths from coronary heart disease totaled 9.4 million, from stroke 5.8 million, from lung problems three million, and from influenza and pneumonia together almost 3 million. By the end of 2020, COVID-19 deaths will be third in order, more than the number of deaths from lung problems. As of Dec. 26, 2020, the USA had 330,000 deaths attributed to the COVID-19 virus, the majority sixty-five and older.[1]

In 2015 in the USA, there were 2,626,418 deaths or 7,195 deaths each day of that year. If we assume that an average of 2,500,000 deaths occurred each year from 2000 through 2016, then a total of 40,000,000 deaths occurred in that sixteen-year period. Many funeral homes were necessary to care for and prepare those individuals for burial or cremation. In the USA in 2019, there were 19,136 funeral homes.[2] Some of the dead were from drowning, homicides, fires, and other situations wherein the bodies were never recovered.

In some years going back in USA history, there were many deaths above the average numbers, for example in times of war. During the Civil War, 620,000 deaths of soldiers occurred; WWI had 116,000 deaths, WWII had 405,000 deaths, the Korean War had 36,500 deaths, the Vietnam War had 58,000 deaths, the Iraq War had 4,500 deaths, and the Afghanistan War had 2,350 deaths.[3] At the end of 2020 there were forty armed conflicts in the world, from Chechnya to South America and, including the drug cartel wars in Mexico adding thousands of lives lost, mostly civilians, the total deaths numbered over 100,000 for the year.[4] Many of these bodies resulting from wars have not been recovered. The bodies of many, though recovered, are horribly mangled with parts lost. Is God keeping track of all war dead? Are the souls of all these soldiers under God's keeping?"

Additional deaths occur prior to birth by miscarriages or induced abortions.[5] In 2020 there were 930,000 medical abortions in the USA. That is 186 abortions for every 1000 live births and amounts to 106 per hour. In addition, there are thousands more chemical induced abortions each year. According to WHO statistics there are millions more abortions worldwide. Thus, millions of embryos or fetuses die before birth each year. What is the fate of these failed pregnancies? Is God taking care of all these souls? Will they continue to develop in heaven, be born and live to age thirty-three? What personalities will they have? How will they be educated?

The leading causes of death in the USA are heart disease (614,348 deaths/year) and cancer (591,699); 40,000 American women each year die from breast cancer and respiratory ailments (147,101 deaths).[6] Deaths are divided into non-communicative (heart, lung, kidney, diabetes, cancer) making up 68%, and communicative (bacterial, viral, nutritional) making up 23%, with injuries making up 9%. Communicative diseases include HIV, tuberculosis, pneumonia, malaria, smallpox, seasonal flu, the 1918 Spanish pandemic, COVID-19 in 2020/2021, and diarrhea. The number of COVID-19 deaths in the USA so far near the end of March 2021, is over 500,000, more than the total number of USA deaths in WWI, the Korean War and Vietnam War combined. In Los Angeles County, CA, one person died from COVID-19 every ten minutes and on some days in the USA 4,000 people died of the virus.[7]

In 2013 worldwide there were 1.25 million vehicular accidental deaths or 3,500 each day of that year.[8] Traffic accident deaths in the USA in 2014 numbered 32,675 (90 each day) of which 4,586 were motorcycle accidental deaths. The majority of motorcycle deaths are due to head/brain injuries. There were 6000 pedestrian deaths in 2016 in the USA, or sixteen on each day in that year, the increasing numbers attributed to distraction while texting.[9] In addition to 40,000 deaths related to motor vehicles, other accidents in 2019 will kill thousands of Americans; from falls 36,000; from poisoning 65,000.[10] These numbers represent a huge number of diagnoses every day for God.

In 2012, 6.6 million children worldwide died before their fifth birthday or 18,082 each day. About 44% of these latter deaths were neonatal (within twenty-eight days of their birth). Poverty is a big issue worldwide and hunger goes along with poverty. In 2016, 7,665,000 individuals died from hunger worldwide, or 21,000 each day. In a 48-hr. period in March 2017, 110 individuals died in Somalia. In Somalia, Nigeria, Sudan, and Yemen, it was estimated that five million people were suffering from malnutrition.[11] A continuing high death rate due to starvation will be expected for some time. Perhaps anorexia deaths would fit into the hunger death category. Poverty is seen in the USA, the richest country in the world.[12] In 2018 over thirty-eight million people in the USA lived below the poverty line; that is 11.8 percent of the USA population. The danger to health is that people who are living in poverty, for example a family of two parents and two children with income below $25,500, do not have a healthy diet, leading to various adverse effects on the brain and the body in general that contribute to earlier deaths. (see Chapter 36)

About one in five deaths totaling eleven million worldwide are related to unhealthy dietary choices according to data published by the Lancet journal.[13] People do not eat enough whole grains, nuts, seeds, and milk and milk products. Processed meat, salt, and sugar make up too much of our diets. The deaths worldwide include nearly ten million from cardiovascular disease, thousands from cancer, and thousands from Type 2 diabetes. In the USA 171,000 deaths in 2019 were linked to poor diet, ranking forty-third worldwide. The UK ranked twenty-third. The lowest rates of poor diet related deaths were in France, Spain, Japan, and Israel. Highest rates of death due to poor diets were in Afghanistan and the Marshall Islands. What will be the dietary choices in Heaven? Will it matter what residents of Heaven eat? In any case, according to the Bible, there will be no deaths, pain, or suffering (Revelation 21:4)! No deaths? That will be billions and billions of people living forever and all worshiping God!

Alcohol-related deaths are very high. Almost one million people died from alcohol-related causes from 1999 to 2017 in the USA. Death certificates that mentioned alcohol numbered 72,558 in 2017, 199 every day, indicating alcohol played a role in 2.6% of all deaths that year. Alcohol-related deaths can involve overdoses, injuries, and chronic diseases. Furthermore, hospitalizations increased during that period of time. Imagine the adverse effects on families and friends.[14]

Deaths due to opioid overdoses numbered 33,000 for the year in 2015 or ninety per day. Drug overdoses in 2016 numbered 52,000 and drug overdose was the leading cause of accidental deaths; 20,000 due to prescription pain killers (opioids) and 13,000 due to heroin overdoses.[15] About 68,000 people in the USA died of drug overdoses in 2018, 186 each day; opioids were involved in two-third of the cases. Very worrisome is that a very powerful opioid, 100 times more powerful than morphine, is now of great concern. This opioid, fentanyl, was implicated in over 18,000 overdose deaths in 2016.[16] Fentanyl is coming into the USA across the border from Canada; a 10.5 lb. seized amount was reported which would be enough to kill millions of people by overdoses. A quantity equivalent to a few grains of salt is enough to cause an overdose. Other items encountered at the USA northern border include cocaine, opium, guns, stolen gift cards, Rolex watches, and counterfeit makeup.[17] The USA represents 5% of the world's population but consumes 80% of the opioids.[18] Other drugs called "stimulants" include methamphetamine and cocaine. Different parts of the country have different numbers of deaths from different drugs. For example, drug overdose deaths per 1,000 population are very high in West Virginia but very low in N. Dakota. Drug use and overdose deaths have increased greatly during COVID-19.[19] Will God be able to diagnose the drug involved in a death and how that drug caused the death?

We can ask if there will be borders between states and countries in Heaven and whether people and materials will be free to cross the borders both ways. Perhaps there will be no borders of any kind, just one huge area with everyone mingling together or apart as they wish.

Worldwide 800,000 people take their own lives each year by suicide. In the USA, in 2017, more than 47,000 people took their own lives; that is 130 lives lost per day to suicide, now the tenth leading cause of death in the USA. The states with the highest rate of suicides are Montana, Wyoming and W. Virginia and the states with the lowest rates are New Jersey, Massachusetts, New York, Connecticut, and Maryland. Men commit suicide 3.5 times more often than women, white males more than others. Firearms account for 50% of the suicides (American Foundation for Suicide Prevention). Interesting data would be to see if there is a correlation with religion in the two sets of states.[20] Suicides have increased by 33% from 1990 to 2019 and suicides are now the second leading cause of death in the USA for young people (ten to thirty-four years of age.)

The dramatic increase in suicides is correlated in large part to an increase in depression and mental illness. The World Health Organization states that 300 million people worldwide suffer from depression which is the leading cause of disability.[21] The Manhattan Project for Depression is underway as a 500-million-dollar effort to understand and treat depression and includes researchers from neuroscience, molecular genetics, psychology, economics, and engineering.[22] Depression is a complex phenomenon. Will God find it just as complex? Will Heaven residents have depression? Will the souls of these young people carry with them their depression and suicidal thoughts, or will God ensure that suicidal thoughts, even depression, are not going to be seen in Heaven?

Suicide rates have increased dramatically among USA youth, showing a 56% increase from 2007-2017. Possible causes are social media and smart phones, bullying, and lack of community. Today's teens are the most anxious and depressed ever. Seventeen percent of age nine-twelve students reported thinking seriously about suicide in 2017, 22% of girls, 12% of boys, and almost half of all gay, lesbian, or bisexual youth. Schools are becoming more and more aware of suicide symptoms and are talking and listening to students.[22]

Suicide is prevalent among veterans. Between 1999 and 2014 in the USA, over twenty veterans committed suicide each day. The late country singer Charlie Daniels tweeted that number regularly.[23] Veterans should get preferential treatment from God, regardless of their home country, be it USA, Japan, Germany, Vietnam, Syria, China, or Russia, whether they die from war or suicide. Why is God allowing so many suicides among veterans? But will they receive that treatment? How will interactions in Heaven occur between the deceased from countries that were enemies or are enemies?

Suicide is linked to depression, and it seems that to decrease suicide levels it will be important to decrease the frequency of depression. One woman is "innovating to stop suicide." Her point is that 300 million people around the world suffer from depression according to the World Health Organization but not even half receive treatment for their depression. Thus, she launched a free peer-support app called "Be-a-Looper," to let people check in with friends and give themselves a numerical rating for their mental well-being. Each person can thus have a support group to rally around them. Be-a-Looper is now active in seventy-six countries and is saving lives every day.[24] Will Be a Looper be available in Heaven?

Homicides, which numbered 16,425 in the USA in 2019, and can result from firearms, knives, bludgeoning with a baseball bat, strangulation, asphyxiation, and more.[25]

There are many, many different causes of death, discussed by Michael Largo in his book, *Final Exits*.[26] Listing the various ways people can die, Largo goes through the alphabet A to Z. Here are some of the numbers. As examples, there are twenty-nine different ways to die beginning with the letter S, twenty-seven begin with B, twenty-six begin with A, etc. through the alphabet. The fewest, only three, begin with X, Y, or Z, and only four with K and Q. A total of 299 different ways of dying are listed and discussed, including the number of deaths due to each cause listed during a certain period of years, all very fascinating. Some causes beginning with A include abandonment, air bags, alligators, arsenic, and anorexia. Under B are listed balloons, baseball, bicycles, bingo, black death, and body piercing. Under S are included scorpions, sea diving, shame, sexually transmitted diseases, Siamese twins, sperm allergies, and sneezing. God must diagnose each of these causes and correct/heal the situation for each of the deceased as he restores the bodies.

Of interest is to look more closely at a sample of the deaths Largo discusses. "Ague" was recorded as the cause of death on 319,334 death certificates from 1850-1920. Ague was a catch-all term to include deaths from shakes, chills, and fevers, in other words not well-defined causes, not unlike saying someone died of natural causes or old age. Now hundreds of well-known diseases would fit into the "ague" category. There is a web site which is keeping track of deaths from about twenty causes with continuous updates. For example, from Jan. 1 to Jan.17, 2017, there were 28,026 deaths from heart problems or over 1600 each day in that short time period.[27]

Another website, for the year 2018 worldwide, lists 83 different causes of death with coronary heart disease having 9,405,000 deaths (# 1); stroke 5,775,313 deaths (# 2); lung disease/ailments 3,032,444 deaths (# 3); influenza/pneumonia 2,947,050 (# 4); Alzheimer's/dementia deaths 1,976,848 (# 5); low birth weight child deaths 1,022,063 deaths (# 13); HIV AIDS 1,011,748 deaths (# 14); suicide 788,851 deaths (# 17); birth trauma 678,355 deaths (# 20), malnutrition 342,092 deaths (# 34); iodine deficiency 2054 deaths, (# 77). At the bottom of the list were Vitamin A deficiency with eight deaths and hookworm with one death.

The average life expectancy in the USA is dropping and is now 78.5, ranked thirty-fourth in the world.[28] This low ranking of the USA is possibly because of increased numbers of younger and middle-aged people dying from drug overdoses, alcohol-related deaths, and suicides. In 2016 the number of people killing themselves with guns (22,928) was nearly double the number of people dying from guns fired by others (14,415). Alcohol-related deaths of 25-34 yr. old individuals, mostly due to liver cirrhosis, increased 65% from 1999 to 2016.[18] God will have to repair many bodies damaged in various ways. Consider the brain of a person suffering from depression damaged severely by a self-inflicted gunshot. What a challenge that brain will be for God to diagnose and restore!

NOTES

1   WorldLifeExpectancy website, accessed February 2020, worldlifeexpectancy.com/world-rankings-total-deaths; *NBC Nightly News*, December 20, 2020.

2   statista website, "Number of funeral homes in the United States from 2004 to 2021," accessed January 2020, https://www.statista.com/statistics/882963/number-of-funeral-homes-in-the-united-states/

3   Wikipedia website, "United States military casualties of war," last edited February 8, 2023, https://en.wikipedia.org/wiki/United_States_military_casualties_of_war.

4   S. Tuttle, "The Other 2020," *Northern Express*, December 21/28, 2020.

5   ALL (American Life League,) website, "USA Abortion statistics," accessed December 12, 2020, https://www.all.org/?s=USA+Abortion+statistics.

6   *Time*, October 14, 2019, 44.

7   *NBC News*, March 2021.

8   World Health Organization website, "Road traffic injuries," accessed February 2, 2020, https://www.who.int/health-topics/road-safety#tab=tab_1.

9   *USA Today* online, "Pedestrian deaths spiked in 2016," published March 30, 2017. https://www.usatoday.com/videos/news/nation/2017/03/30/pedestrian-deaths-spiked-2016/99811908/.

10 Stephen Tuttle, "Human Error," *Northern Express*, December 14, 2019, 6.

11 *Detroit Free Press*, March 5, 2017, 5A.

12 *Cheboygan Daily Tribune*, September 12, 2019, 1A, 3A.

13 *Detroit Free Press*, April 4, 2019, 11A.

14 Data from National Institute on Alcohol Abuse and Alcoholism, *Detroit Free Press*, December 2020, A5.

15 CDC website, accessed March 2020, https://www.cdc.gov/drugoverdose/index.html.

16 *Detroit Free Press*, February 10, 2019, 6A; March 25, 9A.

17 *Detroit Free Press*, January 30, 2020, 1A, 6A.

18 Mitch Albom, "Why is living shorter, dying sooner a new trend?" *Detroit Free Press*, March 31, 2019, 22A.

19 *Detroit Free Press*, January 22, 2020, 13A; CDC Center for Disease Control and Prevention, Website accessed December 2020.

20 *Cheboygan Daily Tribune*, September 10, 2019, 1A.

21 *Discover Magazine* November 2019, 68-72.

22 neaToday website, January 2020, https://www.nea.org/advocating-for-change/new-from-nea/peer-programs-helping-schools-tackle-student-depression-anxiety.

23 *Detroit Free Press*, July 7, 2020, 11A.

24 *Time*, Oct 21/28, 2019, 101.

25 John Sandford, *Storm Prey* (New York: G.B. Putnam's Sons, 2010.)

26 Michael Largo, *Final Exits: The Illustrated Encyclopedia of How We Die* (New York: HarperCollins, 2006.)

27 CDC website, "Deaths and Mortality," last edited January 17, 2023, https://www.cdc.gov/nchs/fastats/deaths.htm.

28 CDC website, "Leading Causes of Death," accessed March 2020, https://www.cdc.gov/nchs/fastats/leading-causes-of-death.htm.

11

INFORMATION GOD
NEEDS AT DEATH

WHEN A PERSON dies, God needs information in order to decide whether to accept the person's soul into Heaven or into an intermediate Heaven. If there is no soul (see Chapter 4) how can God preserve information about the deceased? If there is a soul, how can a spirit, a non-material entity, preserve this information? Religious people to whom I have raised this question give the following answer: "I don't know how but God will do these things. God can do everything."

The Bible reminds us as stated in John 5:28-29, "For the hour is coming in which all that are in the graves shall hear his voice and shall come forth, they that have done good enter unto the resurrection of life and they that have done evil enter unto the resurrection of damnation." At the Rapture, the general belief is that God will combine the souls of the deceased with the bodies (James 5:20). And in Revelation 20:13, we read, "The sea gave up the dead who were in it and death and Hades gave up the dead who were in them, and they were judged, each one according to what they had done." Does this mean that even those who have accepted Christ, and have been born again, are still going to be judged? John 3:3 says "...except a man be born again he cannot see the kingdom of God." If only accepting Jesus is sufficient to gain entrance into Heaven, then do those "born again" have to be concerned if their transgressions are going to be known to God? If

Jesus is going to judge everyone by their ungodly deeds and words, does it matter the quantity or how awful the transgressions are? Will a murderer get to Heaven if he/she accepts Jesus? Things are not so clear.

Genesis 2:7 says, "And the Lord God formed man of the dust of the ground..." and Genesis 3:19 says, "...for out of the ground was thou taken, for dust thou art and unto dust shalt thou return." Ecclesiastes 3:19-20, says "...yea they have all one breath, so that a man hath no preeminence above a beast...all are of the dust and all turn to dust again." In order for living cells to be made, organic molecules are necessary to make nucleic acids (DNA and RNA, and proteins (enzymes and structural), carbohydrates and many more. If after decomposition there is nothing but dust (decomposed molecules or ashes) in graves, at the bottom of lakes/seas, or in urns, at the time of the resurrection, how can each be "judged according to what they have done?" God must be keeping a record. It is of interest to this dust topic that a Japanese space craft with samples from an asteroid has returned to earth. The Japanese scientists hope to find organic and non-organic molecules that will give clues as to how these molecules are distributed in the solar system and how they might be related to life on earth.[1] The USA has a space probe on Mars. Will it find organic molecules there?

Revelation 21:4 says, "And God shall wipe away all tears and there will be no more death, no sorrow, no crying and no pain." When a person dies, God has to do a diagnosis and make decisions about that person, regardless of how the person died. The analysis is like that of a coroner called to examine a deceased person or a detective examining a homicide victim, but God has to be more thorough. Chapter 10 discusses the many ways people may die. God has to know the cause of death, the name of the person, features (face and body) and personality, the nationality and language, memories and brain activities, age, sex (including gender, LGBTQIA), information about the family such as parent and/or grandparental status, the person's present and past health, history of diet, drugs, HIV status, alcohol, smoking, concussions, stroke, heart attacks, disabilities (hearing, sight, smell, physical ability/arthritis), dementia, Alzheimer's disease, genetic defects, surgeries, organ/tissue transplants or donations, intelligence, education, religious background, good deeds, and wealth, and more. Wealth is added based on the Bible verse, Matthew 19:24, "It is easier for a camel to go through the eye of a needle than for a rich man to enter into Heaven." One would think God would acquire his information prior to the person becoming dust. Note that the Bible says God created man from dust and to dust he will return. But please, dust cannot carry information about that person.

Individuals who have been adopted are also a challenge as the birth parents may not be known and may not want to be known. The adopted individual is not biologically related to the parents who raised him/her nor to the individual's siblings. What will God do with regard to this individual in Heaven? Will God favor the adoptee's parents and family? Will the biological parents, siblings or relatives be searched out and brought into the person's life? Or will God decide to leave well enough alone and not bring the individual together with the biological family. The difficulty would be in the case of the adoptee wanting to meet with biological parents but laws in some states make it difficult to do so and thus the only chance to meet the parents and family would be in Heaven. Other adoptees may not want to meet their biological parents or may not have been told they are adopted.[2]

According to Alcorn,[3] the souls of all deceased persons will go to an intermediate Heaven and reside there until the Rapture, when the decision about going to Heaven or Hell is made. In the intermediate Heaven people may be given a temporary body. Since the bodies left on earth would decompose, God would have to make the above diagnoses and record that information for when bodies are raised from the dead to ascend into Heaven. The idea of restoring the body into a thirty-three-year-old in excellent health, especially the brain with all its complexities (memories, thought processes, personality), is far-fetched given the rapidity and thoroughness of decomposition, not to mention cremation destruction of everything. From medical records God could access health information, such as that listed above, but also the number of hospital visits, types of medications and for how long administered, number of strokes or heart attacks, falls, type of cancer and history of the cancer (number of surgeries, length, and type of chemotherapy), and more. Hospitals and doctors are by law required to keep medical records for a period of time, usually fifty years is cited, according to HHS.gov, but that number may vary. Access to those records is provided for law enforcement (if a crime may be involved in the death), the coroner/funeral director, organ donation people, family members, and the executor of the estate (HIPAA Privacy Rule). Records would also be available from the dentist, ophthalmologist, audiologist, urologist, dermatologist, otolaryngologists, and other medical people. Medical records would be particularly useful to God when the deceased is older but could be useful even for younger individuals if death is caused by disease/cancer/genetic conditions. Before modern medicine, God must have kept his own data on the health of people.

God must also decide exactly when a person is dead, like the Wicked Witch of the East in the *Wizard of Oz* who is thoroughly examined and pronounced "really, really, sincerely dead" by the Munchkin's coroner. The issue of when death occurs is brought up by John Troyer, Director of the Centre for Death and Society, Univ. of Bath.[4] Troyer's dad was a funeral director and was asked for help exhuming a body thirty years after burial. The concrete around the casket had cracked and water had filled the casket which resulted in a "big, brown, soupy mess." Nothing could be learned by analysis of this body! Troyer then discusses how life support machines raised questions about when someone is "really dead!" It certainly is not just when the heart stops; perhaps when the brain is dead the person is dead. But organs (cells and tissues) can still be alive as seen by transplants of organs like kidneys or liver from medically declared dead individuals into patients whose own organs are threatening to die; the patient's body can be kept "alive" for weeks while under life support and waiting for an organ donor.

Implants can make life better for the living. Lens implants might not be so easy to diagnose but millions of people now have artificial lenses. The first lens implant was done in Arizona in 1972. Prior to that, God was seeing many lenses with cataracts and supposedly he replaces them with the person's own lenses which he has restored to good health and function. Now more than 2.4 million lens implants are performed in the USA each year with that number increasing.[5] God is seeing more artificial lenses in the deceased. Ophthalmologists will tell you that the plastic lens will last forever (meaning one's lifetime on earth) but since Heaven is forever, maybe God will not have to replace the artificial lenses of the resurrected.

Women who die before menopause might very well be menstruating. In Heaven will women menstruate? Certainly, women will be at an age (early thirties) when they will still be menstruating. In order to stop menstruation God will have to stop the flow of women's hormones, i.e., progesterone and estrogen. Won't this hormonal change influence a woman's physiology and personality? What about women who die with IUDs (intrauterine devices)?

These are small, plastic devices containing synthetic hormones designed to prevent pregnancy. If there is no sex in Heaven, God will not have to reinsert IUDs. After a woman's body undergoes degeneration in the grave, IUDs will remain along with lens implants and maybe some bone and tooth fragments. How crazy is this? After the 2016 election, with the threat of a repeal of the Affordable Care Act (ACA), a 900% increase in IUD insertion appointments occurred at Planned Parenthood clinics nationwide. The ACA provides free insertion with private health insurance. Modern IUDs are very safe compared to the Dalkon Shield of the 1970s which resulted in infertility and even death in tens of thousands of women. God had to deal with those injuries and deaths and get rid of those defective Dalkon Shields.[6]

God might also find useful information of a digital nature. Popular Science (Jan. 2019) discusses the preparation of a person's digital life for his/her inevitable death. This information could be financial accounts, photos, videos, notebooks, email, social media accounts, phone records and contact lists. A person can make arrangements as to who could have access to this information, such as by providing passwords. Most states have laws allowing a person to declare who has access to digital information. Google and Facebook can help a person make arrangements for dealing with digital information. This information can be programmed to delete itself after a period of time. Will God have access to this information?

The average expected lifespan in 2012 was 78.6 years; Hawaiians have the longest life span and Mississippians the shortest. In the continental USA Minnesotans have the longest life span. Even within a given state lifespans vary from county to county.[7] Life spans in Michigan's eighty-four counties in 2014 varied from the highest of 82.7 years. for Keweenaw County to the lowest of 75.3 years for Wayne County,[8] an eight-year difference. The causes of death might very well be somewhat different between those two counties. God could find that information useful. But whatever, most deaths are of older people with a full half being over seventy-five. If everyone in Heaven is going to be thirty-three years of age, God has work to do dealing with the infirmities of old age and in 2020 and perhaps 2021 the adverse effects of the COVID virus since most people die at sixty years of age or older. Even if the gender is not given God must have that information in his records. If not, would God diagnose the gender? Does gender matter in Heaven?

In one Sunday newspaper, forty-one names were listed in the obituaries and sixteen pictures were included, eight women and eight men. Most interesting was that seven of the pictures were clearly chosen from when the deceased was considerably younger. Similarly, from the Dec. 2020 pictures, most were of the deceased at a younger age but only two looked anywhere near early thirties. Perhaps the pictures will help God to assemble the body, especially the face, of those individuals to closely match what they would have looked like at thirty-three years of age, as everyone in Heaven is presumably going to be that age.[3] Egyptians added a number of personal items to the deceased tomb to be sure the spirits identified the individual correctly for the afterlife and thus a picture of any age could help God in identifying the deceased, especially after decomposition or cremation. A challenge for God would be if the deceased was horribly burned in a fire, was homeless, had no family, no birth certificate, no drivers license, and no photos were available. To help identify decomposed remains, faces can be constructed to "fit" the skull. God will have to do many of these reconstructions.

What about embryos, fetuses, infants, children, and teens? What determines what a person is going to look like or what their personality will be like at thirty-three years of age? Perhaps genetics is the biggest factor, but environment (experiences, diet) has a role as well. And how will relatives and friends deal with an "instant" case of aging? The worst thing is that a child who dies at age five would instantly find herself/himself in Heaven at age thirty-three with her/his thirty-three-year-old grandparents, but with no experiences such as school, sports, movies, TV shows, college education, work, marriage, parenting, and on and on.

The cause of death is rarely given in these obituaries. The major causes of deaths are provided in Chapter 10. In the state of Michigan, the leading twenty-five causes of death are listed with the leading seven being heart disease, cancer, chronic respiratory disease, suicide, drug overdose deaths (mostly opioid-related) and motor vehicle (traffic) accidents.[9] In 2018 opioid deaths surpassed traffic deaths in frequency. Opioid deaths also are generally of younger people and the numbers above of death listings do not include very many younger individuals; perhaps families choose not to list opioid deaths of family members. Also, some of those whose ages were not given could be opioid deaths. More and more deaths are being attributed to drug overdose, liver disease, and suicide, increases great enough to be

lowering the life span of Americans.[7,8] Additional deaths result from falls
and poison.[10] In Dec. 2020, deaths caused by COVID-19 followed only
heart disease and cancer as a leading cause of death in the USA.[11] Will
God sort out all of these deaths, in all cities, in the entire USA, and in the
entire world?

The DNA of children can be sequenced to determine genetic variants
and the likelihood (tendency) to acquire alcoholism, diabetes, cancer, and
other diseases.[12] Presumably the DNA of the aborted fetus or embryo could
be similarly examined by God. But when only dust remains, or ashes,
DNA is no longer intact. During cremation all organic material in the
body, all organs, tissues, and cells, and the carbohydrates, lipids, proteins,
and nucleic acids (DNA and RNA), will burn and go up in smoke. The
puzzle then is how God can keep track of the characteristics of a person
from just dust or ashes without DNA and the intact brain with its billions
and trillions of neurons and synapses. Investigators in one mid-Western
state are using new 3D image technology to help identify a body found in
1985 in a shallow grave. The facial image obtained from the skull indicates
how the woman appeared at the time of death and perhaps will lead to her
identity.[13] How will God reestablish facial features of the deceased when
they arrive in Heaven? Does God remember the faces of all people when
they were thirty-three? How will he establish the facial features of infants
and fetuses when they are thirty-three? If a death occurs as an infant, how
will this person in Heaven, at thirty-three, recognize family?

NBC news (Aug. 14, 2018) dealt with the question of whether we are
all "tracked" daily via Google's computers. Google can apparently follow
an individual's I-phone or Android signal and follow a person into a cab,
into Starbuck's for coffee, to their work site, and to the grocery. But the
tracking is done via an electronic signal. Google wants information to assess
where the person might shop and for what items. Even members of the US
house and senate were erroneously matched to mug shots of criminals.[14]
How would God follow and recognize individuals in different countries
who use different languages, and keep track of each one of seven billion
people? Computers are being programmed to recognize people by facial
characteristics but are having difficulty with distinguishing people's faces
of different nationalities. RealNetworks technology has 1600 data points
for each face it sees. It took eight million faces and more than eight billion

data points to obtain useable technology that can now identify a face with almost 100% accuracy. Now multiply eight billion times the trillions of people who have died. That is a lot of data for God to keep track of. One application of facial recognition technology is to make it safe to enter and leave schools. Any unfamiliar face would block entry and set off an alarm.[15] God has apparently "tracked" people for centuries, far before computers were invented. We can only hope God can be more than 100% accurate about recognizing people. We must hope also that when a person gets to Heaven, he/she will recognize grandparents, parents, siblings, children, relatives, and friends and be recognized by them.

Within seconds after death the body and brain begin to deteriorate and therefore God has to do the diagnosing quickly. Even worse cases are if the person is killed because of brain damage in an accident, war, or due to homicide or suicide, with immediate neurological damage occurring. Perhaps most important would be analysis of the person's brain, the health of that brain, and knowledge of the person's total neurological information, yes, every memory and experience, including prayers, praises to God, and religious experiences or not. God will have to know every time the person said a swear word, told a lie, and had an evil thought. Consider that a computer hacker took fifty gigabytes of NYC taxi data and mapped the movements of a taxi for a single day. Presumably God is doing the same mapping, but he has to keep track of all 13,237 taxis of NYC and taxis throughout the world.[16]

In Chapter 10, the number of deaths each year and each day worldwide are discussed as well as the ways people die and the most frequent causes of death. There are 161,600 deaths worldwide each day or a little over 100 deaths each minute.[17] Sometimes that number of deaths per day can take a big jump, due to circumstances, like wars, volcanic eruptions, ship-wrecks, and fires. An example is the 1944 revolt in Warsaw, Poland, against German Nazi occupation, which resulted in the deaths of 18,000 fighters and 180,000 Polish citizens, 3,143 each day of the sixty-three-day revolt. Many of the bodies have not yet been found. More deaths likely resulted from the injured and those expelled by the Nazis.[18] Another example is the fire of 1918 in Esko, MN and surrounding area, when 453 lives were lost in one day (Finnish Amer. Reporter, Aug. 2018). A third case is volcanic eruptions. When Mt. Vesuvius erupted in 79 AD over 13% of the population of Pompeii died, most likely from the heat and then also from ash which buried them. In the past 200 years seventeen volcanoes have killed 200,000 people. The worst was Tambora, in Indonesia, which erupted in 1815, and killed 92,000 people. In each of these cases, God would have been busy diagnosing and deciding how to deal with each death and to collect information on each individual for eventual acceptance into Heaven. There would be very little body tissue and therefore limited information due to decomposition through the decades. Note also that 173 children were killed on the same day, in less than hour, in the Newtown shootings[19] providing a huge challenge to God. On Oct. 1, 2018, an earthquake off the coast of Indonesia and the accompanying tsunami killed over 1,200 people. When the Empress of Ireland went down in 1914 after colliding with another ship over 1,000 lives were lost. These multiple deaths that occur suddenly and unpredictably are a far cry from the view that God will take the deceased into his arms, call him/her home, and lead the individual to a place already prepared (John 14:2-3).

In Spring of 2020, mainly from March through April, the COVID-19 pandemic was killing thousands of people worldwide. More COVID-19 deaths were associated with certain pre-existing health problems including diabetes, obesity, asthma, and hypertension; these factors combined with the virus lead to more deaths.[20] God will have to diagnose not only the immediate cause of death, like the virus, but also these other health conditions so that all the deceased individuals will be in perfect health in Heaven. (see Revelation 21:4).

According to I Corinthians 15:51-58, in Heaven we will receive a new and glorified body. But not so fast! Our body and especially our brain are what make each of us who we are. In Chapter 9 the number of deaths worldwide through the ages is discussed, realizing that many bodies have never been found, are completed decomposed, or cremated. Often there is no body to be restored to perfect health. If the deceased are given a new body, whose body will it be? Will each body be unique? What about embryos and fetuses and children who have died? Will they receive adult bodies and what information will their brains contain? Will they recognize their parents? The children should all go to Heaven but not all parents will. What then? Will they be recognized by other Heavenly residents? Will they still visit separately with divorced parents? Does it matter to God what Heaven residents look like as long as they praise him twenty-four hours a day?

The mature human brain has 86 billion neurons which make over 100 trillion synaptic connections; each brain will have different connections depending on age, experiences, and heredity. Francis Collins of the Natl. Inst. of Health points out that an adult human brain has a million, million, million megabytes of information or 100 terabytes. One terabyte is 1000 gigabytes or 1 million megabytes. A human brain has enough information to fill millions of 4 drawer filing cabinets with text.[21] Challenges for God will be to deal with the embryo before the brain has begun to develop, to deal with a fetus brain, which would have very limited experiences/memories, or a child's brain that is just beginning to acquire memories. Also, what about brains of fetuses, children or adults who are mentally disabled? Or people who have had concussions, now with chronic traumatic encephalopathy, dementia, or Alzheimer's (see Chapters 23 and 27). Stroke victims have various portions of the brain damaged. The neurons and their connections begin to deteriorate soon after death. How will God restore the brains of the billions of deceased with the exact neuronal and synaptic patterns in Heaven that were present on earth? Each day the world generates 2.5 quintillion bytes of information. Every minute 500 million tweets, seventy million photos on Instagram, four billion videos on Facebook (Meta) and 300 hours of new content on U-tube are generated.[22] But Hebrews 4:12 says, "The Word of God is discerning of our hearts intents and thoughts" and Proverbs 15:3 says, "The eyes of the Lord are everywhere, beholding evil and good." We cannot hide, his eyes see everything. He is everywhere.

Transferring information from brain to brain, telepathy, has not been accomplished. One difficulty is that the electrical impulses/signals are very weak and can be detected only by electronic enhancement. Perhaps God has this enhancement ability so that he can detect and record our thoughts, even in 1000s of different languages.[23] Mark Zuckerberg, President of Meta, optimistically said, "One day I believe we'll be able to send full rich thoughts to each other using technology."[24]

God will be challenged by speech and speech problems. Expectations would be that everyone in Heaven can speak clearly and communicate with God, Jesus, the Holy Ghost, angels, family members, spouses and friends and there will be much singing and rejoicing.[3] But millions of both children and adults can have many, many kinds of speech problems most of which are due to unknown causes. Known speech problems are due to cleft palate, tooth problems, hearing loss, mouth and tongue movement difficulties, brain injuries or disorders, tumors in the mouth, stroke, viruses, diseases, autism, or cerebral palsy.[25] A certain number of these people with speech problems will die each day and God will have the challenge of diagnosing the degree of speech difficulties and will hopefully insure that the individual's speech in Heaven is healthy and understandable. What language will Heaven residents be given? What about sign language? To Rev. 21:4 could be added, "no speech difficulties." The same issues can be considered for problems with vision, hearing, taste, and smell. Various diseases, birth defects, and disabilities are considered in Chapters 10, 18 and 19. Many ailments are associated with the ear, nose, and throat. A brochure obtained from an otolaryngologist's office lists thirty-six separate medical conditions including hearing disorders, pharyngitis, sleep apnea, voice disorders, and tinnitus. People may not die from any one of these conditions but in Heaven God will not want to see any of these conditions. Thus, pre-death or immediate post-death, diagnosis must include these thirty-six medical conditions.[26]

Most hospitals/health centers have departments of Physical, Occupational, and Speech-language Therapies. In a brochure of one such local hospital are listed nineteen different therapies, including for vertigo, dizziness, imbalance, pelvic floor incontinence, pelvic pain, stroke, accident, and breast cancer. Many people regularly visit their local health center for rehabilitation specific to their health condition. God would have to know what difficulties the deceased was having that required therapy, figure out the cause, and "cure" the ailment, whether due to aging, trauma, disease, or something else. Alternatively, the patient may be given therapy in Heaven. Perhaps the soul carries a blueprint, so to speak, of the body which it left behind, and that blueprint tells God what the medical history of the deceased is. Or, by telepathy, God withdraws/gathers up all the information in a person's brain at the time of death and stores it until the Rapture.

Since the end of the Korean war, the USA and North Korea have at times returned/exchanged bodies of dead soldiers. In 2018 North Korea provided fifty-five boxes presumably containing the remains of some of our soldiers killed and buried over sixty years ago. Needless to say, most of the tissues have deteriorated leaving only the skeletal components, all be it incomplete skeletons, perhaps even missing the skull. Worse, each box may contain remains of more than one soldier, and some may be Allied soldiers as well as USA soldiers. Since dog tags are seldom included, the Defense POW/MIA Accounting Agency will have a difficult task and to aid in identifications they will use circumstantial evidence, dental records, and chest x-rays (radiographs). If there are no dental records or chest x-rays of the soldier available from sixty-five years ago then making an identification may not be possible.

A similar problem is seen along our southern border. In 2017 there were 415 immigrant deaths along the USA-Mexico border. Often only incomplete skeletons are brought in by border patrol and even determining the sex and age of each is difficult. The big challenge is to identify those deceased and notify loved ones in Mexico or wherever but money for up-to-date forensic equipment and DNA analysis is in short supply.[27] Has God already found a place "by his side" for these deceased people?

Families in the USA are happy to obtain closure and wish to have a full military funeral with full deserving honors. Even if a partial skeleton leads to conclusive identification, the family may be satisfied and accept closure. The Accounting Agency wants each ID to be based on science. The ultimate would be DNA sequence analysis but obtaining enough tissue to provide DNA will be difficult. The DNA of either mitochondria or of the nuclear chromosomes could provide enough sequence to show relationships to a family and thus lead to identification.

From the Korean war alone, there are 7,800 soldiers not accounted for and for all previous wars, that number is 83,000. Some of those will never be recovered, for example deep water losses in aircraft or ships. Further complicating the situation in Korea is that some bodies might still be buried, in temporary cemeteries, the military being unable to recover them because the Chinese entered the war. Some bodies were buried in the fox holes where they were killed, perhaps several in the same foxhole, and have been mixed together during recovery.[28]

What kind of a God can gather and analyze all the above information? Patricia Beall Gruits[29] describes God as follows: God is eternal and everlasting; he has lived in our past and will live in our future (Isaiah 46:9, 10). God has not changed and will not change (Mal. 3:6). God is omnipotent, almighty, all powerful and he can do everything (Gen. 17:1; Psalm 62:11; Matt. 19:26). God is omniscient, all knowing (1 John 3:20; Psalm 139:4). God is omnipresent, he is everywhere (Jer. 23:24). God is infinite, knows no bounds or limitations in power or space (Rom. 11:33). But God is a spirit and has never been seen; he is without flesh or blood, yet God created humans in his image, with brains and bodies and blood. No problem for God?

The total information on earth, from the stone age and epic poems, is 10^{56} or a trillion, trillion, trillion, trillion gigabytes. Human texts, pictures, and videos equal 10^{21} bytes or 2 trillion gigabytes. New information produced by humans equals 2 trillion gigabytes each year.[30] In 2012 the Higgs boson (or God particle) was confirmed. That name, God particle, was appropriate because presumably God created all matter from bosons. But in July 2018, it was shown that the Higgs boson decays into bottom quarks, even more fundamental particles. These findings came from studies with the Large Hadron Collider (LHC), located under the Alps, and operated by the European Organization for Nuclear Research, also known as CERN (French acronym). CERN utilizes 20% of the world's computing resources; an enormous amount of data is analyzed. To date, the LHC has produced one exabyte of data and by 2026 will have produced thirty exabytes.[31] One exabyte is one billion gigabytes. That is two to the sixtieth power. Yes, theists will say God can digest and understand all these data, no problem.

The question is: How does God store all the information he has to gather and how does he analyze all of it, especially given that he is a spirit? The typical answer from theists to that question is: "I don't know how he does it but I know he does it!"

NOTES

1   Mari Yamaguchi, "Japan Capsule Carrying Asteroid Samples Lands," *Detroit Free Press*, December 6, 2020, 13A.
2   *Detroit Free Press*, January 3, 2020, 13A.

3   Randy Alcorn, *Heaven: A Comprehensive Guide to Everything the Bible Says About Our Eternal Home* (Illinois: Tyndale Momentum, 2004.)

4   John Troyer and Rachel Feltman, "Tales from the Field: 'a trip to the other side'," *Popular Science*, September/October, 2017, 76.

5   Kindermann Eye Associates, https://www.kindermanneye.com; Barnet Dulaney Perkins Eye Center, https://www.goodeyes.com. Websites accessed in June 2020.

6   Maya Dusenbery, "Why Women-and Men-Need Better Birth Control," *Scientific American*, May 2019, 40-47.

7   Wikipedia website, "List of states and territories by life expectancy," last edited March 23, 2023, https://en.wikipedia.org/wiki/List_of_U.S._states_and_territories_by_life_expectancy.

8   "Which Michigan counties have the longest, shortest life expectancy?," *Michigan Live*, published March 27, 2018, https://www.mlive.com/news/erry-2018/03/07f0cf7208/what_michigan_counties_have_th.html

9   *Detroit Free Press*, January 15, 2019, 16A.

10 "Accidents or Unintentional Injuries," CDC website, last reviewed January 17, 2023, https://www.cdc.gov/nchs/fastats/accidental-injury.htm

11 *NBC Evening News*, December 6, 2020.

12 *NBC News*, January 3, 2019.

13 *Detroit Free Press*, September 5, 2014.

14 *Northern Express*, August 13, 2013.

15 Safety vs Privacy, *Detroit Free Press*, October 23, 2008, 1C.

16 Wikipedia website, "Taxi," accessed in December 2018, https://en.wikipedia.org/wiki/Taxi.

17 Our World in Data website, "Number of deaths by cause, World, 2019," accessed January 2020, https://ourworldindata.org/grapher/annual-number-of-deaths-by-cause.

18 *Cheboygan Tribune*, August 2, 2018.

19 *NBC News*, December 12, 2013.

20 *Detroit Free Press*, April 10, 2020, 5A.

21 *Scientific American*, February 5, 2016.

22 Answers Issue, "What's this all about?," *Time*, July 6-13, 2015, 42.

23 *Smithsonian Magazine*, May 2016, 45-50.

24 The View, "Verbatim," *Time*, July 20, 2015, 26.

25 Center for Parent Information & Resources website, accessed January 2019, www.parentcenterhub.org; Cincinnati Children's website, accessed January 2019, www.cincinnatichildrens.org.

26 Pamphlet referenced from Northwoods Ear, Nose & Throat, PC, Petoskey, MI.

27 *Indy Star*, December 21, 2018, B1

28 *Detroit Free Press*, June 21, 2016; Tom V. Brook, *USA Today*; Paula Hancocks, Yoonjung Seo and Joshua Berlinger, "War Dead Remains Returned," *CNN*, August 1, 2018.

29 Patricia B. Gruits, *"Understanding God and His Covenants,"* (Michigan: Peterpat Publishing, 1985.)

30 *Brown Alumni Magazine*, January/February 2019, 17.

31 Wikipedia website, "Large Hadron Collider," last edited March 6, 2023, https://en.wikipedia.org/wiki/large_hadron_collider.

12

ILLNESSES, DISEASES, DISORDERS

THE CONCEPTS OF Heaven, Hell, Jesus and God were developed far before concepts in medicine and science. Christ was born in the year 0000, Muhammad was born in the year 0570, and the Black Death raged through Europe in 1348. Some chapters of the Bible were written before Christ was born and some were written during the first few centuries after Christ's birth. Through history and even today, many people put more faith in the Bible and prayer than in medical science. Microscopy was not invented until the 1650s and bacteria were not recognized to be disease causing agents until the 1850s. Richardson and Morris[1] begin their book on the history of medicine with a discussion of medical beliefs in Mesopotamia and make the point early on that the leaders of society practiced superstition rather than religion and believed that illnesses were caused by upsetting the deity by a wrongdoing. Healthy people avoided contact with the sick to avoid also incurring the wrath of the deity. Treatment of the sick involved incantations, spells and the like. The diseases and injuries of the time, as far back as 2700 BCE, were many of what we see today and included arthritis, tuberculosis, dental caries, hernias, fractures, poliomyelitis, and parasitic diseases but causes were not understood. Over many centuries treatment of the sick and injured was divided between seers who used divination, priests who performed incantations and exorcisms, and physicians, who used drugs, surgery, and bandages.[1] Information about injuries, diseases, and cures had to be spread by mouth as writing was not yet available. God must have known about these early medical problems and ailments in societies, but he provided no help to advance medicine. People who suffered from or died from one or more of these medical ailments/illnesses, such as tuberculosis, as noted from examination of mummies, were believed to go to an afterlife but that was not the Heaven referred to in the Bible. So, what was the fate of these early deceased people? Is God caring for their souls? Are their souls carrying their medical histories? Can God resurrect their decomposed bodies?

Consider medical practices by the early Egyptians living during the time period of Mesopotamia, 2700 BCE. They also believed that disease and bodily suffering were the result of transgression of a sacred law; practical medicine was not encouraged by the priesthood. The deceased body was not allowed to be desecrated and thus mummification was practiced. The idea was to preserve the body until the time of resurrection and reuniting with the spirit. Even though anatomy was largely understood at the gross level, that knowledge was not applied to medicine.[1] Women practiced medicine minimally or not at all, but some gynecological disorders were recognized and treated.

The Egyptians developed papyrus and medical texts were written and made available. Nine main medical papyri have survived to modern times, all dating to around 1550 BCE and are believed to be interpretations of older writings and are rather difficult to understand. They were copied by scribes without any sense of meaning or continuity.[1] Examination of mummies shows that Egyptians suffered from the same injuries and illnesses as Mesopotamians. Not only was the pharaoh divine but each part of his body was divine and granted its own physician. Consider two titles of physicians: Guardian of the King's right eye; Shepherd of the King's anus.

The Babylonians (1500 BCE) still believed that disease and illnesses were punishment due to wrongdoing and took action to placate the deities instead of seeking a physician. Payment for medical services to the doctor was based on status in the community; curing a freeman was worth ten shekels; son of a plebian, five shekels; a slave, two shekels (paid by the owner). If a doctor treated a person and the person died, the doctor's hands were sometimes cut off.[1]

Egyptian medicine spread to many countries along trade routes, but mainland Greece was mostly independent about medical practices (1500 BCE). Their physicians and religious-based healers got along but competed. Mineral baths were combined with priest's visits, often at night while the patient was asleep. Bloodletting was still practiced.[1]

Efforts of one person, Hippocrates (430-425 BCE), resulted in advances in medicine by his own medical practice but also by encouraging medical practice through his writings without inclusion of religious or supernatural influences, i.e. via his doctrine of the four humours - red blood (blood humour), serum (yellow bile), red blood cells enmeshed in fibrin (black bile), white blood cells and platelets (phlegm), and the Hippocratic oath which is a statement of medical ethics still followed by students of medicine today. The oath in short states: "perform to the best of your ability, maintain the patient's privacy, encourage the next generation of physicians."[1]

Aristotle and Alexander (370-321 BCE) further contributed to understanding human anatomy and medicine. The roles of the brain and the heart were not clearly discerned, and the soul was considered a real entity. The book of Daniel prophesied Alexander's coming to Jerusalem (Daniel 11:2-5) but Daniel was written 200 years after Alexander's time. Whoops! Not exactly prophesy. The physicians Herophilus and Erasistratus (325-250 BCE) made further advances toward understanding anatomy and physiology. Understanding the flow of blood through arteries, capillaries, and veins was still not completely clear but understood well enough for bloodletting from either veins or arteries. Erasistratus, in the third century BCE believed in bloodletting to treat and cure many diseases. Bloodletting, begun in Egypt and also in Greece, was practiced from antiquity to the early 20th century. The idea was that illness was caused by too much of the blood humour. Thus, some blood had to be removed to gain a balance of the humours. Later it was thought that blood carried diseases and by bleeding a patient the disease could be rid from the body. Christian writings even advised which Saint's Days were best for bloodletting. A French sergeant who was injured by a sword underwent bloodletting off and on for 2.5 months, losing a total of thirteen pints, some by seventy-two leeches, and recovered amazingly enough. But not everyone recovered from the procedure. President George Washington, sixty-seven years old, underwent bloodletting because of a sore throat, lost 40% of his blood, and did not recover. Some suggest that the loss of that much blood may not have been the cause of death but certainly put him at ease, like an opioid would (//en.wikipedia.org/wiki/bloodletting). Galen, born in 129 CE, was one of the significant medical people of the time. He further developed the theory of the four humours and encouraged wound washing methods to prevent infections.[1]

Interestingly the BCE belief that only God can heal was carried smoothly into the CE, yes, the same belief. In both cases observations of healing reenforced the "healing by God" beliefs. Christianity was established in the Roman Empire by 300 CE and had an adverse effect on medicine in espousing the belief that illness was associated with sin and thus God alone could heal a person. A child recently died in the USA because the parents depended on God to heal and did not take the child to a doctor. Sad! God obviously did not heal the child. If the child had lived and been healed, God would have no doubt been given the credit. Presumably God heals these children in Heaven but unfortunately, they have been denied their youth here on earth. Medicine thus stagnated for many centuries, helped by the view that Christ's second coming was imminent, and everyone would be in Heaven in perfect health. Here we are more than 2,000 years later and preachers are still telling us the return of Christ is imminent! Furthermore, since only God could heal and cure illness, why even practice medicine?

With the development of Islam (00-1037) good medical practice rebounded. Illness was somewhat less related to religion. Many medical works, including those of Galen, were translated in Baghdad into Islam and done so by scholars and done very well. But public health and hygiene were very bad, and pollution was everywhere, especially in rivers into which waste found its way. Sadly, while Roman cities (170-180 CE) had clean water, baths and toilets for the rich, common people had to deal with open sewers, polluted rivers, and diseases such as the plague and smallpox. There were too few hospitals for the large populations in cities (Cairo, Baghdad, Damascus, for example). Poverty, hunger, and malnutrition were common as were diseases (dysentery, leprosy, malaria, tuberculosis, and typhus). In the Middle Ages, 12th to 15th centuries CE, medicine did not progress much. Scholars wrote but not on relevant medical questions and the writings were question oriented. For example, "Was a big head better than a small head?" "Was the heart the organ of touch?" Illness was still associated with sin, a result of Christianity's influence. Bloodletting was still practiced.[1]

During the time of the Black Death (Bubonic Plague), Giovanni Boccaccio (1313-1375) wrote his book, *The Decameron*, what some believe to be the first novel, and which apparently influenced Chaucer, Spenser, and Shakespeare. Boccaccio vividly described the black death.[2] This terrible disease killed one-third of the population of Europe, about thirty million people. Again, the plague was believed to be a punishment for sin or a response to astrological events. We now know it is caused by a bacterium, *Yersinia pestis*, which is spread by fleas.[1] There was so much death that a "death dance" was invented which was danced over the buried remains of those that had not repented. Bodies collected at night were buried in mass graves the next morning. Presumably those that had not repented went to hell whereas those that had repented went to Heaven. God was able to make those decisions, but how? There were thirty million deaths in a matter of a few years of people of all ages and different nationalities?

God was so prevalent in the lives of people that it is not surprising none dared to raise the question of whether there is a God, a Heaven, and a hell, and ignorance of science did not help. Consider that all metals were thought to be related and that gold was the apex. Thus, alchemists tried mixing mercury and sulfur hoping for gold. Also, the word alchemy was applied to human nature and was concerned with the transmutation of the lower nature of man to the higher or divine nature, meaning unity with God. The aging process was thought to be reversible, thus Ponce de Leon's search for the Fountain of Youth. Astrology did not help to advance medicine and science. Do some people still believe in astrology? Sadly, yes. Women were believed to have defective souls and were considered intellectually, physically, and morally inferior to men.[1] Today we have women leading countries and in the USA several highly qualified women vied for the democratic presidential nomination and a woman is Vice President.[3]

Printing was invented by Gutenberg in the sixteenth century and allowed the dissemination of knowledge throughout the developing world.[4] Information like Leonardo da Vinci's and Calcar's anatomical drawings (1500s) were made available to all and helped the advance of medicine.[1]

Medicine and science continued to show advances with discoveries by William Harvey, Robert Boyle, Antonie van Leeuwenhoek, and so many others between the 1500s and 1600s. Understanding blood circulation, heart function, and respiration were some of the advances.[1] Microscopic anatomy (cells and microbes) and the understanding of pathology (causes of disease and death) followed in the second half of the seventeenth century. Bacteriology, the start of modern medicine, began to influence medicine in the mid nineteenth century. Note that modern science and medicine have only been around for a little more than two centuries.[1] Think of the ignorance in the world for almost twenty centuries and the erroneous influence of religion! Humanity has suffered greatly from religion! Fortunately, science and common-sense rules today and much of the world has excellent training available for medical doctors, nurses, and technicians, high powered up-to-date medical research, the National Institutes of Health (NIH) and Center for Disease Control (CDC) in the USA and equivalents in many other countries, and top-notch hospitals.

Internet sources give the number of documented different human diseases in the world to be in the thousands.[5] As many as three-fourths of these diseases have no cure. Diseases are caused by viruses, bacteria, fungi, gene mutations, and vitamin and mineral deficiencies. Many are under-diagnosed including Lyme disease, lupus, fibromyalgia, hypothyroidism, hemochromatosis, chlamydia, hepatitis C, irritable bowel syndrome, sleep apnea, ovarian cancer, and heart disease.[1,6] The latter two illnesses could be a cause of death if not diagnosed and not treated. The former nine illnesses a person can live with but must deal with the pain and suffering. Of course, a person could have more than one of the above diseases. Could God diagnose these illnesses and cure/correct them so as to avoid suffering and pain in Heaven? Lyme disease is caused by a bacterium, *Borrelia burgdorferi*, that is carried by a tick. The tick bite transmits the bacterium to the person who then shows the symptoms of Lyme disease which are overall aches, pain, and fever. Lupus is an autoimmune disease in which case the person's own immune system attacks the person's own tissues. Then there is idiopathic multicentric Castleman disease, first described 1954, with about 7,000 new cases each year in the USA. Castleman's causes the immune signaling molecules called cytokines to go crazy and to become too abundant; the patient's immune cells begin attacking his/her healthy tissues. A patient, who was a doctor, remembered that after kidney transplants an immunosuppressant drug was used to prevent the kidney recipient's immune system from rejecting the transplant. He tried the drug, called sirolimus, and it worked. He has been free of symptoms for six years.

His organs were no longer being attacked and his skin was free of blotches. Most important was that he could be a husband and father and practice medicine.[7] Fibromyalgia results in overall aches and stiffness of joints and muscles. Hemochromatosis is a hereditary condition wherein the person's iron quantity in the blood and body is too high, causing liver failure among other tissue sufferings. Chlamydia is a sexually transmitted bacterial disease which causes problems in the reproductive tracts of both women and men.[1]

God not only has to know the symptoms and thus recognize the disease, but he has to know how to treat the condition and/or cure it. But most symptoms appear only in a live body! With even a recently deceased body diagnosing illness would be a challenge.

There are many infectious diseases and health conditions caused by agents.[1] Acquired immunodeficiency (AIDS; HIV) syndrome is caused by the HIV virus. Measles, the common cold, chicken pox, smallpox, hepatitis A, B, and C, the seasonal flu and COVID-19 are virus-caused. The Center for Disease Control reports that each year up to 56,000 people in the USA die from the seasonal flu; over 150 every day. From Feb. 2020 to April 2021, the COVID19 virus killed over 560,000 Americans and many more worldwide.[8] COVID-19 is a pandemic, causing sickness and death worldwide. One country being hit very hard is Peru, a nation with thirty-two million people. The daily death number in Peru was 4,500 during the week leading to June 2, 2020. The quarantine in Peru is being undermined by the socio-economic conditions. Nearly 45% of homes lack electricity forcing people to buy food daily from crowded markets, which are centers of infection.[9] How is God dealing with these virus-caused deaths, in Peru, in the USA, and worldwide, especially in India where COVID is presently surging?[10] Are all the souls in his safe-keeping? Is God keeping Heaven free of the virus?

People with the flu often die from flu-associated illnesses, like pneumonia, heart failure and chronic obstructive pulmonary disease (COPD), a disease of the lungs. Lung disease is the third leading cause of death worldwide.[11] Conditions which contribute to COPD include: smoking, air pollution, poor housing, jobs that have dust and pollutants in the air, genetics, childhood events (pre-term birth, secondhand smoke), and vaping (using e-cigarettes). The fluid in vaping products has been linked to severe lung problems and deaths especially in our nation's youth.[12] Some cases of

COPD are caused by Alpha-1 antitrypsin (gene) deficiency, a condition in which the lung tissue fails to fight off infections. The protein can be purified from plasma donors and infused into the lungs of COPD patients to prevent further damage.[12] How will God deal with these illnesses? Were God's "cures" different before the cures of modern medicine were developed? Did God curse himself for creating disease-causing viruses and bacteria?

It is instructive to look at hepatitis, a disease that targets the liver, as a model of medical investigations into virus-caused illness. Hepatitis A and B were the first to be investigated and vaccines were then developed against these problem diseases by identifying and then targeting the specific virus that causes each. When people who were negative for hep A and B received blood transfusions, they sometimes developed liver disease which alerted the medical community that there was another virus that was blood-borne. Dating back to the '70s and '80s the work of Harvey J. Alter, Charles M. Rice and Michael Houghton, using molecular and immunological methodologies, cloned the virus and identified it as the liver damaging agent in the blood transfusions. The world health organization estimates that there are seventy million cases and 400,000 deaths from hep C each year worldwide. These three shared the 2020 Nobel Prize in medicine for their findings that will lead to controlling, if not eradicating, hep C.[13] These hep C deaths are people of different ages, nationalities, and medical histories and must be a major challenge to God.

Will there be smoking in Heaven? The view that smoking and chewing tobacco cause cancer is well-accepted. The effects of smoking marijuana or vaping are not so clear, and the news frequently deals with these issues. Marijuana has been legalized in many states as a recreational drug and/or as a treatment for various medical conditions. Doctors and hospitals have "geared up" to be ready for medical emergencies due to marijuana becoming legal in Michigan and other states. Emergency rooms have seen patients with agitation, psychosis, anxiety, fast heart rate, high blood pressure, and vomiting, which are all marijuana associated symptoms.[14]

In order to provide legal permission to treat a condition, the State Medical Board of Ohio requires opinions of experts, medical evidence that the patient with the condition will benefit from marijuana, and also letters of support from doctors. Some conditions that have not received approval for medical marijuana treatment include anxiety, autism spectrum, depression, insomnia, and opioid use disorder. A recent request for use of medical marijuana comes from long-suffering fans of the Cincinnati Bengals and Cleveland Browns football teams who cite the pain of defeat over and over. At least one fan has suggested that the same misery is seen in Detroit Lions football fans and therefore medical marijuana treatment is warranted for them as well.[15] When fans of losing teams get to Heaven, God is going to be puzzled as to why they are in such a state of depression!

Bacteria cause whooping cough (pertussis), meningitis, tuberculosis and pneumonia. Malaria and African Sleeping sickness are caused by protozoa. Autoimmune diseases are caused by the immune system of a person going awry and attacking healthy tissues; examples are type 1 diabetes, rheumatoid arthritis, multiple sclerosis, and lupus.[16] There are more than 200 different types of cancer.[17] There are thousands of different kinds of diseases and 75% have no effective cure.[18] Many, many diseases and ailments have evolved in human societies since the Bible was written. Will God be able to sort them out individually and cure the person carrying the particular disease or ailment?

The six deadliest diseases in history are smallpox, the black plague, tuberculosis, malaria, Ebola, and cholera.[19] The total number of people who have died from these diseases must be in the billions. Does God have medical history information for all of these deceased people so that they can be cured when they are resurrected? Smallpox was the first disease to be treated by using a vaccine. It is caused by the Variola virus.[20] There have been forty-nine epidemics and pandemics in history, seven of cholera alone, from 1961 to the present. Cholera still persists in SE Asia.[21] The AIDS epidemic began in the USA in 1981 when 184 cases were recognized, then 650 were recognized in 1982, 2100 in 1983, and 4,500 in 1984. Many were fatal. One view of some Christians is that AIDS was sent to punish gays. What is God's view we can wonder? AIDS is spread via sex between two women, a man and a woman, or two men. A husband or wife who is not gay can acquire AIDS from the HIV infected spouse.[22] Who will get to Heaven?

Measles is a virus-caused disease that was quite prevalent prior to 1963; in each year prior to 1963 over three million people in the USA got measles, thousands of those got serious brain infections, and over 500 people died. Measles was seldom seen in the developed world after a measles vaccine (mumps, measles, rubella; MMR vaccine) was developed and licensed to immunize a child or adult.[23] The vaccination program subsequently included whooping cough (pertussis), mumps, and rubella (a form of measles). In the 2000s, largely due to wrong information suggesting immunization led to autism, many parents stopped immunizing their children. Other parents do not immunize for religious reasons. When a certain percentage of the population is not immunized, a disease can spread rapidly. A Midwest state was scolded by the Center for Disease Control for having a vaccination/immunization rate of only 60% in 2019.[24] In 2019, measles killed over 4,000 people in the Congo (Ebola has killed thousands more).[25] Is God caring for the souls of these people?

When combined with poverty, especially poor nutrition, children can die from a disease that is not normally fatal. This was happening in Madagascar in 2019 where there were 115,000 cases of measles and over 1,200 deaths. Only 60% of Madagascar's people have ever been vaccinated; 50% of the children are malnourished.[26] The 1,200 deaths and additional children who die from the combination of measles and malnourishment will be a challenge to God in Heaven. He will have to diagnose how both measles and malnourishment caused death and then he has to bring those children back to good health. Will he then age them to thirty-three years of age? What challenges!

A controversial issue is that health insurance costs more or does not cover people with health "pre-conditions." One such pre-condition is diabetes, which is a disease of mainly two types, 1 and 2. Type 1 diabetes can develop in childhood or any time after that and is a situation wherein the pancreatic islet cells stop producing insulin. Insulin regulates blood sugar and is necessary for life. Type 1 diabetics take insulin daily, usually as a self-administered injection. Insulin is very costly. Healthcare costs for diabetics are higher than for non-diabetics and insurance does not adequately cover these costs. There are 34.2 million Americans with type 1 diabetes, one of every ten. One in three have pre-diabetes.[27] Why does God allow anyone, especially children, to have these kinds of health conditions? Worldwide 4.8 million deaths each year are caused by diabetes, over 13,000 every day. Many millions have already died from diabetes through the ages. Diabetes can lead to heart disease, stroke, kidney failure, limb amputations, and blindness. Apparently, half the deaths from diabetes are undiagnosed to be diabetes. Thus, the challenge for God. When a diabetic dies, not necessarily from that illness, God must diagnose diabetes, which kind of diabetes, and correct the body condition leading to that form. In the case of Type 1, the pancreas Islet cells have to be re-engineered by God, a new gene for insulin added, and control elements inserted into the genome to again regulate insulin production. God has to also diagnose the health complications associated with diabetes. After all, there will be an abundance of carbohydrate foods in Heaven.

Possibly on the horizon is a cure for Type 1 diabetes. An investigator has bioengineered stem cells with the insulin gene. These stem cells are then put into a small device that is implanted under the skin of the diabetic patient. The device allows sugar (glucose) to pass in to trigger insulin production and the insulin can pass out of the device to regulate blood sugar in the body. Cells of the immune system cannot pass into the device and thus cannot reject the insulin producing stem cells.[28] Will God do this bioengineering by magic? Good luck with that wishful thinking!

The diabetes medical community was elated in 2018 because the Food and Drug Administration approved a new insulin delivery system for Type 1 diabetics. The device is called MiniMed™ 670G System and delivers insulin regulated by monitoring the patient's blood glucose levels. The patient no longer has to inject herself/himself with insulin or use an insulin pump and thus the high and low swings in blood sugar levels are avoided. Low blood sugar levels increase the odds of dementia. Would such a device be available in Heaven?[29] This single publication includes articles on stroke and heart disease, food as a prescription, cancer cells in lymph nodes, laser cataract surgery, eye care, high-risk pregnancies, robot assisted surgery, hip replacement surgery with the direct anterior approach, sleep apnea, and dentistry. Can it be possible that none of these medical conditions will be present in Heaven or that they will be present and not only treatable but curable?

Type 2 diabetes is an illness wherein insulin is produced but the body cells are resistant to the insulin, so glucose uptake is not correctly regulated. Genetics and lifestyle are contributing factors. Symptoms include frequent urination, thirst, fatigue, weight loss, slow healing of cuts/wounds, and sometimes blurred vision. More than thirty-four million Americans are diabetic, 95% with Type 2, which causes 1.6 million deaths each year. Another

eighty-eight million are pre-diabetic.[30] With Type 2 patients dietary cut-
back of sugar/carbohydrates is critical and added complex carbohydrates,
fiber, and fruits and vegetables are called for along with regular exercise. A
person's genetics and epigenetics as well as diet (obesity) can be risk factors.
In 2019 over 40% of Americans were obese and that figure is predicted
to increase to 50% in the next decade. Nearly five million US teens and
children are obese, and the Academy of Pediatrics recommends weight loss
surgery for these youngsters. As with obese adults, many of these obese
youngsters already have diabetes, sleep apnea, high blood pressure, and liver
disease, all of which are associated with obesity.[31] Will people carry Type 2
diabetes with them into Heaven? Will God cure Type 2 and/or ensure diets
are regulated appropriately?

Yes, some people carry diseases like Type 2 diabetes much of their life.
The aged carry this and many more ailments/diseases, including cancer,
heart disease, dementia, and arthritis, sometimes until they die. Now re-
searchers believe that these and other health issues have a common trigger,
which is low-grade inflammation. Good supporting evidence came from a
clinical trial involving 10,000 patients with a mean age of sixty-one, from
thirty-nine countries, that were given an anti-inflammation drug. The drug
lowered the incidence of heart disease, lung cancer, gout, and arthritis. This
low-grade inflammation can lead to chronic inflammation and thus can
further adversely affect the gut lining, the arteries, the liver, brain, joints
and muscles and trigger diseases such as diabetes, cancer, dementia, heart
disease, arthritis, and depression. To protect oneself from chronic inflam-
mation lifestyle choices are important: avoid stress, tobacco, excess alcohol,
weight gain, inactivity, poor sleep, and poor diet.[32] Will God diagnose the
level of low grade and/or chronic inflammation in the deceased? How will
the environment of Heaven avoid inflammation?

The earliest known diseases were tuberculosis, cholera, typhoid, and
leprosy.[1] Cholera was described by the physician Hippocrates in 400 BC.
It is caused by a bacterium and is spread via polluted water. Typhoid was
recorded as an early disease among humans in 420 BC by the historian
Thucydides (Thuycydides). Typhoid is also caused by a bacterium. Evidence
of tuberculosis (TB) has been noted in mummies being examined by ar-
cheologists, mummies from hundreds of years BCE. TB is caused by the
bacterium, *Mycobacterium tuberculosis*, and is still very much with us in

the world today, causing 3,500 deaths every day, 1.3 million every year worldwide. People have been dying due to TB for thousands of years. Many others die of other causes but have TB and carry the *M. tuberculosis* bacterium with them. God has been rather lax in dealing with TB; in fact, he has done nothing. An estimated two billion people worldwide carry a form called "latent TB" which has no symptoms, but which can develop into full-blown TB. Microbiologists are hard at work to develop antibiotics which control both forms of the bacterium.[33]

The Bible often mentions leprosy and states that Jesus twice healed people with leprosy. In Matthew 8:2-4, when Jesus had come down from the mountain, a leper approached him and asked to be made clean. Cleansing was the word for a cure for leprosy. Jesus touched the leper and made him clean. In Luke 17:11-19, Jesus was on his way to Jerusalem and when he passed through a village, he heard a group of ten lepers over on the side of the road asking for his mercy. Jesus told them to go to a priest and when they started out they were cleansed. Jesus apparently cured them of leprosy from a distance. Just by his thought process? Did he send microwaves? One of the cured, when he saw that he was healed, came back to Jesus, fell down on his face at Jesus's feet, glorified God in a loud voice, and gave thanks. Jesus wondered about why the other nine did not come back. Leprosy is caused by the bacterium, *Mycobacterium leprae*, as shown by a Norwegian, G.H. Armauer Hansen, in 1873, and thus leprosy is also called Hansen's Disease. Leprosy was the first disease shown to be caused by a bacterium. Studies of the leprosy DNA sequence show that there are four strains in the world and that the *M. leprae* bacteria and the disease originated in E. Africa. The estimation is that 180,000 people worldwide are infected with leprosy. Leprosy was treated by promin in the 1800s. Beginning in the 1960s, like most bacterial diseases, leprosy treatment was with antibiotics, usually Dapsone, Rifampicin, and Clofazimine. Antibiotics are given for 6 months or longer. It is difficult to cure a person's leprosy. Leprosy can leave disfiguring sores on the skin and nerve damage that are not reversed by antibiotic treatment.[34] Jesus must not have known the cause of leprosy, yet he somehow killed off the *M. leprae* bacteria and healed the sores and nerve damage throughout the bodies of those ill people. We can wonder why he didn't cure leprosy throughout the world while he was in the "curing" mood. The leprosy bacteria are slow growing, and a person exposed may not show symptoms for months or years. Thus, many people die of other causes but may be carrying the leprosy bacteria, something God must diagnose.

Chapter 10 on causes and number of deaths touches on epidemics and endemics. New diseases can arise from mutations in bacteria and viruses. Antibiotic resistant bacteria are getting more and more commonplace. New viruses are appearing. One of the latter is the virus that causes EEE disease, Eastern Equine Encephalitis, which has symptoms like West Nile virus infection but further examination of patients with EEE and the symptoms resemble those of both encephalitis and meningitis, but some are unique; there is no cure. Patients have weakness, inability to walk or talk, brain swelling, and confusion. The patient sleeps almost continuously so it is also called "sleeping disease." The virus is transmitted via mosquito bites.[35] Another relatively new virus is the zika virus, which is carried by mosquitoes. The worst symptom of zika is seen when an expectant woman is infected and passes the virus to her fetus. The fetus can then be born with a small brain, a condition called microcephaly, and also can have other neurological defects.[36]

Additional illnesses caused by viruses include the common cold, adenovirus infections, parainfluenza, SARS (severe acute respiratory syndrome), norovirus, rotavirus, hepatitis A, B, and C, genital herpes, hemorrhagic diseases (Ebola, yellow fever, and dengue), and at least four neurologic virus diseases (polio, meningitis, encephalitis, and rabies).[37] In 2020-21 we had COVID-19, taking the lives of 3,000-4,000 USA citizens every day.[38]

Vaccines save millions of lives worldwide, mostly children. Vaccines are available to immunize people against pneumococcal disease, rubella, measles, hepatitis A and B, chicken pox, polio, diphtheria, and whooping cough. These diseases, which killed millions decades ago, are now seen infrequently or not at all. Vaccines are readily available in the industrial world but are a challenge to provide to poor countries, such as Bangladesh. Other countries, like Pakistan, have strong resistance to getting vaccinated. Even in the USA there are people who resist being vaccinated or having their children vaccinated.[39]

A new flu-like illness that was first noted in China had killed several dozen people there by Jan. 25, 2020. Within days it had spread to S. Korea, Japan, Italy, and then reached Europe and the Americas, including the USA.[40] The causative agent is COVID-19 and some feared a possible pandemic caused by this virus so precautions (masks, frequent hand washing, and isolation of patients) were being taken in whatever country or state new patients appeared.[41] By May 19, 2020, COVID-19 was in fact a full-scaled worldwide pandemic, continuing into May 2021. There was a rush to develop a vaccine against the COVID-19 virus which was challenging the medical community worldwide. An ambitious vaccination program, utilizing two vaccines and then two more, is now underway worldwide to control the Coronavirus disease.[42] Every state in the USA had cases of COVID-19; schools, restaurants, and bars were closed, athletic events and tournaments were called off or postponed and citizens were urged to carry out social distancing (stay home if possible and do not get closer than six feet to another person). Shortages were reported in department stores and groceries.[43] The elderly, sixty years of age and older and the unvaccinated are most vulnerable to being killed by COVID-19.

There was a rush to develop a vaccine to halt the spread of COVID-19 and after the Chinese posted the genetic sequence of the virus the pharmaceutical industry had targets to aim at.[43] While the likelihood of one or more vaccines being developed was high, it was months for the first one, the Pfizer vaccine, to be thoroughly tested and put into use. Those that succumb to COVID-19 or EEE virus will carry that virus to their grave. Will those viruses be killed by embalming fluid? Will viruses be carried to Heaven, or will God find them and stamp them out? Will there be vaccines in Heaven? Ticks carry the bacteria that cause Lyme disease and mosquitoes carry the virus for EEE. Will ticks and mosquitoes be present in Heaven?

Trillions of bacteria, viruses, and fungi live on and inside our bodies. Together these microbes are called the "microbiome" and are important to good health. When a person's microbiome of the mouth, lungs, skin, or gut, gets out of whack, from illness, poor diet, antibiotics, stress or obesity, the person's immune system can also get out of whack and can lead to inflammations and diseases such as forms of arthritis or lupus.[44] A healthy microbiome is also important to a healthy gastrointestinal tract. This microbiome was present in early humans. Archeologists in Sweden discovered a piece of birch bark chewing gum and analyzed it for DNA and microbes (bacteria and viruses). The individual's entire DNA sequence, yes, the entire genome, was in that piece of primitive gum, which was dated to 5,700 years ago, along with DNA of oral microbes and dietary remains.[45] Researchers have analyzed the skin and feces (gut) microbiome of Amazon rainforest people and concluded that the diversity of gut species is twice that of those of us in industrialized countries. They conclude that our modern lifestyles, with processed foods and antibiotics, are killing our microbial diversity and that we need to collect and preserve as many different microbes as possible to avoid losing any. People's personal micro-biomes of the gut, mouth, lungs and skin (microbiological communities) are believed to play a role in disorders including inflammation associated with forms of arthritis, obesity, diabetes, bowel diseases, and Alzheimer's.[46] Perhaps God will assure healthy foods in Heaven that encourage a healthy microbiome. And when God restores bodies for life in Heaven he should provide them with the trillions of bacteria, viruses, and fungi for healthy microbiomes.[47]

When God restores the bodies of people in Heaven, will these bodies carry both the healthy and disease-causing microbes along with them? Will God ensure Heaven residents have healthy microbiomes? 1 Corinthians 15:51 and 1 Thessalonians 4:14-18, say that both the dead and living will be taken up to Heaven on the judgment day. The living will take their microbes, such as their microbiomes, along with them so presumably Heaven will have bacteria, viruses, and fungi, both good and bad forms. As crowded as Heaven will be, God will have the challenge of preventing diseases and preventing the spread of diseases. Will people maintain the immunizations of the deceased in Heaven? Will there be antibiotics? Will there be antibiotic resistant microbes? Will there be vaccines? When fetuses or children die, will God give them healthy microbiomes in Heaven?

Will there be medicines in Heaven such as aspirin, Aleve, Tylenol, ibuprofen, acetaminophen, hydrocodone, heroin, hydromorphone, oxymorphone, oxycodone, oxycontin, and Vicodin? Will there be addictions in Heaven to such medicines? Will addictions to marijuana, vaping, opioids, caffeine, nicotine, alcohol, and foods be seen in Heaven?

Based on factors such as health and housing, the "livability index" can be determined for any one state. One mid-western state had a livability index of fifty, on a scale of 0-100. (aarp.org/livabilityindex). The individual states of the entire USA have been ranked based on the percentage of sixty-five-plus age citizens as to their health being very good to excellent. The percentages vary from a high of 48.4 to a low of 32.4. Thus, more than half of the people in the USA do not consider themselves healthy.[48] Will God restore their health in Heaven to 100%?

Perhaps God will make use of "smart toilets" which can spot signs of disease by analyzing the molecules of the user's urine. The smart toilet will preemptively detect urinary tract infections, kidney disease, diabetes and other metabolic disorders, and determine how prescription medicines are being metabolized to perhaps modify the doses. The user's daily life can be analyzed too – amount of sleep, exercise, how much alcohol or coffee consumed, and amount of over-the-counter medicines consumed. The device, perhaps on the market by 2025, uses a mass spectrometer, which can sort out thousands of molecules in just one microliter of urine.[49] Such a device could be of diagnostic use to God when someone is first admitted to Heaven.

The Children's Environmental Health Network reported the environmental health of children in three states in 2019 and plans to do the same for the remaining forty-seven states when funding is obtained. Eight indicators were examined for the three states: safe drinking water, air quality, warming temperatures, toxic chemical releases, neuro-developmental disorders, asthma, pediatric cancer, and blood lead levels. The child poverty rate varied among the three states from 20% to 12%. Poverty significantly harms the health of children and their families and children of color are disproportionately poor and likely more susceptible to adverse health outcomes.[50] Will the environmental health of Heaven be the very best?

Some states in the USA are ranking counties as to their level of healthiness. The two main issues are how long people live and how healthy people feel. Health behaviors that influence how well and how long we live are monitored. These are: tobacco use, diet/nutrition, obesity, exercise, alcohol and drug use, sexual activity, clinical care, social and economic factors (education, employment, income, family and social support, community safety) and physical environment (air and water quality, housing, and transit). In Heaven there should be little concern for any of these except physical environment and diet. People will still have to eat and exercise and will have to have transportation. How will God provide for the many billions in Heaven? Will there be health care?[55] Will the physical environment of Heaven always be conducive to healthy residents?

Will God correct all these challenging health issues in the environment of Heaven and in individuals when they die and reach Heaven, regardless of their age? If health is being challenged in the USA, what about in the poor nations of Africa and S. America? Why is God allowing poor health to exist?

The challenge to God will be to recognize diseases, whether or not there are obvious visible symptoms. God must carry out some kind of diagnosis for ailments and diseases, at the time of death, as well as ascertain the cause of death.

The good news for God is that symptoms can indicate many specific diseases, for example sexually transmitted diseases such as chlamydia, gonorrhea, herpes, syphilis, and HIV/aids. Symptoms can also indicate arthritis, Lupus, infections, and bowel diseases.[51] But symptoms will be visible only in living persons. If a person dies in an accident, will God know what disease(s) the deceased has? Will the soul carry these symptoms up to Heaven?

When visiting the dermatologist, dentist, audiologist, ophthalmologist or physical therapist, patients are rather routinely asked what prescriptions they are taking. Will God have a medical record for each person, perhaps each person's list of medications? Consider God looking at the list of medications for an individual who recently died from an automobile accident and sees that the person has been taking ten different pills every day for type 2 diabetes, high blood pressure, high cholesterol, irregular heartbeat, arthritis, kidney stones, urination problems, anxiety, back pain and sleep apnea. Now add hearing aids and lens implants. Imagine God going down the list and correcting all the ailments including the head injury from the accident. What a challenge!

Possibly everyone in Heaven will be at the age of thirty-three, the prime of life.[52] The older deceased people will thus lose excess weight, have restored hearing and vision, have no malfunctional body parts, and be cured of arthritis, cancer, diabetes, and/or other diseases of old age. When God adds age to a young person who dies, will he recognize what ailments the individual already has and those that would have shown up in that person if aged on earth?

Instead of assessing each and every person who enters Heaven with regard to what the person's various ailments and diseases might be, God could be following each individual through their life on earth so at the time of death, he already knows the health conditions of each person, all eight billion of earth's residents. Thus, along with following everyone's thoughts, he follows everyone's health. In each case, God has a formidable challenge. Many individuals have more than one health problem, often several. And in some cases, the exact ailment is not even defined although the symptoms are clearly observable. In fact, there are many ailments and diseases that are unknown to most of the public. When a person is diagnosed with cancer or a disease, that individual and/or family member/friend/spouse often searches out everything available about that cancer or disease. For most diseases and cancers there is a history, a set of symptoms, treatment options, and prognosis. For example consider heart disease.[53] There are 120 million Americans with heart disease. Most of them are overweight. Symptoms may be shortness of breath, lack of energy, and chest pain. Some already have stents in their heart blood vessels or have had bypass surgery. Will God repair these hearts or keep the people on prescriptions and exercise/ weight loss programs?

Mexicans are dying from the Covid-19 virus at a rate of 12% of those infected whereas in the rest of the world only 4% of the people infected with Covid-19 are dying. That high death rate in Mexico of Covid-19 patients is believed due to the generally poor health of the Mexican population and thus the associated pre-existing medical conditions. According to a university study the response, or lack of, of a person's immune system can predict the severity of the Covid-19 response. Age is also a predictor as older people are hit harder by the virus.[54] God will have to diagnose those pre-conditions, the status of the immune system, and the age of Covid-19 arrivals in Heaven! God is probably saying, "come on people, pray harder for good health, too many unhealthy people are coming up to Heaven!"

In the deceased, whatever the age, how will God recognize the damage done by poverty while that person was young? How will God correct cognitive (brain power) injury and emotional damage that occurred as a youth?

Some of the rarer diseases will be most challenging. One of these is tardive dyskinesia, which is seen as involuntary and repetitive body movements (tongue jutting, grimacing, frowning, lip smacking), and is associated with long term use of dopamine receptor blocking medications to treat neurological or gastrointestinal ailments. It was first recognized in the 1950s and is seen more often in those older than fifty and in more women than men. There are roughly 200,000 tardive patients in the USA.

It is sort of the opposite of Parkinson's disease in which case patients find it difficult to move whereas tardive patients have difficulty stopping movement.[56] Will God diagnose tardive patients and correct the condition? A very big challenge!

Wegener's polyangiitis is another particularly challenging disease to diagnose and treat.[57] This disease, named after Friedrich Wegener, who described it in 1936, is one of many autoimmune diseases; in this case the body makes antibodies, called antineutrophil Abs, that specifically attack the small and large blood vessels of the body. Effects on the heart, lungs, kidneys, upper respiratory tract, and/or the nervous system lead to symptoms and treatments. The disease can occur at any age, remissions and relapses are seen, and life expectancy is mid-sixties. Drugs that suppress the immune system are the treatment of choice and these drugs have a long list of potential side-effects. A total of fourteen common signs and symptoms are associated with Wegener's, but several doctors are needed to diagnose the disease with certainty; required are a dermatologist (skin doctor), an ear, nose, and throat specialist, a pulmonologist (lung), neurologist (nervous system), nephrologist (kidneys), and a rheumatologist (joint and immune system specialist). If a person dies of this disease, God either already knows he or she had the disease, having followed this person from year to year, day to day, or God can diagnose the disease after the person dies. But, of the fourteen Wegener's symptoms, twelve are <u>symptoms seen only in a living person</u>, such as numbness in limbs, weakness, cough, fever, and hearing loss. Two of the symptoms, sinus and nose congestion and blood in the urine, could presumably be seen in a dead person, but they are symptoms seen associated with other ailments (the common cold and prostate problems). Perhaps God can survey that dead body, as with a CT scan, and detect those specific Abs attacking blood vessels. But the specificity of an Antibody is based on the amino acid sequence in its structure and that specificity is often not known or certainly not understood. God has a formidable challenge with Wegener's disease and the 200,000 people in the USA who have this disease.[57]

Has God been familiar with each and every one of the ailments and diseases and been able to correct the conditions in Heaven residents? When a person dies does God keep a record of the person's cause of death and a history of the ailments that person had?

Adults, teens, children, and infants benefit from comprehensive diagnostic and treatment centers that are near home. There is often at least one treatment center serving one or two counties even in low population areas of a state.[58] Like these health centers, God will have to have a set of tests to diagnose the thousands of diseases and ailments that a person may have died from but God also will have to do the same diagnosis for people who died in accidents or other non-disease causes, not wanting to resurrect a body that is diseased, certainly not one carrying the COVID-19 virus, HIV/AIDS virus, or any other virus, even the common cold virus.[59] Yes, huge challenges for God.

NOTES

1   Robert Richardson and Hilary Morris. *History of Medicine.* (UK: Quiller Publishing, 2005.)

2   Wikipedia website, "Giovannia Boccaccio," last edited February 7, 2023, https://en.wikipedia.org/wiki/Giovanni_Boccaccio.

3   *NBC News,* July 31, 2019.

4   Jackie Vlahos, "How the Gutenberg Press Revolutionized Printing," Printivity insights (website), March 13, 2023, https://www.printivity.com/insights/2021/10/07/gutenberg-press/.

5   Quora website, "How many diseases are known on this world?," accessed March 2, 2020, https://www.quora.com/How-many-diseases-are-known-on-this-world.

6   Editors, "Ten Minutes of Exercise can Improve Memory and More," *Readers Digest,* April 9, 2019. 44-46.

7   *Readers Digest,* May 2020, 69-70.

8   *NBC Nightly News,* April 13, 2021.

9   Ciara Nugent, "Why Peru's COVID-19 problem spiraled - despited a strict lockdown," *Time,* June 15, 2020, 9.

10 *NBC News,* April 23, 2021.

11 WebMD website, search on Cold and Flu Deaths, accessed March 2020; *NBC Nightly News,* December 6, 2019.

12 COPD Foundation website, "Treatment and Medications for COPD," accessed February 2020, https://www.copdfoundation.org/Learn-More/I-am-a-Person-with-COPD/Treatments-Medications.aspx; *Detroit Free Press,* November 15, 2019, 1A.

13 *Detroit Free Press*, October 6, 2020, 8A.

14 *Detroit Free Press*, November 15, 2019, 1A.

15 *Detroit Free Press*, January 9, 2020, 2A.

16 Benaroya Research Institute website, accessed March 2020, www.benaroya-research.org.

17 Cancer Research UK website, "What is Cancer?," accessed March 2020, https://www.cancerresearchuk.org/about-cancer/what-is-cancer.

18 Springhouse Publishing, *Professional Guide to Diseases* (Philadelphia: Lippincott Williams & Wilkins, 1982.)

19 Quora website, accessed February 2020, https://www.quora.com/search?q=Top%2010%20deadliest%20diseases.

20 World Health Organization website, "History of the Smallpox Vaccine," accessed February 2020, https://www.who.int/news-room/spotlight/history-of-vaccination/history-of-smallpox-vaccination.

21 Jo N. Hays, *Epidemics and Pandemics: Their Impacts on Human History* (California: ABC-CLIO, 1st edition, 2005.)

22 Gilead / HIV website, accessed March 2020, https://www.gileadhiv.com.

23 Wikipedia website, "Measles vaccine," lasted edited February 17, 2023, https://en.wikipedia.org/wiki/Measles_vaccine.

24 *Detroit Free Press*, September 4, 2019, 13A.

25 *Detroit Free Press*, October 20, 2019.

26 L. Bezain, "Madagascar's Measles Kills 1200," *Detroit Free Press*, April 15, 2019, 13A.

27 CDC website, "National Diabetes Statistics Report," last reviewed, June 29, 2022, https://www.cdc.gov/diabetes/data/statistics-report/

28 *Time*, November 4, 2019. 42.

29 Michael Poehlman "Fine-Tuning Insulin Levels-Even While Sleeping," *MyNorth Medical Insider*, 2018, mi5.

30 World Health Organization statistics; *AARP Bulletin*, September 2019, 40.

31 *Time*, November 4, 2019, 48; *Detroit Free Press*, October 28, 2019.

32 Mike Zimmerman, "The Cure for Everything," *AARP Bulletin* #9, November 2019, 11.

33 Laura Luptowski Seeley and Sarah Zwickle, "Detection & Discovery: A new era of antimicrobial resistance research," *Connections Magazine*, Winter (2020): 17.

34 Co-author Chris M. Matsko, "How to Cure Leprosy," wikiHow (website), updated January 20, 2023, https://www.wikihow.com/Cure-Leprosy; Kelli Miller, "Leprosy (Hansen's Disease)," WebMD (website), reviewed November 12, 2022, https://www.webmd.com/skin-problems-and-treatments/guide/leprosy-symptoms-treatments-history; Reviewed by Deepak S. Patel,

"Leprosy," FamilyDoctor.org (website), last updated March 2021, https://familydoctor.org/condition/leprosy/.

35 *Detroit Free Press*, August 29, 2019, 6A.

36 CDC website, Zika Virus, updated November 2, 2022, https://www.cdc.gov/zika/.

37 Jill Seladi-Schulman, Reviewed by Daniel Murrell, "Viral Diseases 101," healthline(website), updated March 29, 2019, https://www.healthline.com/health/viral-diseases

38 *NBC Nightly News*, January 27, 2021.

39 Cynthis Gorney, "Why Vaccines Matter," *National Geographic*, November 2017, 114-132; *Arthritis Today*, July/August 2019, 32.

40 *NBC News*, January 29, 2020; NBC News, March 1, 2020.

41 *Detroit Free Press*, January 25, 2020, 1A.

42 *NBC Nightly News*, January 28, 2021.

43 *NBC Nightly News*, March 18, 2020; Time, February 17, 2020, 47.

44 *Arthritis Today*, July/August 2019, 32.

45 Jensen, T.Z.T., Niemann, J., Iversen, K.H. et al., "A 5700 year-old human genome and oral microbiome from chewed birch pitch," *Nature Communications* 10, 5520 (December 2019). https://doi.org/10.1038/s41467-019-13549-9.

46 Jonathon Keats, "Save the Microbes!," *Discover Magazine*, July/August, 2019, 90.

47 *Arthritis Today*, July/August 2019, 32.

48 *AARP Bulletin*, September 2019, 40.

49 K. Wheeler, "Urine luck," *Detroit Free Press*, December 24, 2019, 1C.

50 *Cheboygan Daily Tribune*, January 3, 2020, A12.

51 TestResult.org website, "CBC Interpretation," accessed February 23, 2020, https://testresult.org/en/test/cbc;

52 Randy Alcorn, *Heaven: A Comprehensive Guide to Everything the Bible Says About Our Eternal Home* (Illinois: Tyndale Momentum, 2004.)

53 *NBC Nightly News*, November 16, 2019.

54 Yale School of Medicine website, "Clinical Trials at Yale," accessed February 20, 2020, https://medicine.yale.edu/ycci/clinicaltrials/; *NBC Nightly News*, August 2, 2020.

55 *Petoskey News-Review*, Saturday, April 6, 2019.

56 Wikipedia website, "Tardive dyskinesia," last edited March 11, 2023, https://en.wikipedia.org/wiki/Tardive_dyskinesia.

57 Mayo Clinic website, "Granulomatosis with polyangiitis," accessed March 5, 2020, https://www.mayoclinic.org/diseases-conditions/granulomatosis-with-polyangiitis/symptoms-causes/syc-20351088.

58   Family Medicine Pamphlet, McLaren Northern Michigan, https://www.
     mclaren.org/northern-michigan/mclaren-northern-michigan-home.

59   Richard Conniff, "How Pandemics Change Us," *National Geographic,* August
     2020, 40.

13

PLAGUES IN HISTORY

BEFORE THE GERM theory of disease was understood, before bacteria and viruses were recognized as causative agents of disease, and before the immune system and immunity were understood, many millions of people in the USA and worldwide died from diseases.[1] Consider the following numbers for just a sample of years:

- In 1900 there were 21,064 cases of smallpox (virus caused) in the USA and 894 died.
- From 1900-1904 there were 48,164 cases of smallpox in the USA and 1,528 deaths.
- In 1918 there were 675,000 deaths in the USA from the Spanish flu (virus caused).
- In 1920 there were 469,924 cases of measles (virus caused) in the USA and 7,575 deaths.
- In 1920 there were 147,991 cases of diphtheria (bacterium caused) in the USA and 13,170 deaths.
- In 1922 there were 107,493 cases of pertussis (whooping cough; bacterium caused) in the USA and 5,099 deaths.
- From 1951-1954 there were over 16,000 cases of polio-caused paralysis (virus caused) in the USA and over 1,800 deaths.

Has God diagnosed and cured all these people and does he now have them in Heaven?

In the late 1700s, a crude vaccine for smallpox was developed but was not widely accepted and not used widely. In the 1800s, crude vaccines for rabies, typhoid, cholera, and plague were developed but many deaths from these diseases resulted until better vaccines were developed and became widely accepted. Consequently in the 1990s, due to more vaccinations, the number of cases of smallpox, polio, measles and other diseases dropped sharply or disappeared completely.

Smallpox is thought to have originated in N. Africa in 10,000 BC, as the first agricultural settlements became established. Facial lesions of Egyptian mummies dated to 1050 indicated smallpox was present. Then it was brought to India and Europe in the fifth and seventh centuries. Smallpox was epidemic in the Middle Ages and probably was instrumental in the decline of the Roman Empire. Spanish and Portuguese brought smallpox to the new world where it decimated the Aztecs and Incas in S. America and Native Americans on the east coast of N. America. The slave trade brought in more smallpox to Europe and the Americas. In 18th century Europe, 400,000 cases per year of smallpox were seen and one-third of the survivors were blinded. The fatality in infants was near 90%.[2]

Edward Jenner (1749-1823), a British biologist, noted that milkmaids rarely had smallpox. He knew that cattle could contract cowpox and thus reasoned that the milkmaids in contact with cows had developed an immunity to the cowpox which also worked against smallpox. But many were skeptical and he had to work hard to prove his case. He used the pus from cowpox sores and later from smallpox sores and "inserted" the material into wounds cut on the body of a young boy. The boy did not get smallpox. The Latin word for cow was "vacca" which led to the name "vaccination" for this procedure. This was the first attempt to vaccinate people for a disease. In the 1800s royal families accepted the method and its acceptance spread through England and Europe.

But before immunizations, millions of people died from infectious diseases.[3] Between 1347 and 1700 there were at least 100 plague epidemics in Europe. Where are the souls of these deceased?

Some of the deadliest disease outbreaks in history are the following:[4]

Bubonic Plague (Black Death), 1347-1351. The world
population was 450 million. More than twenty-five mil-
lion died. The characteristic feature was black skin spots,
thus the name black death. Attributed to the bacterium
Yersinia pestis. Two more resurgences occurred, in 1665-
1666, and in 1894, with twelve million more deaths.

Spanish Flu. 1918-1919.[5] This was history's worst epi-
demic, and the number of deaths surpassed all the mil-
itary deaths of WWI and WWII combined. It was ini-
tially not reported (censored), to maintain troop morale,
in Germany, The United Kingdom, and France, so the
prevalence and virulence of this virus was not generally
known. But Spain, being neutral in the war, allowed news-
papers to publish death numbers. This led to misleading
views that it began in Spain, and thus the name Spanish
Flu.[6] More likely it began in Kansas and from there spread
to the military who carried it overseas. Over 50 million
died worldwide from this pandemic; 675,000 in the USA.
Depending on the country/city/village, anywhere from
1 – 100 % of those infected died from the virus.

A pandemic occurs when a new and very virulent form of disease virus
enters the population and spreads worldwide. The 1918 virus infected the
upper respiratory tract, the nose and throat, making it easily transmitted,
but this virus also infected tissue deep in the lungs, damaging the tis-
sue making it susceptible to viral and bacterial pneumonias. In the first
twenty-five weeks, twenty-five million died. In 1991 it was gone, and the
reason is unknown. It might be the first case of an H1N1 disease. At the
military Camp Devens near Boston an average of 100 soldiers were dying
from this flu each day. In Philadelphia, 12,000 deaths occurred in a six-
week period, 759 in a single worst day, but averaging 241 per day. Some
worried that if the flu had continued its rampage, most if not all of human-
ity could have died off. But suddenly the initial pandemic ended, and two
lesser bouts followed but not as deadly or widespread, possibly because the
human immune system of the survivors learned to recognize it and/or the

virus lost its ability to infect deep into the lungs. Thus, the virus evolved into a seasonal influenza virus. But let us not relax too much for a deadly bird flu virus is causing 100s of deaths in China.[7] Needless to say, medical researchers worldwide are working hard to develop a universal flu vaccine to prevent another pandemic.[8]

What makes these flu deaths challenging to God is that the deaths occurred in a short period of time and involved many different nationalities, different language speakers, different races, different age groups, people with different health issues, and people with different religious backgrounds. Books have been written about pandemics, perhaps influenced by the 1918 pandemic. One novel, *Station Eleven*, by Emily St. John Mandel, depicts such a pandemic that killed off most of the world's people, leaving behind bands of people roving about wastelands, with no electricity, automobiles, trucks, trains or planes and no grocery stores. Interestingly, religion did not disappear, with some bands being led by self-proclaimed prophets with many wives.

> HIV-AIDS. Brought to the USA from the Congo where the first case was seen. HIV was recognized in 1981 as a disease. In 2011 there were sixty million people infected worldwide and twenty-five million died. In 2012, thirty-five million worldwide were infected with HIV. Since the early 1980s in the USA, 1,216,919 people have been diagnosed with AIDS of which 12,233 have died, 6,721 directly from AIDS. Tuberculosis deaths are often seen associated with HIV-AIDS. Most of the diagnoses were gay and bisexual black men, then next were white gay/bisexual men, Hispanic/Latino gay/bisexual men, black heterosexual women, black heterosexual men, Hispanic/Latino heterosexual women, and the fewest in white heterosexual women. Worldwide AIDS has killed thirty-two million people, a huge challenge for God.

> Plague of Justinian: 541-588. Rats on boats brought this disease to the Roman Empire. Twenty-five million died. 5,000 died per day in Constantinople. 40% of the

population died. The Emperor Justinian had the plague
but recovered. This may have been the first outbreak of
the bubonic plague.[1]

Plague of Antonine, 165-180. Named after the Roman
emperor Marcus Aurelius Antoninus who died of the dis-
ease. There were five million deaths in those fifteen years,
sometimes 2,000 in one day. One fourth of those infected
died. This may have been smallpox.

Cholera received honorable mention (honorable?) but did not make
the top five.[9] Cholera killed millions of people worldwide beginning in
1817 with six more waves, the seventh still underway. In 1854 a physician
traced cholera to a single well in London. When that well was closed, the
epidemic subsided. Cholera is caused by a bacterium, *Vibrio cholerae*, most
often in contaminated water or food and the resulting diarrhea caused se-
vere and rapid dehydration. Even now, 1.4 million cases and thousands of
deaths per year are seen worldwide. In 2015 there were 172,454 cases spread
over forty-two countries. Many deaths are believed to not be reported.
Treatment is early oral rehydration.

The Great Plague of London, 1665-1666, should also be mentioned;
75,000-100,000 people died, one-fifth of London's population. It was
thought spread by a bacterium on fleas, but some think it may have been
bubonic plague. It has similarities to hemorrhagic fever, a virus disease.

After AIDS, from 2000 to 2020, the world has faced additional pan-
demics including Influenza, SARS, Swine Flu, MERS, and West African
Ebola, all virus-caused, totaling 1,000s of deaths. At present the world
is in the midst of the coronavirus pandemic. The origin of this virus is
debated but most fingers point to China, where it was first reported. As
of July 2020, COVID-19 had resulted in over 19,200,000 infections and
over 718,000 deaths worldwide; 5,000,000 infections and 160,000 deaths
in the USA and had not leveled off. (Centers for Disease Control; World
Health Organization, Wikipedia: June 10, 2020; NBC News, August 15,
2020). If God had any control over diseases, would he allow COVID-19 to
cause deaths of children, nuns, preachers, veterans, the elderly, those with
pre-existing conditions, or anyone?

Where are all these deceased people today? Are their souls in Heaven? Did God record their cause of death and the ravages of the diseases on the bodies, and does he have enough information to restore the bodies in Heaven and unite them with their souls? Will there be viruses and bacteria in Heaven?

Many animals have been and still are involved in spreading disease-causing organisms, such as viruses and bacteria, to humans; these include mosquitoes, bats, rodents (rats), poultry/birds, camels, chimpanzees, and pigs. It is estimated that there are 827,000 viruses in the animal world with the potential to infect humans.[4] Will these animals be in Heaven, still carrying the viruses or bacteria?

NOTES

1   Center for Disease Control website, "Summary of Notifiable Diseases, United States, 1999," accessed, February 2019, https://www.cdc.gov/mmwr/preview/ mmwrhtml/mm4853a1.htm; Henry E. Sigerist, *History of Medicine* (New York: Oxford University Press, 1951)

2   World Health Organization website, "Smallpox," accessed January 2019, https://www.who.int/health-topics/smallpox#tab=tab_1.

3   "Outbreaks: Protecting Americans From Infectious Disease 2013," Robert Wood Johnson Foundation (website), December, 2013, https://www.rwjf. org/en/insights/our-research/2013/12/outbreaks--protecting-americans-fro m-infectious-disease-2013.html.

4   R. Conniff, "Stopping Pandemics," *National Geographic*, August, 2020, 46-75; Maryn McKenna, "Virus Hunters," *Smithsonian Magazine*, July-August 2020, 56-67.

5   John M. Barry, "Journal of the Plague Year," *Smithsonian Magazine*, November 2017, 34-43.

6   Wikipedia website, "Spanish flu," last edited March 11, 2023, https://en.wiki-pedia.org/wiki/Spanish_flu.

7   Melinda Liu, "The Birth of a Killer," *Smithsonian Magazine*, November 2017, 44.

8   Maryn McKenna, "How to Stop a Lethal Virus," *Smithsonian Magazine*, November 2017, 52.

9   Wikipedia website, "1854 Broad Street cholera outbreak," last edited March 7, 2023, https://en.wikipedia.org/wiki/1854_Broad_Street_cholera_outbreak

14

GENETIC DISEASES

BECAUSE OF THE general notion that humans are somehow "special" and "more advanced" than other living organisms, the thought was that humans would have many more genes than mice or flies or other animals. Sequencing of both animal and plant genomes has now been completed and their number of genes coding for proteins is now known. During evolutionary time the number of genes in the human genome became established at 20,500 but, somewhat surprisingly, mice also have a similar number. Furthermore, only about 1% of the genes of humans and mice are different. Even flies have 13,500 genes, not that many fewer. Humans, mice, and flies share many genes. For example, a gene necessary for eye development is found in humans, mice, and flies, and also in other organisms that have eyes. Many genes are now known to be conserved across the living world, consistent with the theory of evolution. The chimpanzee has nearly the same number of genes as the human, yet we consider the chimp a "lower" primate. Only fifty genes of the human genome have no equivalent (homolog) in the chimp.[1]

Genes are the genetic component of chromosomes and are made up of DNA. DNA is a double helix composed of two complementary strands of nitrogen bases which are thymidine, cytidine, guanosine, and adenine. Each of these nitrogen bases is combined chemically with a 5-carbon sugar (ribose or deoxyribose) and phosphorous to make nucleotides. The sequence of the nucleotides along the DNA, through an intermediate called messenger RNA, determines the amino acid sequence of proteins. Proteins are the main structural and functional components of cells; their structure and function give cells characteristics (nerve cells, blood cells, connective tissue cells, epidermal cells, pancreas cells). Some well-known proteins are the following: insulin, made by the pancreas and which regulates sugar metabolism; globin, which makes up hemoglobin of red blood cells and carries oxygen through the body; keratin, which is the structural component of skin epidermis, hair, and fingernails; and dystrophin, a protein in muscle that is essential for muscle function.[2]

Changes that are found in the normal sequence of the DNA are called mutations. Mutations of the DNA of genes that code for these proteins have adverse effects on health, in other words they cause disorders in normal structure or function of a tissue or organ due to absence of the protein, too little of the protein or a non-functioning or poorly functioning protein. Three types of mutations are most commonly seen. A mutation can be a change to one pair of nucleotides, called a point mutation; or a deletion of a portion of a gene; or addition of trinucleotide repeats, which can extend the length of a gene. There are 100s of known single gene disorders, a veritable plethora of disorders each caused by a mutation in a single gene.[3]

A total of seventy of these single gene disorders are alphabetized, beginning with albinism and ending with Wilson's Disease, and are listed in the edited volume, *Genetic Disorders Source Book*.[4] Here are some disorders caused by mutations in single genes: Cystic fibrosis causes difficulty in breathing due to mucus buildup; Type 1 diabetics are unable to manufacture insulin; people with sickle cell disease have misshaped red blood cells that struggle to get oxygen transported through their bodies; epidermolysis bullosa, caused by a keratin mutation, results in epidermal problems; and mutations in the dystrophin gene result in Duchenne muscular dystrophy. Type 1 diabetics must receive daily doses of insulin by injection as the defective Islet cells of the pancreas of diabetics cannot be replaced, even after decades of research with animal models and tissue culture systems. There is no cure for epidermal keratin malfunctions; muscular dystrophy, even with the mutated dystrophin gene sequenced and the mutation identified and located, has not been cured; only recently has the normal globin gene been given to Sickle cell patients and shown to have some corrective influence. Given these difficulties, the Bible says that in Heaven there will be no illness and no pain.

God will presumably recognize if a new resident in Heaven has a genetic disorder, identify it, and find the appropriate chromosome and the DNA sequence at fault. Then God will correct the defect in every one of the thousands of cells in the pancreas, red blood cells, epidermis, and/or muscle, wherein the mutated gene is having its adverse effect. Best of luck to the deceased and to God, and these are the easy genetic mutations.

Here are some more challenging genetic disorders, most of which have treatments but have no cures: Angelman syndrome, Canavan disease, color blindness, Cri du Chat syndrome, Prader-Willi syndrome; Tay Sachs syndrome; bipolar disorder; Marfan syndrome; multiple sclerosis; nonketogenic hyperglycemia; Pitt Hopkins syndrome; progeria; ectodermal dysplasia; Potter syndrome; Sanfilippo syndrome; amyotrophic lateral sclerosis (ALS; Lou Gehrig's Disease); autosomal dominant neovascular inflammatory vitreoretinopathy; Rett syndrome; Huntington's disease; fibro dysplasia ossificans; Batten disease; and myofibrillar myopathy![4] Looking at a few of these in the medical literature or even on the internet, one can see just how difficult it will be, if not impossible in most cases, to correct these conditions by medical doctors/scientists or God.

Fibrodysplasia ossificans progressive (FOP) is a rare disease in which case connective tissue turns to bone, especially after bruising or injury.[5] A mutation involving the body's tissue repair mechanism causes fibrous tissue (muscle, tendon, ligament) to become ossified (forms bone) spontaneously during normal life or especially when damaged. Joints can become frozen. The "extra" bone has resulted in the name "Stone Man Disease." Surgical removal of the extra bone results in even more bone formation. One in every one million people are affected in the USA. Children initially do not show extra bone symptoms but are born with deformed big toes. The first symptoms usually occur between the ages of four and ten. The extra bone growth begins in the neck and proceeds downward – shoulders, back/chest, arms, down to the feet. Eating and breathing are adversely affected along with joint movement resulting in a shortened life span. One well-known case of FOP is Harry Eastlack (1933-1973) who began to show symptoms at ten years old and by the time of death at thirty-nine, had completely ossified, even unable to move his lips. He donated his body to science which is at the Mutter Museum in Philadelphia. Another well-known case of FOP is Jeannie Peeper, born in 1958, she reached fifty-three in 2013, and was documented in an article in the Atlantic magazine, June 2013. At four years old, she was diagnosed with FOP due to her big toes being short and crooked and she could not open her mouth wide like her siblings. She established the Ossificans Progressive Foundation which brought many FOP patients together to support each other and that foundation helped establish research efforts. There are an estimated 2,500 cases of FOP in the world, 700 of which have been medically confirmed.[5]

The challenges to God can be appreciated when the cause of FOP is examined. FOP is caused by an autosomal dominant allele on chromosome 2q23-24. A mutation in this gene, which codes for activin-like kinase (ACVR1), is responsible for the disease. ACVR1 encodes activin receptor type-1, a BMP (bone morphogenic protein) type-1 receptor. The mutation results in a substitution of codon 206 from arginine to histidine in the ACVR1 protein and this change causes abnormal activation of ACVR1, too much BMP4 stimulation, and thus too much bone formation; the stem cells that make bone are seemingly in overdrive. Understanding FOP may lead to therapeutic agents, some of which have been or are presently being tested, and may lead to better treatments of other bone diseases and improved fracture healing.

God has two main challenges with FOP individuals. 1. If a child with the genetic mutation dies before symptoms, God will presumably recognize that the mutation exists in that child and must correct it in Heaven. Note (see above) that God must recognize the number 2 chromosome and find codon 206 and the mutation must be corrected in all cells. 2. If a person showing FOP symptoms dies or has died of the disease, God must be able to generate a new body free of excess bone and with cells that do not have the mutation. Will God be able to deal with the complex molecular biology of FOP? When someone dies with FOP, does their soul carry the mutation?

Many diseases affecting human health have a genetic causation and those affecting the nervous system are the most agonizing. Some, like amyotrophic lateral sclerosis (ALS; also called Lew Gehrig disease) and Huntington's disease, do not exhibit symptoms until adult life. In others, symptoms appear during childhood and shorten life considerably. One of the latter is Batten's Disease, which is a rare inherited disorder of the nervous system that is fatal.[6] When someone dies with FOP, does their soul carry the mutation? Symptoms appear in childhood, as early as four years old, and include progressive vision loss, personality changes, and slow learning. Seizures and loss of motor function lead to clumsiness, stumbling, and Parkinson-like symptoms. Patients become wheelchair bound, bed-ridden, and die prematurely. A Hollywood producer, Gordon Gray, and his wife received a double dose of Batten when finding out that both of their young daughters have Batten. The Grays established the Charlotte and Gwenyth Gray Foundation, named for their daughters, with the hope of raising $10-12 million to find a cure. Batten is one of several disorders known as neuronal ceroid lipofuscinoses (CLNs). Over sixty different mutations in the NCL gene have been associated with Batten disease, which differ slightly one from another, mainly in the timing of when symptoms first appear, but all adversely affect the nervous system. The most commonly found mutation deletes about 1000 base pairs of the CLN3 gene, thus resulting in a shorter protein with poor function. Note that there are adult-onset forms of Batten disease. The frequency of childhood (juvenile) Batten around the world varies from country to country and occurs in up to eight per 100,000 births. The gene is referred to as CLN3 and is located on the short arm of chromosome 16. The position more specifically is referred to by geneticists as 16p12.1 and is from base pair 28,466,652 to 28,492,301. The gene product is a protein that resides in the membranes inside neuronal cells and may be involved in the organization of the cell framework, movement of cell components, and/or in the normal function of lysosomes, which are cell structures that breakdown and recycle various molecules.[6]

Chromosome abnormalities are challenging as well. In the Genetic Disorders Source Book[4] are listed 13 chromosome abnormalities which result in a disorder. The most common are loss of a chromosome or the gain of a chromosome. The healthy human genome has 23 pairs of chromosomes or 46 total (22 pairs of autosomes plus the XX or XY sex chromosome pair.) During the first cell division of meiosis, which is called the reduction division, chromosomes separate into daughter cells so that the resulting gametes, eggs or sperm, have only 23 chromosomes. Thus, when fertilization occurs, the normal number of chromosomes is back to being 46. But in that first meiotic division, which takes place in the gonad, chromosomes may not separate in one of the pairs, so that the resulting gamete may have an "extra" chromosome or it may be missing a chromosome. The most common chromosome abnormalities are trisomy 21, which results in Down's Syndrome; an extra X chromosome or missing X chromosome results in conditions called Klinefelter's Syndrome, XXY, and Turner's Syndrome, XO. Each of these syndromes results in mental deficiencies and physical difficulties, and the latter two result in sexual function deficiencies. There are syndromes much more severe with extra 10 and 13 chromosomes, called trisomy 10 and trisomy 13.[4,7] One can wonder how God is going to deal with these chromosomal abnormalities. Is he going to remove the extra chromosome from every one of the 10 trillion cells in the body. Will he add the missing chromosome to all the cells? If he is going to add the missing chromosome, from where will he get it? Will he manufacture it? Will he use magic?

The third type of genetic disorder is the type that is both genetic and environmental, of which there are ten identified in the handbook.[4] These are addiction, Alzheimer's disease, mental illness, asthma, cancer, Crohn's disease, diabetes, hypertension, movement disorders, and obesity. In these cases, there may be more than one gene involved (multigene effects) and the abnormal expression may be lower or higher than normal, influenced by environmental factors. Medical scientists are presently attempting to understand these complex disorders and how genes and the environment bring them about.[4] God will not want Heaven residents to suffer from any of these multigene disorders.

A few more words about mental illness are warranted because of increased societal concerns. There are more than 200 different forms of mental illness; some of them are depression, bipolar disorder, dementia, schizophrenia, post-traumatic stress disorder (PTSD), and anxiety disorders.[4] Depression was in the news in 2020 and 2021, due to COVID-19 and associated effects of virtual learning, including decreased social opportunities and adverse effects on sports. Mental illness is also associated with social unrest, and political unrest. One unfortunate effect of these was an increased suicide rate (school-aged youth, police, veterans, and more). In 2020, in one major mid-western city the number of calls to the police department related to mental health numbered 7,300 (twenty every day in just that one city). Mental disorders such as depression are associated with a combination of genes and environmental factors. Efforts are underway to increase the number of mental health workers in schools, police departments, hospitals, and the general community.[8] How will God diagnose the various mental disorders and how will he correct them? Will there be mental health service available in Heaven? Will the soul carry mental disorders?

The difficulties of identifying, characterizing, treating, and curing human genetic diseases were discussed on public TV in 2020.[9] Two very challenging diseases wherein progress is being made are Sickle Cell disease and Spinal Muscular Atrophy (SMA) disease. In Sickle cell, red blood cells which normally carry oxygen to all parts of the body form sickle shapes which tangle up and block circulation. SMA results in loss of muscle function because the SMA protein is abnormal. Years and years of research by many laboratories around the world have identified the genes involved in each of these diseases, the protein products of the genes, the function of those products, and why the mutation leads to a defective protein thus causing the disease. In Sickle cell disease it was found that there are two globin genes, one is active in the fetus and the other is active after birth. The protein is globin, which makes up hemoglobin. The mutation is in the adult globin gene. The treatment is thus designed to turn off the adult globin gene and turn on the fetal gene to make a good globin. Likewise, in SMA, there are two genes, SMA 1, which in the normal form makes enough of the SMA 1 protein but in the mutant form makes very little, and SMA 2, which makes the good protein but very little of it. SMA 1 is the mutated gene. The strategy is therefore to turn on SMA 2 more strongly to provide enough of the SMA protein to function at the nerve/muscle junctions. A drug was discovered which does that, called spinraza (nusinersen) and is now available to patients as an injection under a physician's guidance.[10]

An exciting advance in understanding a devastating genetic disease, ALS, was reported in Scientific American, June 2017, p. 46. ALS is either genetic, i.e., runs in families (10% of the cases), or sporadic (random appearance with no family connections; the remaining 90%). Together, these cases number 6,000 new diagnoses per year in the USA. There is no cure for ALS; the nerve-muscle interactions fail and death results from respiratory failure as the breathing system fails. Most diagnoses are between the ages of forty to seventy years of age with a two-to-five-year life expectancy after diagnosis. The new finding came from examining the DNA sequences of the genetic cases and comparing them to healthy individuals without ALS.

The finding was that a DNA sequence on chromosome #9 had many re-peated "letters" in ALS patients, thus disrupting the function of this gene. The position of those undesirable repeats was C9ORF72 (chromosome 9; open reading frame # 72). Clearly even one chromosome is a challenge to understand. The excitement came because this finding raised the possi-bility of using an antisense oligonucleotide (ASO) to silence that repeated sequence and perhaps improve the outlook for ALS patients. The ALS Foundation says that fifteen people in the USA die from ALS each year. Since Lew Gehrig died of ALS in 1941, many additional people have died from this genetic disease. Could God "cure" ALS when these patients get to Heaven? How would he go about that cure? The repeats on chromosome 9 would have to be removed to get normal genetic expression there and then all the failed neuromuscular systems would have to be re-established, the first being the breathing apparatus. There is air in Heaven so presumably Heaven residents will be breathing! And likely dancing and participating in many other activities.

Kabuki Makeup Syndrome cannot be left out of this chapter. First defined by Japanese medical scientists in 1980, the characteristic of this disease is a permanent facial transformation that is similar to that of Japanese Kabuki theater actors, a very distinct style; long and thick eyelashes and arched eyebrows but in addition flattened nose tips and protruding ears. In addition, microcephaly (small head and small brain), weak muscles, eye problems, short stature, scoliosis of the spine, hip and knee problems, cleft palate, dental problems, ear problems, early puberty, heart problems, and early death often by seizures.[11] This syndrome is the result of a mutation in the KMT2D gene (80%) or the KDM6A gene (6%) but sometimes the syndrome is seen in absence of mutation to either gene. The KMT2D gene is on the long arm of chromosome #12, position 13.2, in between base pr 49018975 and base pr 49061895. The KDM6A gene is on the X chromosome, position Xp11.2, between base pr 44873175 and base pr 44972024.

The KMT2D gene codes for a lysine specific methyl transferase that is found in many cell types and has the role of transferring methyl groups to lysines (an amino acid present in histone proteins). Histones are proteins that are associated with DNA (genes) of chromosomes and methylation is a way of regulating genes. The KDM6A gene codes for a demethylase, which removes methyl groups from histones. If either one of these genes is mutated, the respective enzyme is not formed or is non-functional and the respective histone methylation or demethylation does not occur, disrupting gene regulation and thus giving the Kabuki syndrome.

Women with Kabuki were simply ignored and not schooled in makeup application. Men were considered to be eccentrics in wearing makeup. Thus, Kabuki often went undiagnosed.[11] Why the genes on the 8th chromosome suddenly malfunction or rearrange in sequence for no apparent reason is not understood. The facial changes can be evident at birth or can develop at puberty or in adult women after giving birth and are followed by heart abnormalities and death by seizures. If a child or person dies before the syndrome is exhibited, would God be able to diagnose the impending illness? Can God correct the odd facial features in Kabuki? Can God correct the mutations in the two genes in all the relevant cells?

Every year 7.9 million infants, 6% of world births, are born with a serious birth defect and 3.2 million are disabled for life.[12] The causes are due to inherited and/or environmental factors. In the USA there are 120,000 infants born with birth defects per year; every 4.5 minutes a baby with a birth defect is born.[4,5] Some of the common inherited ones are Down's Syndrome, caused by trisomy 21; Edward's Syndrome, caused by trisomy 18; and Patau Syndrome, caused by trisomy 13. Edward's and Patau infants are rare compared to Downs and die shortly after birth. One of every 800 USA births is a Down's child. With increasing mother's age, the frequency of Down's increases so that at 50 yrs. of age, women give birth to Down's children at a frequency of 1/12. Down's children can live to be an adult but Edward's and Patau children do not survive even early childhood. Some parents might not want their Down's child to be "normal" and love her or him just as is (see Chapter 18). The Down's child might be perfectly happy as well, even in Heaven. Infants are also born with defects caused by single gene mutations. Examples are phenylketonuria, Sickle cell, and Tay-Sachs disease. Chromosomal and single gene defects in these infants adversely affect the heart, brain, spinal cord, the palate, kidneys, lungs, and the eye. Delayed growth is often seen. God has an enormous challenge to diagnose the defect, correct the defect in all the cells, and restore good health in these millions of infants. After embalming, not a single living cell exists. After burial and years of decomposition, not a single intact cell exists. After cremation, only ashes remain. From where is God going to get healthy cells with the individual's genome intact and free of the mutant gene?

What a challenge for God to diagnose these ailments, identify the contributing genetic and environmental factors, and cure the ailments.

NOTES

1   David P. Clark and Lonnie D. Russell, *Molecular Biology Made Simple and Fun* (Illinois: Cache River Press, 1997); William S. Klug and Michael R. Cummings, *Concepts of Genetics* (New Jersey: Pearson, 2003)

2   J.D. Watson and F.H.C. Crick, "Molecular Structure of Nucleic Acids: A Structure for Deoxyribose Nucleic Acid," *Nature* Volume 171, (1953): 737-738; Isaac Asimov, *The Genetic Code* (New York: Clarkson N. Potter, In., 1962); Klug and Cummings, *Concepts of Genetics*.

3   Wikipedia website, last edited May 19, 2023, https://en.wikipedia.org/wiki/List_of_genetic_disorders; Klug and Cummings, *Concepts of Genetics*.

4   Sandra J. Judd, Editor, *Genetic Disorders Sourcebook*, 5th Edition (Michigan: Omnigraphics, 2014.)

5   GARD website, "Fibrodysplasia ossificans progressive," last updated February 2023, https://rarediseases.info.nih.gov/diseases/6445/fibrodysplasia-ossifican s-progressiva; J.B. Lees-Shepard, & D.J. Goldhamer, (2018). "Stem cells and heterotopic ossification: Lessons from animal models." *Bone, 109*, 178–186. https://doi.org/10.1016/j.bone.2018.01.029.

6   NIH website, "Batten Disease," last reviewed January 20, 2023, https://www.ninds.nih.gov/health-information/disorders/batten-disease.

7   Klug and Cummings, *Concepts of Genetics*.

8   Omar Abdel-Baqui, "It Happens Far Too Often," *Detroit Free Press*, January 31, 2020, 1A, 7A-9A.

9   The Gene – An Intimate History, episodes 1 and 2, "101, 102" directed by Chris Durrance, written by Geoffrey C. Ward; Barak Goodman & David Blistein, *WCMU PBS*, April 7 and April 14, 2020.

10 Biogen website, accessed April, 2020, https://www.biogen.com; https.//www.spinraza.com.

11 Michael Largo, *Final Exits: The Illustrated Encyclopedia of How We Die*, (New York: William Morrow & Co., 2006); Wikipedia website, "Kabuki syndrome," last edited December 1, 2022, https://en.wikipedia.org/wiki/Kabuki_syndrome.

12 CDC website, "Birth Defects," last reviewed December 22, 2022, https://www.cdc.gov/ncbddd/birthdefects/index.html.

15

IDENTIFYING MUTATIONS AND GENE EDITING

WOULD IT BE a good thing if we could genetically engineer ourselves as we do with plants and animals? The fact is humans have been genetically engineering plants and animals for centuries but only with the help of nature and our own selection. Charles Darwin and Alfred Russel Wallace presented to the world the concept of survival of the fittest, the idea that in nature those organisms that have the most favorable traits, i.e., best genetic characteristics, will survive under different environmental conditions. Some of these traits in plants are tolerance to droughts or floods, light tolerance, speed of growth, reproduction timed with seasons (light and temperature reactiveness), thorns to ward off browsers, bad-tasting chemicals to keep from being eaten, large numbers of seeds or spores, seeds that can be spread by wind or animals, and colorful flowers to attract pollinators, to name a few. Likewise, animals have survival traits: speed, camouflage, claws, talons, sharp teeth, feathers, and flight, able to live on land or in water, swimming ability, and hibernation. These are traits that help to not being prey, help catching prey, and help reproduction.[1]

We humans have been the "selector" especially as agriculture was developed. Starting with wild plants and animals, we selected for desirable traits in crops (corn, wheat, barley, and other grains);[1] apples, oranges, cherries, and other fruits:[2] and in animals (dogs, cats, horses, cows, pigs, chickens, sheep, and goats).[1] We have placed really strong selection on dog breeds; dogs originated from domestication of wolves. And we are still selecting for desirable traits in plants and animals. Just look at seed catalogs, visit a county fair, or watch a dog or horse show.

From the work on peas of the Austrian monk Gregor Mendel (1822-1884),[3] the view that genes determine traits became established in biology and agriculture. Scientists then soon recognized that genes can be mutated and that mutated genes have different effects on traits. Furthermore, X-rays and some chemicals were found to behave as mutagenesis agents. When fruit flies, *Drosophila melanogaster*, were x-irradiated, various mutant forms were seen in the next generation, eyeless, wingless, and various other odd traits. Mutagenic agents could cause mutations in plants as well and in other animals, such as mice. In flies, genetic studies had revealed the number of chromosomes and from mutagenesis studies, a gene, such as for eye color, could be assigned to a specific location on a specific chromosome. Slowly, the functions of many genes were elucidated in not just flies but in many other animals and also plants.[3]

The molecular genetics methods of genome research are costly and require bright scientists and modern, fully equipped laboratories. The Human Genome Project (HGP), the goal of which was to sequence the entire human genome, involved a tremendous amount of work by hundreds of scientists in dozens of laboratories, and was completed in 2003 at a cost of $4.7 billion.[4] A United Kingdom project, the 100,000 Genomes Project is underway; the govt. and private sources in 2016 made $300 million available, the aim being to complete sequencing of 100,000 genomes in 2017.[4] The sequencing of one genome now takes only days, compared to years previously. Now anyone can have their genome sequenced without too high a cost and several companies provide sequencing sufficient to determine family lineages. Some thought that sequencing and deciphering the exact order of the 3 billion nucleotides (A, T, C and G) of the human genome would lead to identification of many if not all the genetic diseases and their correction. But many diseases in adults are caused by mutations in multiple genes or were not genetic at all. Also, sequencing was costly initially, now not so much, and in infants, mutations are the leading cause of deaths. Fortunately, in 2019 and 2020, whole genome sequencing is being applied to diagnostic and therapeutic uses in infants, especially in the case of single gene mutations, like cystic fibrosis, beta-thalassemia (anemia) and Tay-Sachs disease. Estimates are that one third of newborns in neonatal intensive care units in the USA are there because of a genetic disease.[5] In the next paragraph an application of genetic engineering knowledge is described.

Consider a mutation of the OTC gene, which is located on the X chromosome. The OTC gene codes for an enzyme, ornithine transcarbamylase, which is important in processing nitrogen. If the gene is mutated in a boy, ammonia builds up to a toxic level and the boy must take dozens of pills daily to provide the functioning OTC. The Y chromosome does not carry functional genes therefore one mutant gene on the X is disease causative in men. In women, one OTC gene may be mutated but if the paired X has a normal OTC gene, then functional OTC is produced, and the woman is healthy. Having both mutant X chromosomes would be rare and would require a woman with one X mutated having a child with a man who carries the mutated OTC gene on his single X chromosome. Even then the probability of that genetic combination would be 50%. Now let us say that a woman has a brother with the OTC mutation, and she wants to have a child but knows that she might be a carrier of the OTC mutation. And if she had a boy, he could inherit the mutant OTC gene and have the disease. What could she do? She asked the laboratory at the Center for Pediatric Medicine at Children's Mercy Hospital in Kansas City to collect a half dozen of her eggs and prepare them for *in vitro* fertilization (IVF). Then the eggs were fertilized by a sperm donor, known to not have the OTC deficiency by prior DNA sequencing using cheek swab cells. Sequencing of her DNA showed that she was indeed a carrier of the OTC mutation, but the sperm donor was normal, thus there was a 50% probability that any one of the fertilized eggs would have the X chromosome with the OTC mutation. Next the six fertilized eggs were allowed to undergo cleavage divisions for 3 days at which time doctors harvested one cell from each of the 6 cleavage stage embryos. After a laboratory analyzed the DNA of each of the 6 cells, one was chosen which did not have the OTC mutation on either X chromosome. That embryo was implanted into her womb, and she ultimately gave birth to a healthy girl baby.[6] This same technique can be used to search early embryos for other mutant genes, even genes on non-sex chromosomes, and also for chromosomal abnormalities such as trisomy 21

(Down's Syndrome). Note that this method involves 6 or more embryos only one of which is chosen for childbirth. What will God do with the other 5 embryos? Some of those will be free of the mutation in question but others will carry the mutation. Where will God keep these embryos until resurrection? Will these early embryos have souls and what becomes of them when the embryos are discarded in the hospital?

When a newspaper editor modifies a story prior to publication or a writer edits her or his own story or book, changes are made in the words and sentences and their context, sometimes changing the meaning but usually just improving the wording. Molecular geneticists and medical scientists have developed a new technique to edit genes. Editing genes involves a combination of 3 techniques: deleting, repairing, and replacing DNA (a gene) within a living cell. The idea is to develop treatments for inherited disorders and ultimately other diseases, including HIV. Critics say that parents might want smarter and stronger kids and that tampering with the genome might have undesirable consequences. Britain gave the OK for scientists to edit embryo genes.[7]

To edit genes prior to 2013 required two methods – zinc finger nucleases (ZFNs) and transcription activator-like effector nucleases (TALENS) – and allowed the splicing of DNA at a specific location. These together provided programmable, sequence-specific DNA binding modules linked to a non-specific DNA cleavage domain. Double strand breaks are induced that can stimulate homolog-directed repair at specific genome locations.[8] But the CRISPR/Cas9 methodology was then developed and is much faster, easier, and more accurate. CRISPR stands for *clustered regularly interspersed short palindromic repeats*. First an RNA guide molecule locates the DNA (gene) that needs to be fixed/repaired. Then Cas9 protein attaches and cuts out the defective DNA sequence. A good strand of DNA is then inserted in place of the bad one.[9] Chinese medical scientists reported in April 2016, that they had edited the DNA of human embryos. One gene being edited is that of Sickle Cell Anemia, which is a single mutation in the beta globin gene that adversely affects oxygen carrying capacity of red blood cells, resulting in anemia. The strategy is to edit (correct) the faulty gene from stem cells (somatic cells) of the blood, not germ cells (reproductive cells), so that the edited gene cannot be passed on to offspring.[10] A father and 3 daughters have thalassemia which is a blood disorder that leaves them weak and anemic. They each have to be hospitalized every 3 weeks to obtain a blood transfusion, which they say is cumbersome but realize they are still lucky for it to be available. CRISPR could "cure" the thalassemia in this family of four.

Chinese scientists have tried CRISPR on human embryos with a mutant thalassemia gene but so far without success. [11] But the world medical community prohibits the use of CRISPR in humans, for moral reasons. Nevertheless, CRISPR can be used in model animal systems, like mice, worms, and fruit flies, to examine genes that are mutated in humans. One gene examined in this way is the amyotrophic lateral sclerosis gene (ALS), a mutation that results in neurons dying and thus loss of muscle function, including muscles of speaking and swallowing. The CRISPR methodology involves cloning the ALS gene of humans and then inserting that mutant gene into the worm, *C. elegans*. The neurons of the worm die, and muscle function is adversely affected. This model system may result in "cures" for the worm ALS and ultimately therapies for humans with ALS. [12]

The 2020 Nobel Prize in chemistry was awarded to two scientists for their development of the CRISPR methodology, Jennifer Doudna of the USA and Emmanuelle Charpentier of France. [13]

Another gene editing method involves the mitochondrial genome. Yes, the energy generators of cells, the mitochondria, have their own DNA that is separate from the nuclear DNA. This DNA codes for proteins involved in mitochondrial functions. Mitochondria are inherited strictly from the mother as all the mitochondria of the embryo come from the egg; none come from the sperm. There are disease mutations in mitochondrial DNA as there are in nuclear DNA. To correct for these mutations, mitochondria from donors that have no mutations can be injected into the fertilized eggs with the mutated mitochondria. The technique here is called mitochondrial replacement therapy (MRT). The nuclear genome of the embryo would be from both parents (egg and sperm nuclei), but the mitochondria would be from a donor with no mitochondrial disease mutations and thus the result would be a three-parent embryo. When that embryo develops, is born, grows up, matures, and reproduces, the mitochondria would become part of the eggs of that individual if female and thus be passed on to the next generation. Thus, the worry by critics. If an older woman decides to have a child, her eggs are also older, and the mitochondria of her eggs are older.

The eggs are not as viable as has been seen from *in vitro* fertilization (IVF) studies. To rejuvenate her eggs, mitochondria from a younger woman's eggs or from her own egg stem cells (younger cells) can be injected into her eggs.[14] According to some, scientists should be allowed to proceed with MRT but must be cautious.[15]

The puzzle is how God could sequence and edit the DNA of all people who get to Heaven, thousands to millions per day, and correct the bad, disease-causing mutations, both in the nuclear chromosomes and the mitochondria. The Human Genome Project led to identification of 1,800 previously not known disease causing genes. We can see that the molecular methods are very challenging. Can God just use supernatural methods, wave his magic wand, and correct all defects and make the body well again? Maybe God can give each person the same genome so that everyone will have the identical genome, with the same DNA sequences. But whose DNA sequence will he use as the model? Perhaps the genome of Jesus? What could be more perfect? But then wouldn't everyone have the same identical bodies and same personalities? No, that cannot be what God would do. Lucy would still want to be Lucy, with her memories, interests, and personality. Jim would still want to be Jim, and not be Jesus. Does God have everyone's DNA sequence, genetic mutations and deletions included, in his memory bank, and is he up-dating each sequence as new mutations occur? It is unlikely that the soul, which is non-matter, can carry genetic information. The body of the deceased is meanwhile decomposing in the ground.

A preacher was asked how God will correct for a genetic defect in a small child that has died and insure a healthy body again of thirty-three years old. The preacher hesitated and then answered, "who cares how he will do it but he will just do it." That is a very unsatisfactory answer and is wishful thinking!

NOTES

1   Charles Darwin, *On the Origin of Species by Means of Natural Selection* (London: John Murray, 1859); Philip Appleman, Editor, *Darwin* (New York: W.W. Norton and Co., 1979)

2   www.crops.org/about-crops/genetics; Zhang Zhihao, "Crops with Roots in Space Produce Heavenly Results," *China Watch*, presented by China Daily, 2020; K. Matheny, "A fruitless future?," *Cheboygan Daily Tribune*, February 1, 2022.

3   William S. Klug and Michael R. Cummings, *Concepts of Genetics* (New Jersey: Pearson, 2003)

4   NIH website, "The Human Genome Project," last updated September 2, 2022, https://www.genome.gov/human-genome-project; en.wikipedia.org/wiki/100,000_genomes_project.

5   NIH website, "Chapter 4, Newborn Screening," accessed February 2021, https://www.ncbi.nlm.nih.gov/books/NBK132148/.

6   *Popular Science*, August 2014, 53-55.

7   *Detroit Free Press*, February 2. 2016, 2A.

8   Thomas Gaj, Charles A. Gersbach and Carlos F. Barbas, "ZFN, TALEN, and CRISPR/Cas-based methods for genome engineering," *Trends in Biotechnology*, Volume 31, Issue 7, July 31, 2013, 397-405.

9   *Bloomberg Businessweek*, June 25, 2015.

10 *Popular Science*, March/April 2016, 35.

11 David Cyranoski and Sara Reardon, "Chinese scientists genetically modify human embryos," *nature* online; published on web, April 22, 2015, https://www.nature.com/articles/nature.2015.17378.

12 Tim Murphy, "Re-programming Mother Nature," *Brown Alumni Monthly*, November/December 2019, 16-17.

13 *NBC News*, October 7, 2020.

14 Alice Par, "Controversial New Way to Make a Baby," *Time*, May 18, 2015, 43-46.

15 *Bloomberg Businessweek*, March 7-13, 2016.

16

CANCER

CANCER IS ONE of God's most challenging human ailments. There are over 100 different types of cancer; probably every body tissue is subject to one or more types of cancer, an intimidating fact. Some of the names of cancers are themselves intimidating, for example, pheochromocytoma, myeloproliferative neoplasm, Langerhans cell histiocytoma, acute lymphoblastic leukemia, atypical teratoid/rhabdoid tumor, gestational trophoblastic disease, and more. Cancers are seen worldwide and thus most if not all languages will have names for the various types. Cancers are usually named in two ways, either after the organ or tissue in which it is found or by the cell type which becomes cancerous. Some of the most well-known types of cancer are lung, breast, ovarian, bladder, liver, colon/rectal, kidney, blood (leukemia, lymphoma, etc.), pancreatic, bone, uterine, brain, prostate, and thyroid. About 10-15% of cancers are rare cancers, seen in only a small number of patients.[1] Most cancers are caused by (linked to) environmental or genetic factors (see below) but many cancers have unknown causes. Pancreatic cancer makes up 3 % of all cancers but is on the rise because increased obesity and diabetes, both of which are risk factors. Just 9% of pancreatic cancer patients survive for longer than 5 years after diagnosis. Only colon cancer has a higher rate of death and pancreatic cancer may soon overtake colon cancer. The islet cells of the pancreas make a hormone, insulin, and the pancreas is thus an endocrine organ. These insulin producing cells can give rise to a deadly but rare form of cancer.[2]

There are many different cancers the names of which often have the suffix "oma" which means mass or cancer. Here are some: Myeloma is cancer of the myelin sheath cells and is often expressed in the brain. Neuroblastoma is cancer involving neurons. Melanoma is cancer of the skin melanocytes. Lymphoma is cancer of the lymph cells. Mesothelioma is cancer of the cells that line the lungs. We can add many more cancers named for the tissue in which they are found, such as lung cancer and small-cell lung cancer, cancers of the kidney, cancers of the digestive tract (mouth, tongue, esophagus, stomach, pancreas, small and large intestines, and colon.) There are many different cancers involving the blood. There are cancers of muscle, breast, ovary, cervix, and testicles. The list goes on and on. Each of these cancers exhibits a set of symptoms and specialists for each type of cancer carry out the diagnosis and treatment protocol. Some cancers are deadly early on while others can be treated with irradiation and chemotherapy. New drugs have been developed that target certain types of cancer.

With many cancers, surgery is utilized to remove the cancer or the entire cancerous organ. A person may die of some other cause while carrying a cancer, such as a neuroblastoma. If such a person dies and goes to Heaven, God would have to recognize that a neuroblastoma is present and then kill off the offending cells. Perhaps an accident is the cause of death of the person with the neuroblastoma. Would God be aware prior to that person's death that a neuroblastoma is present? In one mid-western state over 60,000 people died of cancer in 2012; that is about 180 every day. In that state in 2012 cancer was diagnosed in almost 155,000 people with lung, breast, prostate, and colon/rectal cancers as the most frequently diagnosed, in that order.[3] The year 2020 showed a record decline in the USA cancer death rate, attributed to success against lung cancer, in incidence and cure rate. But cancer remains the number two leading cause of death. An estimated 609,000 Americans died from cancer in 2021, an average of over 1,670 each day.[4]

Imagine the challenge to God in diagnosing the type of cancer in these deceased individuals, identifying the causative agent, and curing the cancer. Consider that 1.6 million Americans are newly diagnosed cancer patients each year. Thus, many people likely die of causes other than the cancer that they carry. In these deceased individuals God would presumably recognize that a cancer exists, and he would cure it. But how would he recognize the cancer in a dead body? And how would he cure the cancer in that restored body in Heaven, after years of decomposition of the tissues or after cremation here on earth? Does the soul carry cancer?

Let's look more closely at one type of cancer, cancer of the lung; lung cancer is the top cancer-killer worldwide with 1.7 million deaths each year; 90% of lung cancer patients die from it.[5] There are three types of lung cancer, each with its peculiar characteristics. In the USA about 160,000 lung cancer deaths occur each year (440 every day).[6] Studies show that 85% of lung cancers can be attributed to smoking and nearly 40% of Americans are current or former smokers. Smoking has many adverse effects on health. Each day, more than 3,200 youths smoke their first cigarette. The nicotine in tobacco smoke is terribly addictive. Proposals have recently been made to make cigarettes with a lower level of nicotine, thus perhaps fewer people will get addicted and avoid the carcinogens generated from burning the tobacco. The estimation is that 5.6 million of today's children and teens will die prematurely in adulthood because of smoking, mostly from lung cancer. Already in 1964 the surgeon general declared that smoking increases deaths. Yet, since then, over twenty million people in the USA have died of smoking-related diseases including diseases caused by secondhand smoke. Even though it is more likely for a smoker to get lung cancer than a non-smoker, non-smokers can also get lung cancer. Thus, smoking is not the only cause of lung cancer. Nor can it be predicted who is going to get lung cancer or when the cancer will begin.

Of women with lung cancer, 24% are non-smokers. Of men with lung cancer, 15% are non-smokers. Lung cancer incidence has increased in women over the past 20 years whether or not they smoke, a troubling trend that is under study.[7]

There is good news concerning finding and treating lung cancer and causing death rates to drop; advances have been made in refinements in surgery, diagnostic screening, diagnosing by advanced bronchoscopy, and treating by targeted stereotactic ablative radiation. Genetic testing can identify cancer cell mutations allowing targeted immunotherapy using newer pharmaceuticals.[8] When a person dies of lung or any other cancer one can wonder if when that person is resurrected how God will know the cause of death and how he will rid the cancer from that formerly decomposed body which has been in the grave for countless years. Even more challenging will be for God to restore a body from cremains!

Now consider the challenge to God when a person dies who is a smoker but does not have full-blown lung cancer; God will be expected to know that the person is a smoker and whether a single lung cell or several cells are pre-cancerous (destined to give rise to cancer) and what the change is in that cell, for example if a mutation has occurred that will ultimately result in uncontrolled cell division. Then God must take the necessary steps to prevent the cancer from arising in that person in Heaven.

Another challenge to God is the person who decides to end their life because they have a terminal cancer, and the treatment to attempt to control it has ravaged his or her body. These situations, referred to as assisted dying, are now legal in 6 states plus the District of Columbia. The patient does not die from the cancer but instead from a combination of drugs, administered by a physician. God has to recognize that the person had a terminal cancer or other fatal disease and has to cure that condition and deal with the assisted dying situation as well.[9]

We can consider a similar but even more difficult challenge to God with regard to mesothelioma, cancer of the lining of the lungs, which is associated with asbestos exposure and cigarette smoke. Here, a person may have had a job which resulted in exposure to asbestos (construction/plumbing) decades ago. The cancer is like a time bomb not knowing when it is going to arise but different in that not everyone exposed to asbestos gets mesothelioma. A fellow sued his former company in 2016 because he got mesothelioma but was not awarded any money because it had been more than 10 years since the exposure. Did God know that this fellow had been exposed and that he was going to get the cancer? What if he had died before the cancer arose? Would God have corrected the cancer-causing "defect" so he would be healthy in Heaven? If he died because of the cancer, God would have the challenge of removing or killing the cancer cells so that his lungs would be healthy in Heaven. Will there be cigarette smoke, asbestos and other carcinogenic chemicals in Heaven?

Metastatic cancer is a great challenge to cancer scientists and to medical doctors treating these patients. Metastatic cancer is cancer that has spread from its tissue/organ of origin to begin growths in other locations. Many people die not from the original cancer but from metastatic cancer. Among people diagnosed with early stage breast cancer, up to 30% will develop recurrent, metastatic cancer and die; a total of 40,000 deaths from metastatic breast cancer occur each year.[10] A woman can have a double mastectomy, chemotherapy, lymph node removal, irradiation, and hormone treatment and the cancer can still come back, often somewhere other than the breast, such as in the brain.[11] God will have to find every cancer cell that has escaped the original breast tissue cancer and rid the body of those cancerous cells. Investigators reported in 2017 that the key to cancer metastasis was found to be related to the density of cells within the tumor. When a tumor reaches a certain level of density, the cells release two proteins called Interleukin 6 and Interleukin 8, which tell some of the tumor cells to break away and go to other body places. Drugs that inhibited the interleukin receptors prevented much of the metastasis in mice. Thus radiation/treatment of the tumor in its original location might be more efficient.[12]

One hundred people die each year in the USA from melanoma alone. There are 4 stages. The cancer starts in the skin (stages 1 and 2), moves to the lymph nodes (stage 3) and then to vital organs such as the brain and liver (stage 4).[13] When these people get to Heaven, God will presumably cure their bodies of cancer, even if it has metastasized to the brain or elsewhere. What if a person dies with melanoma in an early stage without showing symptoms. Will God recognize that early stage and remove those early-stage cancer cells? If so, how does he do it?

Cancer investigators now recognize that many, if not most, cancers are caused by mutations in genes that result in their protein products behaving wrongly, either to no longer prevent abnormal cell growth or to enhance abnormal cell growth. These changes in genes are of two types. There are genetic changes that can be inherited from parents which are called *germline mutations*. A second type are *somatic mutations*, which can arise in any cells of the body and are associated with aging, diet, sun exposure, or chemicals in the environment, such as carcinogens in tobacco. Somatic mutations are the cause of most cancers.[14] Cancers shed cells and molecules into the blood and scientists have developed tests, called liquid biopsies, that can detect these cancer molecules. The type of molecule provides information as to what gene is mutated and thus what kind of cancer it is. Treatments and possible cures can then be planned. In the summer of 2020, the US Food and Drug Administration approved two blood-based tests, developed by two different companies, one that tracks 55 genes involved in solid tumors and another that analyzes 300 additional cancer-related genes.[15] Blood unfortunately is replaced by embalming fluid by the funeral home and would not be available for God to examine. Perhaps God could collect a sample of a person's blood immediately upon death. Or maybe God monitors everyone's blood on a daily schedule.

In the USA 110 women die each day from breast cancer, one every 13 minutes; much research is being directed at diagnosing and curing this cancer.[16] The slogan of the research efforts is "breast cancer is unacceptable" and the goal is to reduce the number of breast cancer deaths by half in the USA by 2026. An important advance was the discovery of two genes in association with breast cancer, the BRCA1 and BRCA2 genes. The mutant forms of these genes result in the bodies inability to adequately repair damaged DNA thus leading to cancer cell growth. Subsequently, these two genes were shown to be connected with ovarian cancer as well. Then in 1995 the search began for other breast cancer genes. Researchers now have a more complete picture of the genes that are involved in breast cancer.[17] A team looked at the genetic code in 560 breast cancers and found 93 sets of genes that if mutated, can cause breast cancer. This form of research can target specific genes for drug treatments and thus can lead to more personalized treatments for cancer. The Food and Drug Administration has so far approved 30 tests for specific mutations involved in cancer therapy.[18] Gene testing for these two mutations is highly recommended so that women with either mutation can take steps to lower their risk of breast cancer. Another gene associated with breast cancer is the HER2 gene. Each year about 50,000 women are diagnosed with the HER2 form of breast cancer; most are curable. But breast cancers that are HER2-positive are particularly aggressive and can metastasize to other parts of the body, including the brain, and in those cases the patient is most often not cured and dies. A twice daily pill called Tukysa™, developed by Seattle Genetics, is showing encouraging signs of fighting these HER2-positive cancers that have spread.[19]

Researchers have searched for other mutant genes in other cancers. Two of these are the BRAF gene in melanoma and the KRAS gene in colon-rectal cancer. Few cancers are caused by inherited gene mutations. Most are caused by somatic cell mutations associated with environmental factors including body weight, diet, smoking, alcohol, asbestos, and lack of exercise.[20] Unfortunately there is an "overlap" between breast cancer and heart disease.

Radiation therapy for breast cancer can lead to blocked heart arteries, problems with the heart valves, and irregular heart rhythms. Likewise, chemotherapy for breast cancer can weaken the heart and lead to blood clots and high blood pressure. Women may have breast cancer but die from heart disease or may die of breast cancer but already have heart disease. The good thing is that exercise and a healthy diet are preventative for both cancer and heart disease.[21] Will God ensure an environment in Heaven that is healthy and how will he do that while dealing with the billions of people there?

Diagnosing cancer: blood tests can identify molecules in the blood, called biomarkers, that are an indication of lung cancer. Chemicals in the breath can show a profile indicative of certain cancers. Saliva swabs can show changes from normal and are indicative of lung or air passage cancer. Screening, such as by digital mammography, can detect breast cancer. If cancer is detected in the breast, the patient must decide whether to have surgery, such as by lumpectomy, followed by chemotherapy, and whether to have reconstructive surgery or to accept a flat chest. Some women choose reconstructive surgery, with or without nipple reconstruction, and now can have tattoo art on the reconstructive breast if desired.[22] Will God restore the breast? Will it be necessary for a woman to have breasts in Heaven? Some women say their breasts do not define who they are and may opt not to have reconstructive surgery. History affects whether a woman will have breast cancer: age at first menstruation, number of children, age at menopause, amount of body fat, and general health.[23] One would hope that God would consult with all Heaven residents having had cancer surgery with regard to whether they want that tissue/organ renewed.

Colorectal, breast, and prostate tests for cancer are soon to be approved.[24] The PIK3CA mutation is in several types of cancer but most often in endometrial cancer (uterine cancer). Mutations like this can now be targeted by specific drugs. If you have lung cancer, knowing your genetic code is important. Maybe 4 % of the people with lung cancer will have a genetic marker called the ALK gene translocation and can be treated with a drug made by Pfizer that shrinks these tumors in up to 60% of the patients. But only about 3% of cancer patients get genetic screening of their tumors – physicians are not trained to deal with genetic screening and there is a large cost. A new company has been started, Human Longevity, which is involved in sequencing about 40,000 genomes in 2016 and a million by 2020. There are now over 125 genetic variants that have been identified in 12 types of cancer.

Thirteen years and 2.7 billion dollars were required to sequence the first human genome; the sequence was completed in 2003. Great promise was expected with regard to human health and that promise is now being realized.[25] One reason is because a genome can now be sequenced in less than a week and for only $1000 dollars. But money is still a requirement and there is a need for lots of it. The more research laboratories involved the better. A large amount of money, $250 million, was donated in 2016 by billionaire Sean Parker, the founder of Napster (music file sharing), co-founder of Plaxo, Causes, Airtime and Brigade, and the first president of Facebook. The money is going to 5 of the top cancer research centers, including Sloan Kettering Memorial and Stanford University. Johns Hopkins University received $125 million from Michael Bloomberg and other philanthropists. These funds are directed to further research into immunotherapy treatment of cancer patients. Parker complains that immune therapy should be moved up from "last resort" to "front-line" in treating cancer. The new Parker Institute for Cancer Immunotherapy in San Francisco will fund "high risk best ideas" that might not have a chance for funding from other sources. The Parker Institute will coordinate cancer research across 6 cancer centers. Parker admits to always being interested in the immune system because of his constant battle with allergies and asthma. Major league baseball has supported the "Stand Up to Cancer" mission which has funded cancer research and treatments.[26]

The immune system can work against cancer as evidenced in the following cases: Case One: the patients own immune cells are genetically enhanced to attack and destroy the cancer cells by a procedure called "chimeric antigen receptor T-cell therapy." Case Two: which has been utilized in melanoma patients, a vaccine is generated to then "immunize" the patient against their cancer. [27] So far these immunotherapy methods have been restricted to only melanoma and non-Hodgkin's lymphoma patients. Pending more research dollars, many more human trials may soon be started to attack additional cancers. Already the FDA has approved over a dozen immunotherapy agents for a range of cancers.[28] These newly developed cancer treatments, which involve both DNA sequencing of the cancer cell's DNA and then genetically engineering cancer-fighting immune cells, are reasons for some optimism.[29] Will God use these new methods along with the traditional radiation and chemotherapy treatments?

The saddest cases of cancer are those seen in children. In the case of childhood leukemia, a cancer of blood cells, there is relatively good news as 90% of the cases can be cured. Much more devastating is Diffuse Intrinsic Pontine Glioma (DIPG), a cancer of the glial cells of the child's brain stem, the pons, which controls breathing, blood pressure, and heart rate.[30] Glial cells are the cells that surround and support the neurons. There are at least a half dozen different cancers of glial cells, DIPG is one of them. In this cancer only 1% of the cases survive 5 years after diagnosis. If a child exhibits symptoms of DIPG, 3 tests are carried out: computerized tomography (CT scan), magnetic resonance imaging (MRI) and magnetic resonance spectroscopy (MRS). From the findings of these tests and depending on the child's age, health, tolerance of the child for treatments, and extent of the cancer, treatments are begun which are generally radiation and experimental chemotherapy. Surgery is not possible with DIPG. In 2017 a mutated gene called PTEN was discovered that seems to be associated with the growth of this cancer and offers cautious optimism towards a future treatment. These kids are entering Heaven at a very young age with brains ravaged by cancer. These childhood cancers will present monumental challenges for God. Why doesn't God prevent cancers in children or at least cure the cancers when they do form in children? Why not let these kids grow up on earth with family, friends, and schools?

Efforts to understand and cure childhood cancers are underway at St. Jude Children's Research Hospital in Memphis, TN.[31] A researcher there explains the approach to having a child's cancer cell DNA sequence compared with the sequence of normal cells. What has been learned is shown on a circle plot. Around the outside of the circle plot is something that looks like a colorful bar code. Inside, a series of city skylines. Through the center are colored arcs. The diagram represents everything that could go wrong in a child's cell to cause cancer. The circular visualization shows real mutations found in 3,000 pediatric cancers at St. Jude's, and includes gene sequence mutations, structural variations, too many or too few gene copies, and chromosome cross connections or rearrangements. Another idea being pursued at St. Jude's is that the microbiome (the 40 trillion bacteria in a 150 lb. person) is involved in cancer treatment. Still another factor is diet. What a person eats, their exercise regimen, and general living habits, can affect the risk of cancer.[32]

Each day worldwide 6,580 people die of lung cancer and another 2325 die of liver cancer. That is 6,983 deaths every day for just those two cancers.[33] Where is God housing all these souls of deceased cancer patients? Will they all ultimately receive new lungs and/or livers? Or completely new bodies?

A quarterly magazine, Cure, provides cancer updates, treatments, research progress reports, and education.[34] God has the challenge of keeping up on all these topics.

Not only will God have challenges in diagnosing and curing cancer of the deceased who are in Heaven but also in insuring that no cancer-related genes are present in the residents of Heaven and that environmental carcinogens are absent. Consider the billions of people who are already in the intermediate Heaven and will ultimately be in the new-earth Heaven; these are formidable challenges for God. How is God maintaining the cancer history of the deceased if their bodies are decayed, lost or burned? It does not seem likely that the soul carries the cancer history of the deceased. The brain, face and body carry a person's uniqueness. Residents of Heaven would want their uniqueness but be free of cancer!

NOTES

1   American Cancer Society website, Cancer Facts & Figures 2018, accessed March 2020, https://www.cancer.org/research/cancer-facts-statistics/all-cancer-facts-figures/cancer-facts-figures-2018.html; Michelle Crouch, "13 things genius scientists wish you knew about cancer," Reader's Digest, September 2016, 118-122.

2   K.J. Shamus, "Pancreatic Cancer," Detroit Free Press, March 30, 2019, 8A; Detroit Free Press, August 16, 2019, 1A.

3   Cheboygan Daily Tribune, August 3-4, 2013.

4   Cheboygan Daily Tribune, January 14, 2021, B6.

5   *Cheboygan Daily Tribune*, August 3-4, 2013; M. Chafkin, "Robots Could Replace Surgeons in the Battle Against Cancer," *Bloomberg Businessweek*, April 2, 2018, 28-30.

6   A. Sifferlin, "Surviving Lung Cancer," *Time*, August 12, 2013; 2018 Cancer Guide, *Detroit Free Press*, August 19, 2019.

7   *Time*, November 18, 2019, 27.

8   *Parade Magazine*, December 1, 2019, 8; *Detroit Free Press*, January 9, 2020, 19A.

9   *People*, October 21, 2019, 89-91.

10 *Detroit Free Press*, June 8, 2014; MBCAlliance website, accessed February 2020, https://www.mbcalliance.org.

11 Kate Pickert, "The Overlooked," *Time*, October 14, 2019, 48-52.

12 *Detroit Free Press*, June 25, 2017, 9A.

13 AIM at Melanoma website, accessed March 2020, https://www.aimatmelanoma.org; Carie Wells, "Researchers say they have unlocked key to cancer metastasizing and how to slow it," *Detroit Free Press*, June 25, 2017, 9A.

14 Jessica Wapner, "Why Gene Tests for Cancer Don't Offer More Answers," *Scientific American*, September 1, 2016.

15 A. Park, "Why doctors are turning to the blood to learn more about tumors," *Time*, October 19, 2020, 25.

16 Susan G. Komen website, accessed February 2020, Komen.org/unacceptable.

17 *Detroit Free Press*, May 3, 2016.

18 Jessica Wapner, "Why Gene Tests for Cancer Don't Offer More Answers," *Scientific American*, September 1, 2016; *Detroit Free Press*, October 16, 2016, 2F.

19 *Detroit Free Press*, April 18, 2020, 9A.

20 *Detroit Free Press*, May 23, 2016, 5A.

21 *Cheboygan Daily Tribune*, February 25, Tuesday, A5.

22 *Cure magazine*, Spring, 2019, Volume 18, 68.

23 McLaren Northern Michigan Hospital pamphlet on Breast Cancer Awareness; *Cheboygan Daily Tribune*, October 18, 2019.

24 *Bloomberg Businessweek*, October 13-19, 2014, 39.

25 *Bloomberg Businessweek*, October 13-14, 2014, 84-85; *Popular Mechanics*, June 2017.

26 Stand Up to Cancer website, accessed February 2020, https://standuptocancer.org/?s=MLB.

27 *Bloomberg Business*, August 5-11, 2013.

28 *Reader's Digest*, September 2016, 118.

29 Robin Marantz Henig, "Could Immunotherapy Lead the Way to Fighting Cancer?" *Smithsonian Magazine*, April 2018, 44-55; Alice Park, "After Cancer

Took His Mother, James Allison Taught Our Immune Systems How to Fight It," *Time,* February 17, 2020, 16-17.

30 Detroit Free Press, November 12, 2015, 2C; Boston Children's Hospital website, accessed February 2020, https://www.childrenshospital.org/conditions-treatments; Dana Farber Boston's Children's Hospital website, accessed February 2020, https:// www.danafarberbostonchildrens.org/

31 *Popular Mechanics,* June 2017.

32 Life Styles section, "The Cancer Guide," *Detroit Free Press,* August 18, 2019, 1Q-4Q.

33 "Lung & Liver Cancers," *Bloomberg Businessweek,* April 2, 2018, 28.

34 *Cure,* Winter 2020, Volume 19.

17

DISABILITIES

A DISABILITY IS a physical or mental impairment that substantially limits one or more major life activities.[1] Disabilities can show up at the time of birth or at any time after that, all the way to old age. In the USA, of non-institutionalized persons, 49 million are disabled; just about one in five of the population has some kind of disability. Twenty-four million persons in the USA have a severe disability. Worldwide there are 1 billion disabled people. Of those under five years of age 0.8 % are disabled; of persons five to seventeen years of age, 7.2% are disabled; of persons seventeen years of age and older, 9.2 % are disabled. Disabled people suffer from difficulties with hearing, vision, cognition, self-care, movement (ambulation) and independent living. Many disabilities such as autism, cystic fibrosis, and mental retardation adversely affect learning in the young but in the aged disabilities adversely affect mobility. Disabilities are thus categorized as mental or physical or sometimes both.[2] (Note that disabilities are also discussed in Chapters 14 and 18)

Some disabilities are recognized already at birth or shortly after. One of these disabilities is Joubert Syndrome,[3] which is a rare autosomal recessive genetic disorder that has an adverse effect on the development of the cerebellum, the part of the brain that controls movement, coordination and balance. The cerebellum can be entirely missing. The brain stem can also be affected. Other effects of Joubert Syndrome are cognitive delays, cleft palate, breathing difficulties, extra toes and fingers (polydactyly), abnormalities in the face, retina, kidney, liver, skeleton, and the endocrine system. About thirty gene mutations are associated with Joubert Syndrome and the chromosome locations of twenty of these are known. Only one is on the X chromosome. Joubert is considered one of the ciliopathies because it affects the cilia of many different cell types. In the worst cases of Joubert, kids never crawl, walk, talk, or eat and have difficulty sleeping and even breathing. They die sometimes within weeks of birth. A similar syndrome is Dandy-Walker Syndrome which also affects the cerebellum and is another ciliopathy but is less-well characterized.[4] Another rare condition is holoprosencephaly, in which case the entire brain is missing.[5] The parents of one of these severely disabled newborns will still love him/her. Death often occurs within days, or at most, weeks.

Blindness is certainly disabling; one condition leading to blindness is Leber Congenital Amaurosis (LCA), caused by a genetic mutation influencing the retina. The gene was identified and sequenced and a "normal" copy of the gene can now be injected into the eye of a person with LCA and in most cases the blindness is cured. Fortunately, it is a small gene and affects a "friendly" area to examine and treat, i.e., the retina. Most mutant genes are not so easy to treat. Other treatments for genetic diseases include stem cell and bionic implants. The most common cause of blindness in the world is cataract formation, very correctable if the medical expertise is available.[6] These disablities represent many challenges for God in diagnosing and correcting the genetic mutation and the physical deformity and disability.

Non-religious parents will sometimes have their disabled children baptized, thinking that would insure the child had a soul which would reach Heaven. Parents with disabled children most often say, "She/he is now in a better place." After her son died, one mother said, "I was robbed of the child I wanted. I was robbed of the child I loved." Having a child that has holoprosencephaly, born without a brain, parents will still love the child, even if the child lives only a day or two. A disabled child may have multiple surgeries, sometimes almost one a month, in an effort of the parents to have the child eat, walk, and talk.[7]

Cerebral Palsy (CP) refers to any disability that is caused by damage to the cerebrum before birth or any time within the first 3 years of life. The extent of the disability varies greatly. One CP individual, call him Eddy, is only 4 feet tall, has hands and arms but they are only 30% functional. He can only walk with hand-held crutches or ambulates with a wheelchair. He is bright, received his Ph.D., has published several journal articles, and now teaches in college. Asked what he would like in Heaven from God he said, "arms that are 100% functional." Static encephalopathy (SEnC) is similar to CP, varying from severe to mild in symptoms.[8]

The Charge Syndrome is a rare autosomal dominant genetic disorder. The mutant gene is on one of the twenty-two pairs of autosomes and one copy is sufficient to cause the disorder. The wildtype (normal) gene on the other chromosome is not sufficient to override the effect of the mutation. The mutation is in the chromodomain of the helicase DNA-binding protein -7 (CHD7) gene. The Charge Syndrome is accompanied by coloboma, a hole in the iris and/or retina of one or both eyes. Many organs and tissues are adversely affected in the Charge Syndrome including the brain, heart, nose and throat, genital tract, ear and more. Surgery on the heart increases the life expectancy and other surgeries can help the patient to succeed in walking, talking, and eating, but mental retardation still occurs. Charge persons live from one year or less, to five years of age, and even to seventy-five years if surgery is successful.[9]

Hydrocephalus and spina bifida both lead to disabilities. Hydrocephalus is a condition of water on the brain, really cerebrospinal fluid (CSF), not water as such. This abnormal accumulation of fluid puts pressure on the brain. The condition can be congenital (genetic or uterus effects) or acquired during life caused by injury or stroke. Of all pediatric hospitalizations, 0.6% are due to hydrocephalus. Genes, spinal tube defects, spina bifida, encephalocele, diabetes, hemorrhage, meningitis, cancer, or injury can contribute to hydrocephalus. Symptoms associated with this condition which would not be tolerated in Heaven, are headache, vomiting, sleepiness, irritability, seizures, nausea, vision problems, coordination problems, incontinence, memory loss, and slow developmental progress. The condition can be fatal. The main treatment is to put a shunt into the brain and drain excess CSF but there are many complications with shunts. The Hydrocephalus Clinical Research Network is involved in researching this condition.[10]

Every day in the USA eight babies are born with spina bifida (SB). SB is a birth defect wherein the neural tube does not close properly in the embryo stage, leading to one or more protrusions of the spinal cord as development continues. The spinal cord normally closes on the twenty-eighth day of pregnancy, but many factors might result in incomplete closure: environmental factors in the uterus, low folate in the mother, family history, medications, diseases (diabetes, meningitis) and obesity (mother). Mothers having had two previous children with SB have an increased chance of another SB child. More SB is seen in white and Hispanic female babies. SB affects walking and mobility, the legs and spine are disfigured, scoliosis is seen, bowel and bladder control are affected.[11] What a challenge for God.

One mother after surgery to correct cleft palate in her child commented, "Who is this baby? I loved the old one." The question is whether surgeries "hide" or "disguise" the disability/disfiguration that is still there. Should we strive for "normality?" Hitler tried this by murdering 270,000 people with disabilities. Many countries and states have passed laws to keep the "unsightly" from public view. Where should a line be drawn? Consider people who are obese, anorexic, deaf, blind, are addicts, bipolar, have AIDS, or have cancer and on and on? It is perhaps vital that we cling to our own lives with all the challenges, limitations, and particularities, including disabilities. We need differences for evolution to occur. Genetic variation is important for survival of all populations, microbial, plant, and animal. What is better? To be born with disabilities or not to be born at all? God will have to decide what to do in each individual case, perhaps with input from family members and the wishes of the deceased.[2]

About 85% of disabled children live with their parents until their parents become disabled or die. The parents of the severely disabled sometimes have the child's breasts, uterus, and ovaries removed. They want the child to remain small and immature, so they are able more easily to lift and ambulate the child as they care for the child. Roughly half the children put up for adoption are disabled. Parents want "typical" children. Having a physically or mentally disabled child is stressful and ages parents ahead of time.[2]

Mental illness is increasing in frequency in every country in the world. Many people in the world are receiving psychotherapy for a variety of mental issues, including depression, obsessive compulsive disorder, phobias of various kinds (fear of flying, heights, dogs), post-traumatic stress disorder, suicidal thoughts, attention deficit disorder, attention deficit hyperactivity disorder, other mental illnesses, and more.[12] Most often the treatment involves modern cognitive behavioral therapy, with 10-20 weekly sessions with a therapist. Now short-course therapy is being recommended which involves education, understanding, tolerance, and accelerated relief.[13] A person's mental health is becoming more and more recognizable and acceptable by individuals, family, friends, and employees. How will God deal with all these conditions? Except for suicide, most mental conditions are not the cause of death but may lead to death. If for example someone dies of a heart attack, will God recognize that the person also had one or more mental conditions and then make sure that the person is free of that condition in Heaven?

Depression has become a common and debilitating condition and is now one of the main causes of disability worldwide. Together with anxiety, depression costs the global economy over $1 trillion a year in lost productivity. The World Health Organization estimates there are 300 million people suffering from depression in the world. Among millennials (ages 24-39) depression is the fastest growing health condition in the USA. Employers (companies/workplaces) are more and more recognizing depression as a serious health condition and over 60% of employees feel comfortable discussing their mental health at work. There are different forms of depression including Major Depression, Persistent Depression, and Bipolar Depression. Some of the indications of depression include low self-esteem, tiredness, sleep problems, abuse, diseases (diabetes, cancer), family history, and addictions. Youth are exhibiting higher numbers of mental health issues, including depression and anxiety, which can lead to suicide. Suicide is the third leading cause of death for fifteen- to nineteen-year-olds in the USA. Childhood trauma, referred to as adverse childhood experiences, is one of the leading causes of depression in young people.[14] The Bible says there will be no sadness and no pain in Heaven which means that God will have to diagnose depression in the deceased and rid the person of this debilitating ailment. But how? Will he "clean up" the brain? Will he rid the brain's memories of adverse childhood experiences? God should recognize that deaths from suicide are likely caused by depression. But many people hide their depression. If they die from some other illness or an accident, how will God know they were depressed?

Consider that 151,000 people die in the world every day and one in five is disabled; that means 30,000 disabled people die every day in the world. These are people of different ages (birth to old age), living in different countries, speaking and writing different languages, and exhibiting different disabilities.[15] How will God decide how to process these people? Will each soul carry with it the disabled condition? Will God have a "blueprint" of the disability, so that when the body and soul are reunited at the resurrection he can then determine what to do? Will he immediately "correct" the disabilities? If so, how will he ensure that family members recognize the formerly disabled person? Will he accept the disabled condition in Heaven?

NOTES

1   K.J. Shamus, KJ, et al., "50 and older eligible for vaccine," *Detroit Free Press*, March 14, 2021, 4A.

2   Institution on Disability website, accessed January 2020, www.disability-compendium.org; Andrew Solomon, *Far From The Tree*, (New York: Scribner, 2012.)

3   NIH website, accessed January 2020, https://rarediseases.info.nih.gov/diseases/6802/joubert-syndrome.

4   Wikipedia website, "Dandy-Walker malformation," last edited October 7, 2022, https://en.wikipedia.org/wiki/Dandy–Walker_malformation.

5   GARD website, "Holoprosencephaly," last updated February 2023, https://rarediseases.info.nih.gov/diseases/6665/holoprosencephaly.

6   David Dobbs, "A Cure In Sight," *National Geographic*, September 2016, 30-53.

7   Solomon, *Far From the Tree*, 962 pages.

8   Musculoskeletal Key website, accessed February 2020, https://musculoskeletalkey.com/static-encephalopathy.

9   GARD website, accessed February 2020, https://rarediseases.info.nih.gov/diseases/29/charge-syndrome.

10 NINDS website, "Hydrocephalus Fact Sheet," last edited March 2023, https://www.ninds.nih.gov/health-information/disorders/hydrocephalus

11 Mayo Clinic website, "Spina bifida," accessed March 2018, https://www.mayoclinic.org/diseases-conditions/spina-bifida/symptoms-causes/syc-20377860.

12 C. Shamus, article on Depression, *Detroit Free Press*, October 9, 2019, 1A.

13 Claudia Wallis, "Psychotherapy in a Flash," *Scientific American*, Volume 320, Issue 4, April 1, 2019, 20.

14 healthline website, accessed March 2020, https://www.healthline.com/health/depression; Mandy Oaklander, "When Every Day is a Mental Health Day," *Time*, February 3, 2020, 73-75.

15 CDC website, accessed March 2020, www.cdc.gov/nchs/fastats/deaths.htm.

18

HEAVEN'S PEOPLE; FAR FROM THE TREE

REVELATION 7:9 TELLS us that in Heaven there will be "a great multitude, which no one could count, of all the nations, and kindreds, and people. and tongues." Certainly that will be a tremendous mixture of different people. On earth we see that people exhibit a range in characteristics such as health, height, weight, personality, intelligence, ability, and language, and we can ask which of these might be in Heaven. Most people on earth fit into an average range on any one characteristic and would be positioned in the main portion of a bell curve with fewer people at the extremes. God might expect the majority of people to be those average types and he would welcome their love, praise, and adoration. But the exceptions, especially those at the extremes of the bell curve, are of most interest to consider, and will be challenges for God. Andrew Solomon identifies ten of these exceptions in his book *Far From the Tree* and in a movie of the same name based on the book.[1] The analogy is to consider a fruit tree in which case most of the fruits fall straight down from the branches and the seeds grow into trees that are easily recognized as that same type of tree producing the same type of fruit, year after year. But some smaller number of seeds produce trees with different fruit, such as being larger and juicier and more flavorful, or smaller and less juicy and flavorful. Thus, the saying, "she/he did not fall far from the tree," means that an individual is very much like the parents. But others fall a long distance from the tree and are much different from the parents and "fell far from the tree." These latter individuals, specifically dwarfs, the deaf, and schizophrenics, are subjects in Solomon's book and this chapter is largely based on that book and movie. Other individuals that Solomon includes as falling far from the tree are Down's Syndrome people, autistics, prodigies, and those with other disabilities. These are discussed in separate chapters.[1]

DWARFS

Dwarfs present many challenges for God in Heaven. Dwarfs can also be referred to as "little people" but the word midgets is not acceptable. Dwarfs are people who do not grow taller than 3 feet and can be much shorter. The world's shortest man died at age seventy-five in 2015 at just twenty-one inches tall. He was from American Samoa. The next shortest man was 23.5 inches tall and lived in the Philippines.[2] On her 18th birthday in 2011, Guinness World Records declared a woman from India to be the world's shortest woman. She is two feet tall and twelve pounds in weight. Her goal is to become an actress. She has many fans and admits, "Fame is fun!"[3]

There are approximately 200,000 little people in the USA and several million worldwide.[1] In Africa, the aka, efe, and mbuti peoples are dwarfs, sometimes called pygmies, each with their own language.[4] On the Island of Flores in Indonesia is a cemetery of little people that was discovered in 2004.[5] Will God give deceased little people "normal" height in Heaven or keep them at their earth height? Would they want to stay as a dwarf? What would the parents want? Where are their souls now? Are their souls little too? Little people present many challenges for God.

Achondroplasia is the most common form of dwarfness and is caused by a mutation in the fibroblast growth factor receptor 3 gene (FGFR3). About 70% of little people fall into this category. These people have short arms and legs, a more typical body, and a large head. Other types of dwarfism are hypochondroplasia, skeletal dysplasia and spondylometaphyseal dysplasia.[1] There are over 200 genetic mutations associated with these forms of dwarfism. Three other genes that when mutated result in dwarfism are the genes for fibroblast growth factor 3 (FGF3), pituitary growth hormone, and collagen type II. The main adverse effect of these latter three mutations is on the growth of the long bones but also seen are mental retardation, hearing loss, depression, spinal column problems, large hips, head too large, arthritis, and jaw, tooth and other abnormalities, more challenges for God. The adverse effects are sometimes seen *in utero* in the fetus; expectant parents abort the pregnancy in roughly ¼ of those pregnancies. How does God deal with these "little" fetuses? Most often the dwarfism shows up at age two or three.[1] A rare subset of dwarfism is Majewski Osteodysplastic Primordial Dwarfism Type II (MOPDII) that at any one time affects only about 100 people in the USA and Canada combined. These dwarfs have proportional growth but are still very small, maybe only 3'6".[6]

Little people have a higher rate of childhood death and later in life a higher rate of depression. There can be discrimination against little people. Some little people have limb lengthening surgery which can result in fourteen inches of added height. Little people can marry average height people or other little people. Often little people married to little people are very happy but can also be happily married to average height people.[7] Little people can be gay or lesbian, can get diseases such as cancer, can be autistic, and can have Down's Syndrome, thus, other than being short, can be like average people, they can have a job, have girl/boyfriends, get married and have children.[1]

Perhaps the most severe form of dwarfism is spondyloepiphyseal dysplasia congenita, in which case the little people have club feet, cleft palate, wide set eyes, a small mouth, and a barrel chest. To correct the physical characteristics some dwarfs undergo as many as 30 surgeries. Some little people have hearing loss, mental retardation, and suffer from depression. Some are in constant pain because of the physical deformities.[1] This form of dwarfism must be particularly challenging for God. It goes without saying that in order to diagnose little people when they die God must be an anatomist, geneticist, molecular biologist, and psychiatrist.

God has several challenges with dwarfs. Is the soul of a little person also little? Will he give them average height or keep them as dwarfs? Will he correct the various physical and mental non-average conditions and the mutated genes seen in little people so that in Heaven the person is more average? Consider that some parents would not change their dwarf children even if they could. Many little people are quite happy. Little people have a yearly get-together, the Little People of America Convention, which is much enjoyed, and boys and girls can make associations. There is also an annual athletic competition for little people, one was at Michigan State University, with 400 little people competing from seventeen countries in many different athletic events.[8]

Will God insure activities for little people in Heaven? What about the fetus that has been aborted that was already exhibiting dwarfism? Will he give that person an average body in Heaven? Will God correct each of the 200 mutant genes as they show up in souls/bodies of little people? How will parents recognize their children in Heaven if they are no longer little?

THE DEAF

The deaf present many challenges for society in life and for God when they die. The Lexington Center for the deaf in Queens, NY,[9] is the most-well known and most highly respected school for the deaf and provides education for 350 students from pre-school to high school. The school is run by the deaf for the deaf. When asked if they might want to change, one student answered, "I am black and deaf and proud and I do not want to be white and hearing." In 1817 the USA had an Asylum for the Education and Instruction of the Deaf in Hartford, Conn. Much progress for deaf people was seen in the next 50 years, mainly due to the French, i.e., Gallaudet, developing sign language and the founding of Gallaudet College in 1857,[9] authorized by President Lincoln to grant degrees to the deaf. Now all but two states have a school devoted to educating the deaf. But still, at the time of WWI, 80% of deaf children were being educated without sign language. A former president of the Natl. Assoc. of the Deaf (NAD) said, "It is my hope that we all will love and guard our beautiful sign language as the noblest gift God has given to deaf people." Sure, God gave humans deafness and then gave the deaf sign language. Really? Are the deaf going to be hearing in Heaven or will there be sign language in Heaven? Every deaf person who enters Heaven should be asked if she/he wants to be hearing.

Sign language is most easily learned when begun early in life. A two-year-old with deaf parents can know 300 words in sign but if the parents are hearing, the child may only know 30 words and have a mental disability from then on. Ability to learn sign language regresses after 36 months and tails off at age 12 but even at 20 yrs. of age one can learn sign language. Deaf children of deaf parents who learn sign language at home as a first language, do better at written English, score higher in other academic areas and are ahead in maturity, social interactions and getting along with strangers. If one of these children were to die in an accident, from disease, or cancer, would God give them English (or French, Spanish, German, Finnish, etc.) or would God have a place for them, with other deaf children or adults, in Heaven? Consider that the deaf love sign language and some words like "milk" are milkier in sign than if spoken. The deaf using sign language can take pleasure in the distinctions between dry, arid, parched, desiccated and dehydrated. Also, a film company begun in 1982 captioned films which showed gun shots, ringing telephones, and doorbells. No sound was left out.[1] Perhaps God will give everyone the ability to understand and use sign language (see Chap. 32). Will God know that sign language on earth is not universal? Each language has its unique sign language.

One of every 1000 newborns in the USA is born completely deaf. Two of every 1000 newborns have partial hearing loss. Three of every 1000 will lose their hearing before age 10. Still others lose hearing as adults, particularly with old age. The children born deaf are "congenital deaf" individuals and 50% of those involve one or more genes.[1] More than 120 genetic mutations are involved in deafness; 1/5 of these mutations are dominant and 4/5 are recessive. At least 1000 of our 20,000 genes affect the ear and hearing.[1] The identification of connexin 26 (GJB2 = gap junction beta 2) being involved in deafness in 1997 was a breakthrough and 26 mutations in this gene are now known. Connexin is a gap junction protein that functions in the cochlea, where sound waves are converted to electrical signals. The connexin 26 gene is located on the long arm of chromosome 13, position 12.11, between base pairs 20,187,463 to 20,192,975.[10] Is God going to understand this type of molecular genetics information in every language on earth?

Most connexin gene associated deaf children are born to hearing parents, with the parents each being heterozygous for the connexin gene.

Heterozygotes have one normal gene and one mutated gene. One normal gene is sufficient for hearing. When two heterozygotes mate, there is a 25% chance of the offspring being hearing and not be carriers of the mutated gene, a 50% chance of being hearing and carrying the mutated gene, and a 25% chance of being deaf and having both copies of the mutated gene. Most deaf (70%) are non-syndromic and thus have no other recognizable characteristics (see above) associated with their deafness and most of these have the autosomal recessive gene in double dose with the remainder having the autosomal dominant gene or having a mitochondrial mutation. The other 30% are syndromic and exhibit other "abnormal conditions" (such as effects on the eyes and face).[1]

Not surprisingly the cochlea is involved in deafness as its gap junctions in the hair cells involve K+ ion relaying and then electrical signaling to the brain's hearing center. Many deaf individuals have cochlear implants, particularly those who at one time were able to hear but then lost their hearing. Cochlear implants are less helpful to someone never having been hearing, unless done before the age of two.[1] God will have to recognize those deceased people who have the implants.

Loss of hearing in the elderly can be due to genetic or environmental causes. When God gives the elderly their thirty-three-year-old bodies he will have to correct the hearing loss.

At the National Association of the Deaf yearly convention, discussion groups include AIDS, gays, domestic violence, and other topics. In other words, deaf people, like dwarfs, have a range of personality, behavioral and physiological characteristics and behaviors.[11]

Will God communicate with the deaf in sign language? Does God know sign language and its variations? Note that there are many different sign languages in the world. One deaf woman said she talks to God only by the thought process, not speech, but even so her thoughts will be in her native sign language. Think about it! Will God understand the thought process if it is in sign language? There are a little over 7,000 languages on earth as of 2021, and there is much concern that half of these will be gone by 2100. Many languages have already become extinct. One that might soon be lost is sign language. But will sign language be in Heaven? When a deaf child enters Heaven, will God assess the cause of deafness as environmental or genetic? If genetic, will God examine the genes and correct the condition, for example replacing the mutated connexin 26 gene with a normal gene? If there will be air and sound in Heaven[12] then hearing will be important unless sign language is available. It does not seem logical that God will provide hearing ability to all of the deaf as there is the experience factor. Music such as Mozart, rock and roll, R&B, experienced as a deaf person would be difficult to comprehend all of a sudden as a hearing person. Sign language is also discussed in Chapter 32.

SCHIZOPHRENIA

One of every 100 people in the USA, about 3 million, have schizophrenia (SP).[1, 13] This mental disease poses several difficult challenges for God as the reader will recognize from the following description and discussion and which will be clearly defined at the end of this section. Schizophrenia (SP) is broadly categorized as someone exhibiting the following symptoms: psychotic hallucinations, psychic disorganization, lack of motivation, loss of language, withdrawal, decrease in functionality in society, and loss of emotional contacts. The SP individual experiences images that are most often terrible and hears voices which sometimes are commands to carry out bad behaviors. But the voices can ultimately in some cases become friends and the SP person may sometimes converse with the voices for hours daily and there may be a concomitant gradual deterioration of personality. The SP individual is ultimately unable to attend school and cannot hold a job. The SP individual is often aware of these changes. SP is a developmental disorder that is inscribed in the brain perhaps even before birth but is degenerative and appears usually at adolescence or later. Like Alzheimer's disease, SP eliminates the former person. Parents, siblings, other family, and friends must deal with the progressive changes and see the SP individual change, literally before their eyes, into another person entirely, at adolescence or later. SP is thus different from Down's Syndrome, which is recognized at or before birth, or autism, which is recognized at 3 or 4 years of age. The young SP individual is often a personable son or daughter, with many friends, talented in school, sports, and/or music, with plans and goals for the future. SP individuals sometimes retain certain memories, even going back to childhood, and can sometimes play sports, like tennis, that they were good at in the past.[1] Will God tolerate SP in Heaven?

The causes of SP have been postulated about since ancient times and rigorously investigated more recently.[1] Both genetic and environmental factors play roles. Because the brain is involved, causes point to the neurotransmitters dopamine (DOPA), glutamate, norepinephrine, serotonin, and GABA; one or more of these neurotransmitters are believed to become deregulated leading to an excess of DOPA in one or more neural pathways. Treatments are often antipsychotic drugs which regulate neurotransmitters and lower DOPA. Sometimes there are undesirable side effects of the drugs. Treatment and care are improved as noted by the number of SP patients in institutions in 1971 being 500,000 whereas in 2000 that number was 170,000. Solomon describes the personal histories of several SP individuals and the challenges associated.[1] Mother and/or fathers will often spend all their waking hours caring for their SP son or daughter. The suicide rate of SP individuals is high, obesity is prevalent, and alcohol and drug use are high.

SP does run in families but the inheritance is not straightforward.[1] A first degree relative with SP is a predictor and increases one's chance of SP by 10%. But even without such a relative SP can appear and parents of an SP individual are usually normal. SP individuals have a low reproductive rate, yet the incidence of SP is staying the same or even increasing. In identical twins, if one twin is SP the chance of the other being SP is 50%, not 100% as might be expected. Clearly environmental factors play a role in incidence. These factors might be childhood head trauma, drug or alcohol abuse. Many causative genes as well as protective genes are believed involved. Parents of a child with one or more of the causative genes will worry and fret about the child's future.

A report of a newly identified gene associated with SP was published in 2013.[14] The critical observation was that the incidence of SP in a remote northern part of Finland was 3%, three times higher than elsewhere in Finland, which is about 1%. This remote region of Finland is home to rural communities that were founded by a small number of families and thus have a restricted genetic background, indicative of inbreeding, as in some animal populations. Sequencing the DNAs of the northern population led to identification of a genetic deletion, 22q11.22, that appeared more often than elsewhere in Finland or in other parts of the world. The gene with the deletion was cloned and studied and named TOP3beta, a gene that codes for a protein called topoisomerase that is involved in messenger RNA translation and transport, directly involved in protein synthesis. Thus, in individuals with the defective gene, the mRNA is malfunctional in the brain tissue, resulting in the neurotransmitter problems, and thus, SP. The investigators have found eight variations in this gene highly associated with SP, giving symptoms from mild to severe. But caution is warranted as environmental factors may be influential as well.

According to the Bible, we can assume that SP individuals would not be present in Heaven. To insure that result, God will be challenged. First, a child not yet showing symptoms of SP may die from an accident, cancer, or other disease who was destined to be SP by his/her genetics or exposure to environmental factors. When God accepts this child into Heaven does he recognize that the child's fate on earth was to be SP? Does he correct the genetic defect in the TOP3beta gene? Does he neutralize the environmental factor, such as head trauma? God will need to have a complete genetic and environmental history of that child. But this assessment will be complicated by the fact that the associated genetic deletion is not a guarantee of SP. God will have to make a determination. Second, in an individual with SP God will have to determine which of the many variations of SP the person has, taking into account the environmental effects, parental and institutional care, if any, and drug treatments, if any. Note that the longer a SP person is on drugs the less effective the drugs become. Third, SP persons are often abusers of drugs and/or alcohol and are obese so God will have to correct for the adverse effects of these factors. Fourth, SP individuals commit suicide at a rate higher than the normal population. Finally, SP individuals commit terrible crimes, including murder(s). Will God forgive these individuals because of their SP and accept them into Heaven? How will God deal with their interactions with their victims in Heaven? If a SP individual largely recovers and has only fleeting symptoms, will God forgive the individual for sins committed during the time SP was running rampant in that person?

NOTES

1   Andrew Solomon, *Far From The Tree*, (New York: Scribner, 2012.); *Far From the Tree*, directed by Rachel Dretzin (2017; Brooklyn, NY: IFC), DVD.

2   Meg Wagner, "World's shortest man dies at 75," *Daily News* online, September 4, 2015, https://www.nydailynews.com/news/world/world-shortest-man-dies-75-article-1.2348805.

3   Emily Strohm, "Meet the World's Shortest Woman," *People*, August 10, 2020, 69.

4   Encyclopedia.com website, accessed November 2019, https://www.encyclopedia.com/humanities/encyclopedias-almanacs-transcripts-and-maps/efe-and-mbuti.

5   nova website, video access no longer available, https://www.pbs.org/wgbh/nova/video/little-people-of-flores/

6   Abdel-Salam GMH, Sayed ISM, Afifi HH, et al. Microcephalic osteodysplastic primordial dwarfism type II: Additional nine patients with implications on phenotype and genotype correlation. *Am J Med Genet A*. 2020;182(6):1407-1420. doi:10.1002/ajmg.a.61585.

7   *People*, May 22, 2017; *People*, June 12, 2017.

8   *Detroit Free Press*, August 9, 2013.

9   Lexington School for the Deaf website, accessed November 2019, www.lexnyc.org/; Wikipedia website, "Gallaudet University," last edited March 21, 2023, https://en.wikipedia.org/wiki/Gallaudet_University.

10 Adi D. Sabag, Orit Dagan, and Karen B. Avraham, "Connexins in hearing loss: a comprehensive overview," *Journal of basic and clinical physiology and pharmacology*, Volume 16, 2-3 (2005): 101-16. doi:10.1515/jbcpp.2005.16.2-3.101.

11 ENT health website, "Genes and Hearing Loss," accessed December 2019, https://www.enthealth.org/be_ent_smart/genes-and-hearing-loss/.

12 Randy Alcorn, *Heaven: A Comprehensive Guide to Everything the Bible Says About Our Eternal Home* (Illinois: Tyndale Momentum, 2004.)

13 Sharecare website, "Understanding Schizophrenia Symptoms and Severity," accessed November 2019, https://www.sharecare.com/mental-health-behavior/understanding-schizophrenia-symptoms-severity.

14 Rachael Rettner, "'Schizophrenia Gene' Discovery Sheds Light on Possible Cause," *Scientific American* online, LiveScience on January 28, 2016, https://www.scientificamerican.com/article/schizophrenia-gene-discovery-sheds-light-on-possible-cause/.

19

PRODIGIES AND
GENIUSES

PRODIGIES ARE CHILDREN who show exceptional ability at an early age, sometimes at two years old and usually before age ten. Their IQ is generally high, but varies from 100-147, as studied in one group of thirty prodigies.[1] What is exceptional is the working memory of these youngsters. A child might come home from church and play the hymns that were played at the church service. A child might be composing music at age five. Another child might be doing complex mathematics at age eight. Another might be fluent in several languages by age ten. Parents are very much involved in supporting the child's ability and providing opportunities for the child to engage in his/her exceptional ability. Sometimes parents "push" the child too much by wanting fame and fortune. There is no obvious delineation between parents supporting, pressuring, and forcing the child to conform to what they imagine and wish for her/him at present and in the future. The child is usually willing to work hard and to practice and study.[2]

Most prodigies are recognized in music, mathematics, and chess – note Mozart, Einstein, and Kasparov – but are seen in many other areas as well. Prodigies have been identified in physics, chemistry, computer science, engineering, literature, art, law, philosophy, evangelism, languages, and athletics.

Prodigies are rarer than persons with disabilities. It has been calculated that one prodigy is born for every 100 million births, at the most, and probably fewer.[3] Creativity and psychosis map to the same area of the brain and both show reduced dopamine D2 receptors in the thalamus. Will God "correct" the brain of the psychotic and save the brain of the prodigy?

A website lists ten prodigies of the twenty-first century; here is the list by number without names and with no priority order:

1. Earned a physics degree at sixteen, now is a Ph.D. student in physics.
2. Carried out a successful surgical procedure at seven years old, now is working on a cure for cancer.
3. Built an atomic fusion device at age fourteen.
4. At three years old could recite the alphabet forward and backwards. Now is working on a Ph.D. in quantum physics.
5. Entered a Ph.D. program in mathematics at age nine.
6. At age eleven won a mental calculation contest against other contestants from 16 countries. Calculated, in his head, the square root of ten six-digit numbers in less than 3 minutes.
7. Played the violin at age two and in a concert at age three.
8. Played piano at age three and composed at age five.
9. Read children's books before one yr. of age; scored 99.9 on the Mensa IQ test.
10. Entered a Ph.D. program in mathematics at age eleven.[4]

Sadly, there have been many prodigies amongst the female sex, but they have not all been allowed to flourish. Sometimes parents would "hold back" their little girl prodigy because of bias against girls and women. Girls were meant to grow up to marry and have children. Will God have these female prodigies develop and use their special talents in Heaven?

Again on the internet one can find a list of prodigies historically, going back into the 1600s.[5] Some of those we are most familiar with are Ludwig Van Beethoven (music), Pablo Picasso (art), Johann Amadeus Mozart (music), Isaac Newton (astronomy), Albert Einstein (mathematics/physics), Tiger Woods (golf), Bobby Fisher (chess), Alan Turing (computers), James Watson (with Rosalind Franklin and Francis Crick; DNA; double helix structure), and Irina Krush (chess). Wikipedia lists 180 prodigies, some alive today, categorized into subject areas. But 180 is not many compared to the total number of people who have died through history. Is that a sufficient number to entertain all the average people? Of the deceased, where are these prodigies today? Are they in Intermediate Heaven? Did God give them bodies? If they are in Heaven as souls without bodies, can they interact in Heaven, and can their special abilities be appreciated? When their original bodies decompose will their genius be lost, or will God somehow restore their brains as He combines their souls with their bodies?

So, what defines a genius? According to Claudia Kalb[6] the truest measure of a genius is when a person's work resonates through the ages and sometimes the single discovery is a meteoric contribution to the field. There might be one main contribution or many. There are many factors believed to contribute to a person's genius, including intelligence, creativity, hard work, and good fortune. Consider some geniuses: Galileo, J. Kepler, Leonardo da Vinci, Confucius, Miles Davis, Charles Darwin, Michelangelo, and Marie Curie (also see list of prodigies above). Some of these were not prodigies in their youth. Note for example that Charles Darwin was quite an ordinary student as a youngster. In other cases, some very bright youngsters did not amount to anything exceptional as adults. The major contribution of most geniuses was not made until they were in their early 30s, rarely after age 40, and often that contribution was not considered significant until decades later. As is the case with prodigies, women geniuses were often suppressed, denied formal education, deterred from advancing professionally, and unrecognized for their contribution. Mozart's older sister showed genius in music too, but her father cut that short when she reached marrying age.

Is genius a product of nature or nurture? It seems that connections between the left and right sides of the brain, in the corpus callosum, might be greater in number in geniuses – where there are 200 million nerve fibers but studies of the sections of the brain of Einstein or of other geniuses have revealed nothing that stands out. No single gene has been identified as relevant to genius, but a study is underway to see if DNA of a genius is unique – this is a study of Leonardo da Vinci, who was an amazing genius, contributing to art (the Mona Lisa and Last Supper paintings), anatomy, engineering, optics, and other areas even though he had simple beginnings being the son of a notary and peasant woman. Mathematics genius Terence Tao, expert in fluid dynamics, says, "what matters is hard work directed by intuition, and a bit of luck!" Certainly if a potential genius is growing up in poverty and oppression there would be little chance for the genius potential to be reached. Darrin McMahon, historian, said, "If genius can be singled out and cultivated and nurtured, what a tragedy that thousands of geniuses or potential geniuses have withered and died."[7] Maybe God will "rescue" these geniuses.

Maybe God will make some of the very young, even embryos and fetuses that die, into prodigies or geniuses. In 2018 two medical institutions reported that problems had occurred with regard to keeping fertilized eggs (zygotes) and early embryos in the frozen state and many if not all had thawed. The cold temperature of liquid nitrogen, -384 degrees F, is critical to keeping these frozen tissues from dying. We may never know the exact number but let us say there were 2,500 that were killed due to the thawing. Women who were saving their eggs, zygotes, or early embryos for possible pregnancies in the near future were understandably upset. Note that in one study of 1,500 frozen eggs, only 9% were used in attempted pregnancies. Apparently the remaining 91% were discarded. Instead of storing eggs, a woman may choose to have the eggs fertilized (in vitro fertilization) and then have the early 100 cell stage embryos stored. Perhaps unfertilized eggs (oocytes) do not yet have souls, but fertilized eggs (zygotes) and early embryos might be expected to have souls. Religious people would assume and certainly hope that God would save the souls of these zygotes and early embryos. Perhaps God will have them all develop in Heaven and have some develop and grow up into prodigies or geniuses. God would have to give all of these individuals, whether or not prodigies, a body. What kind of body? Will God know what kind of brain to give them? How will he provide the nurturing by parents and teachers, the good fortune, the experiences, that are necessary for the development of a prodigy or genius? Each would have to have the proper schooling, parenting, encouragement, and opportunities that prodigies and geniuses have here on earth.[8]

NOTES

1   David Z. Hambrick, "What Makes a Prodigy?," *Scientific American* online, September 22, 2015, https://www.scientificamerican.com/article/what-makes-a-prodigy1/.

2   Andrew Solomon, *Far From The Tree*, (New York: Scribner, 2012.); A. Solomon, "How Do You Raise A Prodigy?," *NY Times Magazine*, November 4, 2012.

3   Jeff Nilsson, Milton Silverman & Margaret Silverman, "The Fate of Child Prodigies," *Saturday Evening Post*, July 7, 2016; David Z. Hambrick, "What makes a child prodigy?," *Scientific American* online, September 22, 2015, https://www.scientificamerican.com/article/what-makes-a-prodigy1/.

4   Merv Crux, "10 Modern Child Prodigies," ListVerse website, edited July 9, 2013, https://listverse.com/2013/07/09/resend-10-modern-child-prodigies/.

5   Wikipedia website, "Child prodigy," last edited March 20, 2023, https://en.wikipedia.org/wiki/Child_prodigy.

6   Claudia Kalb, "What Makes a Genius," *National Geographic*, May 25, 2017.

7   Wikipedia website, "Darrin McMahon," last edited February 6, 2023, https://en.wikipedia.org/wiki/Darrin_McMahon.

8   Walter Isaacson, "The Price of Genius, Alan Turing Story," *Time*, Dec. 1-8, 2014, 66-76; Claudia Kalb, "What Makes A Genius?," *National Geographic*, May 25, 2017.

20

BRAIN

THE BIBLE SAYS God is a spirit and no one has seen him (John 4:24); he is much larger than the earth and everything on it, larger even than the entire universe (2 Corinthians 16: 9); he is omniscient (all knowing) and seeing both evil and good (Psalms 139:4; 1 John 3:20; Proverbs 15:3); he is omnipotent, meaning all powerful (Genesis 17:1; Ps 62:11), and omnipresent, meaning he is everywhere at all times (Jeremiah 23:24). But then the Bible says God created Adam (man) in his own image and he created Eve (woman) from a rib of Adam. (Genesis 1:21). From the Bible then we can picture God, a bearded man sitting on his thrown, looking sort of like Santa but without his corn cob pipe. Presumably, in his Adam-like brain, God has accumulated all the information that has been gathered from the beginning of human history; that would be from the time of primitive humans doing cave drawings and inventing languages, fifteen million years ago, to the present. Estimates of the amounts of information gathered through human history have been reported and are astounding! Consider that the thirty-seven volumes of natural history written by Pliny the Elder in 77 CE would equal 3.06 megabytes in computer data. The entire Encyclopedia Britannica, published in 1768 in three volumes, would add another 3.6 megabytes. The Canon of Medicine adds 7.5 megabytes. The English version of Wikipedia containing 5.5 million articles, adds 27,000 megabytes. Microsoft's brush with an encyclopedia on CD Rom,

1993-2009, called Encarta, adds 1600 megabytes. The entire internet adds 1 followed by 18 zeroes megabytes. Every year another 1.1 zettabytes (1.1 followed by 14 zeroes) is added to the amount of human information.[1] This is an enormous amount of information for God to have accumulated. In what form is God maintaining this information? An electronic form does not seem likely. Since God is spiritual, can he convert this information to a spiritual form? Where and how would God store all this information? The theist answer "I don't know but he does it" hardly seems sufficient.

As the human line of primates evolved, those with the highest brain capacity survived, leading to the line of pre-humans, called humanoids (see chapter 31). The brain of modern humans has a tremendous capacity; there are 85-100 billion neural cells (neurons) in the brain and each neuron has synaptic outgrowths called axons (nerve processes). Neurons interact with other neurons and with other parts of the body via connections at the ends of axons called synapses. A human brain has over 150 trillion synapses.[2] The activity of the brain is electrical, 0.07 volts contained in each neuron which equals the voltage of almost 500 million car batteries.[3] Every day each human brain is loaded, on average, with an estimated 34 gigabytes of added information; this is information reaching the brain through the senses: sight, sound, taste, smell, and touch. The total capacity of a human brain has been estimated to be a quadrillion bytes, an amount that has recently been increased by a factor of ten.[4a]

God being "all knowing" and "everywhere at all times" suggest that he is keeping track of everyone's thoughts and memories and has been doing this through the ages. Currently the earth has over eight billion people and will increase to nine billion within two decades, maybe sooner. Over 108 billion people have already died.[4b] Thus, God presumably has a record of the thoughts, experiences, and memories of some 116 billion people. That is lot of brain capacity to have at hand. In what form does God maintain this information? How does God keep it organized to have each person's information separate and identifiable and be able to keep accumulating additional brain information each day for each person? There are basically two kinds of memory; one is declarative, which is the kind you can put into words, such as names of people and places, your date of birth, social security number, and how to spell ophthalmologist. The second kind is procedural which describes the things you understand but cannot easily put into words such as: swimming, driving a car, eating a grapefruit, and comparing colors.[5] Will God be able to distinguish between the memories in the brains of teachers, doctors, attorneys, pharmacists, auto mechanics, and farmers of different ages and different countries?[5]

There are over 7,000 languages in the world. Some 200 languages have been lost. That is a total of 7,200 languages. Will God restore the brain pathways for each of these languages in the people who spoke them? Or will God give everyone in Heaven the same language? The electrical activity of each person's brain is unique to that person like a fingerprint.[6] How will God restore each person's unique brain in Heaven?

Santiago Ramón y Cajal, born in 1852, crafted detailed illustrations revealing the major pathways, structures and cell types of the brain. Cajal's work led to the understanding that the brain is a vast network of individual neurons and supportive cells. He received the Nobel prize in 1906 and is known as the Father of Neuroscience. This understanding of the brain came 2,000 years after the Bible was written. The brain has three major divisions including the cerebrum, the enlarged upper part with the role of thinking and conscious mental processes; the cerebellum, an enlarged portion behind (dorsal to) the cerebrum and involved in the coordination of muscles and equilibrium; and the medulla oblongata, a somewhat pyramidal portion which continues posteriorly and coordinates brain connections with the spinal cord. The medulla functions to control blood pressure, heart rate, and breathing.[7]

The beautiful, detailed map of the brain developed by the German anatomist, Korbinian Brodmann, in 1909, based on one property, cell arrangement, is still used. But now the brain's divisions have been redefined incorporating 100 properties such as the cerebral cortex thickness and all the wiring and activity involved during various tasks. A total of eighty-three functional regions are now known and almost 100 new ones are predicted with further analysis. Various functions may be pinpointed to a specific region and how that region contributes to brain development, aging, and disease can be understood.[8]

There are dozens of smaller structures important to the mental and physical health of a person. The basal ganglia for example are important to movement, language, and thought, but when degenerating causes Parkinson's disease. The hypothalamus, a pea sized structure of neurons, controls sexual function, hunger, thirst, blood sugar and salts, growth, and sleep, working through the hormones of the pituitary gland.[5]

When kidneys or livers fail, patients can look for transplants from the deceased or even from healthy people who are willing to give up one kidney. Not so with brains. But many people donate their body, including their brain, or just their brain, to research laboratories. The Harvard Brain Tissue Resource Center stores around 3,000 brains. When a donor dies, a pathologist (names are listed in a network) is called who removes the brain from the deceased person, packs it on ice, and a courier picks it up and rushes it to the Brain Center. There the brain is photographed, weighed, examined and cut in half. One half is placed in a fluid that firms it up while the other half is cut into hundreds of small pieces and frozen in liquid nitrogen. The small pieces are sent to laboratories throughout the world and provide enough material for many studies, including Parkinson's and schizophrenia.[3] It seems farfetched to think that God is going to restore the donated brains and bodies of the deceased at the resurrection.

Every year from 150-200 million babies are born in the world. That is over 385,000 births every day, over 16,000 per hour, 260 per minute, four each second.[9] God must stay up to date on these new brains of babies born each day, as they progress through life. (see Jeremiah 1:4-5, before I formed you in the womb I knew you; Psalm 139:13-14). God has to make a record of the information in each of the fifty-seven million brains of people who die each year. Where does God keep all this information and in what form? What about all the embryos that are aborted/miscarried? Be reminded that about 15% of all pregnancies end in miscarriage. Many fertilized eggs fail to implant. Additional embryos and fetuses are aborted. Even a teenager's brain is only 80% complete.[5] What information does God put into these brains when he resurrects these embryos and teens? Will these individuals recognize their mothers and fathers, grandparents, siblings, and friends? What will be their language?

A proper environment is needed for brain development in the embryo, fetus, and child; correct nutrition, emotional care, and cognitive stimulation are essential. Will these needs be provided in Heaven? Also, much of a child's environment is provided by parents and schools. In teen years hormones influence brain development and new neurons and new pathways are molded. We see happiness, humor, religiosity, appetite, and also depression,

manic addiction, indecisiveness, delusional and aggressive or passive be-
havior, and more.[10] At least twenty-five years are needed for the brain's
full normal development with input from peers, siblings, parents, teachers,
experiences, books, movies, TV, computers, and the internet. Retirees are
still learning! How is God going to insure that people who died before TV
or computers or the internet or climate change are going to interact with
people who died in 2020? That perhaps will be more challenging than
grandparents interacting with their grandchildren!

There is evidence indicating that brain health (size, shape and func-
tion) of a newborn is adversely affected by poverty (and the associated poor
diet, weak parenting, and poor education opportunities). Studies show that
one of every three children in the USA lives in poverty and that poverty
adversely affects cognitive and emotional development of the brain.[11] Over
thirty million people, almost 12% of the USA population, lived below the
poverty line in 2018. That "line" would be an annual income of $25,000
for a family of four (parents and two children), or an individual living
alone with an annual income of less than $13,000.[12] So why not give every
household a modest subsidy, say $333 a month, to help the household avoid
poverty? Andrew Yang, democratic candidate for USA presidential nomi-
nation in 2020, campaigned on the idea of giving every American a $1000
monthly universal basic income. That idea had been suggested earlier[13] and
tried in Finland.[14] Results so far are not conclusive. But God must know
which children are born into poverty. Why does he let that happen? Also,
God could prevent child abuse, whether sexual, mental or physical, but still
he does nothing to stop it. Why not? Wouldn't God want healthy brains
coming to Heaven?

There is evidence suggesting that if parents talk to their baby from
birth to year three and on, that child will know many more words and do
better in preschool and kindergarten and thereafter. Why? Because 80%
of a child's brain development occurs during its first three years. Research
shows that the number of words a child is exposed to during the first few
years of life will have a large positive impact on the child's brain develop-
ment, language acquisition, and readiness for school. A minimum expo-
sure of the child to 15,000 words a day is recommended. Children from
disadvantaged backgrounds hear fewer words.[15] We can hope that all the
miscarried and aborted embryos that are in Heaven will somehow develop

through childbirth and thereafter be exposed to the 15,000 words every day in a language in Heaven.

When a person enters Heaven, one would think God would provide their original brain with all of its memories, good and bad, up to the year they died. Maybe God would correct depression, mental illnesses and psychoses. The brain's neurons begin to die within a few minutes of death and all the connections that give us memory are rapidly lost.[16] Those memories make up a person's personality and along with facial and other body features enable friends and family to recognize them. The brain provides a person the ability to recognize family and friends, and to have use of all their senses. When God makes a seventy-year-old person more youthful, down to thirty-three years old, would it make sense that he would subtract that person's memories between the years thirty-three to seventy? No. Those memories, good and bad, are as important if not more so than those of any other period of time. Yes, desirable is a brain free of diseases like Alzheimer's or other dementias, damage from strokes, concussions, other injuries, or cancer. And memories lost due to any of the latter would hopefully be restored. Would God accept an Alzheimer's patient who has lost most of her/his memories without restoring those memories? One would hope not! But what about a one-year-old child? If God makes this child a thirty-three-year-old, what memories would he impart into that individual's brain? Would it make sense to have that child grow up in Heaven with parents, siblings, and friends and go to school and have sports and music, and a computer and iPhone? The brain is a huge challenge to God.

Note that stroke patients lose portions of their memory even if they get prompt medical treatment. In the world, each year, fifteen million people have a stroke; five million recover, five million die and five million become permanently disabled.[17] Almost 800,000 people have strokes each year in the USA. Of those, 140,000 die; 385 deaths each day are due to strokes. Stroke is the leading cause of disability among seniors in the USA. Why? Because a stroke results in brain cells dying. A stroke can be ischemic, caused by lack of blood and oxygen to a part of the brain, or hemorrhagic, caused by bleeding in a portion of the brain. The symptoms of a stroke, of either kind, depending on where in the brain the stroke is, might be inability to walk, talk, read, write, recall the past, plan the future, lack of all or some movement, feeling of dizziness, loss of vision, and/or headache.

Which symptoms appear can alert medical staff to where in the brain the stroke might have occurred.[18] Perhaps God makes use of such records for stroke patients?

As soon as a stroke is recognized and medical staff are available, the patient is given a blood clot dissolving drug. The quicker blood flow to the part of the brain that is affected by the stroke is restored the less damage to the brain occurs. Blood clotting mechanisms and blood clot breakup are a big part of hospital efforts. In one large mid-western hospital, a program was established in 2019 that is centered on blood and blood clotting. Patient's lives will be in good hands. But what about God's hands? Will patients who die from strokes or patients who live after a stroke but never fully recover be fine in Heaven? How will God repair the damaged parts of the brain? Will God make a note of the damage at the time of the stroke and the location of the damage? How will God repair and restore all the millions of neurons and synapses of the 385 people in the USA and the many more worldwide who die of a stroke every day? Will God use stem cells? Stem cells derived from a person's bone marrow have been injected into the brains of stroke patients and have relieved some patients of the adverse effects of the stroke.[19] A Mobile Brain Scanner is soon to be on the market and available to diagnose brain injury and stroke. The device records an electroencephalogram in 5 minutes and the results can be compared with data of healthy brains.[20] Will God have such a device?

God must see the unfairness in the USA with regard to strokes and heart attacks. Blacks, especially black men, by percent, have more strokes and heart attacks and have more deaths resulting from each. There is evidence that a gene carried by blacks results in more salt retention and thus associated high blood pressure.[21] Will God correct this unequal situation between blacks and whites in Heaven? Will the diet in Heaven be so healthy that no health issues are caused by what residents of Heaven eat? Feasting in Heaven might have to be curbed and regulated by nutritionists.

The percentage of children born with attention deficit hyperactivity disorder (ADHD) has increased in the past twenty years and is now seen in 10% of all children.[22] ADHD is a big challenge. Then we also have neurodegenerative diseases like ALS and Parkinson's and birth defects like Down's Syndrome and cerebral palsy. Another brain disorder is post-traumatic stress disorder (PTSD). Now add autism, dyslexia, stuttering, and schizophrenia and we see that these conditions are diagnosed 10X more often in boys than in girls. But depression, anxiety and panic disorders are diagnosed 2X more often in girls than in boys. There seem to be many bizarre syndromes associated with brain disorders. People with Anton-Babinski syndrome are blind but refuse to believe it; people with Riddoch syndrome cannot see objects unless they are in motion; in Capgras syndrome sufferers become convinced that those close to them are imposters, and in Cotard delusion, sufferers believe they are dead and cannot be convinced they are not.[5] God will have a challenge to correct these odd syndromes!!

There are over 100 different cancers of the brain and nervous system and many are seen in children. Many of these cancers are of the brain's supportive cells, astrocytes and glial cells, called astrocytoma's and glioblastomas, respectively, adding to God's challenges dealing with the brain.[23] In one brain tumor center in the Midwest about 200 new patients are diagnosed with glioblastoma every year.[24] Glioblastoma has an average survival of twenty months, even with the best treatment (surgery, radiation, chemotherapy). The cause of this devastating cancer is not known. Rarely do any glioblastoma patients survive ten years after diagnosis and scientists do not know why some patients do; scientists are studying these few long-term survivors to possibly learn how to cure this cancer.

Death is defined as "irreversible cessation of all functions of the entire brain, including the brain stem."[25] At the time of a person's death God has to diagnose the brain for any and all of the brain's disorders/diseases. That is a formidable task because our best scientists do not understand these disorders. The list includes Alzheimer's disease, autism, depression, epilepsy, Parkinson's disease, schizophrenia, stroke, trauma to the brain, and many others.[26] Worse yet, epigenetic phenomena can be involved. Epigenetics involves chemical changes, like an added methyl group to a nitrogen base in the DNA, that are over and above the information in a gene or genes, changes that influence how the information in a gene is expressed into a phenotype. These epigenetic changes in DNA can be associated with traumatic events. For example, children of Holocaust survivors were three times more likely to be diagnosed with PTSD, anxiety, depression, and substance abuse, then their peers.[27] The question was raised in early chapters as to whether God should change anyone who does not fit into the definition of normal and here we go again. If a person has lived with Down's Syndrome, or autism, or stuttering or any disorder, will God correct that condition, and can we assume the person will then be happier? And will the family be happier? Since dementias like Alzheimer's are usually disorders that appear gradually in older people and then get progressively worse, God would seemingly rid persons of those disorders. But would God have a record of what that person's memories were when the dementia began? Would God then restore those memories which had been lost?

In Solomon's book, *Far From The Tree*, the various phenotypes of children that are very different from their parents are discussed. God has to recognize these individuals and theoretically keep their abilities, or lack of, when they reach Heaven. Their parents will possibly not want them changed, whether musical or mathematical geniuses, Downs children, deaf, blind, or otherwise different![28]

Do we all have in our brains the ability to be a genius at something? Evidence of a yes answer to that question comes from observing instant savants. These are people who experience a blow to the head and thus have a traumatic brain injury but instead of losing brain power they gain an ability they did not have before, such as exceptional musical, mathematical or artistic ability, even as they may suffer from the brain damage in their everyday activities. Dementia patients can show this expression of latent special ability as their general mental ability declines.[29] The brain is obviously very complex and different abilities and capacities are distributed in different portions. One can wonder how God will deal with these savants in Heaven. Will he repair the brain damage and have the person revert to their original self? Or will he repair the brain damage and maintain the savant ability? Would a savant or a person of high IQ, perhaps a member of Mensa, want to have God decrease her/his mental capacity? No! Would God want to have only people in Heaven of average intelligence or below average intelligence? No!

God made man (Adam) in his image. Then he made Eve from one of Adam's ribs. If he made Adam in his image, as it says in the Bible (Genesis 1:26-27), then God must look something like Adam. And if God has a kingdom, then he must be like a king and sits on his throne. More than once in the Bible, clouds and air are mentioned as being in Heaven, and speech and trumpets can be heard in Heaven or coming down from Heaven. Thus, not surprisingly, we see the depictions of God in the comics and in books of a bearded old fellow sitting on his throne amongst the clouds. How can that bearded old man handle all the information mentioned above?

The question is: "Just how difficult can it be to re-form a once healthy human brain and retain all its information in the original ordered form?" The human brain can hold 1 petabyte of information, equivalent to one million flash drives of 1 gigabyte each. The answer is: "Very, very, very difficult if not impossible."[30] But at least one person set as his goal to do just that. In 2009 a neuroscientist dedicated himself to eliminating all mental disorders. This ambitious project, The Human Brain Project, centered in Europe with an estimated price tag of $1.3 billion, began in 2012 and was to run ten years, to 2023. He set out to build a model of the "normal" human brain, yes, all 86-100 billion neurons and the 100 trillion connections that link the neurons to each other. Thus, he could then compare the model of the healthy brain with what is going on or not going on in the not healthy brain, beginning with the brain of an autistic child. There are 600 known brain disorders and the goal is to see the world as these brains see it, then corrections/cures can be designed and carried out. This neuroscientist and his fifteen post-doctoral researchers have so far simulated the behavior of a one million-neuron portion of the rat brain. He envisions 6,000 neuroscientists from around the world providing data toward his model.

Not to be outdone, the USA in 2013 started the Brain Initiative which was funded for $300 million and supports 500 investigators in 100 laboratories. The optimistic and ambitious view is that the research will lead to better understanding and treatments for Alzheimer's disease, depression, autism, epilepsy, Parkinson's disease, schizophrenia, stroke, brain injury, bipolar disorder and other disorders of the nervous system.[31] But a pause is necessary here because one well-known neuroscientist reminded everyone that the round worm, *Caenorhabditis elegans*, a model research organism, has exactly 302 neurons but its behavior and how it works is still poorly understood. To understand the complexities of over a dozen different neurotransmitters being released at one or more of the dozen or so synapses, attaching to a dozen or so receptors, altering voltages by opening and closing one or more of over 350 ion channels, is a major challenge. And note that there are different types of neurons. The electrical interactions in the brain are not well-understood but can be detected by electroencephalograms (EEGs). Deep brain stimulation can sometimes relieve patients of

Parkinson's symptoms.[32] Some of the many research projects related to the brain are underway at the Marine Biology Laboratory, Woods Hole, MA.[33]

There are additional brain projects. The Allen Brain Atlas project, funded mainly by $100 million from Paul G. Allen, was begun in 2003, and is still progressing. The goal is to understand neurobiological diseases. The project combines genetic findings with neuroanatomy findings. The main emphasis will be creating gene expression maps of mouse and human brains.[34] Another brain project, begun in 2009 and sponsored by the Natl Inst of Health for $38 million, is the Human Connectome. The goals of neuroscience research are to elucidate human brain functions by associating functional connections with anatomical components. The research will be centered in five universities.[35] When money was released for these projects, another neuroscientist said maybe these goals could be reached with the fruit fly, a model organism, because we are not ready to tackle the human brain in simulations. An Ivy League university was given a gift of $100 million toward neuroscience research.[36] The University of Michigan received a gift of $5.8 million toward bipolar disorder research and patient treatment and care.[37] Bipolar disorder is a poorly understood condition in which the patient has severe up and down swings in behavior, with the down swing often accompanied by depression.[38] If God created man in his image, why did he create people with such a wide range of mental disorders? And how is God going to diagnose these disorders in the deceased and correct them? Or will these disorders occur in Heaven?

How much computer computational power will be necessary for these projects? That amount has been estimated to be 100 petabytes of RAM and an exaflop to make simulations possible.[39] One petabyte = 10 to the 15th power. One exaflop = a quintillion calculations per second. Then there are those who think artificial intelligence will surpass the human brain and those at the same time who say "no way."[40] Perhaps the new quantum computer touted by Google might begin to compete with a human brain. This computer performed a calculation in 3 min and 20 sec that would require the world's fastest supercomputer 10,000 years to complete. Google is no doubt thinking of a practical application for this quantum computer. The future for this computer must be optimistic as the federal government has released $1.2 billion toward quantum research in the USA.[41]

The Religious Orders Study, begun in 1994, involves accumulating

data on catholic nuns, priests, and brothers in the church with regard
to their brain health, specifically dementia, Alzheimer's, and Parkinson's
Disease. The study included 1,168 people. There were 574 deaths and 539
autopsies. Postmortem brain imaging was performed on seventy-two brains.
An initial report on the findings was reported.[42] A total of 248 scholarly
references were included and discussed. The findings seen up to that date
were: 1. A continuum of cognitive ability and neuropathology exists; 2.
Mixed pathologies were associated with each other; 3. Evidence of neural
reserves was seen. 4. There are environmental and genetic risk factors. No
new treatments and no new cures were reported. Clearly the brain is very
complex and the best scientists are only slowly making progress on under-
standing the aging brain.

Already mentioned are three excellent model organisms: fruit fly, round
worm, and mouse. Another model organism is the zebra fish, which has
100,000 neurons. This fish lays up to 200 eggs per week and the embryos
are very transparent and can be manipulated. One neurobiologist with
money from the Human Brain Initiative Project says whole brain imaging
can provide "patterns, sequences, clusters and correlations" but can be just a
lot of data without any understanding. He has succeeded in recording every
blip in the brains of transparent baby zebrafish while they were adapting to
water flow (swimming against the current). Zebra fish are being examined
as they react to drugs and alcohol and may provide data helpful to our
understanding of sleep and anxiety.[43]

A study funded by The Brain Initiative was published in a leading jour-
nal in 2019 that examined cellular functions up to four hours post-mortem
in pigs (four hours after death). Researchers obtained pig brains from a
slaughterhouse and then in the laboratory perfused the brains with a com-
plex concoction similar to pig blood that "promotes recovery from anoxia,
reduces reperfusion injury, prevents edema, and metabolically supports the
energy requirements of the brain." Microcirculation and molecular and
cellular activity was restored to a certain extent, but no claims were made
that any "normal brain activity" was recovered nor the capacity of brain
function. Sixteen biologists co-authored the paper.[44] How is God going to
restore normal brain activity in the deceased when the brain has decom-
posed or is now part of cremains?

The paragraphs above emphasize how difficult it to understand the brain of even the simplest of animals, much less humans, and point out the challenges to God in restoring brain functions and memories in the deceased, especially if the brain has been physically injured, damaged by a stroke, has cancer, or is diseased. And we should be reminded that the human genome project took thirteen years at a cost of $4.7 billion. Now many, many additional genomes have been sequenced in both the animal and plant worlds and useful results and applications have been forthcoming, relevant to understanding human, animal, plant, and microbial diseases and normal biology as well. But understanding the brain is a much more difficult project than was sequencing the human genome. According to Alcorn[45] there will be animals in Heaven. If so, God must assure that their brains have the memories and abilities to make them good pets and companions. Wishful thinking indeed!

Due to injury or disease, a person may be unconscious; but being unconscious is not a simple matter. One can be anesthetized, concussed, or in a coma (a vegetative state), each of which has degrees of depth. Apparently there are thousands of people in the world who are minimally conscious and unable to communicate.[5] If death occurs in any of these states, God must ascertain the cause of the condition and correct it. Also, now and then a situation arises wherein a person has been put on life support. In cases wherein there is no longer brain activity and/or no longer blood circulation to the brain, the medical people involved conclude that the patient is dead and life support is discontinued. The life support keeps the heart beating, the blood circulating; the body is warm, seemingly still alive. But the definition of death is whether or not the brain has activity. In some of these cases, even though the brain is "dead" the family wants the life support to continue. The fact is that God has already no doubt deemed the patient dead and the soul has left the body. God has already made his diagnosis of the patient's health, including brain health, and ultimately can restore the patient to perfect health in Heaven. What wishful thinking we have here and it is so comforting to the family and loved ones. A candidate for president remembered his mother's comment, "You are not dead until you see the face of God."[46] OK, that would make sense to a theist.

God must have a perfect duplicate of all the information of a deceased person's brain. If he were to wait until resurrection, the brain will have decomposed in the grave, or at the bottom of the ocean, or was burned up during cremation and nowhere to be found. The chemical analysis of the brain shows that the elements that make up most of the brain are carbon, hydrogen, nitrogen, and oxygen, for a total of slightly less than three pounds. The remaining elements, found only in trace amounts, are sulfur, phosphorous, cobalt, iron, rubidium, selenium, zinc, chromium, silver, cesium, scandium, and antimony. The brain has a blood circulatory system too, important to the life of the billions of neurons and their trillions of synaptic connections.[47] Were the brains of Adam and Eve this complex at the get go?

Perhaps God did not count on evolution resulting in selection for such a complex organ as a brain. Perhaps God is going to wait until humans figure out all the details of the healthy, diseased, and injured brains, and he will then apply that information to restore healthy brains to the people in Heaven.

NOTES

1   Wikipedia website, "Pliny the Elder," last edited, March 26, 2023, https://en.wikipedia.org/wiki/Pliny_the_Elder; Sara Chodosh, "How much space does all of humanity's knowledge take up?," *Popular Science*, March 24, 2019.

2   Francis S. Collins, "Medical Sciences Age of Discovery," *Time*, November 4, 2019, 40-41.

3   Ellen Airhart and Nicole Wetsman, "your brain is just a pile of wet, fatty goop," *Popular Science*, Spring, 2018, 6-7.

4a Janeen Interlandi, "New Estimate Boosts the Human Brain's Memory Capacity 10-Fold," *Scientific American*, February 5, 2016; Salk website, accessed March 2020, https://www.salk.edu.

4b Hannah Ritchie and Edouard Mathieu, "How many people die and how many are born each year?," Our World in Data website, January 5, 2023, https://ourworldindata.org/births-and-deaths.

5   Bill Bryson, *The Body: A Guide for Occupants*, (New York: Double Day, 2019.)

6   Emily S. Finn, "Brain activity is as unique - and identifying - as a fingerprint," "The Conversation website, published October 12, 2015, https://theconversation.com/brain-activity-is-as-unique-and-identifying-as-a-fingerprint-48723.

7   Websters Collegiate Dictionary, Ninth Edition, (Massachusetts: Merriam-Webster, 1989); Daniel Yetman, "What Does the Medulla Oblongata Do and Where's It Located?" healthline website, last updated December 22, 2021, https://www.healthline.com/health/medulla-oblongata.

8   Teal Burrell, "Redefining the brains divisions," *Discover Magazine*, January/February, 2016, 55.

9   The World Counts website, "How Many Babies Are Born Each Day?," accessed March 2020, https://www.theworldcounts.com/stories/how-many-babies-are-born-each-day

10 David Eagleman, *The Brain: The Story of You*, (UK: Vintage, 2017.)

11 Joan L. Luby, et al., "Poverty and The Developing Brain," Dana Foundation website, published April 15, 2022, https://dana.org/article/poverty-and-the-developing-brain/

12 *Cheboygan Tribune*, September 12, 2019, A1.

13 Kimberly G. Noble, "What Inequality Does to the Brain," *Scientific American*, Volume 316, Issue 3, March 2017, 44.

14 *Finnish American Reporter*, July 2020.

15 *Detroit Free Press*, September 24, 2019, 1A, 6A.

16 Karen Nitkin, "The Challenges of Defining and Diagnosing Brain Death, Johns Hopkins Medicine website, published November 7, 2017, https://www.hopkinsmedicine.org/news/articles/the-challenges-of-defining-and-diagnosing-brain-death.

17 CDC website, Stroke Facts, accessed February 2020, https://www.cdc.gov/stroke/facts.htm.

18 Jill Bolte Taylor and Sophie Bushwick, "a stroke erased my sense of past or future," *Popular Science*, September/October 2017, 75.

19 Kara Platoni, "Rethinking the Brain," *Smithsonian Magazine*, December 2017, 39.

20 Michael Belfiore, "This Mobile Brain Scanner Promises to Assess Injuries Where CT Scans Can't," *Bloomberg Businessweek*, July 23, 2018, 25.

21 *NBC News*, April 30, 2019.

22 *Cheboygan Tribune*, September 17, 2018, A4.

23 Lauren Martin, "What are the different types of brain cancer?," MedicalNewsToday website, posted June 9, 2021, https://www.medicalnewstoday.com/articles/brain-cancer-types

24 *Detroit Free Press*, May 26, 2019, 14A.

25 Charles Patrick Davis, Editor, "Medical Definition of Death," *MedicineNet* website, reviewed March 29, 2021, https://www.medicinenet.com/death/definition.htm.

26 Francis S. Collins, "Medical science's age of discovery," *Time*, November 4, 2019.

27 *Discover Magazine*, March 2017, 53.

28 Andrew Solomon, *Far From The Tree*, (New York: Scribner, 2012.)

29 Adam Piore, "The Amazing Science of Instant Savants," *Reader's Digest*, March 2018, 77.

30 Yves Fregnas and Gilles Laurent, "Neuroscience: Where is the brain in the Human Brain Project?," *Nature*, 513, September 3, 2014, 27-29; Stefan Theil, "Why the Human Brain Project Went Wrong - and How to Fix It," *Scientific American*, Volume 313, Issue 4, October 2015, 41.

31 F.S. Collins, "Medical Sciences Age of Discovery," *Time*, November 4, 2019, 40-41.

32 David Noonan, "How to Plug In Your Brain," *Smithsonian Magazine*, May 2016, 64-66.

33 Marine Biological Laboratory, "Illuminating the Brain," *Catalyst*, Volume 7, No. 2, Fall 2012.

34 Wikipedia website, "Allen Brain Atlas," last edited November 1, 2022, https:// en.wikipedia.org/wiki/Allen_Brain_Atlas

35 Wikipedia website, "Connectome," last edited April 1, 2023, https://en.wikipedia.org/wiki/Connectome

36 *Brown Alumni Magazine,* May/June 2018, 11.

37 *Cheboygan Tribune*, September 11, 2019, A2.

38 Veterans Crisis Line, "Call," accessed March 2020, https://www.veteranscrisisline.net/get-help-now/call/

39 Wikipedia website, "Brain," last edited April 9, 2023, https://en.wikipedia.org/wiki/Brain.

40 *Bloomberg Businessweek*, May 21, 2018, 40.

41 *Detroit Free Press*, October 24, 2019, 1B-3B.

42 David A. Bennett, Julie A. Schneider, Zoe Arvanitakis, and Robert S. Wilson, "Overview and Findings from the Religious Orders Study," Curr Alzheimer, 9(6) July 1, (2012): 628-645. doi: 10.2174/156720512801322573

43 Ariel Sabar, "Flashes of Genius," *Smithsonian Magazine*, July/August 2015, 60-63, 110-114.

44 Z. Vrselja, S.G. Daniele, J. Silbereis, et al., "Restoration of brain circulation and cellular functions hours post-mortem," *Nature*, Volume 568, April 2019, 336-343.

45 Randy Alcorn, *Heaven: A Comprehensive Guide to Everything the Bible Says About Our Eternal Home* (Illinois: Tyndale Momentum, 2004.)

46 *Time*, February 10, 2020, 33.

47 Ellen Airhart and Nicole Wetsman, "your brain is just a pile of wet, fatty goop," *Popular Science*, Spring, 2018, 6-7.

21

BRAIN RESEARCH

THE COMPLEXITIES OF the brain are revealed when trying to understand and treat medical problems such as concussions, chronic traumatic encephalitis, depression, autism, Parkinson's, epilepsy, schizophrenia, Down's and other chromosomal/genetic syndromes, Alzheimer's disease and other dementias. Nevertheless, much research has been and still is directed at understanding these complexities. That research is overwhelmed by the 100 billion neurons and associated axons and the even greater number of their interconnections (several trillion), plus all the supportive cells. Then consider determining which neurons are firing at a given moment when the firing is at millisecond speeds. After working out the complexities of the "normal" brain, medical research will try to find out the differences in the diseased brain. Can God know what any one person is doing and thinking, what information their brain is storing, at any moment in time? How will God recognize the diseased brain, the brain deficiencies after concussions, or the brain suffering from Alzheimer's disease? How will God preserve this information after a person dies and before neurons and synapses breakdown and the brain decomposes? Every year 56 million people on earth die (World Population Review, 2022.)

One neuroscientist's approach is to design electrode arrays that make detailed recordings of activity in the brain, ultimately hoping to understand neurological disorders, like epilepsy and paralysis due to brain signaling mixups. These arrays of electrode implants can sample across almost any area of the brain. The system can perhaps help to understand the origin of the subtle brain signals that give rise to seizures.[1] Another approach is studying pain and the brain and one finding is that pain does not cause magnetic resonance scans to light up. No one has been able to detect pain in a person; pain is impossible to decode. Only the person experiencing the pain can detect the pain. Chronic pain is a real issue, such as that of fibromyalgia. An MD with a degree in electrical engineering has found that people who suffer from chronic pain, such as back pain, show subtle changes in the gray matter density across brain regions.[2] There will be no pain in Heaven (Revelation 21:4) so God must be able to diagnose causes of pain and then correct the situation. Neuroscientists in many other laboratories are growing human brain tissue, seen as floating clumps in tissue culture. Skin stem cells from patients are induced to form these clumps of brain tissue. These mini-brains contain some of the parts of the fetal brain but a complete fetal brain has not yet been achieved in tissue culture. When mini-brains are grown from cells obtained from patients with autism or other brain-related ailments, the structural and/or functional characteristics are different from those of healthy patients. Evolutionary aspects of brain development are also being studied in these approaches.[3]

Studies show that each person's brain exhibits a distinct pattern, so-called whorls, that can be used as a distinguishing feature of that person with near perfect accuracy. A research team used functional magnetic resonance imaging (MRI) to examine brain activity in over 100 healthy male adults. The participants could be identified from one another with 99% accuracy. This neuroimaging methodology might be applicable as a fingerprint for mental health, for example to determine which individuals in a group of teens might be at risk for schizophrenia.[4]

Plant chemicals, such as curcumin and galantamine, are being investigated with regard to their anti-oxidant properties. Using mouse models for human conditions, such as Alzheimer's disease, these chemicals have shown beneficial effects.[5]

Why is neuroscience such a challenge? Maybe a bit of neural knowledge will answer this question. Neurochemicals (neurotransmitters) cause neurons to fire an electrical signal down a long pathway, the axon. The end of the axon, the synapse, connects to another neuron. More neurotransmitters are released at the synapse which attach to receptors and alter the voltage by opening or closing ion channels. There are dozens of neurotransmitters and as many receptors to receive them and more than 350 types of ion channels. Also, there are many different neurons. Thousands, if not millions of brain cells, have to talk to each other in order for a person to perform the most basic task, like lifting a glass of water.[6] What about memory, basic math, algebra, calculus, or going from A to B and following a map or GPS, and pain and pleasure, etc. etc.? Yes, neuroscience is very challenging because of the complexities of the brain and nervous system.

To simulate the human brain would require an estimated computational speed of 100 petabytes of RAM and an exaflop to make simulations possible (note gigaflop, teraflop, petaflop, and then exaflop – computational speed references). Supercomputers will be required and the world already has over 500; the performance of these supercomputers is measured in FLOPS (Floating Point Operations Per Second.) The Indiana University Supercomputer has a theoretical peak performance of 934 Teraflops (10^{12}.)[7]

One goal of supercomputers is to map the human brain, every neuron and all synaptic connections. This map would be the longest dataset ever collected about anything in history.[8] What kinds of datasets of people's brains has God accumulated through history? What a challenge.

The complications with brain simulations are that the brain differs from one individual to another and even in the same individual day to day, hour to hour, and minute to minute. To hope to determine what an autistic or schizophrenic individual is seeing, or to understand any of the 600 known brain disorders, is a huge challenge. Many scientists are unhappy with the human brain projects and say, "numerical simulations and big data are essential in modern science but they alone do not yield understanding. Building a massive data base to feed simulations without connective loops between hypotheses and experimental tests seems like a waste of time and money." Another scientist recorded every blip of brain activity in a transparent baby zebrafish, which was noted as a landmark feat and published in Nature magazine, but says of his lab's work, "we discovered these whole brain imaging results are not that useful" and is moving on to other neuroscience studies.

Smaller science is also involved in brain research.[8] The Beaumont Hospital in Royal Oak, Michigan, is now home to a new three-story, $22 million Neuroscience Center for both adults and children, for diagnosing and treating individuals with neurological conditions including Alzheimer's disease, concussions, brain tumors, and Parkinson's disease. Consider also that most universities have neuroscience programs with course work and research opportunities for students and faculty.

For God to diagnose, heal and correct neuronal ailments and diseases of the deceased is going to require Big Science on His part and Big Faith on the part of priests, pastors, families and friends.[9, 10]

NOTES

1   Cassandra Willyard, "How It Works: A System That Reverses Paralysis," *Popular Science*, July 9, 2014, 59.

2   Conor Feehly, "Why Does Pain Hurt?," *Discover Magazine* online, posted August 13, 2021, https://www.discovermagazine.com/mind/why-does-pain-hurt.

3   NBC Nightly News website, Tanya Lewis, "Mini human brains grown from stem cells," aired August 28, 2013, https://www.nbcnews.com/healthmain/mini-human-brains-grown-stem-cells-8c110207644.

4   Simon Makin, "The Brains Whorl," *Scientific American*, January 2016, 22.

5   Mark Mattson, "Brain Health: What Doesn't Kill You," *Scientific American*, July 2015, 40-45.

6   Ariel Sabar, "Flashes of Genius," *Smithsonian Magazine*, July-August 2015, 60-63.

7   University Information Technology Services website, "Understand measures of supercomputer performance and storage system capacity," last modified March 13, 2023, https://kb.iu.edu/d/apeq

8   NOVA Next, Samia Bouzid, "The Supercomputer That Could Map the Human Brain, *PBS* online, June 6, 2018, https://www.pbs.org/wgbh/nova/article/brain-mapping-supercomputer/.

9   *Detroit Free Press*, Aug. 3, 2014.

10 Stefan Theil, "Trouble in Mind," *Scientific American*, October 2015, 36-42.

22

CONCUSSIONS

FROM CHAPTERS 20 and 21 we know that the brain is a very complex part of the body. Dealing with the injured or diseased brain of the deceased is one of God's biggest challenges, with traumatic brain injuries and concussions very prevalent.

A concussion is a mild form of traumatic brain injury (TBI) that alters the way the brain works. The concussions topic has been in the national news because of a law suit filed by a group of thousands of former National Football League (NFL) players in which the NFL is accused of not warning players adequately of the dangers of playing this violent game, not taking adequate precautions to avoid head injuries, and not recognizing and treating players correctly after head injuries.[1] Also impacting this topic was the movie "Concussion" released in 2015, which documents the serious nature of concussions. The concussions lead to subsequent changes in the brain now referred to as chronic traumatic encephalitis (CTE) which has 4 stages, stage 4 being the most severe. A well-known NFL quarterback who led his team to a win in the super bowl, died of cancer. Because he predicted a CTE diagnosis years in advance, he asked his family to donate his brain to science after his death. Sure enough, his brain showed signs of Stage 3 CTE. His physician said the disease was widespread throughout his brain with severe damage in regions involving memory, learning, and emotion. The physician added that CTE has been found in the brains of former NFL players of every position with the exception of kicker. Players in positions that involve more head injuries are at greater risk of CTE, which unfortunately can only be diagnosed in the brain after death. Suspicions of CTE are expressed when a player suffers one or more of the following: headaches, memory loss, confusion, depression, behavioral changes, and progressive dementia. In 2014 the NFL estimated that nearly one-third of former players will develop dementia, Alzheimer's disease, Parkinson's, ALS (amyotrophic lateral sclerosis) or other brain disorders.[2] Brains of deceased former NFL players show a rate of evidence of brain injury and associated degenerative disease of 96%.[3] National Hockey League players are also suing their league as hockey head injuries can lead to concussions.[4] The Detroit Free Press reported that the cumulative effects of hundreds of supposedly minor blows to the head can equal the effect of several concussions.[5] One offensive lineman on a college team received sixty-two of these "minor" hits to the head in a single game. A ten-year NFL linebacker could receive 15,000 sub-concussive blows in his football career.

What about youngsters? A group of nineteen boys aged seven to eight were studied while practicing and playing football games. Together these boys had over 3,000 hits to the head in the study period. Even though there were no concussions recorded, the researchers predicted that brain injuries were sustained. The danger of concussions is almost 80% higher at the high school level than college level. A total of eight players died playing high school football in 2013. No players died playing any other sport. Concussions do occur in other sports but at a rate in football (thirty-three per 10,000 players; 2013-14) that is twice that of girl's soccer or basketball or boys wrestling or soccer.[6,7]

An alarming statistic is that many head injuries go unreported. Hospitals record about 2.5 million traumatic brain injuries (TBIs) per year in the USA, or almost 7,000 per day, and deaths can result. Of these, 250,000 are nineteen years old and younger.[6] In the state of Michigan research has shown a link between traumatic brain injury and attention deficit disorder, poor decision making, aggression, mood changes, dementia and Alzheimer's disease. The physical consequences of a TBI include several: (1) Nerve fibers (axons) may snap and some may not regrow. (2) Blood vessels may leak. (3) Fluid can leak into the brain and cause cells to die. (4) Swelling can push brain tissue into the spinal cord, disrupting nerve function. NBC evening news (May 10, 2017) reported that 1,200 injured youngsters visit the emergency room (ER) every day in the USA, fifty per hour, and 11% are head injuries, some being concussions. Because the brain is not fully developed in these youngsters, an injury can have life-long adverse effects. Approximately 20% of USA adolescents have reported at least one concussion. That percentage would be considerably higher if all TBIs were reported. Not only football but boys and girls playing soccer, hockey, basketball, and lacrosse report head injuries.[7]

Another aspect of head injuries is that the injured player may commit suicide, suggesting depression is a consequence of the head injury. Some star players in professional as well as college sports have committed suicide.[8] Another former football player died of pneumonia and was taking a pain medication. An autopsy of his brain indicated Stage II CTE. In the report from the university doing the autopsy, the point was made that this player probably did not die from the CTE or the pain meds but one or both may have contributed to poor judgment, leading to his death.[9]

A study at Johns Hopkins University is designed to investigate concussions in retired National Football League players who have had multiple concussions and are now noticing some memory problems and are worried about depression, suicide, and CTE through subsequent years. Also, a study underway is of current players who have had one concussion. The methods being utilized include positron emission tomography (PET scans) and tests of translocator protein 18kDa (TSPO) abundance. TSPO is increased in the brain after injury. In the case of the current players, eight of twelve areas of the brain showed increased TSPO but no memory problems as of yet.[10] Another marker for concussions was mentioned on Natl Public Radio on May 4, 2017, which involves microRNA analysis of saliva and/or urine. Apparently after a concussion unique microRNAs are released from the damaged area, and some can be detected in the saliva and urine. Certain ones of these microRNAs are associated with greater degrees of head trauma and the person suffering the head trauma and/or the examining doctor, may be able to decide whether resumption of the sport can occur and when.

The movie "Concussion" raises awareness of concussions in football. But CTE has been recognized for decades, described in the 1920s as dementia pugilistica, or "Punch-drunk syndrome", in boxers. God has clearly been faced with diagnosing CTE in brains of the deceased for a long, long time.[11] The medical doctor that first diagnosed CTE in a football player was Dr. Bennet Omalu, played by Will Smith in the movie. When Dr. Omalu last watched a football game, it was the Superbowl. He says, "After the first play, the hitting – pow! - I had to …… shut off the TV because what was going through my mind was what was happening to the players brains at the microscopic level." As mentioned above microRNAs may be a diagnostic measure of the degree of trauma after a blow to the head.

Can God diagnose these microscopic events and correct them? Sadly, that first player diagnosed with CTE by Dr Omalu was living in his truck, had dementia, and died of a heart attack. CTE can only be diagnosed by physicians by examining the brain immediately after death. Once the brain begins to deteriorate, any forms of brain abnormalities will be difficult to diagnose, even for God. But players of many different sports can go through an examination to determine if their brain has already been injured and to what extent. The examination involves an MRI, electroencephalogram, and an electrode hook-up that measures electrical activity of the brain, which together can draw a neurological picture of the brain. That picture can help the athlete in deciding whether to continue with that sport, change sports, or drop out of sports. It is hoped research underway in many laboratories will lead to physicians diagnosing CTE in the living brain within a decade.[12] Can God draw these neurological pictures of brains in the living and know what has to be corrected in those brains in the deceased when in Heaven?

The total injury report for the NFL on 12/28/2015, for ten teams, for one Sunday game of each team, listed four concussions, two injuries to the shoulder, two to the ankle, one foot, two knees and one leg. God will have a challenge diagnosing injuries in deceased former NFL players. Some players have multiple surgeries during their playing careers, including suffering paralysis.[13] The injury report on Monday, Oct. 31, listed thirty-five injuries with six concussions. After assessing the many injuries to his players, one coach remarked, "Injuries happen, this isn't tiddlywinks. It is a violent game so guys get hurt." On Mondays, NFL players go through "picking up the pieces" dealing with physical and mental ailments from the Sunday's games.[14]

There are TBIs that are more severe than concussions and include injuries from falls (58%), being struck by an object or collision with an object (18%); from motor vehicle crashes (ATVs, snowmobiles, motorcycles; 16%) and other injury causes (14%). In one state alone, Michigan, almost 58,500 people will sustain a TBI each year; 46,000 are treated and released, 10,980 are hospitalized, and 1,520 will die (over four per day in Michigan).[15] Consider that from the wars in Iraq and Afghanistan 2.5 million men and women served and 300,000 came home with traumatic brain injuries many of whom are still being treated. The symptoms of TBI include balance problems, headaches, sleep difficulty, dizziness, memory problems, concentration problems, feeling foggy or groggy, and irritability, any or all of which can be long-lasting.[16] It can be hoped that none of these symptoms will be seen in Heaven.

God's challenges are formidable. Consider that when a former player or anyone dies who has had a TBI or who has CTE, God must diagnose the cause of death and contributing factors; CTE, cancer, pain med addiction, depression, and perhaps cognitive deficits and other symptoms. Then God has to correct each of these and insure the perfect health of the person in Heaven and restore the deceased person's memories and personality. There are 100 billion neurons in the brain, with trillions of connections between these neurons. There are billions more glial cells giving support and aid to the functions of neurons. Before the severity of concussions became recognized in the 90's, God still had to deal with players dying. Did God know about CTE, PET scans, TSPO, depression, addictions, and did he understand suicides? Certainly God has challenges diagnosing and correcting concussions.

NOTES

1   Dave Birkett, "Mathis receives outpouring of concern when his concussion is called a brain injury," *Detroit Free Press*, November 19, 2015, 4-5C; Paul M. Barrett, "The NFL Concussion Deal's Surprise Winner," *Bloomberg Businessweek*, September 9-15, 2013.

2   "The N.F.L.'s Tragic C.T.E. Roll Call," *The New York Times* website, February 3, 2016. https://www.nytimes.com/interactive/2016/02/03/sports/football/nfl-brain-disease-cte-concussions.html.

3   The Rundown column, "Health 96%," *Time*, October 13, 2014, 16.

4　*Detroit Free Press*, November 26, 2013; Mary Ann Easterling, "The Price Paid," *Sports Illustrated*, September 9, 2013, 17; Dave Birkett, "Mathis receives outpouring of concern when his concussion is called a brain injury," *Detroit Free Press*, November 19, 2015, 5C.

5　*Detroit Free Press*, September 4, 2017, 5A.

6　*Cheboygan Tribune*, November 15, 2013.

7　*Detroit Free Pre*ss, September 29, 2016, 3C; *Time*, October 9, 2017, 6.

8　Lauren Shute, "Hard Hit," *Sports Illustrated*, December 22, 2014, 14-16.

9　*Detroit Free Press*, August 4, 2013.

10　Lisa Watts, "The Lasting Impact of Concussions on NFL Athletes," *Johns Hopkins Magazine*, Neuroscience, Spring, 2017.

11　*Cheboygan Weekend Tribune*, December, 18-20, 2015.

12　J. DeLessio, "Tackling Brain Trauma Head On," *Popular Science*, January/February 2016, 32.

13　"Injury Check," *Detroit Free Press*, December 28, 2015, 6C.

14　Greg Bishop, "Get-Right Day," *Sports Illustrated*, December 12, 2016, 69-76.

15　Otsego Health and Wellness Bulletin, September/October 2017.

16　"Concussion: Tackling a Tough Issue," *Otsego Health and Wellness Publication*, Fall, 2015, 6.

23

SPINAL CORD

THE BRAIN AND spinal cord develop from the ectoderm of the embryo some of which becomes the neural plate, forms a tube, and is the rudiment of the nervous system. The anterior end forms the brain, and the posterior end develops into the spinal cord. The development of the nervous system is studied by developmental neurobiologists and evolutionary biologists. The changes in the developmental processes leading to the complexities of the nervous system have been documented in vertebrates and the enlargement and complexity especially of the cerebrum can be seen and compared in fish, amphibians, reptiles, birds, and mammals.[1]

The spinal cord (SC) and brain together make up the central nervous system. From its connection to the medulla of the brain, the SC extends downward (caudally, toward the tail in all vertebrates). The SC is surrounded by membranes called the pia matter and dura matter and is protected by bones of the vertebral column, the vertebrae. Inside the central canal of the SC is the cerebrospinal fluid. Three main arteries extend down from the brain along the SC and other arteries extend from the sides to supply oxygen and nutrients. The SC functions are to send messages from the brain to the body and to receive messages from the body and transport them to the brain. To move any part of the body, the brain sends signals through nerves in the spinal cord down to the motor neuron bodies in the ventral part of the SC which then relay the messages through the peripheral nerves to the appropriate muscles. The muscles that a person tells to do something (arm, leg, neck and back muscles) receive signals from the brain, down the SC, to the motor neurons of the spinal cord, and then to the muscles.[1]

A stroke can result in various degrees of paralysis. But partial or complete paralysis can also result from diseases such as cerebral palsy or multiple sclerosis or from physical injury to the spinal cord. There are 17,500 new spinal cord injuries each year in the USA; 81% are in males. One spinal cord injury occurs each hour of the day. Injury to the neck region is more adverse than injuries lower down. The major causes of spinal cord injury include motor vehicle accidents, physical labor, falls, sports accidents, and violence/shootings. Two percent of the USA population suffers from some kind of paralysis; that is 5.6 million people.[2]

Spinal cord injury results in damage to or actual breaking apart of the major nerve bundles passing up and down the spinal cord. There are over a dozen major nerve tracts traveling up, down and through the spinal cord, controlling the senses and motor actions. These nerve tracts travel up and down the spinal cord mainly through the gray matter and white matter. The spinal cord is divided down its length by the dorsal septum and ventral fissure into two halves, with each half containing central nerve tracts making up gray matter and the nerve tracts surrounding the gray matter making up the white matter. We can get some understanding of these tracts by naming just three of them. The Retinospinal tract is involved in regulation of voluntary movements and reflex movements of the body. The Lateral spinal thalamic tract is involved in pain and temperature sensations. The Spinotectal tract is involved in tactile (touch) and also pain and thermal stimuli.[3] Thus a person with a severed spinal cord at the neck cannot move either voluntarily or reflexively, cannot feel heat or cold, and cannot feel pain or touching stimuli.[3]

Walking requires an interplay between nerves in the brain and those in the spinal cord. Electrical signals originate in the brain, pass down to the lumbar region of the spinal cord and there activate motor neurons that result in coordinated contraction of leg muscles. If an injury to the upper spine cuts off this communication, a person loses the ability to walk. Now researchers and physicians, using monkeys that have been paralyzed by injury to the spinal cord, developed a pill-sized electrode array that is implanted into the monkey's brain which communicates by wireless means to stimulate the lower spinal motor neurons to activate the muscles for walking. Still, the system cannot send signals back to the brain to feel touch and pain. But the monkeys could walk relatively normally and thus the system provides hope for humans so paralyzed.[4a] God will have to diagnose paralysis in human patients and recognize that such an implant is in the brain, then repair the spinal cord. Very difficult tasks for sure.

The spinal cord can regenerate in some fish, in some amphibians (larval frogs; salamanders), and in some reptiles (lizards), but very poorly or not at all in birds and mammals. Ongoing research with these species with regenerative ability may provide clues to possibly get the human spinal cord to regenerate.[4b] One major effort to provide funds and needed research to learn how to get the human spinal cord to regenerate was begun by Christopher Reeve with his wife Dana who established The Christopher and Dana Reeve Foundation.[5] Christopher Reeve injured his spinal cord and became paralyzed from the neck down after falling headfirst off a horse. He was wheelchair bound for the remaining short period of his life but stayed optimistic about being able to walk again someday.

Peripheral nerves have very limited regenerative ability to regain function in humans. A severed nerve may regenerate but it struggles to find its original pathway to the muscle or skin or sense organ. Thus severed nerves of fingers can lead to numbness or paralysis of one or more fingers or the hand. If nerves are damaged in the shoulder, the entire arm may be paralyzed.[6]

Consider someone dying who is paralyzed from the neck down. That person is tetra (quadra) plegic; all four limbs are non-functional. God looks at this individual and realizes there is a fair number of medical procedures to accomplish. First is the diagnosis. What is the cause of death? What is causing the paralysis? Does the person have multiple sclerosis? Cerebral palsy? Was the spinal cord injured due to a neck injury? Are there other injuries such as to vertebrae? Did the person dive into shallow water? Did the person fall off a horse? Was the person in a motor vehicle accident? Was the person shot with a firearm? How old was the individual at the time of the injury? How old is the individual now, at the time of death? When did the injury occur? Have all the nerves below the injury site degenerated? Have the muscles, tendons, ligaments, and bones below the injury site atrophied? Have the arms and legs withered? Is the person incontinent? What kind of diet has the person been on? Was the person wheelchair bound and for how long? Months? Years? How tall is the person? Has growth been stunted due to the paralysis? Has the person expressed what he/she might want God to do? Has the family indicated what they might desire? Will God restore only some functions? Standing? Walking? Arm and hand use? Bladder and bowel control?

If there is partial paralysis, for example paraplegia (only legs paralyzed), a similar diagnostic and cure procedure has to be followed by God.

In the bodies of persons reaching Heaven, God will find many devices; there are something like 190,000 different medical devices on the market in the USA. One of these is a spinal cord stimulator that is implanted into the spinal cord; 60,000 patients have one implanted every year in the USA. The main goal of these devices is to reduce pain, usually pain associated with a previous injury. Unfortunately, sometimes there are unwanted side effects. In the use of a spinal cord stimulator, burns or shocks can result. As many as 80,000 such incidents have been reported since 2008. Medical devices are also utilized in treatments for heart ailments, cancer and diabetes, and God will certainly find all of these devices among people reaching Heaven.[7] How will the devices be disposed of in Heaven?

Presumably spinal cord injuries will be repaired by God and the paralyzed person will then have complete mobility and full use of arms and legs. But whoa! Consider what the effort is here on earth to attempt spinal cord injury repair. First note that Christopher Reeve with the best and brightest spinal cord specialists available was wheelchair bound until his death. Let's look at the effort needed to surgically attempt to repair an injured spinal cord. There will be more than two dozen people involved: the surgical team would have one lead person and two or more assistants who are also experts on spinal cord injury. These surgeons would have done residencies in surgery and would have "practiced" on animal models (rats, rabbits, dogs, perhaps monkeys) and would have assisted experienced surgeons in human surgeries. There would be technicians to run the equipment including the lighting, monitors, and computers. There would be surgical residents, nurses, anesthesiologists, imaging people, radiologists, blood coagulation specialists, neuroscientists, physiologists, imaging techs, and engineers.[8]

Sadly, all of this effort has led to only slow progress. How can God deal with these paralyzed people? Will he give the person a new spinal cord? A new lower body, perhaps even from the neck down? We must keep in mind that paralysis can also result from strokes and diseases. Saying that God will "magically" heal all these paralyzed people is going far beyond science.

NOTES

1   Joy B. Phillips, *Development of Vertebrate Anatomy* (Missouri: CV Mosby Co., 1975.)

2   WebMD website, "Type of Paralysis," accessed February 2020, https://www.webmd.com/brain/paralysis-types; WebMD website, "Spinal Cord Injury," accessed March 2020, https://www.webmd.com/pain-management/spinal-cord-injury-treatment.

3   Kenhub website, accessed February 2020, https://www.kenhub.com/en/library/anatomy/the-spinal-cord.

4a Kevin Stacey, "Spinal Tap," *Brown Alumni Monthly*, January/February 2017, 17.

4b A. Benraiss, et al. "Neurogenesis during caudal spinal cord regeneration in adult newts." *Development genes and evolution* vol. 209,6 (1999): 363-9. doi:10.1007/s004270050265; Patrizia Ferretti, et al. "Changes in spinal cord regenerative ability through phylogenesis and development: lessons to be learnt." *Developmental dynamics : an official publication of the American Association of Anatomists* vol. 226,2 (2003): 245-56. doi:10.1002/dvdy.10226; David Stocum, *Wound Repair, Regeneration, and Artificial Tissues.* (Texas: R.G. Landes Co, 1995) 34-35.

5   Christopher & Dana Reeve Foundation website, accessed January 2020, www.christopherreevefoundation.org/.

6   Wikipedia website, "Neuroregeneration," last edited March 30, 2023, en.wikipedia.org/wiki/neuroregeneration

7   Mitch Weiss and Holbrook Mohr, "A painful reality with spinal-cord stimulators," *Detroit Free Press*, November 26, 2018, 9A.

8   John Sanford, *Bloody Genius*, (New York: G.P. Putnam's Sons, 2019), 199-200.

24

EPILEPSY

EPILEPSY IS A group of related neurological disorders characterized by sudden recurrent episodes of seizures or convulsions with sometimes loss of consciousness, accompanied by abnormal electrical activity in the brain. Epilepsy was described in Babylonian texts 3,000 years ago. Initial causes were suggested as excessive phlegm in the brain or evil spirits. Treatment included boring holes in the patient's skull or exorcism.[1] There are different types of epilepsy and different types of seizures. Epilepsy is newly diagnosed in 150,000 people yearly in the USA. More than 2 million USA adults and half a million children have epilepsy.[2] The abnormal brain electrical activity is diagnosed with an electroencephalogram (EEG). Electrodes are attached to the patients scalp and electrical activity is recorded. Epilepsy patients show a typical abnormal pattern of activity. A blood test is also a diagnostic tool. A complete blood count is determined from a blood sample of the patient. The blood analysis may indicate anemia, infections, diabetes, allergies, or liver damage – any one or more may be related to the seizures. Blood work also helps to determine what anti-seizure medications to prescribe.[2]

Most children with epilepsy also show other health issues. Epilepsy triples the risk of Attention Deficit Hyperactivity Disease (ADHD) in children.[2]

Causes of epilepsy are abnormal and spontaneous electrical signaling in the brain, possibly brought on by birth difficulties, head injuries, drug/

alcohol use by the mother, tumors, or stroke. But 70% of the cases have no known cause.[2]

Treatment of epilepsy usually involves one or more of the following drugs: Dilantin®, levetiracetam (Keppra), topiramate (Topomax) or Aptiom®. Valproate is another drug but is seldom used by pregnant mothers because it is linked to lower IQs of newborns. More recently cannabidiol shows promise.[3]

One patient whose seizures had become frequent and unbearable, and whom had not been helped by medications or neural surgery, enrolled in an experimental treatment program at the Mayo Clinic. Two electrical stimulators were implanted under the patient's clavicles and wires from them were threaded up her neck under the skin to deep regions of the patient's brain, the thalamus and hippocampus, so that the electrical current would affect signaling that neurons use to interact. Since the devices were implanted, in six months, the patient only had one major seizure. Neuroscientists anticipate this deep brain stimulation might be used to treat not only epilepsy but also depression, Parkinson's, and other neurological ailments. Such devices could also carry out constant recordings of electrical activity in the patient's brain.[4] Another device can be implanted under the patient's skull; this device senses abnormal electrical activity and then sends a charge which can stop the seizure.[5]

Epilepsy kills 3,000 people per year (eight per day) in the USA.[6] God would not want to see people suffering from epileptic seizures in Heaven thus people with epilepsy could expect to be cured of this ailment when they get to Heaven. Therefore, God would have to recognize epileptics who die, even if for other reasons (drowning, falls, driving accidents, burning). How would God do the diagnosis? Would he be able to do an EEG or blood work? Can God record electrical activity in the brain? Would God disconnect such implanted devices as above. If a person dies during an epileptic seizure, God would have to know which form of epilepsy the new Heaven resident had. A double challenge for God would be if the child/teen/adult had both epilepsy and ADHD.

Here is an example of diagnosis using modern medical approaches. Evelyn was born on New Year's Day, 2012. Doctors, other medical personnel and her parents realized she had problems immediately. She had seizures every few minutes and her blood sugar fluctuated way too much. Drugs did not help so doctors took blood samples from Evelyn and her parents and sent them to the hospital laboratory for genetic testing (for a molecular diagnosis). Technicians extracted DNA from the blood samples, copied it millions of times, cut it up into small fragments with ultrasound, and loaded the samples onto chips. The chips were loaded into Illumina's HiSeq 2500 sequencer which read all the sequences in 28 hours. A supercomputer took the information and reordered it by aligning the genetic fragments with a reference genome. Then the supercomputer searched for differences in the sequences of the DNA samples of Evelyn and her parents compared to the reference sample. There could be millions of differences, but most are harmless. A bioinformatics software program determined that Evelyn had a mutation in her SCN2A gene. This gene encodes a neuronal voltage gated sodium channel protein that functions in brain neurons. Her parents did not have that mutation. Thus, the mutation must have occurred in the sperm or egg that led to Evelyn's development. That mutation results in Ohtahara syndrome, which is a rare form of pediatric epilepsy. New medications and a low carbohydrate diet led to significant improvement in Evelyn's health, and she was ultimately released from the hospital with her seizures controlled. Additional diagnoses such as this are regularly performed at Children's Mercy Hospital in Kansas City, MO.[7]

We can wonder how God could make such a diagnosis in a deceased infant, teen, or adult, and then cure the ailment.

NOTES

1   David Noonan, "The Science of Health: The Epilepsy Dilemma," *Scientific American*, Volume 316, No. 4, April, 2017, 28-29.

2   Epilepsy Foundation website, accessed December 2017, https://www.epilepsy.com/about/impact.

3   WebMD website, "Epilepsy Resource Center, accessed January 2018, www.webmd.com/epilepsy.

4   Murray Carpenter, "Electricity Tamps Down Epilepsy," *Popular Science*, November 2015, 40.

5   David Noonan, "The Science of Health: The Epilepsy Dilemma," *Scientific American*, Volume 316, No. 4, April, 2017, 28-29.

6   CDC website, "Sudden Unexpected Death in Epilepsy (SUDEP)," last reviewed, May 12, 2022, www.cdc.gov/epilepsy/communications/features/sudep.htm

7   Melinda Wenner Moyer, "Infant Possibilities," *Popular Science*, August, 2014, 52-57.

25

BLOOD

BLOOD IS A very important component of the body and must itself be healthy for the body to be healthy. The blood has a cellular component and a fluid component. The blood carries oxygen from the lungs to the body and carbon dioxide from the body to the lungs. Blood carries nutrients (protein, carbohydrates, fats, vitamins and minerals) to the body and metabolic wastes to the kidneys and liver.[1] If residents in Heaven are going to talk, sing, walk, run, dance, and play music, they will have to eat and breathe, thus, blood will be important.

In 1658 Jan Swammerdam, a Dutch naturalist, showed with a microscope that there are cells in the blood. In 1695 Anton van Leeuwenhoek, a Dutch microscopist, identified the red cells of the blood. In 1842 Alfred Donne, a French physician, identified platelets in the blood. In 1879 Paul Ehrlich, a German-Jewish physician, developed a method of staining and counting blood cells.[1] This is a good moment to reiterate that the Bible was written much earlier; the Old Testament from the 1600s-400s BCE and the New Testament from 70-120 CE.[2a] Not much was known about science at the time the Bible was being written, yet people believe vehemently in the Bible even today.

The red cells of the blood are called erythrocytes and originate from the bone marrow as hematopoietic stem cells (erythroblasts) which differentiate into erythrocytes in the blood. Erythrocytes synthesize hemoglobin which is the oxygen carrying protein of the body. Hemoglobin is composed of 2 alpha-globin peptide chains and 2 beta-globin peptide chains which together surround a molecule of heme, an iron containing compound, to which oxygen binds. Oxygen levels in the body are thus dependent upon the number of erythrocytes, the amount of alpha- and beta-globin chains, and the amounts of heme and iron. People with too little iron in the blood and tissues are said to be anemic.[1]

Many diseases do not necessarily show obvious symptoms, but the medical community has diagnostic tools. Consider the many diseases of the blood influencing any one of the cell types of the blood including the numbers and functions of red cells, platelets and lymphocytes, and thus adversely affecting the health of the individual. A complete blood count can reveal many different diseases. Blood is a very complex mixture of substances, and more than 150 ailments/diseases can be detected and diagnosed by examining blood components. A metabolic panel of chemicals, such as the high- and low-density lipoproteins, other lipids, oxygen, iron, vitamins, and hormones such as growth hormone, prolactin, estrogen and progesterone, and thyroxine. Levels of these chemicals can indicate diseases or ailments (slow growth of infants, lower fertility in women, lower energy levels); each can be instructive. Enzyme markers can indicate risk for cancer, liver disease, stroke, or celiac disease.

The medical establishment is fast developing a simple blood test to detect some additional medical conditions and characteristics including concussions, Alzheimer's disease, and other dementias. But blood tests are time consuming and not so straightforward. Thus, a test is being developed for malaria that does not require a blood sample nor a microscope or trained technician. A finger is placed in a "cradle" and magnets and a beam of red light can detect changes in red blood cells caused by the malaria parasite. This one-minute test can result in medical procedures and medications to be obtained very quickly to combat this terrible disease; the test is being developed in Uganda where malaria is one of the leading causes of death.[2b] What kinds of tests will God have available?

Two genetic diseases of the blood are beta-thalassemia and sickle cell disease, and each affects the beta-globin peptide, but a different portion, and each is a recessive gene disease. Both diseases are targets of gene therapy. Here is how the therapy would work.[3] Blood cell precursors, called hematopoietic stems cells, are taken from the bone marrow of a sickle cell patient. In people with these diseases all their cells have a mutant beta-globin gene on each set of chromosomes. The mutant cells are treated with CRISPR/Cas9 which cuts out the mutant globin gene and inserts a wild-type (normal) gene. (see chapter 15). The "corrected" stem cells are injected into the bone marrow of the patient. The progeny of these stem cells will have "normal" beta-globin and will not cause the cells to assume the sickle shape. Similarly, CRISPR/cas9 is being used to exchange the mutant gene responsible for beta-thalassemia resulting in red blood cells with healthy oxygen carrying capacity.[4]

Another "genetic fix" has been described for hypertrophic cardiac my-opathy (HCM) which results from a defective gene identified as MYBPC3. The mutant gene causes thickening of the heart muscle and severe effects on blood circulation. In this case what is suggested is that a man with the MYBPC3 defective gene provides a sample of his sperm and the CRISPR/Cas 9 method is used to replace the defective gene in the sperm. A fertilized egg resulting from the "corrected" sperm would then develop into a person that would not exhibit HCM.[3]

God would either identify patients with one of these genetic diseases before they die or diagnose the disease at the time of death. Presumably God would correct these genetic diseases in ALL of the patient's cells when the patient reached Heaven. Therefore, there would be no genetic diseases of the blood in Heaven. This is really wishful thinking and requires that God is a molecular geneticist.

Platelets are part of the white cells of the blood and have an important role in blood clotting, called coagulation. The blood must clot in the case of injuries. But, we don't want blood to clot such that a clot will travel to the heart, shut off blood to a portion of the heart and cause a heart attack. Likewise, we don't want a clot to travel to the brain and shut off blood to a portion of the brain and cause a stroke. If a person is hospitalized with an injury to a foot, care must be provided to prevent a blood clot from traveling from the site of injury to the heart or brain. Hospitals invest a lot of effort and research on anti-coagulation agents to prevent these blood clots from forming. One Midwest hospital has a physician designated the Anti-coagulation Quality Physician, to lead this effort and to insure that the entire staff in that hospital is alert to proper procedures with each patient.

In addition to platelets, which are involved in and very necessary for blood clotting, there are lymphocytes and leukocytes in the blood, both having roles in infection and disease prevention and cleaning up debris from the blood. They are also called T and B cells and originate from the bone marrow and/or lymph nodes and the spleen. The T and B cells are also called white cells. Some white cells mature in the thymus gland. White cells can give rise to many types of cancers, generally called leukemias and lymphomas. Symptoms of these cancers are swollen lymph nodes, pain in the bones, weakness and fatigue, easy bruising and bleeding and frequent infections. Cancers of the blood can result from genetic mutations, chemicals in the environment, or chromosome translocations. The adverse effect is to turn-on oncogenes, genes involved in cancer. Treatment is chemotherapy, radiation, or stem-cell transplantation.[5]

Because of disease and/or injury, a person can lose blood and be in need of a blood transfusion to prevent death. But blood cannot be donated willy-nilly to a recipient because the donor's blood type has to match the recipient's blood type. The blood types are determined by antigens that reside on the blood cells of each person, named A, B, AB, and O. The immune system of a person with A type blood would consider donated blood from a person with B type blood to be foreign and would develop an immune reaction to that "foreign" substance, the B antigen. Likewise, B people cannot accept blood from an A person. AB blood would be foreign to either an A or B type person. But an AB person could accept blood from any type person and is called the universal recipient. O type blood has neither type of antigen, so it is the universal donor. But O type people can only accept O type blood.

Another factor to consider in blood donations and in pregnancy is the Rh factor. People are either Rh + or Rh -. The main Rh antigen is called the D antigen. If it is not present on the mother's blood cells but is present on the blood cells of the fetus, the mother may react to the "foreign" antigen of the fetus's blood circulating through the placenta. These Abs tax the fetus blood cell making system and may cause many problems in the fetus and even death.[6]

There may not be any diseases in Heaven and thus no need for blood transfusions in that regard. But with the activities mentioned above there very well could be loss of blood due to injury and thus the need for blood donations. Maybe God will just wave his magic wand when a person needs blood. Or, God may have "blood banks" as we have on earth. God made man in his image so that might mean God has an unlimited supply of O blood which he can donate to anyone.

Here is an interesting but tragic true case. Ken (not his real name) was employed as a cashier in a party store in a mid-west state. At home one weekend Ken severely damaged his left hand while using a chain saw to clear out fallen trees in his yard after a storm. He was away from work for three weeks while his hand was healing. He returned to work on a Tuesday even though his hand was still swollen and wrapped up and he was his natural enthusiastic self who loved to talk sports with customers, especially about his favorite college team. He was the biggest sports fan ever. On Wed. Ken was not feeling well and that evening he suffered a stroke and died. A blood clot from his injured hand may have migrated to his brain. He was only fifty-five years old. Will God heal up his hand? Will God diagnose the stroke damage and give Ken his healthy brain back filled with sports information? In Heaven will he have the opportunity to talk sports? Will Ken get to play sports in Heaven?

Childbirth safety standards have been the subject of analysis.[7] Each year in the USA almost 700 women die and nearly 50,000 suffer severe injuries associated with giving birth to a child. Black mothers die three to four times the rate of white mothers. Hemorrhage and hypertension are the leading causes of maternal deaths and injuries, and both are preventable. Women suffer strokes because their high blood pressure is not treated quickly enough. Bleeding is extreme and not recognized. Ignoring hemorrhage and hypertension related to giving birth makes the USA the most dangerous place to give birth among developed nations. Two children every day in the USA lose their mothers at the time of their birth. The deceased mothers lose the opportunity to raise the child. Will the mothers and children meet in Heaven? At what age? Will they recognize each other in Heaven?

When a person dies the cells of the body die and that includes all the blood cells. When a person is embalmed the blood plasma is replaced by embalming fluid. When God resurrects a body, new blood cells in the correct proportion, each with the genome of the deceased person, must be added to the vascular system, the arteries and veins. The latter must be restored and cleaned of embalming fluid. The bone marrow and spleen must be restored in their functions of generating new blood cells. The new cells must be capable of differentiating into new arteries and veins and into the typical cells of the blood, including red cells, lymphocytes, macrophages, and platelets, in the correct proportions. All the plasma proteins necessary for clotting must be synthesized. Hemoglobin and all the other proteins of the blood plasma and blood cells must be synthesized. The vascular system has to be coordinated with the heart and blood vessel restoration. The blood represents many challenges to God.

NOTES

1   Campbell Biology, 10th Edition, Reese, Jane B. et.al.; www.timetoast.com/timelines/bloodhistory

2a   Biblica® website, "When was the Bible written?," accessed March 2020, https://www.biblica.com/resources/bible-faqs/when-was-the-bible-written/

2b   Jackie Marchildon, "Ugandan Man invents 1-Minute Malaria Test That Doesn't Require Blood," Global Citizen website, June 15, 2028, https://www.globalcitizen.org/en/content/uganda-bloodless-malaria-test.

3   Ma, Hong et al. "Correction of a pathogenic gene mutation in human embryos." *Nature* vol. 548,7668 (2017): 413-419. doi:10.1038/nature23305

4   Charlotte Harrison, "First gene therapy for β-Thalassemia approved," *Nature Biotechnology*, Volume 37, September 8, 2019, 1102-1103, https://www.nature.com/articles/d41587-019-00026-3.

5   "Blood cancer," City of Hope website, last updated June 21, 2022, https://www.cancercenter.com/blood-cancers.

6   Wikipedia website, "Rh blood group system," last edited March 12, 2023, https://en.wikipedia.org/wiki/Rh_blood_group_system.

7   A. Young, "Childbirth Safety Standards Could Save Mothers," *Detroit Free Press*, April 22, 2019, 9A.

26

AUTISM; ALZHEIMER'S

AUTISM

THE HISTORY OF autism is a "disturbing" story and is very sad and disheartening. In the 1940s, diagnosis of autism was essentially a death sentence.[1] Even in the 1960s, doctors and psychologists often encouraged parents to institutionalize their autistic children, saying they could not be helped. A study of cases in one state hospital showed that these children never had visitors and died without family or friends nearby to show some comfort and compassion. The cemetery of one hospital holds the remains of nearly 800 former patients, each marked with only a metal name tag.[2] Is God caring for these deceased autistic individuals? Will God ensure that they have loved ones in Heaven to interact with? We can wonder if these patients and autistic people through the decades to the present, were and are received in Heaven and if God corrects the autistic condition. Decades ago these autistic individuals were referred to as idiots, maniacs, or morons, based on their behaviors or lack of same. God could have done something to help autistics on earth but he didn't.

A range of symptoms is exhibited with autism, making a definition difficult. Here is an attempt at a definition: "A group of complex disorders of brain development, exhibited in varying degrees. The autistic person has difficulties in verbal and non-verbal communication and in social interaction and expresses repetitive behavior." But autistic people may be exceptional in music and academics. Finally, through the years, parents and physicians came to the realization that autistic individuals could be treated to lessen the symptoms, even if there is no cure. Not only is there no cure but the causes of autism remain unknown.[3]

One form of autism, now included in the "autism spectrum" definition, is Asperger's Syndrome, first described by the Viennese pediatrician, Hans Asperger. Asperger's is a mild form of autism seen in boys, in which case language development and intelligence are normal or even above normal but social skills and communication are lacking. Even then, Asperger's people want to fit in, and they work hard on social skills. They may be obsessive and collect things and know facts, like baseball statistics. They are somewhat clumsy and awkward.

In autism, the development of the brain is certainly involved. The characteristic features of autism begin to show up at six, nine, and twelve months and continue to appear at sixteen months and two years and thereafter, when the child does not use words or uses only two-word phrases. There are worst case scenarios: no language, no comprehension, aggressive behavior and violence, not sleeping for days. There are mild cases such as some speech, some communication, some social interaction, and not so much repetitive behavior. A study in Finland has made use of the fact that autistic people seem to have a natural affinity for computer games and technology.[4] Autistic individuals have trouble looking into a person's eyes but when playing a computer game do not have this difficulty with the virtual characters. Such games seem to keep the interest of autistic people and help them pay attention and perform tasks and lead to a better understanding of how to treat autism in any one person.

The causes of autism are not known but investigations have provided some clues.[5] Genetic factors seem to be involved. One thought is that each parent may have a subset of perhaps 200 genes, not enough to show symptoms, but a child may inherit the total 200 from each parent and thus display symptoms. In identical twins, the concordance is not 100% but varies from 60-90%. One twin may have autism but the other may not. And one twin may have a greater or lesser degree of autism than the other twin. Fraternal twins have a 20-30% concordance; thus, environment has a role. At least 5,000 genes are involved in brain development and the cerebrum, cerebellum and limbic parts are all likely involved in autism. Estimates are that 1,000 genes could play a role in autism disorders. Genes likely interact in autism, i.e., they show pleiotropism, as is the case in epilepsy and attention deficit hyperactivity disorder (ADHD). An ingenious study was summarized in Discover Magazine,[6] in which the investigators sequenced the entire genomes of thirty-two children with autism and compared the sequences with each other and with the genome sequences of non-autistic kids. Half of the thirty-two had genetic variants linked to social anxiety, epilepsy, other signs of autism which impact social interaction, language development, and behavior. Also, four gene variants were identified that had not previously been connected to autism. Will God know what the products of these genes are and how they contribute to autism?

In April 2016, our nation's largest ever autism research study was launched seeking to gather DNA and other information from 50,000 USA families with autism. Data will be gathered from twenty sites across the country on genetic, behavioral, and environmental factors possibly involved in autism from toddlers to adults.[7]

The challenges to God in Heaven will be to diagnose autism in individual cases and decide whether to correct the autism condition. That decision will require understanding what level of autism the individual has and what genes or environmental conditions might be involved. Will God be able to sequence the entire genome of every person who dies? What if a child dies as a fetus or at birth, will God know that this child would have been autistic and proceed to correct the genes? Are the environmental factors involved in autism not going to be present in Heaven?

ALZHEIMER'S

Alzheimer's is a terrible, devastating affliction and one of the most puzzling to affect people of middle to old age. There is no cure, and the cause is not understood. Genetic and environmental factors may play roles. There is an early onset Alzheimer's, affecting individuals of forty to sixty years of age, and a late-onset Alzheimer's, affecting individuals of sixty years old and beyond. More than five million Americans over sixty years of age currently have Alzheimer's disease and by 2050 that number is estimated to climb to fourteen million.[8] In the USA this form of dementia causes the deaths of nearly 100,000 people every year, 274 every day; this disease is the sixth leading cause of death in the USA.[9] The number of Alzheimer's patients is expected to reach 100 million worldwide and sixteen million in the USA as the nation's seventy-six million baby boomers reach old age. Medicaid and Medicare will spend over $150 billion caring for patients with Alzheimer's and other forms of dementia which is about 260 times more than NIH is spending on looking for prevention and cures.[10] Note that Alzheimer's is one of eight different forms of dementia.[11] In Heaven, will God cure Alzheimer's and the other dementias in all these millions of sufferers?

Aloysius Alzheimer, a German physician, had a patient admitted to the Hospital for the Mentally Ill and Epileptics in Frankfort in 1901. This woman, Auguste Deter, was confused and delusional, thinking people were trying to kill her, and she became wild and out-of-control. She continued to get worse and when she died five years later, Dr. Alzheimer examined her brain hoping to find clues as to her mental deterioration. What he found among seemingly healthy brain structures were small clumps of hard bundles of protein called amyloid plaques and also, extending from nerve bundles were protein fibers, called tau, that were thickened and tangled.[12] These amyloid plaques and tau tangles are still today the characteristic features of the brains of Alzheimer's patients, and are believed to be the cause of the mental deterioration in such patients and much research is directed to understanding their roles.

According to neurologist Rudolph Tanzi, of Harvard Medical school, the present mantra is: prediction, early detection, and intervention.[13] Research has led to the finding that amyloid plaques, clusters of protein fragments called beta-amyloid peptides, collect outside of neurons in the brain and screw up the signaling system between neurons, disrupting communication and leading to progressive memory loss, confusion, and difficulty doing simple physical tasks. The tau protein, in contrast, has adverse effects inside nerve cells, accumulating as thin strands that choke the neurons, inhibiting electrical signal passage, and finally leading to death of the neurons. Furthermore, tau can cause a cascade of events that spreads and leads to more damage to the memory and cognitive circuitry of the brain, speeding up the mental deterioration associated with Alzheimer's.

The relationship of amyloid plaques and tau protein is complicated by a possible role of inflammation. Nevertheless, clever and persistent research methods are slowly uncovering the basics of Alzheimer's.[13]

During the years 2010-2015, more than a dozen errant genes have been associated with Alzheimer's. These so-called "renegade" DNA sequences may provide insights into causes of Alzheimer's and if these mutant genes can be found early in life, they may be predictors and thus lead to preventative measures. (Linda Marsa, 2015, articles on Alzheimer's). One should note that the way these mutant genes are identified is to compare DNA sequences of Alzheimer's patients with those of healthy patients. Such a study is not done on a few or even a dozen individuals, but on as many as 50,000 people. One such gene is ApoE-4; the mutant form of ApoE-4 is present in forty percent of people with late-onset Alzheimer's. By 2013, an international research consortium identified eleven more mutant genes associated with late-onset Alzheimer's and in 2015 more were added to make the total twenty-one. Some of these genes are associated with neural interaction, how they talk to each other. Others are involved in the immune response and inflammation, supporting the contention that plaques, tangles and inflammation all play roles. Another mutant gene codes for an enzyme that is normally "protective" but the mutant enzyme fails at this role, enhancing the symptoms of Alzheimer's. Another "protective" gene was discovered in a study of over 1,500 individuals in Iceland. Even if these individuals had the APOE-4 mutation, they did not get Alzheimer's.

Women are more likely than men to get Alzheimer's, an observation that was the subject of a presentation at the Alzheimer's Assoc. International Conference on July 16, 2019. The APOE-4 gene seems to raise more risks for women than for men. Tau was more prevalent and more widely distributed in women with mild impairment than in men with mild impairment. Analysis of genes in 30,000 women vs men, half with and half without Alzheimer's, found four genes related to the disease by sex.[15] Is God aware of these four genes and how they relate to Alzheimer's disease?

While there is no cure for Alzheimer's, a 2017 report[16] raises encouragement towards prevention. This study of 1,260 men and women in Finland showed that those who received excellent nutrition, exercised both their body and mind regularly and were monitored regularly by medical personnel, showed improvement on cognitive measures of memory and mental processing speed, compared to individuals in the control group. Nevertheless, symptoms of dementia still occurred, although delayed and lessened. Two additional studies involving thousands of older people buttress the results of the Finnish study and show that a healthy lifestyle results in a lower incidence of Alzheimer's even in people with genes that predispose people to Alzheimer's. One study was at Rush University in the USA and another was in the UK.[17] We can only hope that Heaven will provide the anti-Alzheimer's environment similar to that of the Finnish study and God will cure Alzheimer's in those people who have this form of dementia and also other forms when they enter Heaven.

Electrical stimulation of the brains of patients with Alzheimer's or other forms of dementia has resulted in improvement of the memories of these patients. This may be a breakthrough and awaits clinical trials.[8] Along that line, a blood test for Alzheimer's may be on the horizon.[18] In a study of 3,285 patients in early stages of Alzheimer's the drug aducanumab resulted in less cognitive decline and less amyloid protein build-up in 15% - 27% of the patients. These results have led to additional studies with more patients.[19]

God has four main challenges dealing with Alzheimer's: 1. Recognizing people who die of heart attacks and strokes and other causes before Alzheimer's symptoms appear but have developed the beginnings of the disease. 2. Recognizing people who have Alzheimer's and die because of accidents, heart attack, stroke, kidney failure, pneumonia or other infections, dehydration and other conditions associated with Alzheimer's. 3. Recognizing people who die of Alzheimer's who are older, and their bodies have many of the conditions associated with old age (arthritis, vision and hearing problems, GI tract problems, kidney problems, cancer, vascular problems). 4. Restoring the memories lost during their period with Alzheimer's. Note that God will have an equally difficult challenge in Heaven with deceased stroke patients or with deceased patients with any one of the more than two dozen other neurological disorders.[20]

Will people in Heaven see their parents and grandparents as mentally and physically healthy individuals after seeing them on earth with Alzheimer's or some other form of dementia?

266

NOTES

1   John Donvan and Caren Zucker, *In a Different Key, The Story of Autism*, (New York: Crown, 2016.)

2   John Donvan and Caren Zucker, "The Early History of Autism in America, *Smithsonian Magazine* online, January 2016, https://www.smithsonianmag.com/science-nature/early-history-autism-america-180957684/.

3   Autism Society website, accessed February 2021, https://www.autismsociety.org/.

4   *Finnish American Reporter*, February 2017, 13.

5   Andrew Solomon, *Far From The Tree*, (New York: Scribner, 2012.)

6   Valerie Ross, "Autism genome sequenced," *Discover Magazine*, January/February 2014.

7   J. Aleccia, "Experts seek help for the nations largest-ever Autism research study," *Detroit Free Press*, April 22, 2016, 2A.

8   J. English, "Let's do more to fight Alzheimers," *AARP Bulletin*, OctoberNovember 2015.

9   WebMD Editorial Contributors, "Understanding Alzheimer's Disease: the Basics," WebMD website, reviewed on February 3, 2021, https://www.webmd.com/alzheimers/guide/understanding-alzheimers-disease-basics.

10   The Editors Opinion, "The Inadequate War on Alzheimer's," *Bloomberg Businessweek*, August 10-23, 2015.

11   Alzheimer's Association website, "2017 Alzheimer's disease facts and figures," accessed March 2021, https://alz-journals.onlinelibrary.wiley.com/doi/10.1016/j.jalz.2017.02.001.

12   Wikipedia website, "Alois Alzheimer," last edited April 13, 2023, https://en.wikipedia.org/wiki/Alois_Alzheimer.

13   Wikipedia website, "Rudolph E. Tanzi," last edited March 12, 2023, https://en.wikipedia.org/wiki/Rudolph_E._Tanzi.

14   Geriatric Nursing website, "MRSA in the Elderly 101: The Essential Guide," accessed March 2021, http://geriatricnursing.org/mrsa-in-the-elderly.

15   Marilyn Marchione, "Clues emerge on Women's Alzheimer's disease risks," *Detroit Free Press*, July 18, 2019, 13A.

16   David A. Bennett, "Banking against Alzheimer's," *Scientific American*, April, 2017, Volume 26, 33-37.

17   *Time Health Magazine*, Fall 2019, 12; Resources, "Health and Wellness," *Autism Society website*, accessed May 2023, https://autismsociety.org/resources/health-wellness/.

18 Rachel Nania, "A Blood Test to Detect Alzheimer's Disease Moves Closer to Reality," *AARP Bulletin*, July 29, 2020.

19 Alice Park, "New Hope for the treatment and prevention of Alzheimers," *Time*, November 23, 2015, 16-17.

20 Frank E. Bair, Editor, *Alzheimer's, Stroke, and 29 Other Neurological Disorders Sourcebook* (New York: Omnigraphics, Inc., 1993.)

27

PAIN

IMAGINE ALL THE forms of pain humans and animals endure in their lives: birth contractions, earaches, toothaches, sore throats, ankle sprains, plantar fasciitis, knee pain, back pain, shoulder pain, stomach ache, appendicitis, concussions, migraine headaches, bumps, cuts, burns, infections, and on and on. Revelation 21:4 states: "And God shall wipe away all tears from their eyes; and there shall be no more death, neither sorrow, nor crying, neither shall there be any more pain: for the former things are passed away." And verse 5 states: And he that sat upon the throne said, "behold, I make all things new." These verses are referring to the conditions in Heaven. How will God accomplish that monumental task? To get an idea of how difficult that would be, we can look at how we deal with pain on earth. There is likely no one who has not experienced pain of some sort during their lifetime and since most people who die are elderly, they are possibly experiencing pain at the time of death. God will have to diagnose the kind of pain the deceased was suffering.

"Hospitals ask you to describe your pain on a scale of one-to-ten with ten being unbearable. But there is an eleven, which you can experience on any horseback ride longer than one tenth of a mile."[1] Now a personal note. That one-to-ten pain scale is posted in my urologist's waiting room too but so far I fortunately haven't come close to a ten. I have experienced the "eleven" but not by riding horseback. Instead, the eleven came from riding a bike with my nephew in Alaska to a trout stream that was more than five miles distant along a narrow, winding trail in uneven terrain. And my back side having already reached an eight, we peddled bikes all the way back, thus leading to the eleven. Oh, and the seat was one of those narrow ones with no cushion. Being a regular biker with a thicker back side, my nephew did not suffer the pain that I did and which for me lasted a couple of weeks. But we caught some nice trout while fly fishing and we were in very scenic country! The pain was well worth it!

A very common source of pain is the back, especially the lower back. Back pain can be debilitating and can lead to a person unable to hold a job, play sports, or even walk. New pain remedies, treatments, and prescriptions for pain are discovered regularly but before being put on the market prescriptions must be approved by the Food and Drug Association (FDA). One kind of back pain has the formidable name non-radiographic axial spondyloarthritis (nr-axSpA) for which a pain medication, a biologic called certolizumab pegol (Cimzia), was approved by the FDA in 2019. Nr-axSpA causes chronic, disabling back pain, stiffness, and fatigue but unlike the common ankylosing spondylitis there is no X-ray evidence of structural damage to the sacroiliac joints. Is God going to diagnose nr-axSpA and correct the condition in Heaven?[2] Maybe God will have an unlimited amount of OmegaXL, touted for back and joint pain by none other than a well-known talk-show host, on a 30-minute national television program in 2020. Web sites caution on whether OmegaXL is effective and that one should consult a physician before taking a compound that is advertised on the internet.[3]

Chronic pain can be debilitating. The body can be healed, as after a burn, but the pain pathways to the brain continue to transmit pain signals. Shoulder injuries have a high rate of resulting in chronic pain. Chronic pain is also more likely in HIV, diabetes and cancer patients undergoing treatment. A research goal is to stop the calcium carrying proteins that carry pain signals to the brain without shutting down the normal pain pathways. Pain is an important protection mechanism.[4]

Even in Heaven God should not eliminate pain completely. So, what kinds of pain will people suffer in Heaven? Sitting in a church pew all day could be painful! Growing food for the billions in Heaven could be painful at times.

What is pain? Sensors called "nociceptors" are spread throughout the body and respond to stimuli such as mechanical, chemical or temperature. The signals go up nerves, to the spinal cord, and up to the brain, and if interpreted as "danger" the brain identifies pain. If the interpretation is not dangerous, the pain is minimal or none.[5] The approach to dealing with pain by this Center may involve one or more of the following: pain education, graded exercise, manual therapy, stress management, and sleep hygiene.

Rev. 21:4 may be referring to both mental and physical pain. But let's have a look at physical pain by seeing what the Great Lakes Center of Regenerative Medicine had to say about physical pain and what can be done about it. The Center ran an ad recruiting participants in three days of seminars in three locations in and around Detroit in Sept., 2019. Millions suffer from joint pain, which is pain associated with one or more joints in the body, places where bones connect with bones but with cartilage in between for a smooth, lubricated surface and a soft interface. Joints are in the neck and all along the spinal column. Other joints include the shoulders, elbows, wrists, hands, hips, knees, ankles, and feet. The conditions that can lead to joint pain include arthritis, cartilage damage, loss of cartilage, tendon inflammation, bursitis, and meniscus tears.[6] At the above seminars, the treatment recommended for these areas of pain is stem cell therapy. Stem cells from the skin, which normally will give rise to epidermal cells, can be grown in culture to become pluripotent and give rise to many different cell types, including the cells of the joint, to restore the normal joint conditions, and alleviate the pain in the joint. The idea is that the stem cells can be injected into the site of pain, such as the joint or even the brain after a stroke and will form new and healthy tissue at that site, thus repairing the site, restoring normal function, and alleviating the pain.

Another form of pain suffered by over twenty million in the USA is peripheral neuropathy. This pain has been described as sharp, electrical-like, or burning. Neuropathy is caused by inflammation or damage to the nerves and the associated pain can adversely affect work and play. There is not only pain but also numbness, cramping, and tickling or pricking of the hands and feet. A free dinner was advertised for participants participating in a seminar about a treatment program for neuropathy sufferers.[7]

Many skin ailments, some of which are due to mutations in genes coding for epidermal proteins, such as epidermal bullous ichthyosis caused by abnormal epidermal proteins, and others with unknown causes, such as eczema, all of which cause much pain and suffering.[8]

One way pain is treated is to take a pain medication, such as aspirin, which has been used for decades and is still used to alleviate pain. Other pain medications now available over the counter include Tylenol®, Aleve® (naproxen; vicodin), acetaminophen and ibuprofen (Motrin®). A stronger pain medication can be obtained with a prescription from a physician. Some of these are carfentanil, heroin, hydromorphone, oxymorphone, oxycodone, oxycontin, and vicoden. The problem with these opioids is that they provide a sense of euphoria for the patient and with continuous use the body becomes sensitized to the dose and the euphoria is achieved only upon increasing dosage. The painkiller may become addictive, a major world problem that is now considered an opioid epidemic that kills more than 130 USA citizens every day.[9]

A program on public TV in March, 2020, dealt with how to alleviate pain of many types, but mainly shoulder pain and lower back pain. The theory was that these pains are due to muscles being out of balance causing other parts of the body, like joints, to be out of position causing nerves to react by sending pain signals to the brain. One of the causes of these imbalances was purported to be sitting too much with lack of exercise. The method suggested was to do a set of yoga exercises with the goal being to put muscles of the area in pain back into balance. Several patients, now pain free, attested to the method working. Perhaps God will have Heaven residents doing yoga exercises and staying active and not continually sitting around his throne and worshiping him. But exercises, and especially sports, are guaranteed to cause injuries and thus pain. Perhaps the "new glorified" bodies God gives Heaven residents will be such that they will always be in balance and pain free.

If there is to be no pain in Heaven, then factors that might cause pain, such as activities (dancing, sports, cooking, farming) that could result in injuries or burns, will not be permitted. And care will have to be taken not to partake of too much of the feasts that will be served. Arthritis will be non-existent. Strains and muscle soreness will not be allowed.

What kind of boring life will it be?

NOTES

1   David Petzal, "What is the Meaning of Life?," *Field and Stream Magazine*, December 2019 – January 2020, 70-73.

2   Arthritis Today, August 2019, 28.

3   Consumer Health Digest website, accessed October 2019, www.consumer-healthdigest.com/joint-pain.

4   Chad Galts, "Speak, Memory," *Brown Alumni Monthly*, April/May 2020, 16-17.

5   Jeff Smith, "How do we experience pain?," *Health and Healing Publication*, Summer 2019, 1-4.

6   Mayo Clinic website, "Center for Regenerative Biotherapeutics," accessed October 2019, https://www.mayo.edu/research/centers-programs/center-regenerative-biotherapeutics/about/about-regenerative-medicine#.

7   *Detroit Free Press*, September 15, 2019; Ad about seminar on neuropathy; Center for Regenerative Medicine, *Detroit Free Press*, January 5, 2020, 16A.

8   Human Genomics website, accessed November 2019, https://humgenomics.biomedcentral.com.

9   Doctors Fueled by Greed; *Detroit Free Press*, September 15, 2019, 1A.

28

AGE OF HEAVEN RESIDENTS

WHAT AGE WILL Heaven residents be? One idea is that a person's age in Heaven is the same age they were at the time of their death. Another idea is that a person's age may be that of their prime age on earth, when they were most healthy and things were going great, at the early thirties. Some may have had their best years on earth at a younger age, others at an older age. Ideally, God would let everyone choose the age they want to be. Isaiah 11:6-9 speaks of children in Heaven. Fetuses, infants and children may want to begin at the age they were when they died so as to not miss the "growing up" years. It would be a shame to deprive someone of a childhood. Ideally God will let these youngsters grow up under the tutelage of adults, perhaps even adults who did not have children on earth. Why not even have these kids attend school? Letting kids age in Heaven might be the ideal thing to do except that their experiences will be unlike those on earth. So, there will be challenges facing God just deciding on everyone's age in Heaven. People who die in their teens or twenties might want to start again at that age when they are in Heaven and continue to experience life as they would have on earth, perhaps even being parents. In Heaven, Alcorn[1] says, "whether or not anyone is the size and appearance of a child, we'll all be childlike in the ways that will bring joy to us and to our Father."

The most accepted view is that Heaven residents will be thirty-three years of age, the prime time of our lives on earth, a time when we are healthy, full of energy, and not yet having progressed at all toward old age.[1] This age is presumably the age of Jesus when he was crucified and ascended into Heaven. Jesus is going to transform bodies according to Philippians 3:21 which states: "Who shall change our vile body that it may be fashioned like unto his glorious body, according to the working whereby he is able to subdue all things unto himself." The subject of the age of people in Heaven has been dealt with in considerable depth.[1] The church's consensus in the thirteenth century was that everyone would be resurrected as they would have appeared at age 33, even if they died much younger than that, even as an infant. The medieval theologian Thomas Aquinas favored the age of 33 for Heaven residents because children have not yet reached that ideal age and those older have already passed that prime age.[1]

Having thirty-three be the age of everyone in Heaven creates three challenges for God. The first is how to decrease the age of those older than thirty-three when they died, some being eighty, ninety, and even 100. Note that centenarians numbered over 320,000 in the world in 2012 with most of them in the USA, Japan, China, and India but also in many other countries.[2] Think of all the age-related ailments, internal and external, that would have to be diagnosed and eliminated. Not only will God have to reverse-age all the deceased old people but he will have to heal all their ailments, which are quite abundant and include atherosclerosis (hardening of the arteries), other cardiovascular ailments, osteoporosis, type 2 diabetes, arthritis, hypertension, Parkinson's disease, and dementia (Alzheimer's disease), not to mention poor eye sight and hearing, dental problems, surgeries, injuries, burns, wrinkles, baldness, and more. Of the roughly 150,000 people who die each day worldwide, 100,000 (66%) die of one or more of these age-associated ailments; that fraction is 90% in industrialized countries. In the USA, the Covid-19 virus took the lives of three and even four thousand people each day in late 2020 and early 2021, the majority being older folks.[3] Each year 610,000 people in the USA die of heart disease; one of every 4 deaths. Together that is a lot of deceased people for God to diagnose and deal with.[4] The average life span in the USA is now near eighty for both women and men and more and more people are living to be over 100 years old. A great challenge, therefore, would be for God to reverse aging and to have all these old people become youthful, back to age thirty-three, in perfect health. What will God do with all the memories and experiences in the brains of a 100-year-old when he makes that person thirty-three years old? Will they just be eliminated? Maybe that 100-year-old would be happy just to have fewer ailments and to stay at 100 years old.

Another method of making the old younger is to give blood plasma from young to old. In mice that transfusion is claimed to make old mice younger. A trial in California is underway to test this idea and also to see if young plasma will slow or reverse the ravages of Alzheimer's disease. One might expect that God would know what those "youth" factors are and could infuse them directly into the new Heaven residents without bothering with plasma. Will there be chemistry laboratories and pharmacies in Heaven?

The second challenge God faces is to stop the aging process at age thirty-three. The best we can hope for on earth is to slow the aging process; stopping the aging process seems far-fetched. A magic elixir has yet to be developed/invented, like a pill one could take daily that will stop aging. Beginning with Ponce de Leon people have searched for the "fountain of youth" and yes, dietary suggestions are plentiful and include red wine, green tea, blueberries, kale, and plenty more. Exercise too! Other suggestions to slow the aging process include life-style changes of a physical nature. Crowley and Lodge[5] in their book, *Younger Next Year*, make an abundance of suggestions concentrating on exercise and nutrition but include attitude and behavior as well. Another life-style change many are already trying is a low-calorie diet.[6]

The world has Blue Zones, places where people appear to be healthier and live longer, on average, than the rest of the world.[7] The five Blue Zones listed are: Okinawa, Sardinia, Costa Rica, Greece, and Loma Linda, CA. Correlated with the good health and long lives of these people are the following: less smoking, a semi-vegetarian diet with lots of legumes, nuts, and wine, physical activity that is moderate and regular, maintenance of a healthy body weight, social engagement, stress reduction, having a life purpose, and spirituality/religion. If Heaven is going to be a Blue Zone, the difficulty at the "Get Go" is going to be that most of the residents will be old and overweight! What a challenge to bring these people down in both age and weight! Common sense would tell us that someone who lives longer is going to be healthier throughout their life, but do we know that to be true for people of the Blue Zones? We can all identify with people who have looked "old" early in their lives, but they nevertheless have gone on to live on into their nineties and beyond.

Other zones are related to aging. Consider zip code zones. It is possible to predict life span of people by what zip code zone they live in. Studies that have been carried out in Chicago, Washington DC, and New York show that the zip code zone people live in is a predictor of life expectancy; those in the most impoverished areas with high unemployment, low income, few easily accessible healthy groceries, less green space, less medical care, and polluted air have the shortest life expectancies.[8] Are we surprised? Clearly lifestyle and the environment are factors in aging.

There is much interest and effort into not only living healthier but living longer; some have suggested that someday living to 130 will be commonplace. Consider the Church of Perpetual Life in Florida with the gospel being immortality. Mark Zuckerberg and his wife Priscilla Chan have invested billions of dollars into their science program with the goal being to cure all disease. There is Unity Biotechnology that is developing therapies for age-related ailments. Universities including Harvard and Stanford as well as the National Institutes of Health are working on interventions of the aging process. Several chemical substances have shown promise. One of these, Metformin, is the subject of the only FDA-sponsored study to look at whether a specific drug can slow aging.[9]

There are some cases of immortality in the living world and include a few species of bacteria, perennial plants, and some of the simple animals like hydra and protozoa. One human cell line, the HeLa cell line, appears to be immortal, has been growing in cell culture for many decades, and is commonly used in cell biology research. HeLa is the cell line that was used to develop the polio vaccine. The source of this cell line was a cervical cancer in a patient, Henrietta Lacks. The genome of this cell line has no doubt been modified by rearrangements, mutations, and losses and gains of DNA and thus it would not be possible to clone Henrietta Lacks from HeLa cells. While the cell line is immortal, Henrietta Lacks is not. Variations in the aging process occur in the animal world; in rats, 30% of the population get cancer by three years of age whereas 30% of humans get cancer by age eighty-five. Humans, dogs, and rabbits get Alzheimer's disease, but rodents do not. Old rodents die of cancer or kidney disease but not of cardiovascular disease.[10]

The third challenge concerning age thirty-three is how to age those younger than thirty-three, like fetuses, infants, children, and teens, and then stop the aging process at thirty-three. Perhaps God can learn something from observations and studies of accelerated aging in humans, known as progeroid syndromes.[11] These are rare instances wherein youngsters exhibit old age symptoms and die of old age health problems but at a young chronological age; all are genetic disorders; one or more mutations are associated with each of the premature aging disorders. A total of nine of these disorders have been identified worldwide: Werner Syndrome, Bloom Syndrome, Rothmund-Thomson Syndrome, Cockayne Syndrome, Xeroderma Pigmentosa Syndrome, Trichothiodystrophy Syndrome, Restrictive Dermopathy Syndrome, and Hutchinson-Gilford Progeria Syndrome. Werner Syndrome and Hutchinson-Gilford Syndromes are due to mutations in the gene for Lamin A/C which is a protein involved in function of the nuclear envelope (membrane surrounding the nuclear contents). The mutated form of lamin alters the movement of DNA repair proteins into and out of the nucleus and causes premature aging because DNA cannot be repaired. The other seven syndromes above are all caused by mutations in the DNA repair proteins; these are Req Q protein-like helicases and nucleotide excision repair proteins. Again, if DNA repair is adversely affected then accelerated aging occurs, leading to the syndromes of premature aging.

Werner and Hutchinson-Gilford (H-G) individuals most resemble the natural aging process in showing hair loss, osteoporosis, muscle wasting, and skin atrophy. Also, their growth slows giving them a short stature, a large head, small chin and lower jaw. Aging occurs at an accelerated rate.[12] If God were to age fetuses, infants and children, he might utilize the method of interfering with the lamin proteins, as is the case in these syndromes. But while accelerated, these individuals do not age instantly but gradually through several years and may live into their forties and fifties and then die generally of cardiovascular disease or cancer. In 2006 there were 1,300 cases of Werner Syndrome in the world. The Werner gene shows a range of thirty-five different mutations, each causing the syndrome, each directly or indirectly adversely affecting the WRNP protein; this protein is a 1,432 amino acid long RecQ helicase which unwinds DNA when repair or replication occurs. If DNA is not repaired or there are errors in replication, the problem mushrooms throughout the genome leading to acceleration of the aging process. In H-G Progeria the rate of aging is 7X the normal; the first case was identified in 1886 and only 130 cases are known to date. The syndrome is generally diagnosed by three years of age. Heart and cardiovascular diseases cause death at thirteen years of age on average. The mutations are in the LMNA gene (lamin A gene) and are sporadic as opposed to being inherited. The common mutation is a deletion of 150 base pairs which results in fifty amino acids missing from the lamin A protein and thus causes malfunction of the nuclear envelope.[12]

Another accelerated aging syndrome is Progeroid Neonatal syndrome in which case aging begins in utero and the baby is born already looking like an old person. Death is within six years of life.[13]

When one of the above accelerated aged individuals dies, God will have quite a challenge. God will have to recognize that the deceased is chronologically young but physiologically old. He will have to identify the aging syndrome involved and correct the genetic problem, for example, add the correct sequence of bases to the 150 base pair deletion in the lamin LMNA gene in all cells of that body. Then, if God decides to make the person thirty-three-years-old he may have to subtract the physiological aging and add to the chronological age of the person. But will God somehow add experiences and memories to the person's brain? Alternatively, having corrected the aging genetic problem, God could have the youngster begin at his/her chronological age in Heaven and have the youngster raised in Heaven by his/her own parent or family member previously deceased. The speeding up of the aging process and then stopping it at age thirty-three as well as insuring the person is 100% healthy, will be a huge challenge.

All chromosomes have a unique repeated sequence of DNA at their ends, i.e., the telomere. When cells replicate the DNA in preparation for division, an enzyme named DNA polymerase is involved. But the unique telomeric DNA at the very ends of the chromosome is not replicated by DNA polymerase and instead requires a different enzyme, telomerase, for its replication. Telomere shortening occurs each time cells divide and thus is associated with the aging process. The telomere provides stabilization to the chromosomes and has been studied with regard to whether the length of telomeres is correlated with animal life span or with animal aging. The results of several studies are inconclusive.[14] Higher levels of the enzyme telomerase are associated with telomere lengths and slower aging of cells is seen in tissue culture.[15] Attempts at human gene therapy are apparently being carried out in at least one country. The view is that aging is a disease and like other genetic diseases it is controlled by a gene, in this case the telomerase gene. If a person has an early form of dementia, perhaps increasing telomerase levels in the brain could rescue or at least stall the dementia. Certainly controversy exists around such an attempt and carefully controlled clinical trials are called for.[16]

Presumably God controlled life spans during the time indicated in the book of Genesis. Methuselah was the oldest man of the Bible and died at 969 years of age; Jared lived to 962: Noah lived to 950. Adam, the first man, lived to 930. Some of these old fellows were sexually active throughout their long lives indicating that their sperm cells were healthy. One can wonder if they suffered prostate enlargement as men do now. Sarah was the oldest woman of the Bible reaching 127 years and at ninety had a child with Abraham. Anna, a prophet, lived to eighty-four. God established an average life span of 120 or longer then dropped it severely to forty and now has raised it to near eighty in the industrialized world. But in many countries the average life expectancy is still in the forties.

The Bible says that the "vile" bodies of new Heaven residents will be given "new glorious bodies" fashioned after the body of Jesus (Philippians 3:21) and there will be no more death, sorrow, crying or pain (Revelation 21:4). The challenges with a new body will be how these new residents will be recognized by their spouses, family, and friends. This issue is discussed thoroughly by Alcorn.[1] Presently, recognition is mainly based on facial features. Facial surveillance is now a common part of police work. A face of a badly decomposed deceased body can be reconstructed to aid family and relatives in possible recognition. This forensic facial reconstruction is an amalgamation of artistry, anthropology, osteology, and anatomy. Many companies, such as banks and department stores, employ facial surveillance. We recognize friends and relatives based mainly on facial characteristics. If we look at decades old photographs, family members can often be recognized. So, if God chooses to make an eighty-year-old Heaven resident thirty-three-years-old, that person's face may very well be recognized. But if he ages an infant or child to thirty-three years old, how will he determine what facial features to utilize. In forensics there have been some attempts to determine how a missing person might look after years and years of being missing. Posting these pictures has not provided many successful searches. Facial recognition is becoming better with technology.[17]

DNA has been in the news more and more as a means of identifying a person, whether a possible criminal or a relative. When a person has their DNA sequenced, from then on, that sequence and the person's identity are in the records of the state or national gene bank and/or police files. DNA testing has aided law enforcement in solving decades-old crimes. Millions of people have had and currently are having their DNA sequenced. Crime scene DNA data solved a murder case by asking what family blood line sequences in the data base matched that crime scene sequence. Following the family trees led to the suspect. More than fifteen million Americans have their DNA sequence in consumer databases, 4.6 percent of the 328 million people in the USA population.[18] Perhaps God uses DNA to identify the deceased when, or in addition to, physical features are not available. God could have his own DNA sequences database acquired before birth or immediately at death, before any degradation, so that when Jesus returns and bodies in graves have all degenerated to ashes, or a person has been cremated, lost at sea, or destroyed in war, that individual can be resurrected using that DNA sequence. Alcorn (2004) implies that a person's DNA sequence may determine their ideal age in Heaven. Aha! People will still be regulated by their genes, even in Heaven, just as God presumably created life in the beginning.

Look into a mirror, turn your head from side to side, look up and down, use a hand mirror to look at your face from the side, and now do the same but change the lighting. Look at the sculptures of the presidents on Mt. Rushmore. Certainly we can note features but they are not all easy to describe. What we can say is that we are looking at faces of modern humans and we can identify each president and certainly our own face. It seems that facial recognition is centered in 6 nodes of the inferotemporal cortex of both hemispheres. Some of the neurons in these brain regions are active when viewing a face from the sides and others from the front.[19] Other parts of the brain recognize skin texture and color, eye color, size of the nose, chin and ears, amount of hair and its color, and on and on. Not only will Heaven residents have to have facial features recognizable to others, but Heaven residents will have to have the brain components needed for that recognition. Good sense would indicate that the best thing God could do would be to not change the ages of adults who have accumulated much history and memory while on earth. Sure, give them good health but don't change them to the point that they will not be recognized by family and friends. Embryos, fetuses, infants, children, and perhaps even teens, should be given many years to make friends, acquire memories and a history, and to grow up and attend school in Heaven, under the guidance of elders and God. Maybe God could even let each person decide what age they want to be in Heaven. Alcorn[1] discusses the age of Heaven residents and points out that it is an issue that has been unresolved by the church or the Bible, but the consensus is that everyone will be at or near the age of thirty-three at the prime of life. Alcorn further speculates that children will have the opportunity to grow up in Heaven, perhaps guided and nurtured by their parents.[1] Is Heaven going to be a repeat of earth?

The question of what age Heaven residents will be is interesting to contemplate but there are no firm answers. Whether everyone will be the same age or there will be an assortment of ages, as on earth, God will still have a huge task to provide immortality for all Heaven's residents. If everyone in Heaven is thirty-three and there will be no deaths, then God has to accelerate the aging of children to stop at thirty-three and decrease the age of the elderly.

NOTES

1 Randy Alcorn, *Heaven: A Comprehensive Guide to Everything the Bible Says About Our Eternal Home* (Illinois: Tyndale Momentum, 2004.)

2 Wikipedia website, "Centenarian," last edited April 2, 2023, https://en.wikipedia.org/wiki/Centenarian.

3 *NBC Evening News*, December 7, 2020; February 8, 2021.

4 Jeffrey Kluger, "Covid-19 may lead to a heart-disease surge," *Time*, February 4, 2021, 18.

5 Chris Crowley and Henry S. Lodge, *Younger Next Year* (New York: Workman Publishing Co., 2005.)

6 Andrew Zaleski, "The Forever Man," *Popular Science*, Summer 2018, 108-113.

7   National Geographic, November, 2005; January, 2022.

8   Time Health Magazine, Fall 2019, 9.

9   Honor Whiteman, "Diabetic drug 'slows aging process and increases lifespan,' study suggest," MedicalNewsToday website, June 4, 2014;, https://www.medicalnewstoday.com/articles/277679.

10 Wikipedia website, "Ageing," last edited April 19, 2023, https://en.wikipedia.org/wiki/Ageing.

11 Wikipedia website, "Progeroid syndromes," last edited January 1, 2023, https://en.wikipedia.org/wiki/Progeroid_syndromes.

12 "Werner's Syndrome," FactDr® website, last updated December 20, 2021, https://factdr.com/health/werners-syndrome.

13 NIH/GARD website, "Neonatal progeroid syndrome," last updated February 2023, https://rarediseases.info.nih.gov/diseases/330/neonatal-progeroid-syndrome

14 Scott Gilbert and Michael J.F. Barresi, *Developmental Biology*, (UK: Oxford University Press, 2000.); Mather, Karen Anne et al. "Is telomere length a biomarker of aging? A review." *The journals of gerontology. Series A, Biological sciences and medical sciences* vol. 66,2 (2011): 202-13. doi:10.1093/gerona/glq180.

15 W.S. Klug and M.R. Cummings, *Concepts of Genetics*, (London: Pearson Education, Inc. 2003.)

16 Integrated Health Systems™ website, "Telomeres, Dementia, and Alzheimer's Gene Therapy, accessed May 2023, https://www.integrated-health-systems.com/blog/telomeres-dementia-and-alzheimers-gene-therapy/.

17 Alexander S. Gillis, "facial recognition," TechTarget website, last updated December 2022, https://www.techtarget.com/searchenterpriseai/definition/facial-recognition

18 Kristen V. Brown, "No One is Safeguarding Your DNA," *Bloomberg Businessweek,* March 4, 2019, 26.

19 Doris Y. Tsao, "Face Values," *Scientific American*, February 2019, 22-29.

29

CRYONICS

WHOLE BODY FREEZING

A CRYONICS LABORATORY in a major midwestern city experienced much interest nationally and internationally after accepting the body of a teenage girl from Great Britain in 2016. Her frozen corpse is now stored in liquid nitrogen in a large vat along with vats holding over 145 other human bodies and 125 pet bodies. The idea here is that when a cure is developed for the person's illness, i.e., cause of death, the body will be thawed and reanimated, the cure applied, and the person will continue in life here on earth but with her/his health restored. There are at least two additional cryo-laboratories in the world, one in Arizona and one in Russia. There are both supporters and skeptics of cryopreservation.[1] A professor in the neuroscience and human biology program at a major university says the entire idea is as close to impossible as anything he has heard of. Ask any person running a cell biology laboratory and that person will tell you that even freezing individual cells in numbers just in the hundreds, and being as efficient as possible, there is still a rather large number of cell deaths. Consistent demonstrations of reanimation after cryopreservation of a multicellular organism such as a mouse or pig would provide optimism.[2]

Cryopreservation has 5 main steps. 1. When the body is declared dead it is quickly moved into an ice bath. Injection of chemicals to reduce blood clotting is done and antacids are administered to reduce dissolving of the stomach lining. 2. The blood is pumped out of the body and an organ preserving solution is pumped in. 3. The body is transferred to the cryolab where the temporary preserving solution is replaced with an antifreeze to protect the cells from the deep freezing. The body is placed into a computer-controlled cooling unit. 4. The now-frozen body is placed into a bag and attached to a wooden board. 5. The body is lowered into a vat of liquid nitrogen and continues to cool to -320 degrees. There it awaits reanimation.

The question is whether the soul of the frozen person is still with the body in the liquid nitrogen. According to Dr. MacDougall (see Chapter 4), the soul leaves the body within minutes of death and presumably the effort would be to hurry the process to not only prevent death of cells, especially the brain, but to preserve the soul within the body. The soul and body together will then await reanimation. On the other hand, if the soul has already left the body before the liquid nitrogen deep freeze, then apparently God decided the individual is dead and the soul will be awaiting the body until the rapture. Thus, the frozen body will be no different in the eyes of God than any dead body. But it should be easier for God to restore the frozen body for a life in Heaven since it will not have decomposed. The cryolab in Arizona has the head of a famous baseball player preserved in liquid nitrogen. In this case, the soul of that player would have clearly left the body as the head alone could hardly be considered alive.

Whatever the case, if we assume re-animation occurs prior to the Rapture, will the reanimated body not have a soul or will God keep track of those souls until the Rapture occurs and then restore the souls to the reanimated bodies. God could also give those souls a new body, of his choosing. Is any of this feasible? No! Reanimation has not been demonstrated. A test of the success of whole-body freezing has not been reported.

EGG AND EMBRYO FREEZING AND IN VITRO FERTILIZATION (IVF)

In vitro fertilization involves obtaining a woman's eggs (oocytes) from her ovary or oviduct after ovulation and fertilizing the eggs with sperm from the husband or from a donor. The eggs may be freshly obtained or may have been frozen previously and thawed prior to fertilization. Eggs and/or embryos may be frozen if a woman is still young and has no plans to have a baby for some years. Also, a woman may be scheduled for x-rays or chemotherapy, because of cancer, and not want her reproductive organs or eggs to be damaged. The fertilized eggs are allowed to develop in a petri dish (*in vitro*) and the normal looking early cleavage stage embryos can then be inserted into the woman's uterus. Alternatively, a gestational carrier, another woman, may bring the embryo to birth. Several are inserted in hopes of getting one to implant. Multiple births can result if more than one early cleavage stage implants in the uterus. Some cells may be sampled from the early embryo to test for mutant genes. Sperm may also have been frozen previously. Extra embryos may be donated to another couple, donated to research, or discarded. From 1987-2015 over a million babies were born using IVF. If the woman is thirty-five or younger the success rate is 21% and drops to 1% with women over forty-one years of age. In 2012 there were four million births in the USA and 61,740 by IVF, fewer than 2% of the total.[3] Louise Brown was the first baby born by IVF, in 1978. Since then, 8,000,000 IVF babies have been born.[4]

There is a big difference between freezing a woman's eggs (oocytes) or an early embryo versus a whole body. A cryopreservative can be taken up by an unfertilized egg (oocyte), a fertilized egg (zygote), or by all the cells of a very early embryo, which are then frozen and cryopreserved in liquid nitrogen. With the cryopreservative, ice crystals do not form and therefore the freezing process kills fewer cells. The frozen egg can be thawed later and fertilized; the process is called *in vitro* fertilization (IVF). A frozen zygote or early embryo can be thawed at a later date, implanted into a woman's uterus, and development will be initiated and proceed in a high percentage of cases. Many would argue that a fertilized egg (the zygote) and an early embryo already has a soul. Thus, if these zygotes and/or early embryos are not utilized by a woman, what happens to the soul in each case? At the Rapture God might consider these cases like spontaneous or induced abortions and the zygotes and/or embryos would be restored to adulthood and their souls restored to their bodies in Heaven. There are undoubtedly thousands of zygotes frozen in liquid nitrogen, presenting a huge challenge for God at resurrection. Since small amounts of tissue can survive freezing better than whole bodies, perhaps the cryoprotection labs should have taken a small tissue sample of the person prior to death and frozen that or frozen cells derived from that piece of tissue. If the body is not reanimated, then the possibility of cloning that person would exist.

ANIMAL ANTIFREEZE

Some frogs, fish and some insects can survive freezing but note that they are not deceased, as is the case for humans above. Of the 5 species of freeze-tolerant frogs in North America, the best known one is the wood frog (*Rana sylvatica*).[5] As winter sets in with colder temperatures and shorter periods of day light, the wood frog buries underneath a layer of leaves on the forest floor. When the temperature drops below the freezing temperature, ice crystals form in the skin of the frog, which sends signals to the liver to convert the carbohydrate glycogen to the sugar glucose. The liver releases the glucose into the blood and is pumped throughout the frog's body to all cells. The glucose prevents ice crystals from forming and prevents damage to the cells. The heart then slows down and stops beating. Urea and specialized proteins also assist in this cryoprotection. The frog can withstand thawing and refreezing a number of times. When the weather warms in the spring, the heart resumes beating and any tissue damage that has occurred is repaired. Arctic fish also exhibit cryoprotection enabling them to live in subfreezing water temperatures. Many insects survive the cold temperatures of winter by dehydration, producing alcohol, or making specialized proteins for cryoprotection. Studies of these cryoprotection methods may have provided the human cryolabs ideas for their methods, if not whole body freezing, then at least preservation of organ viability while being transported from a donor for transplanting to a recipient.

Reanimation of a whole body or a head after cryofreezing seems farfetched.[6] Better to consider it a way of preserving the body, even better than mummification, but the various solutions put into the body and then the long-term cryopreservation make it unlikely many cells if any remain viable. There is also little chance that the entire body can then be thawed without considerable death of important cells. Questions remain unanswered about their soul, whether God considers such frozen bodies dead, and whether he will resurrect them.

NOTES

1   Wikipedia website, "Cryonics," last updated February 14, 2023, https://en.wikipedia.org/wiki/Cryonics.
2   Hayley Campbell, *All the Living and the Dead* (New York: St. Martin's Press, 2022) 210-211.
3   Myra J. Wick, *Mayo Clinic Guide to a Healthy Pregnancy*, 2nd Edition, (Minneapolis: Mayo Clinic Press, 2018.)
4   Science Daily website, "More than 8 million babies born from IVF since the world's first in 1978," accessed March 2020, https://www.sciencedaily.com/releases/2018/07/180703084127.htm.
5   American Museum of Natural History website, "Frog Antifreeze," accessed February 2020, https:/www.amnh.org/exhibitions/frogs-a-chorus-of-colors/frogs-and-the-ecosystem/frog-antifreeze.
6   Futurism website, "Isaac Asimov's Cryogenic Predictions," accessed March 2020, https://vocal.media/futurism/isaac-asimovs-cryogenic-predictions.

30

RESURRECTING SPECIES

RESURRECTION IS A main theme in the Bible. There will be a judgment day when God will evaluate each person, whether deceased or alive, both just and unjust, and decide if that person should go to Heaven. (Acts 24:15; John 5: 29) One immediate difficulty with following this theme in the Bible is that the books in which the resurrection is mentioned (John 5:29; Matthew 22:28; Revelation 20:5; Revelation 22:14) were written many years before anything was known about biology or astronomy. The book of Matthew was written somewhere near 70-90 CE and Revelation about 96 CE or earlier.[1] John 5: verses 28-29 state, "Then he is coming when all that are in the graves shall hear his voice and shall come forth. They that have done good unto the resurrection of life; those that have done evil, unto the resurrection of damnation." John 11:25 states, "I am the resurrection and the life; he that believeth in me, though he were dead, yet shall he live." Then in John 11:43-44 we read that he brought Lazarus back to life after four days in a tomb. 1 Corinthians 15:21 states, "...for since by man came death, by man came the resurrection of the dead;" and 15:52 states, "in a moment, in the twinkling of an eye... the dead shall be raised incorruptible and we shall be changed;" and 15:55 states, "oh death, where is thy sting, oh grave, where is thy victory." Revelation 20:13 states, "And the sea gave up the dead which were in it, and death and hell delivered up the dead which were in them, and they were judged according to their works."

Probably none believe more strongly and rigidly about the Bible (scripture) than the Laestadians (Apostolic Lutherans), a movement that began in Sweden and spread to Norway, Finland, N. America, Russia, and Estonia. "In their view the Bible is God's Word and in it God has revealed all that humans need to know to be saved from the power of sin, to live in fellowship with God, and to attain eternal life. They believe that the Bible is the highest authority on faith and life and a person becomes righteous, or acceptable to God, alone by faith, alone by grace, and alone by the merit of Christ."[2] They have a strict life; no movies, no dancing, no skating, no comics, no TV, but church and Sunday school, yes!

Worth looking into here are two books that center on Heaven and deal with when the soul leaves the body, when the body and soul are re-united in Heaven, and what kind of body people in Heaven will have. One book is by Judson Cornwall[3] who says that we will always have a body, even in Heaven. We on earth and forever will be spirit, soul, and body and he cites 1 Corinthians 15: 44,45, 47,49. He says that we will join our Lord Jesus immediately upon exiting our earthly body when we die. Then he reminds us that Christ ascended into Heaven with a glorified body, verse 49, and says that we shall have glorified bodies that have senses and can communicate. Heaven will be real substance, made of real matter, and not be just spiritual, and thus we will have real bodies. But then to confuse the issue he cites Ecclesiastes 12:7, which states that "at death the human spirit leaves the body." He reminds the reader of the parable of the rich man and the beggar Lazarus, communicating with each other between hell and Heaven and able to recognize each other. Christ told the thief on the cross next to him, "You will be with me in paradise." (Luke 23:43). Cornwall does not say where our glorified body will come from and what happens to the bodies in graves and at the bottom of seas. Cornwall goes on to say that there will be joyful reunions in Heaven and that we will recognize one another. Families will get together. Deceased children will still be children and will continue to develop in Heaven. He does not mention miscarriages or aborted embryos/fetuses. He says we will all remember famous religious people like Jesus, the Virgin Mary, past popes, Martin Luther King, Billy

Graham, and others. Cornwall's depiction is straightforward and probably satisfying to most theists.

The second book, by Randy Alcorn,[4] is considerably more comprehensive and raises two interesting possibilities; that there is an intermediate Heaven and that the deceased might have intermediate, or temporary, bodies. While the final or permanent Heaven will be here, on the "new" earth, the whereabouts of the intermediate Heaven is unknown. Revelation 3:4 and 6:11 say that new Heaven residents will arrive naked and be given white robes; new Heaven residents will be immediately clothed. Alcorn doesn't think this is disembodied nakedness. He thinks the "clothing" may be the intermediate Heaven itself. We are reminded that the Apostle John must have had a body when he visited Heaven because he grasped, held, ate, and tasted. In 2 Corinthians 12:3 Paul is uncertain whether he had a physical body. Alcorn[4] argues that the intermediate Heaven must be a physical place because, if not, then Christ must have been floating around for over 2000 years. The Bible also refers to physical forms and items in Heaven such as clothing, which is a physical item. Enoch went to Heaven without dying, with his full body (Gen. 5:24) and Elijah also went to Heaven without dying. (2 Kings 2:12). Moses (having already died) and Elijah appeared physically at the transfiguration with Jesus, in presumably their intermediate Heaven bodies but they were recognizable (Luke 9:28-36). Alcorn says that the deceased who go to Heaven or hell are conscious and recognizable as shown in the rich man/Lazarus story. But we learn in Rev. 6: 9-11 that white robes are given to souls in Heaven. Alcorn thinks that the deceased immediately go to the intermediate Heaven or intermediate hell and have bodies, perhaps intermediate bodies that God gives them since their original bodies are dead and in graves, and that the intermediate Heaven is a physical place. He speculates that it might be in another dimension that we on earth cannot see. God created Adam's physical body and then gave him a soul (Genesis 2:7). But Alcorn[4] says that the soul includes the mind, emotions, will, intentionality, and capacity to worship. But these senses are dependent on a healthy brain. If the brain is buried with the body and decomposed, then what? The people in the intermediate Heaven have physical bodies, have their original appearances, have their original names, a distinct identity, children are still children, and everyone has their five senses. Each person will be considered a separate individual whose life is observed and cared for one at a time. The soul seems to have capabilities even without the brain and body of the deceased. Miscarriages and abortions are not mentioned by Alcorn.[4]

Again, as repeated many times in these pages, the challenge is to deal with the many billions of deceased individuals. In the midst of the coronavirus pandemic, Jan. 2021, 3,000 to 4,000 people died from the COVID-19 virus every day in the USA alone. Now add about 8,000 deaths from other causes. Now add the COVID-19 deaths from around the world and the typical number of deaths from other causes and the challenge of numbers is obvious. And these deceased are all immediately going to the intermediate Heaven? To do what there? To worship God while awaiting the "final" resurrection, when bodies will come out of graves or from the depths of the sea? (Rev. 20:11-13). This is very hypothetical thinking.

Those who doubt the validity of a resurrection (see 1 Corinthians 12-29) might raise the question of how a body can be put back together after it has decomposed in a grave or underwater or has been cremated, leaving no organic molecules. And somehow that body admits to all its transgressions? And the resulting body is a righteous, incorruptible, spiritual body. Theists might answer by quoting Bible verses as in 1 Corinthians 15:35-55 and argue that a new wheat plant can be resurrected from a dead plant by planting the wheat seeds. Only a small bit of the deceased body is sufficient for God to resurrect the entire wheat body. After all, God created Adam from the dust of the earth, as told in Genesis 2:7. And 1 Corinthians 15:38 says that just as a wheat seed will give rise to wheat and no other grain, so will seed of the deceased body give that very same body. But we learned in high school biology that animals do not develop from seeds. A body can be generated from a small amount of living tissue only with great difficulty (see below) and both living tissue and intact DNA are necessary.

Readers of the Bible should be reminded that when the books of the Bible were written, essentially nothing was known about cells, embryology, genetics, or astronomy; cells were first described by Robert Hooke in 1665; Schleiden and Schwann developed the cell theory in the 1800s; Van Leeuwenhoek described many cell types including sperm cells in the later 1800s; Sutton and Boveri described chromosomes in the 1800s; Watson and Crick published the structure of DNA in 1953; Stem cells were described in the 1980s.[5] The earth was thought to be flat with Heaven above and hell below. The earth was thought to be the center of the universe and other planets and the sun revolved around the earth, according to the Ptolemaic or geocentric model of the solar system.[6] Thus when the Bible was being written and on into the early days of astronomy and Christianity, into the fifteenth and sixteenth centuries, it was not unreasonable to consider resurrection. There was no problem accepting resurrection of an entire body, alive or deceased. God could just by magic whisk the body up to Heaven, even after years in the grave or ocean. It is certainly wishful thinking.

RESURRECTING EXTINCT ANIMALS

Many, many animals have gone extinct, including the dinosaurs, saber toothed tiger, passenger pigeon, wooly mammoth, mastodon, some frogs, and the Iberian ibex (a goat). There are many more species endangered that may also become extinct without conservation efforts. The challenge is to bring back to life a species that once lived on the earth, but no living members of the species are now present. Resurrecting a human from the grave, whether recently buried or buried thousands of years ago, would be a similar but more difficult challenge. Consider whether it is possible to bring back to life a dead animal, specifically of a species that is no longer alive on the earth.

There are three possible ways to bring back, i.e., resurrect, a species that is extinct. The first way would be to extract, purify and sequence the entire genome of the extinct animal, put together the DNA sequences into chromosomes that are functional, and which will associate with the typical chromosomal proteins to regulate gene activity, and put this genome (the total set of chromosomes) into a host nucleus that is devoid of its own chromosomes. The host nucleus would be from a somatic cell of a related but extant (living) animal species. This method was implied in the movie Jurassic Park and was used to bring back dinosaurs, including *Tyrannosaurus rex*. The difficulty with this method is that DNA degrades through time and even if intact DNA was obtained, to piece fragments together and make chromosomes would be a very difficult if not impossible undertaking. Consider that we are talking about a billion base pairs or more.

Molecular geneticists have found that constructing a single complete bacterial chromosome that functions is an onerous task. But the C. Craig Ventor Institute finally did just that and unveiled *Mycoplasma mycoides* JC VI-syn3.0, the first artificial organism ever created. It has 473 genes, fewer than the 525 genes in *Mycoplasma genitalium*, the fewest of any organism in nature. 149 of the genes have as yet no known function. Along with CRISPR for gene editing, molecular geneticists can customize cells/organisms for development of highly effective drugs and also find energy alternatives to present day fossil fuels.[7a] If the number of chromosomes in a diploid set of an extinct species is not known, the effort to construct a functional set of chromosomes is even more difficult. Some success has been reported in sequencing a considerable portion of the genome of the wooly mammoth.[7b] Interestingly the mammoth DNA has viral, bacterial, fungal, and plant DNA found along with it which may provide clues about the mammoth's ancient world. Because mammoths have been frozen in the far north for the 10,000 years since their extinction, the cellular and molecular breakdown typically seen after death is not so extensive. When much of the DNA sequence of the mammoth is completed and cloned, the task will be to express the mammoth genes in a host zygote (fertilized egg), perhaps of an Asian elephant, its closest kin, with the aim being to have the mammoth genes regulated by the elephant cytoplasmic signals and then expressed in the correct sequence for mammoth development. Insects such as mosquitoes, stored in amber, have been shown to contain DNA of the species (mammoth?) whose blood they have sucked but again, the DNA is fragmented.

A second way to resurrect an extinct species is to purify and sequence as much of the DNA of that extinct species as is available and splice the fragments into the chromosomes of a similar extant (living) species. Such a method is outlined as a theoretical method of resurrecting the passenger pigeon.[8] The result would be eggs of present-day pigeons that would carry traits of the passenger pigeon. Then with selective breeding, looking for the reddish breast and other traits of the passenger pigeon, through several generations a bird might be obtained that closely resembles the passenger pigeon. This method might work with the mammoth using elephant eggs as hosts. Whoops! Elephant eggs might not be easy to come by and are few in number; the long gestation period of two years poses an added problem.

The difficulty in this method is to obtain a good amount of the DNA of the extinct species, if not the entire genome.

The <u>third way</u> to resurrect an extinct species is by somatic cell nuclear transplantation. A number of species have been cloned in this way, including species near extinction.[9] The first vertebrate animal cloned by nuclear transplantation was the Leopard frog, *Rana pipiens*, a feat accomplished by Briggs and King (1952) using nuclei from embryos.[10] In the next decade, John Gurdon and his colleagues succeeded in cloning another frog, the S. African Clawed Frog, *Xenopus laevis*, from adult somatic cells.[11] The latter effort was significant because the results led to the concept that when a vertebrate goes through development, none of the genes are lost or destroyed. Since then, mice, sheep, and other animals have been cloned by this method, now called somatic cell nuclear transfer (SCNT). Thus, if intact nuclei of an extinct animal were available and suitable closely related host enucleated eggs, the possibility of resurrecting that extinct species would be reasonable. There lays the crux of the problem, to find intact nuclei of that extinct species, with intact chromosomes and DNA that has not been degraded. Of course the cells must be alive or cryopreserved.

Of all the attempts to resurrect extinct animals the most relevant to human resurrection is perhaps that of the resurrection of the Pyrenean ibex.[12] This goat has been extinct since 2005, when the last known individual died. Nuclei were obtained from frozen (cryopreserved) tissue samples of the extinct ibex and individual nuclei were injected into enucleated eggs of an extant (domestic) goat. One offspring was born but it had a lung malformation and died shortly after birth.

The discerning reader perhaps already has wondered if immediately upon the death of a loved one some cells could be collected and cryopreserved. Then, by the third method above, the loved one could be resurrected and brought back to life, albeit as an infant. The expense of the cryopreservation and the subsequent laboratory work would be great. Many, many questions of a scientific and ethical nature are raised given this possibility. What happens to the soul? Would God now have to consider the soul of the clone as well as the soul of the deceased at the resurrection? Another would have to do with parentage. Would the brain be devoid of any experiences and education? Still another would be asking what effect this "new" environment would have and epigenetic effects in general. We are in scary territory here. Finally, there would be no way to duplicate the childhood, teen years, and adult years that the person experienced in her/his life.

The challenge to God is immense! The number of people God has presumably already taken to Heaven and those he will later accept into Heaven will possibly number in the billions. Consider that there are eight billion people on the earth now and billions have already died. God has to decide who will enter Heaven and with what kind of body. Since most people who die are old and therefore have various physical and mental ailments, God has to evaluate each, restore the body, and correct the ailments. Philippians 3:21 states, "Who (Jesus) shall change our vile body, that it may be fashioned like onto his glorious body...." This verse may be referring to the views, thoughts, and opinions of bodies here on earth and the "fashioning" may be of a mental and physical nature.

DNA is a biological chemical present in cells in long segments. There are 46 of these long segments of DNA in human cells which, combined with a host of proteins, make chromosomes. The components of chromosomes degrade through time, even in frozen or dried tissues. Only in tissues frozen rapidly at very low temperatures, so-called cryofrozen, is degradation at a minimum (see Chapter 29). Cryofrozen cells will survive because they are given a cryoprotectant to avoid having ice crystal formation break them apart. Human bodies presently are not frozen and are not dried but instead are embalmed and placed into a casket which is then buried in moist earth. The embalming fluid is mainly formaldehyde and might preserve the tissues and DNA for some years, but the cells would be dead. In criminal cases sometimes bodies are unearthed, and tissue samples taken for forensic analysis of the DNA sequence. But there is a limit to how long the DNA is available in pieces long enough for analysis. Sometimes the body is never recovered, such as in ship disasters or accidental drownings, or buried without a casket by a murderer, or burned beyond recovery, or lost during wars or cremated, leaving no recoverable DNA. What about fertilized eggs, embryos, and fetuses, which are spontaneously aborted or chosen to be aborted? How does God keep track of the genetic information in these latter cases?

Another difficulty is that most deaths occur in old age (see Chapter 28). As a body ages the ends of chromosomes, called telomeres, shorten. As telomeres shorten, cells struggle to divide and to function and the organism gets older and older and finally dies of old age or of some disease, such as heart disease or cancer. If God restores people in Heaven to age 33, then the telomere lengths perhaps will be restored. Telomere shortening is a problem with cloned animals, such as sheep, in that the cloning procedure does not restore telomere length. Thus, the cells of the newborn sheep, pig, or mouse are as old as the cells of the donor animal. Only in the case of cattle cloning are the telomeres restored to the length of the original embryo, i.e., a youthful length and therefore the potential lifespan of the clone is as long as that of a typical newborn calf.[13] It is not known if telomere lengths would be restored if humans were cloned.[14] When God restores the health of people who die of old age and restores their youth, presumably their telomeres would be lengthened appropriately. One can puzzle over how people in Heaven can live forever, presumably without telomere shortening. Is it possible that in Heaven there is no cell division because cells and tissues never wear out and cells of the body are thus immortal? Such a possibility would not be consistent with biological concepts.

Does the soul carry information? According to religious belief, when the body dies the soul lives on. Ultimately, at the time of Christ's return, at the resurrection, the soul and body are reunited. If the soul carries information, for example the entire genetic complement of a person (the genome), then the genetic information is there to be expressed into a body. If death occurs at the fertilized egg, embryo or fetal stage, perhaps the soul that leaves takes a genetic blueprint to Heaven to deliver to God. But how this expression would be achieved without an embryo would be a puzzle. And the difficulty would be to achieve development to at least an infant stage and then have it grow and mature in Heaven. The soul would have to carry a blueprint of the body so that when the individual is resurrected the body can be identified by family and friends as the person they knew on earth. That resurrected individual would eat, sing, walk, talk, and especially praise God and do most of what he/she did on earth in the lifetime before death.[4] But such a set of views would not be consistent with scientific concepts (see Chapter 4).

An alternative would be that God has in his capacity to keep a "blueprint" of sorts on every human being on the earth, including pre-birth stages, and thus without a body he can resurrect that person with his divine powers. God would have to have stored the entire genetic sequence, all the genes of all 48 chromosomes, billions of base pairs, as well as the epigenetic modifications, such as methylations, that have occurred through the lifetime of that individual. And those gene modifications, both genetic and epigenetic, might be quite different in the various cell types. Modifications in the brain would be most challenging for God to reproduce in Heaven (personality, intelligence, accumulated knowledge, experiences, injuries, cancer, mental diseases such as Alzheimer's, depression, and Parkinson's). God would have to remember the cause of death and the various ailments the person has, and whether he/she has satisfied the requirements to enter Heaven.

Maybe God will choose to resurrect only certain "types" of people, such as musicians. Consider that he might want to have many Wolfgang Amadeus Mozarts. God would need "Mozart's genome with all the changes beginning in his mother's uterus, his father's music lessons, his parent's friends and his own friends, his diet, the state of music in 18th century Austria, Haydn's patronage, and on and on..." Just to get one Mozart in Heaven would be a challenge![14]

NOTES

1   Bible Study website, "When Was New Testament Written?," accessed May 2023, https://www.biblestudy.org/beginner/when-was-new-testament-written.html

2   A. Palola, "The History of Conservative Laestadianism," *The Finnish American Reporter*, January, 2021, 12-13.

3   Judson Cornwall, *Things You Don't Know About Heaven* (Florida: Charisma House, 2007).

4   Randy Alcorn, *Heaven: A Comprehensive Guide to Everything the Bible Says About Our Eternal Home* (Illinois: Tyndale Momentum, 2004.)

5   William S. Klug and Michael R. Cummings, *Concepts in Genetics* (London: Pearson Education, Inc., 2003).

6   Wikipedia website, "Geocentric model," accessed November 2019, https://en.wikipedia.org/wiki/Geocentric_model.

7a Jonathan Keats, "Biologists Create Organism with Smallest Genome," *Discover Magazine*, January/February 2017, 15.

7b Gibbons, Ann, 2005, New Methods Yield Mammoth DNA Samples, *Science* Vol. 310, p 1889; Webb Miller, Daniela Drautz, Aakrosh Ratan, et al.,

"Sequencing the nuclear genome of the extinct wooly mammoth," *Nature*, Volume 456 (2008): 387-392.

8   Carl Zimmer, "Catching up: A Hundred Years Without Passenger Pigeons, and the Secrets of the Puppet Masters," *National Geographic* on-line, published August 31, 2014, https://www.nationalgeographic.com/science/article/catching-up-a-hundred-years-without-passenger-pigeons-and-the-secrets-of-the-puppet-masters.

9   Raul E. Pina-Aguilar, Janet Lopez-Saucedo, Richard Sheffield, et al. "Revival of extinct species using nuclear transfer: hope for the mammoth, true for the Pyrenean Ibex, but is it time for "conservation cloning"?," *Cloning and Stem Cells*, 2009 Sep;11(3):341-6. doi: 10.1089/clo.2009.0026.

10   Robert Briggs and Thomas J. King, "Transplantation of Living Nuclei from Blastula Cells into Enucleated Frogs' Eggs," Proceedings of the National Academy of Sciences of the United States of America 1952: Volume 38, 455.

11   J.B. Gurdon, "Transplanted nuclei and cell differentiation." *Scientific American*, Volume 219,6 (1968): 24-35. doi:10.1038/scientificamerican1268-24.

12   A Baguisi, E. Behboodi, D.T. Melican, et al., "Production of goats by so-matic cell nuclear transfer," *Nature Biotechnology*, 1999 May;17(5):456-61. doi: 10.1038/8632. J. Folch, M.J. Cocero, P. Chesne, P., et al, "First birth of an animal from an extinct subspecies (*Capra pyrenaica pyrenaica*) by cloning," *Theriogenology*, 2009 Apr 1;71(6):1026-34. doi: 10.1016/j.theriogenology.2008.11.005.

13   R.P. Lanza, et al. "Extension of life span and telomere length in calves cloned from somatic cells," *Science* 288 (2000) 665.

14   L. Eisenberg, "Would cloned humans really be like sheep?," *New England Journal of Medicine*, 340 (1999) 471-475.

31

HUMAN EVOLUTION

IN 1859, CHARLES Darwin's *The Origin of Species*,[1] was published. It was the most important scientific book ever written according to Isaac Asimov. Darwin followed that with *The Descent of Man* twelve years later. These books presented the idea that species on earth, including humans, had evolved from common ancestors, and were modified by means of natural selection. Species were not immutable. No, each one was <u>not</u> specially created by God.[2] There were non-human animals on the earth much earlier than humans.[3] To put human evolution in perspective, it should be pointed out that the earliest animal remains (non-human fossils) that archeologists agree on were uncovered in Newfoundland and are dated to 571 million years ago, shortly after the last glaciation that covered most of the earth in 2 mile thick ice. These early animals were soft-bodied, some were up to a meter in length, and had feather-like fronds. They lived in what is called the Ediacaran period, between 630 and 540 million years ago, along with some other soft-bodied creatures. The variety of animals diversified considerably after that on into the Cambrian explosion. These very old fossils are being found in Namibia, Newfoundland, Siberia, and China.[4]

Accurate dating of old rocks involves measuring the ratio of lead to uranium in zircon crystals found nearby in ash from volcanic eruptions. Many species once in abundance on earth have gone extinct as the earth's environment has changed, for example oxygen level modifications, leading to major extinctions. One well-known extinction occurred during the Permian period 252 million years ago and killed off more than 90% of all marine species. Will God restore these early creatures in Heaven? Due to climate change, mainly the warming of the earth's temperature due to human activities, scientists at the University of Arizona predict over a million plant and animal species will become extinct by the year 2070 as they will be unable to migrate northward or adapt as global warming occurs. This will be the sixth mass extinction in the past 500 million years.[5]

If there is a God and if there is a Heaven, we can ponder about what point in human history God began to accept people into Heaven. And we can ask: When did God begin to put souls into evolving humans? The books of the Bible were all written within a few hundred years before or just after the birth of Christ (BCE, before the common era; CE, in the common era), or 3,000 years ago at most. In Bart Ehrman's 2020 book, *Heaven and Hell; A History of the Afterlife*,[6] the concepts of Heaven, hell and the soul are discussed and presented going back to their origins in the writings of early philosophers such as Socrates and Plato, in the Iliad and the Odyssey, and in the books of the Bible, centuries before the cell theory came about and much before an understanding of genetics. These early philosophers and writers of the Bible were living at the time the world was thought to be flat and no more than 6,000 years old. It is a puzzle why the belief in Heaven is so strong. Is it the survival instinct of humans?

When the history of humankind is examined, we see that there were several lines of *Homo* species in evolutionary time, all of which became extinct except for ourselves, *Homo sapiens*.[7] The earliest humanoids (human-like forms (also called pre- or protohumans) were present on the earth 7 to 5.5 million years ago at which time they had separated into a branch of primates different from the apes; humans and apes have a common ancestor. But did we descend from apes? Oh my? What a horrid thought to most at the time of Darwin. Not exactly, but Darwin's first book could lead to that idea. The wife of the Bishop of Worcester, when Darwin's theory of natural selection was explained to her, said to her husband the bishop, "Descended from apes? My dear, let us hope that is not true, but if it is, let us pray that it will not become generally known." Humans from apes was certainly a controversial talking point back then. At a meeting of the British Assoc. for the Advancement of Science in Oxford, in 1860, Samuel Wilberforce, the Bishop of Oxford, who was anti-Darwin, looked directly at James Huxley, a supporter of Darwin, and demanded of him whether he claimed attachment to the apes by way of his grandmother or his grandfather. Huxley declared that he would rather claim kinship of apes than to someone propounding uninformed twaddle during a serious scientific forum.

That exchange was the talk of the conference. What fun! Darwin finally did state his belief in our kinship to apes in his second book, in 1871, *The Descent of Man.*[1] Was Wilberforce suggesting that one of Huxley's grandparents was an ape? The result of this meeting and Darwin's book caused a fervent search for human fossils but progress back then was still slow. In 1887 Eugene Francois Thomas, a Dutch citizen, set out to Sumatra, the Dutch West Indies, with the sole intention of finding the earliest human fossils, heretofore having been found only accidentally during other activities.[19] Yes, Thomas did find fossils but not without controversy because none were complete skeletons; nevertheless Cro-magnon man, Java man, and *Homo erectus* were deduced from as little as leg bones. Even in 1924 only four categories of human fossils were recognized but soon many more came from fossil discoveries.

Walking on hind legs, bipedalism, came about some 3-2.5 million years ago.[2] Stone tools dating to 3.3 million years ago were found near Lake Turkana in Kenya. Paleoanthropologist Lee Berger says early *Homo* species originated between 3 and 2 million years ago. We are the result of 6 million years of evolution from our ape-like, bipedal ancestors. Bipedalism (walking on hind legs), recognized by the bone structure of the hind legs, evolved 4 million years ago.

Two of the well-known somewhat earlier forms of humans were Denisovans and Neanderthals, both of which roamed the earth as far back as 400,000 years ago up to their extinction some 30,000 years ago, along with archaic humans (*Homo* species other than *Homo sapiens*). Denisovans and Neanderthals over-lapped with early *Homo* species and evidence from DNA sequencing suggests that there was some crossbreeding. Denisovan and Neanderthal DNA has been extracted from parts of their fossilized skulls or other bones uncovered by archeologists, and some sequencing has been accomplished. People who have their DNA sequenced today will often find some small percentage of Denisovan or Neanderthal DNA within their genomes (within their total DNA sequence). These small amounts of DNA are speculated to have been retained because of positive survival influences on hair texture, height, smell, and/or immunity. When the DNA sequences of Neanderthals and present-day humans are compared, there is only a 0.12 % difference.[2,8] Estimates are that 61 genes are different between the human and Neanderthal genomes. One of these genes that is involved in both has been inserted into human stem cells that develop into mini clumps of nervous tissue. The idea is to see how the Neanderthal gene modifies the nervous tissue in culture and may provide information about the evolutionary success of humans vs Neanderthals.[9]

Of modern primates, we are most closely related to chimpanzees and bonobos in which case our DNA sequences differ by only 1-2%. Thus, while we seem to be quite different from Neanderthals and chimpanzees in our appearance, anatomy, physiology, behavior and mental ability, these differences are attributed to only a small difference in our genetics. Humans, chimps, and bonobos descended from a single ancestor species that lived 6-7 million years ago.[2,10] Another primate similar to humans is the macaque monkey, having been studied with regard to human-like culture for many years. Yes, macaques show culture, previously thought to be only a human characteristic. Macaques can learn a behavior, such as washing potatoes before eating them, by observing other monkeys.[11] Macaques and humans share 93% of their DNA sequence suggesting a common ancestor.[12] If Heaven exists, why wouldn't God add these primates to the Heaven population? But do they have souls?

There is a coalition of lawyers and scientists working toward expanding the rights of elephants, great apes, and cetaceans (whales and dolphins). Chimpanzees are being considered first because of the similarity of their DNA sequence to humans and also their consciousness and autonomy. Thus, some argue that they are very human-like and should have rights similar to humans and deserve "personhood" status and legal rights.[13] We might well ask if chimpanzees have souls, do they sin, and will they get to Heaven? Alcorn[14] suggests that animals have "animal souls" (but not human souls) and that animals will be in Heaven. We should note here that chimpanzees, whales, and elephants all have culture (they grieve their dead), language, and use tools. Their brains have spindle cells, as do humans, and these cells are believed to be involved in self-awareness, empathy, and compassion. Their brains evolved millions of years before the modern human brain.[15]

Interestingly, Neanderthal DNA is absent from regions of modern human DNA sequences that are involved with speech and language.[16]

Because we modern humans carry small bits of Neanderthal DNA, archeologists are led to believe that when modern humans migrated from Africa and then into Asia, some 200,000 years ago, some had sex with Neanderthals and Denisovans (already present in Europe and Asia) which resulted in offspring. Evidence reported in 2012 indicates that our early human ancestors also procreated with another group of ancient humans that previously was not known to exist (not yet named). No bones or skulls were found but analysis of the DNA sequences of 405 modern W. Africans, from Sierra Leone and Nigeria, indicate some previously unknown DNA sequences which are not modern human, Denisovan, nor Neanderthal and thus are called "ghost" sequences. The ancient humans provided these "ghost" sequences by mating with the *Homo sapiens* line about 50,000 years ago, near when Neanderthals split off from the modern human tree. Yes, our ancestors "played around" a fair amount. Archeologists are puzzled as to why this "ghost" DNA has been retained in these W. Africans.[17a] Maybe someday paleoanthropologists will find some skull or other fossilized bony remains of these "ghosts." The final 8-10 % of the human genome was reported as sequenced in March, 2022.[17b] Who knew the sequence was not yet complete? This last 8-10% is in a difficult portion of the chromosomes and waited for a certain technology before it could be sequenced. What might be learned from this sequence is not yet known.

From examination of some 6,000 individual fossils from around the world, there are well-documented protohumans (hominids) based on fossil evidence.[18] Studying fossils tells paleoanthropologists the size of the people, their body morphology, their head, jaw and face structure, their ancestry on earth (date), diet, behavior (tools and weapons), and use of fire. If DNA is available, the sequence can be compared with other hominids. Their art and culture can be surmised from things like cave drawings and beads. Dating fossils and artifacts involves many methods using physics, chemistry, and earth science.

Here are the seven most recognized protohumans beginning with the oldest but keep in mind there are over twenty types of hominid recognized

in the literature today.[19] *Homo heidelbergensis*, 700,000-200,000 years
ago, fossils from Africa; *Homo rudolfensis*, 1.9-1.8 million years ago; *Homo
habilis*, 2.4-1.4 million years ago (first Homo; tools used); *Homo flore-
siensis*, 95,000-17,000 years ago; *Homo erectus*, 1.9 million-143,000 years
ago (Africa, India, China, Java); *Homo neanderthalensis* and Denisovans,
600,000-350,000 years ago (tools, jewelry, buried their dead with offer-
ings). A French team working in the Djurab Desert of Chad in 2002
found a hominid nearly seven million years old[18, 19], yes, a bit older than
6000-year-old humans created by God. These *Homo sapiens*, our ancestors
of 60,000-40,000 years ago, adapted to climate changes, they were hunters,
had a varied diet, cultivated plants, and domesticated and bred animals,
used fire, and made shelters.

Studies of the above fossils led to the view that humans evolved from
Ethiopia (east Africa). But the east Africa origin of humans was questioned
by the 2017 finding in southern Africa of fossils of another protohuman
species, *Homo naledi*, aged to 236,000 years ago. Discovered in large num-
bers in a cave, called Rising Star Cave, in Johannesburg, S. Africa. With
no easy access, the bodies of the deceased may have been dropped into the
cave, perhaps in some kind of religious ceremony. The fossil remains of a
Homo naledi child that died 250,000 years ago were found in a particularly
deep part of the Rising Star Cave and reported internationally in 2021.[20]
Paleoanthropologist Lee Berger, suggests that *Homo naledi* coexisted on
the earth with *Homo neanderthalensis* and early *Homo sapiens*. Whichever,
the only line of humans to survive adaptive pressures was that of modern
humans, *Homo sapiens sapiens*.[21] Stephen Jay Gould said it best, "Humans
are here today because our particular line never fractured, never once at any
of a billion points that could have erased us from history."[19]

Two studies reported in the journal *Nature* now report even older fossil
humans found in Morocco (NW Africa). From an abandoned barite mine,
paleoanthropologists discovered the fossils of five individuals including
three adults, a juvenile, and a child. The fossils included skull, jawbone,
teeth, and limb bones. In addition, tools of flint, evidence of fire, and ga-
zelle bone fossils were present. Dating by thermoluminescence revealed the
ages of the flint tools to be more than 300,000 years old. Reconstruction
of the face and head from the fossil remnants suggested a face and skull
structure not very different from modern humans. The scientists postulated

that the evolutionary processes leading to the emergence of modern humans involved the WHOLE of Africa.[22] Religious scholars might want to consider that the Garden of Eden was the entire African continent. Hublin and colleagues returned to the site in 2018 and found remains of more humans, along with tools and artifacts.[23]

The evolution of humans is summarized in Discover magazine, Jan/Feb 2018.[23] Fossilized humanoid tracks were dated to five to eight million years ago in Greece but what form of humans these tracks represent will require more studies.[24] What we can say is that early humans originated in Africa over 200,000 years ago, evolved into modern humans with much genetic diversity through thousands of years, and from there in the next 150,000 to 15,000 years ago migrated in multiple waves into Asia, Scandinavia, Europe, Australia, and across the Bering Land Bridge to N. America; some migrated to S. America. Many sideways and back and forth migrations likely occurred. DNA sequence analyses show that most non-Africans today are descended from a few thousand humans who left Africa about 60,000 years ago. These migrants were closely related to groups who live in East Africa today, including the Hadza of Tanzania. Because they were such a small subset of the African population, these migrants possessed only a small fraction of African diversity.[25]

Human fossils uncovered in Israel were dated to 170,000 years ago; some of the earliest pioneers may not have survived but certainly others did. Evidence presented in 2017[26] from the study of a site in S. California shows evidence of human behavior of 130,000 years ago; bones of an elephant-like mastodon smashed with rocks. Because of the earlier date than other human fossil evidence, these early Californians may have been Neanderthals or Denisovans. Much of what we know about human evolution is presented in Lee Berger's book.[27] Berger says, "today we recognize no less than 13 early hominid species, and the number of new species will grow as the science progresses."

Did these early hominid species have souls? Were they judged after they died? Are they going to be in Heaven along with modern humans? Will they have a language?

The DNA of a twelve- to eighteen-month-old baby boy buried in Montana 12,600 years ago was recovered and indicates the ancient roots of today's Native Americans and other native peoples of the Americas. It is the oldest genome ever recovered from the New World. A total of 125 artifacts buried with the body, including spear points, elk antler tools, and heirlooms, show that the boy was of the Clovis culture, which existed in N. America from 13,000 – 12,500 years ago. The observation that the skeleton and artifacts were powdered with red ochre indicate a burial ceremony. The DNA shows that his people were direct ancestors of many native peoples in the Americas today and indicates that the ancestors of the boy came from Asia via the land bridge no longer in existence.[28] Is this little fellow's soul now in Heaven along with souls of other members of his Clovis culture? At the resurrection, will his body and the bodies of other native Americans come out of their graves and be judged? (John 5:28-29). And what would be the judgment criteria? Christ had not been born. The Ten Commandments had not been written. Baptisms had not been part of the culture. Will God just ignore our ancestors?

At the end of the 1500s CE, all of Europe had about 70 million people. But already about 100 million people lived in what we know as the Western Hemisphere with about 40 million in N. America and Mexico. Many of these were Aztecs and Mayans but there were also the Olmec, Toltec, Culgoa and at least 3 others. These early civilizations already by 8000 BCE had domesticated and cultivated plants, perhaps the most important one being corn. The history of indigenous people in the USA is of great interest.[29] Millions of these early Americans died before Christianity arose. Where are the souls of these early peoples? Is God caring for them? Are their decomposed bodies going be resurrected and united with their souls?

The Great Lakes were carved out by the glaciers; before the glaciers melted completely there was much less water in the lakes and much more shoreline. Observations of stones in patterns on the floor of Lake Huron by University of Michigan archeologists in 2009 suggest ancient ice-age settlements existed on land that is now under the water of Lake Huron. In 2020, native American tribe scientists while studying the bottom of the Straits of Mackinaw found stones arranged in circular and linear patterns on the floor of the straits, again indicating early human activity. This would have been 10,000 years ago, when the area was not yet submerged.[30] Are the souls of these early Great Lake's peoples now in Heaven? Where are their bodies?

The fossil skeleton of "Cheddar Man" discovered in Britain in 1903 and believed to be about 9,000 years old, provided enough DNA to determine characteristics; this earliest known human of Britain had dark brown skin, curly hair, and blue eyes.[31] Did this fellow have a soul and is his soul in Heaven? In 2020 the body remains of a woman hunter along with a hunting kit and meat processing tools were excavated at a site called Wilamaya Patjxa in what is now Peru and dated to be 9,000 years old. Her sex was determined using skeletal and dental analysis. The researchers from the Univ. of California, Davis, say that she is likely one of the earliest female hunters of the Americas. It was customary then for hunters to be buried with the items they take with them when hunting. The researchers looked at published data of burials of people of the late Pleistocene and early Holocene eras at 107 sites in both North and South America. Of these, twenty-seven used big-game hunting tools and eleven were female. Sexual division of labor was more equitable than previously thought.[32] Including the hunting items with the deceased was to enable the deceased to do well in the afterlife, especially hunting for food. Did these people have souls and what was their view of the afterlife? Did God have a role in who goes to the afterlife?

According to Genesis, the first book of the Bible, God created Adam and Eve. DNA analysis can now be utilized to examine the genetic history of humans in attempts to trace us back to these theoretical first humans. This opportunity comes about from knowing that mitochondria are inherited only through women; the oocyte (egg) contains mitochondria and when fertilization occurs the sperm does not contribute mitochondria to the zygote (fertilized egg). Mitochondria have DNA and this DNA undergoes base changes, called mutations, just as nuclear DNA does. These DNA changes are predictable through time in living creatures and can be used to determine the age of the organism. In the case of mitochondrial DNA, scientists can theoretically trace back to ancestral Eve, known as Mitochondrial Eve. Likewise, only men have a Y chromosome. Similar analysis of the DNA of the Y chromosome has been used to determine the ancestral origin of the first man, known as Y Chromosome Adam. A common female ancestor, Mitochondrial Eve, has been dated to between 99,000 and 148,000 years ago. A common male ancestor, Y Chromosome Adam, has been dated to between 180,000 and 200,000 years ago. Perhaps *Homo sapiens* is older than fossil evidence suggests. Or, early humans mated with other hominid species that contributed to the pool of the Y chromosome. The scientists cautiously say, "we are not saying all men and women descended from the same couple or that Y Chromosome Adam and Mitochondrial Eve were the first man and woman, but they are real people whose DNAs (genomes) have been passed down to every living man and woman."[33]

The challenges to God in Heaven are many. When did humans acquire souls? When did he begin to accept humans into Heaven? What were the criteria for the acceptance? When did he define sin? Did he wait until Jesus was crucified? Was God in prehistoric times and now at present accepting humans into Heaven regardless of their religion or lack of? When DNA sequences are compared among different people around the world, including in different parts of Africa, Craig Venter, a scientist involved in the initial sequencing, observed that "the concept of race has no genetic or scientific basis."[34] Grouping people into races by skin color or continental residence is totally wrong! Revelation 7: 9 says that ultimately in Heaven standing before God and Jesus there will be multitudes of people of all nations, all tongues, and all kindreds. We all originated in Africa and although evolution and adaptive changes have resulted in different appearances, we are all humans. Is this the way God sees humans?

NOTES

1   Darwin, Charles, 1859, The Origin of Species. 502 pages. London: John Murray; https://en.wikipedia.org/wiki/On_the_Origin_of_Species. Darwin, Charles, The Descent of Man. 1869; London: John Murray.

2   Kate Wong, "How Scientists Discovered the Staggering Complexity of Human Evolution," Scientific American online, published September 1, 2020, https://www.scientificamerican.com/article/how-scientists-discovered-the-staggering-complexity-of-human-evolution/; Richard Dawkins, The Greatest Show on Earth (New York: Simon and Schuster, Inc., 2009.)

3   Rachel A. Wood, "The Rise of Animals," Scientific American, June 2019, 25-31.

4   Wikipedia website, "Cambrian explosion," last edited May 16, 2023, https://en.wikipedia.org/wiki/Cambrian_explosion.

5   Detroit Free Press, Feb 15, 2020, p. 13.

6   Bart Ehrman, Heaven and Hell: A History of the Afterlife (New York: Simon & Schuster, 2020).

7 Saugat Adhikari, "The 7 Homo Species Close to Present Humans That Existed on the Earth," Ancient History Lists website, accessed March 2020, AncientHistoryLists.com/people/7-homo.

8 J. Shreeve, "Mystery Man," *National Geographic*, October 2015, 36-56.

9 Health, "Neanderthal DNA used to grow a 'mini-brain'," Big Think website, accessed March 2020, https://bigthink.com/health/neanderthal-dna/.

10 Lund University. "What makes us human? The answer may be found in overlooked DNA." ScienceDaily website, accessed May 2023, www.sciencedaily.com/releases/2021/10/211008105736.htm.

11 Ben Crair "On the Origin of Culture," *Smithsonian Magazine*, January/February, 2021.

12 NIH website, "Monkey Genome Gives New Insight Into What Makes Us Human, published April 23, 2007, https://www.nih.gov/news-events/nih-research-matters/monkey-genome-gives-new-insight-into-what-makes-us-human.

13 Kent Roberts, "Chimp Rights," *Brown Alumni Monthly*, May/June, 2014.

14 Randy Alcorn, *Heaven: A Comprehensive Guide to Everything the Bible Says About Our Eternal Home* (Illinois: Tyndale Momentum, 2004.)

15 Charles Siebert, "Animals Like Us," *Popular Science*, January, 2015, 52-54.

16 Ewen Callaway, "Modern human genomes reveal our inner Neanderthal," *Nature* (2014). https://doi.org/10.1038/nature.2014.14615.

17a Merrit Kennedy, "'Ghost' DNA In West Africans Complicates Story Of Human Origins," *NPR Morning Edition*, February 12, 2020. https://www.npr.org/2020/02/12/805237120/ghost-dna-in-west-africans-complicates-story-of-human-origins.

17b Euronews with Reuters, "Scientists finally sequence the complete human genome: Full DNA map could help improve healthcare," euronews.next website, accessed April 2020, https://www.euronews.com/next/2022/04/01/scientists-finally-sequence-the-whole-human-genome-full-dna-could-help-improve-healthcare.

18 Smithsonian National Museum of Natural History website, "Human Family Tree," accessed May 2023, https://humanorigins.si.edu/evidence/human-family-tree.

19 Bill Bryson, *A Short History of Nearly Everything,* (New York: Broadway Books, 2003).

20 Wikipedia website, "Rising Star Cave," accessed April 2020, https://en.wikipedia.org/wiki/Rising_Star_Cave.

21 J. Shreeve, "Mystery Man," *National Geographic*, October 2015, 36-56.

22 Hublin, J. et al. 2017. New fossils from Jebel Irhoud, Morocco and the pan-African origins of *Homo sapiens*. Nature 546: 289-292; Richter, D. et al.

2017, <u>The age of the hominin fossils from Jebel Irhoud, Morocco, and the</u> <u>origins of the middle stone age</u>. Nature 546:293-296.

23 Gemma Tarlach, "Human Evolution Timeline Topples," *Discover Magazine*, January/February 2018, 10.

24 Gemma Tarlach, "<u>Our New Past</u>," *Discover Magazine*, April 2018, 68-69.

25 E. Kolbert, "<u>Skin Deep</u>," *National Geographic*, April, 2018.

26 LiveScience website, "Paleo CSI: Early Hunters Left Mastodon Murder Weapon Behind," accessed May 2023, https://www.livescience.com/1664 1-early-american-hunters-mastodon.html.

27 Lee Berger and Brett Hilton-Barber, *In the Footsteps of Eve: The Mystery of Human Origins* (Washington D.C.: National Geographic Society, 2000).

28 Morten Rasmussen, et al., "<u>The genome of a Late Pleistocene human from a</u> <u>Clovis burial site in western Montana</u>, Nature 506, 225-229 (2014).

29 Roxanne Dunbar-Ortiz, *An Indigenous People's History of the United States*, adapted by Jean Mendoza and Debbie Reese (Boston, MA: Beacon Press, 2019).

30 Winona Ominika, "Introduction: Eastern Woodland Indigenous Peoples in Canada," Great Lakes Guide website, published October 27, 2020, https:// greatlakes.guide/ideas/nations-surrounding-the-great-lakes

31 Robin McKie, "Cheddar Man Changes the way we think about our ancestors," The Guardian website, accessed January 2020, https://www. theguardian.com/science/2018/feb/10/cheddar-man-changed-way-we-thin k-about-ancestors.

32 Wikipedia website, "Sexual division of labour," accessed May 2023, https:// en.wikipedia.org/wiki/Sexual_division_of_labour.

33 Wikipedia website, "Mitochondrial Eve," accessed May 2023, https://en.wiki-pedia.org/wiki/Mitochondrial_Eve.

34 Elizabeth Kolbert, "There's No Scientific Basis for Race-It's a Made-Up Label," *National Geographic* online, published October 22, 2018, <u>https://www.nation-algeographic.co.uk/people-and-culture/2018/04/theres-no-scientific-basis-fo</u> <u>r-race-its-a-made-up-label</u>.

32

LANGUAGE IN HEAVEN

A MAJOR CHALLENGE in Heaven for God will be to accommodate billions of people/souls of different nationalities and for them to be able to communicate with him and each other. Presumably a language would be essential. A language is a collection of dialects that are mutually intelligible. A single speaker's version is an idiolect, an individual's distinct and unique use of language including vocabulary, grammar, and pronunciation. Idiolects are unique in England, the USA, and Australia but are intelligible by each other because they are all English. In the year 2021 there were 7,102 spoken languages in the world being used by humans to communicate. About 2,000 of these languages have fewer than 1,000 speakers and forty-six have only a single speaker. Asia has 2,300 languages, Africa has 2,143, the Americas have 1,060, and Europe has 288. The most frequently spoken language is Mandarin Chinese with 1,213,000,000 speakers, followed by Spanish, English, Arabic, and Hindi (India has twenty-three different official languages). About 50% of the world's populations speak one of the top ten languages. Many additional languages, roughly 500, have gone extinct.[1] Sadly, many languages are dying off every year and estimates are that half of the present languages will have died off by 2100.[2] How will God accommodate the deceased whose languages have already or will become extinct?

The continent of Africa has much linguistic diversity with over 2,000 languages. Why? Because modern humans originated in Africa and have lived there for thousands of years, time enough to evolve much genetic diversity, including language diversity. Nlu and Xhosa, spoken in the southern tip of Africa, represent two of the 2,000 African languages.[3] Will all these languages have a place in Heaven?

What will the situation be in Heaven? Will all of the languages ever spoken on earth be represented in Heaven or just the top ten most common? What about those languages with only one or a few speakers, such as Wintu, of the McCloud River area of California? Or speakers of any one of fifty-four languages in British Columbia, Washington, or Oregon, whose youngest speakers are over sixty years of age? Or Seri, of Mexico, with 650 speakers? Or, AKA, of India, with 1,000 speakers, and with twenty-six words to describe beads but no words to count, except "few" and "many?" Or, TUVAN, of Russia, with 235,000 speakers, who believe the future lies behind and have words like songgaar, which means "go back to the future."[4] In the book, *Vanishing Peoples of the Earth*,[5] ten tribes, clans, and families from around the world are discussed as they strive to keep their traditions alive and well, including their unique language, but they are being irrevocably altered to the extent of being completely lost as a people, not just the language, by the impact of the twentieth century. These include the Lapps of Northern Norway, the Bushmen of Africa's Kalahari, the Nilgiri people of India, the Ainu "Sky People" of Japan, Australia's aborigines, the Eskimos of N. America, the Indians of Central Brazil, the Hopis of SW USA, and New Guinea's Asmat.[5] Will God understand all these languages and be able to communicate in each one?

Consider that a person dying today will go to Heaven speaking one of the 7,102 languages in use today and will encounter and presumably communicate with God, Jesus, the Holy Ghost, and with other people speaking a different one of the 7,102 languages who are already in Heaven. Most of these people will have spoken Mandarin Chinese. Furthermore, this person will encounter individuals who died hundreds of years ago and went to Heaven only to have seen their language go extinct on earth. Will the 500 languages that have gone extinct on earth be spoken in Heaven? Yes, let's hope so because God will want these people to communicate. Many languages are spoken by different nationalities of people, for example English, and the nationality of these people can usually be identified by the idiolect (the accent), expressed when they speak English. People who learn English in India, China, Japan, and Finland can be recognized as to where they were born, grew up, live now, or once lived. Dialects are even noticeable in the same country, for example in the USA. People in the south have a dialect characteristic of where they were raised, similarly with people in some of the northern states, like Michigan's Upper Peninsula, Minnesota, and N. Dakota. Dialects can be recognizable when people of New York City and Boston are speaking. Henry Higgins, the linguist in *My Fair Lady*, claimed to be able to identify which part of London a person was from by listening to the person's idiolect. Perhaps in Heaven there will be only one language and without idiolects but that would require programming the brain of each resident of Heaven to speak/sing, understand, and even write that language.

Native North Americans spoke over 300 languages before Europeans came but only about 160 remain today in 8 indigenous families (Navajo, Cree, Ojibwa, Cherokee, Dakota, Apache, Blackfoot, and Choctaw). A subfamily was composed of the Algonquian languages, which includes Potawatomi, Cree, Montagnais, Naskap, MesKwaki, Kickapoo, Shawnee, Menominee, Cheyenne, Arapaho, Malecite, Abnaki, and Delaware. The reader will recognize some of these. At the time of the European invasion the native Americans that lived around the Great Lakes, as far back as 50,000 years, are known as the Anishinaabeg and their language is now undergoing a revitalization in Canada and the USA.[6] Sadly the early USA government established boarding schools in which youngsters were forced to use English as an effort to eradicate Native American languages. Presently, efforts are underway to revitalize many of the Native languages. In addition to spoken words, the Native American languages included petroglyphs, wampum belts, and books. Books were symbols painted on cloth or bark. Just because these are not alphabetic methods they should not be considered primitive because they are methods increasingly used today, such as emoticons/emoji seen in computer communication, of which there are already over a thousand different ones.[7] God has to be aware of Indigenous peoples' languages as millions were killed as the America's were settled; these deceased must be in Heaven, yes?

There are 200,000 Navajo speakers in the SW USA.[8] In British Columbia, the Campbell River Indian Band, known as the Wei Wai Kum

First Nation, is working hard to maintain their original language, called Liq'wala language, within their community.[9] Thousands of decorated stone artifacts, called prayer stones, have been dated to 3700 BC by archeologists.[10] These prayer stones have religious significance to the Numic peoples of the Great Basin, which is most of Nevada. The Numic are ancestors of today's Shoshone-Paiute, and Ute peoples, whose languages are similar enough to suggest a common ancestor language. The prayer stones provide "puha" or "power" and help to get a deceased spirit into the next world. The most sacred place is the highest peak, the Nuvagantu (where the snow sits), of the Spring Mountains, where portals provide openings into the spirit world. In 1809 a written language was formulated by a Cherokee man, named Sequoyah, which is called a syllabary because the characters represented syllables rather than letter sounds. Cherokees began to use this written form of the language and it is taught and used today, for example the Cherokee Phoenix newspaper utilizes it.[7] Perhaps these native American forms of communication would work well in Heaven.

Consider Yellowstone National Park and its 2.2 million acres, at one time visited by or home to many native American tribes. It has forty mountain peaks 10,000 feet or taller, hot springs, geysers, rivers, lakes and animals, including buffalo. The geysers, hot springs and mountain peaks have always been considered by native Americans as places of great spiritual power. The Crow Indian reservation makes up two million acres of an original eight million acres, and 2.2 million acres represent the present Yellowstone National Park. Archeologists like Doug MacDonald have uncovered evidence of native American tribe activity around Yellowstone Lake especially but throughout the entire area.[11] Ten tribes lived around the lake, including Crow, Blackfeet, Flathead, Shoshone, Nez Perce, and Bannock. Picture ten different tribes, each speaking a different language, all visiting, interacting and likely trading with each other. No, Yellowstone was not a wild wilderness before the USA government claimed it and chased out the native Americans living there, far from it; at least 11,000 years ago Native Americans were very active in these millions of acres and their living sites continue to be discovered, including over 300 around Yellowstone Lake. Perhaps thousands of living sites remain to be found in Yellowstone. Stone fasting beds are indicative of people searching for religious visions. Imagine the many different languages among those Native Americans.[11] Is God presently utilizing them to communicate with deceased Native Americans? Will those languages be spoken in Heaven? Is God caring for the souls of the millions of deceased Native Americans, including the youngsters who died in the boarding schools?

Another native language is the Wôpanâak language, not long ago in danger of becoming extinct but now has been rescued and is even taught in schools.[12] This language, spoken by the Mashpee Wampanoag native Americans of Cape Cod, was lost for more than six generations due to the "violence of settler colonialism and forced assimilation practices of Christianization." Wopanoag words are generally descriptive and can be found buried within English words such as in the Woonasquatucket River in Rhode Island. The "tuck" means river. Also, new descriptive Wôpanâak words can be generated for things in the modern world, such as for the four wheeled automobile, thus, the name yawequat (rolls by four). Wôpanâak is part of the Algonquian language family, which includes over three dozen languages, with considerable overlap. One language may use an M in a word whereas other languages will use an R, L or Y.[12] What will be the fate of these languages as these native Americans get to Heaven? What language are the deceased members of these native Americans speaking in Heaven now?

Sami people in northern regions of Norway, Sweden, Finland, and Russia up to the middle of the 1900s had ten different languages, each called a Sami language. These languages were decimated by assimilation attempts, efforts to get Sami children to learn the main language of the country they lived in, whether Sweden or Finland for example, and to forget the Sami language and Sami customs, called "primitive" by officials. That process was painful and not fair, clearly an injustice. The result is that Finland has 10,000 Sami people but only one-third of them speak Sami. Now a new generation of young Sami language speakers has begun music, TV and even a movie in their basic Sami language. A young man has even begun rapping in a Sami language understood by only ten young people. What has happened is that Sami people have died along with their Sami language. Are these people in Heaven and what language are they speaking?[13]

A language similar to Finnish is Meänkieli, spoken in Northern parts of Sweden since 2000, and has been considered as a "real" language, recognized as a national minority language, and not just a dialect of Finnish. Again, discrimination resulted in school children being forced to drop Meänkieli (like Sami) and to speak only Swedish.[14] Will Meänkieli be discriminated against in Heaven? There must be thousands of Meänkieli speakers already in Heaven. What is their language?

The 2020 census is beginning mid-January in Toksook Bay, a small Alaska town of just 661 residents on Nelson Island and only accessible by boat or plane. The townspeople can be found at home in January but when the spring thaw arrives, they spread far and wide to hunting and fishing grounds. The USA census, which begins in mid-March in the rest of Alaska and the USA proper, provides the questions in thirteen languages but does not include even one of the twenty official Alaska Native languages.[39]

Language is unique to each culture. Consider the Denaakk'e (Koyukon) language spoken by about 150 people in three dialects in ten small villages along the Koyukon and Yukon rivers. Do'eent'aa? How are you? Note that in the Denaakk'e language there is no word for "apportionment" a word used to determine representatives in congress, thus words natives use when dividing moose meat or fish are substituted. So that community leaders can trust and understand the importance of the census, local groups are bringing in language experts and translators. The group of four census workers that will go door to door has two individuals fluent in English and Yup'k. Toksook people do not want to lose any federal funds to which they are entitled so they don't want to be under-counted.[15] Now think about the many language possibilities in Heaven without a universal language. Some groups might be under-counted and miss out on some of God's glory!

Another very interesting people are the Nenets, who live in the Northern Arctic zone of Russia, number about 45,000, and depend very much on reindeer and fish, both often eaten raw, for their livelihood. The Nenet language, which is endangered, derives from a Samoyedic branch of the Uralic language family, somewhat similar to Finnish. The Nenets speak one of two dialects, Forest Nenets or Tundra Language, which are mutually unintelligible.[16] Will the Nenets language be represented in Heaven? One can hardly be optimistic given that two of the Nenets dialects, the Mator and Kamas, have become extinct.[17] Will the Nenets gain a place in Heaven?

The Hawaiian archipelago, born of volcanic eruptions and untouched by humans for millions of years, was discovered as early as 400 CE by

Polynesian navigators. The early inhabitants, who made the islands their home, developed an oral language but had no written language. The first colonizers, led by Capt. James Cook, arrived in the late 1700s. These were followed in the 1800s by Americans including many Protestant missionaries. The goal of the latter was to convert Hawaiians to Christianity, which required converting their native oral language to a written language and by the mid-1800s literacy reached 90%. Then, as more foreigners came to Hawaii, the local culture (foods, music, dancing), including the language, began to be erased, and a new social and political hierarchy came to be, with white Americans at the apex. In 1959, when Hawaii gained statehood, only about 2000 people, mostly older folks, could speak the original Hawaiian language fluently. Now, thanks to universities and high schools including native Hawaiian in the language curriculum, and due to the strong leadership of Hawaiian youth, the language is making a comeback. In 2016, the count was over 14,000 native Hawaiian speakers. Now one sees *ho'okupu* (offerings) of music and dance and people going *holoholo* (taking a walk and chit chatting).[18] What a pity if all these native Hawaiians who became Christians go to Heaven only to find that their native language is not spoken there!

People love their native language. Consider the woman who set up a folding table and chair on the sidewalk in front of her apartment. She called it her "grammar" table and answered questions about grammar to passersby. She explains the difference between "that" and "which," "who" and "whom," and punctuation rules. She loves to talk to people about more than language but mostly about language. She considers herself and those like her "lingual geeks." When these English language lovers get to Heaven hopefully they will be able to communicate in English. The same can be hoped for language geeks in all native languages. How will God manage this situation in Heaven?[19]

The world has specific terms and sayings in regard to sports and other activities like eating at a restaurant and buying tools in a hardware store. Probably only anglers would recognize the following terms: lunker, keeper, undersized, spinning reel, fly reel, braided line, monofilament line, wooly bugger, parachute Adams, jigging, trolling, and the list goes on and on. A grizzled old angler might give a young kid advice such as, "Don't ever weigh or measure your fish, just guestimate them, that way you can report any length or weight and not lie about it."[20] Baseball has at least one term for every letter of the alphabet: at bat, batter-up, center field, designated hitter, error, foul ball, ground ball, home run, etc. Only a baseball fan would know who said, "There is no crying in baseball!" and in what movie it was used. Football similarly has its terms; kick off, first down, field goal, wide receiver, center, tackle and guard, linebacker, quarterback, etc. A legendary coach of a university in the Big Ten conference had the philosophy "3 yards and a cloud of dust" which earned his teams many victories. Who was the coach? What university was it? What does the saying refer to? Will sports terms and sayings be lost forever in Heaven where language will be centered around worshiping God? Will Heaven even have sports like hunting, fishing, baseball, soccer, pickle ball, and football?

God might consider several possible solutions to the problem of language and communication in Heaven. One is that everyone in Heaven speaks the language they spoke on earth before they died but that God gives everyone the mental ability to translate any language being spoken, yes, all 7000 languages being spoken today on earth and the 500 or more extinct languages. But it is difficult enough to learn even a 2nd language, much less thousands! This ability to translate languages instantly is a complex task taken on by Facebook that will require huge amounts of resources, and is a mission in the mind of Mark Zuckerberg, founder and CEO of Meta.[21] The Facebook idea is that humans will ultimately be able to communicate with perhaps most if not all of humanity without any problems in understanding. Visualize yourself visiting a foreign country while carrying your I-phone with the translation capability turned on. The foreigner speaks to you in her native language. Your computer immediately translates the speaking into your native language, and you receive the translation on your screen to be read or perhaps by audio through an ear plug to be heard. Now you speak and your computer instantly translates similarly to the foreigner. Your computer may be programmed to translate one or perhaps several languages other than your native language, depending on your need. It is doubtful that residents in Heaven will carry computers around, thus God giving everyone the brain power to translate any written or spoken language would be necessary. But 7,102 or more different languages would require a lot of brain power! Furthermore, the translation program Google introduced in 2017 was only 92 % accurate translating doctor's orders from English to Spanish and 81 % accurate from English to Chinese. Are these percentages adequate? Microsoft's text translation technology can do seventy languages and speaks forty languages, a far cry from the more than 7,000 languages spoken on the earth today.[22] Maybe Heaven will be divided by communities with different languages, as the world is today.

A second solution would be that communication is only by thought and not by speech. God could give everyone in Heaven the mental ability to receive and send thought messages and to be able to translate those messages. This solution would be necessary if Heaven had no air since sound cannot travel through empty space but thought processes perhaps could. But would a song still sound like a song if received only by thought? Would we not have any musical instruments? And to not be able to hear the English, Australians, Irish, or Scottish speak would be a shame. Furthermore, we think in our native language. One youngster said she prays in thought and assumes that God can read her thoughts. Her thoughts would of course be in her native language.

A third solution would be for everyone to use sign language. From 250,000-500,000 deaf people use sign language in the USA and seventy million worldwide. Deaf people have a gathering every summer which is thoroughly enjoyed by attendees because all use sign language. Romances often get started at these gatherings. Sign language would not require air in Heaven but just like oral languages, God would have to have a universal sign language or give everyone the ability to understand all the different sign languages that have evolved. In *Ask Marilyn*[23] a reader poses the question, "Why isn't there a universal sign language (on earth)?" Note that there is also a tactile sign language, used by deaf/blind people.[24]

A fourth solution would be that God provides Heaven with a universal language which would include all the thousands of words used here on earth (not swear words of course) and the many new ones relevant to Heaven, without any dialects. Such a system could work with or without air, i.e., by oral or thought communication. Everyone entering Heaven would have to learn this Heavenly language, even the elderly and those with Alzheimer's and other forms of dementia. The Mandarin Chinese might be unhappy given that billions speak that language here on earth. People who are linguists might cry "foul" as all their efforts to master a language on earth would now be gone by the wayside. On the other hand, they might accept the new challenge of mastering this Heavenly language.

Perhaps the best and fifth solution would be for God to maintain each of the languages already used on earth, including those gone extinct, for the people who spoke and communicated in these languages on earth, and at the same time give each individual the ability to use a language universal in Heaven. People could maintain their individual identity and still communicate universally when necessary.

From here to the end of this chapter additional various idiosyncrasies of language are discussed. God will have to be aware of all of them. Language has four parts: speaking, hearing, writing, and reading. A reminder of how important writing/reading is came from the Frazz comic on May 28, 2020. Frazz, the school custodian, is talking to one of the young students, maybe eleven to twelve years old, who tells Frazz about his written communication with his Aunt Betsy and finds that it is "much better than the herky jerky zoom time chat and even better than talking." Frazz says, "who would have known?" The youngster says, "I knew about language but I just didn't realize it worked so well written down." So, we have to keep in mind that learning to speak, to understand the speaking, writing, or reading of one or more languages is easier when a person is young, even as a child, when the brain has greater plasticity. Children who grow up in a home where two languages are spoken can be fluent in both and not have an accent. However, most people who go to Heaven are elderly when the brain no longer has plasticity and language learning is difficult. Consider Ron, age eighty, who grew up in a household where English and Finnish were spoken. Even after decades of not speaking Finnish, he was able to relearn to speak everyday Finnish and could pronounce the Finnish words appropriately. Ron never learned to read Finnish very well and struggles to read Finnish today. Tess, in her 50s, is trying to learn Italian in anticipation of doing a tour in Italy. She is thoroughly enjoying a virtual course by a native Italian and Tess is progressing with both pronunciation, vocabulary, reading and speaking, and even doing some writing.

Reading out loud, like to a child, requires cooperation of two areas of the visual cortex, Wernicke's area and Broca's area. The child being read to utilizes still a different brain circuit. Language, including both speech and reading, has been so important to human survival on this planet that it involves a huge amount of the brain.[25] If everyone in Heaven is going to have the brain they had while on earth, minus Alzheimer's, other dementias, stroke damage, tumors, or other pathologies, but have memories and experiences intact, then how can people learn a new language?

A universal language is a reasonable idea; yet there has never been a truly universal language in the entire history of humans, but some came close. Greek was widespread a few centuries BCE. When Alexander the Great died in 323 BCE, the Greek Empire began to fall apart and Latin, the language of the Romans, became commonly used as the Roman army conquered country after country. As the Roman Empire began to break up Latin dialects developed into Italian, French, Spanish, English and others. Latin had a big revival in the Middle Ages but then French and English began to dominate. English became common as the British Empire grew and the United States became influential.

In past centuries, there have been many attempts to establish a universal language. Solresol was invented by the Frenchman Sudre and was based on using the notes of the universal musical scale, do, re, mi, fa, sol, la, si as letters. It could be spoken, written, and sung but was considered silly, monotonous, and difficult and did not catch on. Volapuk, presented to the world in 1880, was initially showing promise but then was recognized as unscientific and too complicated. Perhaps the most successful was Esperanto, developed in 1890 by L.L. Zamenhof, a Polish physician; his reasoning was that a universal language might promote equality, love, and world peace, all of which we could use more of here in the 2020s. Esperanto became prominent in 1890 and stayed popular even after WWI but lost favor during and after WWII because there was too much animosity around the world for agreement on a language. Perhaps also the rise of the English language via the British colonies around the world outcompeted it. But there are suggestions that Esperanto might be making a comeback. Apparently over 200,000 people and maybe up to a million worldwide speak and write Esperanto, mostly in Europe, China, Japan, and Brazil. In fact, some Esperanto speakers live in the USA. One ten-year-old boy who lives in the American West was taught Esperanto as his native language by his dad and the boy demonstrated by saying, "Li satas salti en la naejo por preni pilkon" which translated means, "the dog was going to jump for the ball which he likes to do."[26] You Esperanto speakers/readers will note that the umlauts were left out of the sentence. Apologies!

Some other attempts at a universal language include Interglossa and Glossa, Real Character, Solresol, Ido, Ithkuil, Bojan, and aUI. This last one translates to "space, spirit, and sound," and was developed by Dr. W. John Weilgart, originally from Austria and who now lives in the USA. He claims he learned it from an alien, and it is the universal language of logic and thought and is used throughout the cosmos. Novial, Flexione, and Basic English are all three derived from the existing languages German, French and English respectively.[27]

What about laughter? In every culture laughter sounds essentially the same and even if played backward can be recognized as laughter.[28] The idea that laughter evolved as people evolved is indicated in the movie, *The Quest For Fire*, when a primitive (early) human has an item drop on his head. While bleeding profusely the scene strikes the fellows with him as funny and all, including the fellow with the bleeding head injury, begin to laugh, for the first time in human history!

How about mathematics? How about biology and the macromolecules in living cells (the deoxyribo- and ribonucleic acids; DNA, RNA, and the proteins they code for)? They are universal and research and teaching can be communicated with relative ease within different languages. Even a book title suggests DNA is a language.[29] But given his title Professor Collins probably does not suggest DNA could be used to talk to someone, to communicate as one would do in French or Italian. But DNA is the universal genetic code, and all organisms use DNA in cells to communicate function and structure.

"Hash yer astoe ki Dothraki?" Translated this means "Do you speak Dothraki?" Dothraki is a Sci-Fi language invented by David J. Peterson.[30] He separates the invention of a new language into three parts: sounds, word meanings, and grammar. He doesn't like articles and verbs and points out that Russia gets along fine without them. Finnish also does not have articles but does have verbs. Peterson's languages, yes he has a few now, evolve like existing languages.

After Noah's Flood, everyone spoke only one language. When the waters of the flood dried up, the only people on the earth were Noah, his wife, and his three sons. God instructed them (Genesis 9:1) to "be fruitful, multiply, and replenish the earth." And they certainly did in the next several hundreds of years: Noah's three sons, and their sons, and their sons, etc. Women are not mentioned in Genesis 10, which lists all of the sons, but beginning with Noah's wife and daughters, there must have been many women!!! Noah himself lived 950 years (Genesis 9:29) and his descendants had long lives (Genesis 11). All these people found a plain and settled there. Then they decided to build a tower to reach Heaven and to establish a city around the tower; these people in the city of Babel and tower of Babel were descendants of Noah and spoke only one language. God came down and looked at the tower and the city and decided that one language was not a good idea because they could come up with ideas and actions that were easy to attain given that everyone spoke the same language. Ideas and actions could arise that were unfavorable to God (Genesis 11:6). So, God decided to confound the language so they could not understand each other and thus he scattered the people across the face of the earth, who gave up the idea of building a city (Genesis 11:7,8). This, it seems, is evolution. The story of Babel argues against God providing one universal language in Heaven; imagine the high amount of conniving behind God's back with everyone able to communicate with everyone else! God could not stand for this!

Language evolved as humans evolved, but from what and when?[31] Apparently almost 50% of the world's population speaks one of 400 languages that evolved from a single ancient tongue, called PIE (Proto-Indo-European). PIE spread from central Asia to Europe about 5,500 years ago. This ancient language spread west to Ireland and east to China. There are two hypotheses as to the origin of PIE. One hypothesis is the Anatolian hypothesis – farmers could have spread PIE some 8,000 years ago from the Anatolian peninsula. The second is the Kurgan hypothesis which is that PIE was spread from the steppes north of the Black Sea by nomads on horseback going both east and west as long as 6,000 years ago. As these early language-speaking people died and went to Heaven, God had to pay attention to what language they were speaking and only then could he communicate. And as people enter Heaven with language more and more evolved with more and more words, phrases, and grammatical parts, God has to ensure complete and thorough communication, now with over 7,000 different languages.

Note that Neanderthals, primitive humans that lived from 400,000 to 30,000 years ago, cross-bred with the modern human lineage and some Neanderthal DNA therefore can be found within our genomes, near 8%. This small amount of Neanderthal DNA is not present in the human chromosome portions involved in speech and language (see Chapter 31). This finding seems consistent that Neanderthals did not have speech or language. But wait, perhaps they did have language. Psychologist Sue Savage-Rumbaugh showed that bonobos, members of the apes, can sort-of learn a language, although non-verbal; a bonobo named Kanzi learned up to 300 symbols that referred to words, including his name. Thinking that a primate other than a human can learn a language, even if non-verbal, and communicate in that language, is scary says Savage-Rumbaugh, and raises the question "who are we?" She goes on to say that the idea of humans being special is challenged by science. Darwinian theory puts the idea aside that God created humans as special and language became, in a way, the replacement for religion. We are special because of our ability to speak, and we can generate words to communicate.[32] Are Neanderthals, chimpanzees and bonobos in Heaven and did God give them speech and language?

Jean M. Auel, in her sixth book of the series she calls *Earth's Children Books*, titled *The Land of Painted Caves*, very nicely on p. 225 has the book's main character, Ayla, explain how the people which raised her, called "flat heads," developed language. These flatheads no doubt are Neanderthals, but Auel does not mention Neanderthals. Ayla explains, while being shown a cave by friends, that the flatheads had difficulty communicating in the dark because they relied on visual movements and gestures to converse, and to communicate complex and comprehensive ideas, not unlike our sign language today. "Where the hands were held when the signs were made, the posture, bearing, stance, slight movements of the feet, hands, or eyebrow, were all involved." Youngsters were taught this "sign language" and of course much was learned by experience and use. Sounds were also introduced but minimally; the sounds of speech were secondary.[33]

According to the Bible, the first words spoken on earth were by God to Adam and Eve after he created them in the Garden of Eden. Genesis 1:28 says, "And God blessed them, and God said unto them, "be fruitful and multiply and replenish the earth..." and in verse 29, "...God said, Behold, I have given you every herb bearing seed, which is upon the face of the earth, and every tree..." After he put Adam into the Garden of Eden, God commanded the man saying, "Of every tree of the garden thou mayest freely eat: but of the tree of knowledge good and evil, thou shalt not eat of it..." (Genesis 2:16, 17) And then Adam gave names to the creatures God had created, Genesis 2:20, "And Adam gave names to all the cattle and to the foul of the air, and to the beasts..." God then made Eve from one of Adam's ribs, Genesis 2:22. In Genesis 3:1, a serpent said to the woman (Eve), "Yea, hath God said, Ye shall not eat of every tree in the Garden?" Then Eve spoke to the serpent in Genesis 3:2,3, "we may eat of the fruit of trees of the garden: But not of the fruit of the tree in the midst of the garden." So we have God, Adam, the serpent, and Eve speaking and communicating. What language would they have been using? God must have given each a language that he himself could use, to speak and understand, and which Adam, the serpent and Eve could use to communicate. But a serpent speaking a language? Far-fetched!

The first Bible was written sometime between 1500- and 700-years BCE and was written in Biblical Hebrew with some Biblical Aramaic.[34] The first translation was into Greek. Perhaps the communication in the Garden of Eden was in Hebrew. Whatever the case, those first humans spoke in complete sentences and with nouns and verbs included. But the idea that Adam and Eve spoke in the very first language of the earth is unlikely, even if they did exist as people. More likely the first language was composed of clicks and sucking noises. Our early ancestors depended on such sounds to communicate. Clicks have deep roots, originating 10,000 years ago or earlier. Today clicks are in typical conversation in thirty groups of people, most from Botswana, South Africa and Namibia. Something like 120,000 people use clicks to communicate and some researchers suggest that click languages are as different from each other as English and Japanese. Clicking goes back more than 10,000 years and genetic analysis suggests that click-speaking populations go back to a common ancestor 50,000 years ago or more. Some postulate that communication began between early humans by gestures of the hand and face, then to clicks, which was a way of adding sound, and then to speech.[35] Is "shh" a word? How about "psst"? Horses understand, "click, click" which means to go.

Language is still evolving and new words or old words with new meanings are added to vocabularies each year. *Time* provided these new and revived words of 2019: hot girl, hindutva, flygskam, quantum supremacy, streaming wars, single-use, self-partnered, themself, quid pro quo. Hindutva is an ideology that seeks to define Indian culture through Hindu values. Hot girl is a confident and unapologetic woman. Flygskam is a Swedish word meaning flight shame and refers to a movement encouraging people to stop traveling by plane to reduce carbon emissions. Self-partnered means unattached romantically. Single-use refers to items like soda straws that are used once and then tossed away. Quantum supremacy refers to a computer that uses quantum physics to complete tasks in very short periods of time compared to that of ordinary computers. Quid pro quo means a favor for a favor. Collusion refers to the same interaction of the two presidents. Themself refers to a gender-neutral singular pronoun used instead of himself or herself. They is also being used more and more as a singular form to replace him and her for gender neutral references.[36] Finnish already has a gender-neutral word, "han," which is used to refer to both sexes, and does not have words equivalent to him and her.[37]

The year 2020 has seen the reintroduction of old words and the introduction of new words into the English language. Some of these, related to the Covid-19 virus spreading throughout the world, are pandemic, covid, covidiot, superspreader, bubble, masking, herd immunity, and social distancing. Other new words include, entanglement, bipoc, blursday, on mute, simp, defund, quarantini, doomscroll, and antiracist. The reader will recognize the humor v seriousness of the different words.[38]

Wayne State University (in Detroit) has a program called "word warriors" which seeks to bring back words that have fallen into misuse. This group is concerned that we are robbing ourselves of the "inherent beauty and agility" of English. The most recent word being recommended to be brought back from the past is "stifle" which is to restrain oneself from acting on something. Additional words the group would like to see brought back into use are: cachinnate, coruscate, gewgaw, luculent, mullock, perendinate, redolent, seriatim, somnambulant, and velleity.[39]

While new words are entering the world's vocabularies, other words are being removed or at least recommended to be removed. Every year new words enter the English language while others fall by the wayside through time due to lack of use. Lake Superior State University (LSSU) in Sault Ste. Marie, Michigan, each year invites the public to nominate words and phrases that "seem tired or annoying" and to recommend removing them.

In 2019 the following were listed: influencer, artisanal, chirp, elly, totes, ok boomer, mouthfeel, I mean, literally, and curated. There are now over a thousand banned words and phrases in the Lake Superior State Univ. archive accumulated since 1975 when the process began; new words are added each year as nominations arrive from around the world.[40] The list of some words and phrases recommended by LSSU to be banned in 2021 include many relevant to the coronavirus pandemic. These are: social distancing, we're all in this together, pivot, with an abundance of caution, in these uncertain times, sus, and unprecedented.[41] Two words/phrases that should be banned are "like" and "to be honest" which are totally unnecessary. We can wonder if Heaven will be a place where language evolves beautifully or where it stagnates. From what the Bible says about Heaven it will be a place that is rather boring and dull and therefore language will likely stagnate. What a pity!

Changes in word usage is a common phenomenon as society evolves. Consider words used in the magazine Scientific American during its publishing life of 175 years. The magazine did a frequency study of 4,420 of the prevailing words. Some words persisted, some increased, some decreased, some were lost, and new words appeared. Most interesting are the words **fossil** and **evolution**, which first appeared in the 1950s, **sequence** appeared in 1970, **interbreeding** appeared in 1980, and **genome** and **paleoanthropology** did not appear until the 2000s. **Cosmos, nebula,** and **quantum** first appeared in the 1950s and **multiverse** not until 2000.[42] Many words used around the world, especially in science, medicine, and computer science, it would seem might not be used at all in Heaven. What a pity and how boring an existence. And forever?

Different countries exhibit different words, for example words that reflect happiness. Different words and their use frequency can be plotted by native speakers of a language assigning a positivity of 1-9 for each of 5000 words in that language.[43] The language using the most happy words is Spanish but we all tend to favor positive words. If such a study was conducted in Heaven one might hope for a positivity value far above even Spanish.

What about gender-specific words? Will there even be gender in Heaven? Alcorn reviews opinions about gender in Heaven and then concludes that since God created gender with Adam and Eve there in fact will be gender in Heaven. Most countries are aiming to insure gender equality in the workplace, in theater/movies/TV, in education and in society. Worldwide there is much effort to avoid discrimination concerning indigenous peoples and equality of the sexes is being demonstrated even in national anthems. Some anthems have been modified to acknowledge progress and representation of women. Some national anthems have been modified accordingly. Australians changed the first line in their national anthem from "for we are *young* and free" to "for we are *one* and free." Austria added gender inclusive words by changing "great sons" to "great daughters and sons." South Africa added verses to its national anthem in each of the 5 most common spoken languages in that country; Xhosa, Zulu, Sesotho, Afrikaans, and English. In Canada's anthem "in all thy sons command" was changed to "in all of us command."[44] Will God be happy with these changes? Will he take note of the changes and adapt them to Heaven?

Duolingo is a language learning app that enables people to learn a new language in just minutes a day; English, Spanish, French or German and other languages are being added. No books and no instructors and all for free. The app is designed to be addictive. Already there are 200 million users worldwide.[45] Perhaps God will use such an app to teach everyone a single language.

When God has to deal with individuals who die before they learn a language, such as aborted embryos and fetuses or children who die before they learn a language, we can ask what language God will give them. God also has to give them the brain/mental capacity to learn a language or to instantly assimilate that ability. Language requires learning words, grammar, pronunciation, recognition of sounds, and comprehension. "Growing up, the best way you learn a language is through interaction with peers and people in the community."[46] Language is part of a person's personality. Language is learned through a period of years, beginning as a toddler and continuing on into school, even through college. Giving a language to individuals who enter Heaven as an embryo, fetus, or child not yet having a language would be a challenge. Also, let us not forget about those thousands of people who have died and then having their language become extinct. Is God going to provide that extinct language in Heaven? Presumably God will correct any hearing defects as soon as possible. Adults who were deaf at the time of birth can learn sign language but in reading only reach the

4th grade level. Much effort is being placed on making sure students at the Ohio School for Deaf are successful at reading and writing at an early age.[46]

Written language evolved after speaking by thousands of years. Or perhaps they evolved simultaneously? Some 4,000 years ago in a cave on the Sinai peninsula, some individuals "scratched on the walls of a mine what is now believed by many to be the very first attempt at something we now use every day: the alphabet."[47] In 1905, a husband/wife team, the Flinders Petries, who are Egyptologists, excavated a mine where mining for turquoise had been going on for thousands of years. On the walls of the mine were curious signs, related to hieroglyphs but which were simpler. The Flinders Petries recognized the signs as an alphabet but decoding the "letters" took another decade. The Flinders Petries and others after them reasoned that the miners back then sounded out the name of a hieroglyph for something, like an ox "aleph" and just took the first sound, resulting in an "a" and from the word for a house "bet" came the letter "b" so the alphabet was on its way to become what we have today, given many more changes. Some letters were borrowed from hieroglyphs, others drawn from life, until all the sounds of the language they spoke could be represented in written form. The Egyptologist, Orly Goldwasser, says, "Emojis actually brought modern society something important: We feel the loss of images, we long for them, and with emojis we have brought a little bit of the ancient Egyptian games into our lives."[47]

Writing was likely first used in numbering and describing items, like animals, by marking and etching on stones, clays, metals, or pottery. Evidence of primitive writing later came from the seventh to the sixth millenniums BCE. Early forms of writing were Mesopotamian cuneiforms, Egyptian hieroglyphs, and Chinese characters. One of the first uses of writing was in China, and their characters were used to keep government records. Writing as literature dates back to the twenty-fourth and twenty-third centuries BCE. A big advance was writing on paper. Putting words on paper was perhaps history's most important technology. The first type of paper was papyrus made from plants growing along the Nile River. Writing on papyrus was done by hand and was slow and tedious. It might have taken 3 hours to write a single page. But the writing looked neat because papyrus had natural horizontal and vertical lines which the writer could follow. Next came parchment which came from animal skins, treated in various ways and scraped and sanded to smoothness. Parchment could be folded and pages could be sewed together to make books. Many animal skins were needed for a 400-page book. Finally, wood pulp came to be used to make paper and depending on the tree type and the chemical treatments different kinds of paper were possible. For 600 years only China made paper. Here we are in 2020 and we still use paper made from wood pulp. Then printing was invented, and printing presses followed, leading to the more rapid production of letters, magazines, and books.[48]

Reading and writing would have to be present in Heaven, would they not? Will paper be made? Will there be writing, both printing and cursive, in various languages? Will there be printers and printing presses? Will famous and not so famous authors have the opportunity to write? Will Heaven have poets and poetry? The importance of poetry is indicated by the fact a Nobel prize is awarded yearly to a poet recognized internationally. In 2020 the Nobel prize in poetry was awarded to Louise Gluck, Professor of English at Yale University. She is known for 12 collections and various essays of poetry centered on childhood and family relationships.[49] How sad if poetry was not part of literature in Heaven.

Theists at funerals and after funerals believe and talk about the deceased being in Heaven. Presumably that person would be in Heaven as a "soul" given that their body is still here on earth, in the coffin at the funeral, decomposing in the ground, or burned up during cremation. If the soul is a spirit how can that soul communicate by sight and language without the physical attributes of brain power, thought, and expression of a language, not to mention hearing? Nevertheless, discussing what language will be utilized in Heaven is an interesting and fun exercise.

From clicks and sucking noises, the first human methods of oral communication, as far back as 50,000 years, language has evolved to the over 7000 different languages of the present. Language is still evolving.[50] Will language evolve in Heaven?

NOTES

1   The Intrepid Guide website, "How Many Languages are there in the World? The number May surprise you," edited March 31, 2022, https://www.

theintrepidguide.com/how-many-languages-are-there-in-the-world/; The Linguist List website, "List of Extinct Languages," accessed March 2020, https://old.linguistlist.org/forms/langs/get-extinct.cfm.

2   David Graddol, "The Future of Language," *Science*, Volume 303, Issue 5662, February 27, 2004, 1329); Russ Rymer, "Vanishing Voices," *National Geographic*, July 2012, 60-93.

3   Eizabeth Kolbert, "Skin Deep," *National Geographic*, April 2018, 28-46.

4   Russ Rymer, "Vanishing Voices," *National Geographic*, July 2012, 60-93.

5   G.M. Grosvenor, Editor, *Vanishing Peoples of the Earth* (Washington D.C.: National Geographic Society, 1968).

6   Bucko Teeple, *Kitchigamig Anishinabeg: the People of the Great Lakes* (Michigan: Sault Ste. Marie Tribe of Chippewa Indians, 1994).

7   Roxanne Dunbar-Ortiz, Adapted by J. Mendoza and D. Reese, *An Indigenous Peoples' History of the United States* (Boston: Beacon Press, 2015).

8   Fen Montaigne, "The Fertile Shore," *Smithsonian Magazine*, January/February 2020, 32-40.

9   Wikipedia website, "Campbell River First Nation (Wei Was Kum)," last edited January 6, 2023. https://en.wikipedia.org/wiki/Campbell_River_First_Nation_(Wei_Wai_Kum).

10 Eric A. Powell, "The Prayer Stone Hypothesis," *Archeology*, Volume 72, No. 4, July/August 2019, 38-41.

11 Richard Grant, Richard, "The Lost History of Yellowstone," *Smithsonian Magazine*, January/February 2021, 32-55; G. Spencer, "Manufactured Wilderness," *Brown Alumni Magazine*, June-August 2021, 45.

12 Jack Brook, "A Language, Liberated," *Brown Alumni Magazine*, September-October 2020, 34-39.

13 *Finnish American Reporter*, June 2020, 16.

14 J. Rauvala, "Swedish government taking action for Meänkieli," *Finish American Reporter*, June 2021, 6.

15 Alaska Native Languages website, "Languages," accessed March 2020, https://www.alaskanativelanguages.org/languages; M. Thiessen, "Census to begin in small Alaska town," *Detroit Free Press*, January 20, 2020, 13A.

16 Wikipedia website, "Nenets people," last edited May 2, 2023, https://en.wikipedia.org/wiki/Nenets_people.

17 Gleb Raygorodetsky, "Life on the Edge," *National Geographic*, November 2017, 108-125; Facts and Details website, accessed May 2023, https://factsanddetails.com/russia/Minorities/sub9_3a/entry-5093.html#.

18 Alia Wong, "Beyond Aloha," *Smithsonian Magazine*, December 2020, 29-39.

19 Detroit Free Press, August 3, 2010, 3A and 8A.

20 Robert H. Jones, *Warped Rods and Squeaky Reels*, (Canada: Touchwood Editions, 1997).

21 *Popular Science*, September/October 2016, 46.

22 The World Factbook webpage, "Field Listing - Languages," accessed May 2023, https://www.cia.gov/the-world-factbook/field/languages/.

23 Ask Marilyn, "Why isn't there a Universal sign language?," *Parade magazine*, March 18, 2018, 15.

24 TakeLessons Blog website, "What is Tactile Sign Language & How is it Used?," edited February 11, 2021, https://takelessons.com/blog/2021/02/what-is-tactile-sign-language-how-is-it-used.

25 National Geographic Society, *Your Brain: A User's Guide: 200 Things You Never Knew* (Washington DC: National Geographic Society, 2017), 42.

26 Wikipedia website, "Esperanto," accessed March 2020, https://en.wikipedia.org/wiki/esperanto.

27 The Grolier Society, E.V. McLoughline, Editor, *The Book of Knowledge, A Universal Language* (New York: The Grolier Society, 1952), 1619-1622; David Tormsen, "10 Attempts To Create An Ideal Universal Language," Listverse website, published April 17, 2015, https://listverse.com/2015/04/17/10-attempts-to-create-an-ideal-universal-language/

28 Adam Piore, "Laugh Yourself Smarter," *Readers Digest*, September 2019, 64.

29 Francis S. Collins, *The Language of God*, (New York: Free Press, 2007).

30 Matt Giles, "Inventing Sci-Fi Languages," *Popular Science*, January/February 2016.

31 Elizabeth Culotta, and Brooks Hanson, "First Words," *Science*, Volume 303, issue 5662, February 27, 2004, 1315-1335; Michael Balter, "Language Wars," *Scientific American*, Volume 314, Number 5, May 2016, 63; see also Chapter 31, "Human Evolution," in this book.

32 Lindsay Stern, "The Divide," *Smithsonian Magazine*, July-August 2020, 30-49.

33 Jean M. Auel, *The Land of Painted Caves* (New York: Crown Publishers, 2011).

34 Wikipedia website, "Biblical languages, accessed March 2020, https://en.wikipedia.org/wiki/Biblical_languages; www.Bibleodyssey.org/Bible_basics.

35 Elizabeth Pennisi, "The First Language?" *Science*, Volume 303, Issue 5662, February 27, 2004, 1320-1321; Elizabeth Culotta, and Brooks Hanson, "First Words," *Science*, Volume 303, Iissue 5662, February 27, 2004, 1315-1335.

36 The University of North Carolina at Chapel Hill website, "Gender-Inclusive Language," accessed May 2023, https://writingcenter.unc.edu/tips-and-tools/gender-inclusive-language/.

37 Borje Vahamaki and Stuart Von Wolff, *Mastering Finnish*, V(Canada: Aspasia Books, 2004).

38 2020 The Year In Language, *Time*, December 21/28, 2020, 30.
39 M. Theissen, "Census to be in small Alaska town," *Detroit Free Press*, January 7, 2020, 4A; Wayne State University website, "Wayne State Word Warriors release 2023 list," accessed May 2023, https://today.wayne.edu/news/2023/01/09/wayne-state-word-warriors-release-2023-list-50259.
40 Lake Superior State University website, "2023 Banished Words List," accessed April 2023, https://www.lssu.edu/traditions/banishedwords/#toggle-id-1-closed.
41 Cheboygan Daily Tribune, January 5, 2021.
42 Moritz Stefaner, Lorraine Daston, Jen Christiansen, Daston, "The Language of Science," *Scientific American*, September 1, 2020, 27-33; Martin Rees, "Our Place in the Universe," *Scientific American*, September 1, 2020, 58-64.
43 Jeremy Berlin, "Power of Positive Speaking, *National Geographic*, March 2016, 23.
44 The Brief News, "Anthems anew," *Time*, January 18/25, 2021, 18.
45 Jeff Wise, "Addiction to a Language-Learning App Can Be Good for You," *Bloomberg Businessweek*, January 7, 2019, 19.
46 Ohio School for the Deaf website, Language of Learning, accessed May 2023, https://osd.ohio.gov/home.
47 Lydia,Wilson, "Who Invented the Alphabet?," Smithsonian Magazine, January/February 2021, 22-25.
48 Nova program, Words on Paper, WCMU television, Sept. 30, 2020.
49 The Nobel Prize website, accessed May 2023, https://www.nobelprize.org/prizes/literature/2020/gluck/facts/
50 Elizabeth Culetta, Brooks Hanson, et al., "First Words, the Evolution of Language," *Science Magazine*, Volume 303, February 27, 2004, 1315-1333.

33

HEAVEN AND THE
UNIVERSE

BELIEF IN SOMETHING that does not exist is common. Kids around the world believe in Santa Claus or some likeness of him. In the USA the North American Aerospace Defense Command (NORAD) takes calls from kids on every continent as they await a visit from Santa. In one year, NORAD received over 154,000 phone calls, drew 10.7 million visitors to its website, had 1.8 million Facebook followers, 382,000 YouTube views and 177,000 Twitter followers. Calls were from as far away as Japan and the United Kingdom.[1a] Kids also believe in the Easter Bunny and Tooth Fairy. We adults think nothing of lying to kids about these beliefs. At the same time, we teach kids about God, Jesus, the Holy Ghost, angels, and Heaven. The difference is that the latter beliefs are maintained into adult lives. Few parents sit down with kids and tell them that there is no God and no Heaven. Thus, beliefs in God, Jesus, supernatural angels, the Holy Ghost, and Heaven, persist. Why? Because religion is drummed into kid's heads at an early age. As a car salesman once told me "Believing is the safe thing to do." The Bible says we must believe in Jesus if we want to get to Heaven. We are taught that the Bible is God's word. According to the Guinness Book of Records, the Bible has been purchased by more readers (5 billion) than the Cur'an (800 million) or the Book of Mormon (120 million). The Bible must be the number one read book in the world.[1b]

There are untruths in the Bible because the books of both the Old and New Testament were written before much was understood about how the earth is related to our sun, the other planets, and the stars. The books of the Old Testament were written before the common era (BCE). For example, Genesis, which describes God's creation of the Heavens, earth, and life, was written in 1445 BCE; Daniel was written in 600 BCE, Proverbs in 700 BCE, and Zechariah in 520 BCE. According to the Old Testament, rain, wind, hail, and snow came out of windows in the firmament, including the rain of forty days and forty nights of Noah's flood. The books of the New Testament were written in the first century common era (CE): Peter was written in 63 CE, James in 50 CE, Romans in 58 CE, Acts in 62 CE, Matthew in 60 CE, Mark in 64 CE, Luke in 60 CE, and John in 62 CE. The book of Revelation was written in 68 or 95 CE, depending on sources.[2]

The New Testament writers continued to assume a flat earth.[3a] Ancient cultures believed in a flat earth with a dome-like firmament sitting over it with the stars just above the firmament. Inside the firmament were the sun, moon, and clouds. Some believed that the earth floated on water. Hell was below the flat earth. Heaven was naturally "up" and is still thought of that way. Hell was "down." The earth was believed to be the center of the universe and the sun, moon and stars traveled around the earth. This belief was common throughout Greece until the classical period, in the Near East Bronze Age, in Iron Age cultures until the Hellenistic period, in India until early centuries CE, and in China until the seventeenth Century CE. Pythagoras, 6th Century BCE, and Aristotle, 330 BCE, believed in a flat earth. The famous Flammarion Engraving of 1888, yes 1888, depicted a flat earth with a domed firmament over it and a person's head sticking out of the firmament. It was thought possible to walk to the edge of the earth and walk on the surface of the firmament which was a solid roof. Thus, the universe had 3 parts: the firmament, the earth, and the underworld. The firmament became thought of as Heaven and most believed in one Heaven, but some believed in more than one. So even though the concept of a Heaven just above the earth, in the air, does not make scientific sense, the idea persisted until a spherical earth became the predominant view. The concept of a spherical earth dates back to the 6th century BCE but it was only speculation until Hellenistic astronomy established the concept in the

3rd century BCE and long-distance navigators, like Magellan, also became convinced of a spherical earth.[3b]

It was an exciting but controversial time when astronomy began to reveal the earth's place in the universe.[3b] In 1514, Nicolas Copernicus wrote up an early outline of his heliocentric theory of the earth, indicating that the earth revolves around the sun as do the other planets, but he only shared the theory with friends. In 1540 the first printed version of Copernicus's theory appeared in public. In 1608 Hans Lipperhey (or Lippershey) invented the telescope. In 1755 Kant theorized the Milky Way was a large disk of stars. Previously some believed the white of the Milky Way was real milk from one of the constellations. In 1785 Herschel mapped out the Milky Way and placed our sun in the center of this flattened disk of stars. In 1814 Joseph Fraunhofer invented the spectroscope which is used to study the chemistry and motions of celestial objects. In 1838 Bessel used stellar parallax to calculate celestial distances. In 1914, Harlow Shapley showed from a six-year study that our sun is not in the center of our galaxy but is 27,200 light years from the center. In 1989 the Cosmic Background Explorer was launched and provided evidence that our galaxy, the Milky Way, is a barred spiral.

The theory of Copernicus and his heliocentric view of the earth was slow to be accepted and indicated that religion was the main belief system of that time and for decades to follow.[3b] Copernicus's theory was stated as: *The earth is not the center of the universe; the earth's gravity holds the moon; the earth's motion suggests motion in the firmament, including that of the sun.* The two motions of the earth, rotation and revolution, were slow to be accepted. Even fifty years later, Kepler and Galileo, both of whom provided supporting evidence for heliocentrism, that the earth moves around the sun, were not viewed favorably. Religious leaders, like John Calvin, continued to support the view that the earth was the center of the universe. Calvin asked, "how can the earth stand suspended in the air were it not held up by the hand of God?" In 1633 Pope Paul V gave Galileo prior notice that Copernicanism was not going to be accepted and that Galileo should not defend it. Galileo did not listen, defended Copernicanism, and was convicted of heresy and condemned to house arrest for the remainder of his life. An interesting aside is that Galileo lived through the 1630 plague in Italy but continued to do his astronomical studies.[4]

Sir Isaac Newton, in 1687, outlined his theory of gravitation in his book, *Philosophicae Naturalis Principia Mathematica*, along with his three laws of motion. The book presented a rigorous mathematical framework for Kepler's laws of planetary motion. Newton's theory of gravitation is stated as: *Every particle in the universe attracts every other particle with a force directly proportional to the product of the masses of the particles and inversely proportional to the square of the distance between them.* Now consider the mass of the New Jerusalem as this city is described in the Bible in Revelation 21:16, "and the city lieth foursquare, the length as large as the breadth and he measured the city with the golden reed, 12,000 furlongs, the length, and breadth and height are equal." And the book of Revelation continues, "That great city, the holy Jerusalem, descending out of Heaven from God...had a wall great and high, and 12 gates...3 on the east, 3 on the north, 3 on the west and 3 on the south. And the wall of the city had 12 foundations. And the city lieth four square and length = breadth, 12 thousand furlongs, the wall was one hundred and 40 cubits...the wall was of jasper, the city of pure gold, the walls were garnished with precious stones, the streets were pure gold...there was no need of the sun as God's glory provided light. There was included a tree of life with fruit and a river of life." This "new" Jerusalem is presumably going to replace the old city at the time Jesus returns to the earth, at the Rapture. If furlongs (one furlong = 220 yards) and cubits (one cubit = 21 inches) are converted to feet, this new city is going to be 1500 miles to the side, over half the size of the USA from east to west, with walls 216 feet high. How many people is this size of a city capable of housing? And we can ask where is this new Jerusalem and how can an entire city, with the weight of all that gold and foundations of minerals, be gently set down on the earth? Is it floating up in the clouds being held up by the hand of God or is it being stored somewhere else? Now read Matthew 24:29, "Immediately after the tribulation of those days shall the sun be darkened and the moon shall not give her light, and the stars shall fall from Heaven and the powers of the Heavens shall be shaken." The size of stars was certainly underestimated. Also see Matthew 24:31, "And he shall send his angels with a great sound of a trumpet..." Here again these passages indicate that there is air in Heaven as well as water and fruit trees. Whoa! That is some imaginative writing!

Someone, presumably John, the same John as wrote the book of John, had a fantastic imagination, for sure, but keep in mind that without knowledge of planets, our sun as a star, other stars, galaxies, our atmosphere, how sound travels, and gravity, these ideas may have seemed quite reasonable at the time and to some are still reasonable.[5] Consider also in 1 Thessalonians 4:14-17, "For if we believe that Jesus died and rose again, even so them also which sleep (meaning they are dead in their graves) in Jesus will God bring with him. For the Lord himself will descend from Heaven with a shout, with the voice of the archangel…and the dead in Christ shall rise first and then we which are alive and remain shall be caught up together with them in the clouds, to meet the Lord in the air…and so shall we ever be with the Lord." Verses like these have given rise to cartoon pictures of Heaven, with God and people standing in the clouds. Note that God's shout will be heard, that there are clouds, and believers will meet the Lord in the air. Clearly Heaven was thought to be in the atmosphere. The stars were thought to be in Heaven as noted in Matthew 24:29, "Immediately after the tribulation…shall the sun be darkened and the moon shall not give her light and the stars will fall from Heaven…" Furthermore, Heaven had dimensions as mentioned in Matthew 24:31, "…he shall send his angels with a great sound of a trumpet, and his elect shall gather together from the four winds, from one end of Heaven to the other."

We should be reminded that very little was understood about air and the earth's atmosphere before the 1600s.[6] In the days of Plato and Aristotle, 400-300 BC, all things were thought to be made up of four substances – earth, fire, water, and air. But it was thought that air moved away from the earth's surface. Newton had not yet discovered and described the force of gravity. Finally in the 1600s Isaac Beeckman, a Dutch scientist, showed that air was a substance and had weight. Then Robert Boyle in 1660 invented the barometer and did some weather forecasting, Joseph Priestly identified oxygen in 1774 and showed that it supported fire, and Antoine Lavoisier named oxygen and later hydrogen.[7] Thus, not knowing about the atmosphere or about gravity, writers of the Bible likely thought that air extended far, far above the earth and that God and a Heaven with gold streets were housed up there.

Interesting too is to contemplate angels. Angels are Heavenly messengers which "God uses to convey his word to humans and to carry out tasks for him on earth."[8] Note that angels are often depicted with wings, thus indicating that they live in an atmosphere with air. But angels also have arms and unlike birds have no large breast muscles to power those wings. Early biblical writers had no knowledge of sound, much less how shouts and music travel through air. Those passages in the Bible describing shouting and trumpets are legitimate only if there is air, further indicating that for those passages to be believable Heaven must be in the atmosphere, somewhere above the earth's surface. "Above" at that time was "up" from the flat surface of the earth. Knowing the earth is a sphere, where would Heaven be? Up there? In what shape? Are the thousands of satellites up there soaring through Heaven? Have the astronauts in the space station reported evidence of Heaven? Not!

Consider the concept from the Bible (John 5:28-29) that when a person dies the soul leaves the body and goes to Heaven and when the Rapture occurs, the soul is reunited with the dead body and that individual then resides in Heaven with God, Jesus and the Holy Ghost for eternity.[5] But what happens before the Rapture? Are the billions of souls of all the dead throughout history, and 1,000s more each day (see Chapter 4), disembodied souls, including the soul of Christ, that have been floating on clouds for decades and centuries? One view is that God gives these souls a temporary body and these embodied souls are in an intermediate Heaven,[5] awaiting the Rapture. "...when all who are in their graves will hear his voice and come out – those who have done good will rise to live" (John 5: 28-29). Alcorn[5] argues that the body is physical and the soul (spirit), a non-physical entity, is in that physical body. After all, God created Adam and Eve in body and then breathed into them their spirits (Genesis 2:7). Further indications of people in the Intermediate Heaven having physical bodies is presented by Alcorn[5] as follows: The apostle Paul apparently grasped, held, ate, and tasted things in Heaven (Rev 10: 9-10). Paul says he sensed his physical body in Heaven. Also, the stories of Enoch, Elijah, and Moses are presented as evidence for those in the Intermediate Heaven having physical bodies. "Enoch walked with God, and he was not, for God took him" (Genesis 5:24). The "he was not" has been translated to mean his body was not found, suggesting that he went up to Heaven body and soul. And Hebrews 11:5 says that Enoch did not die so he apparently went up to Heaven with his body and soul. And Elijah was taken up to Heaven in a whirlwind (2 Kings 2:11). Alcorn[5] suggests that Enoch and Elijah went up to the Intermediate Heaven with pre-resurrected bodies and are there awaiting resurrection. Furthermore, Moses and Elijah appeared physically with Christ on the mountain at the Transfiguration (Luke 9:28-36). Moses had died and Elijah had gone up in the whirlwind. Thus they must have each had a physical body in the Intermediate Heaven, perhaps a "temporary" physical body while waiting for the resurrection. If they had physical bodies, presumably air, water, and nutrition would be necessary to maintain them. But how and where?

If Elijah went up in a whirlwind, there must be air in Heaven. But if Elijah was whisked up high enough, the air would be too thin to survive, and he could have died. Angels are always depicted with wings and thus require air. There is music and speech in Heaven, again suggesting air is present. Given the lack of scientific information about the atmosphere when the Bible was written, it is reasonable for these writers to have considered Heaven being above the earth, in the firmament, which is composed of air. No wonder cartoons/comics depict Heaven as God and people floating or suspended among the clouds.

How many souls, perhaps with temporary physical bodies, are in the Intermediate Heaven? According to the Bible (see Alcorn[5]) the souls of all who die initially go to the Intermediate Heaven and only when the Rapture occurs is the decision made as to who goes to the final Heaven to be with God and who goes to hell. We can ask: How many souls are in the Intermediate Heaven? Now we must make some assumptions. Let's assume that souls of early humans, the hominids of 1.5 million years ago, did not possess souls but the *Homo* line of early humans did. We can start counting in the year 700,000 BCE. Modern humans were on the earth 50,000 years BCE. During the Age of Agriculture, the estimate is that five million people lived on the earth. Keep in mind that the life span was probably only twenty to twenty-five years and the birth rate barely kept up with the death rate. In the year 8,000 BCE there were 500 million people. In 1850 there were 1.2 billion people. At present the earth's population is over eight billion and destined to rise to nine billion by 2050. Of all the people alive today, May 2017, that number has been calculated to be 6% of all the people who have died. That latter number is between 102 billion to 108 billion people. Perhaps as many as 108 billion souls with temporary bodies are in the Intermediate Heaven and at the time of the Rapture the souls of those going to Heaven will be united with their bodies with one wave of God's hand. Will that be all in one day or perhaps a billion a day until everyone is accounted for? Note Chapter 11 deals with the information God will need for each of these 108 billion deceased people (Heaven deserving qualities or not, age, health, cause of death and more).

We can consider that the Intermediate Heaven is somewhere else in our solar system, perhaps on another planet. The most earth-like planet is Mars, but no air or water exists there. Even Mars is a tremendously long distance away. A launch to Mars, the Red Planet, is planned for the year 2030, carrying four people the 34,000,000 miles, when Mars is at its closest position to earth.[9] The massive rocket to power the capsule will be 322 feet tall and more powerful than the Saturn V which powered the Apollo moon missions. The estimated travel time is seven months during which the four-person crew would be bombarded by cosmic rays; bones could lose calcium, and eyesight could suffer. After landing on the surface of Mars, imagine an astronaut stumbling down the ramp because of poor eyesight, falling, and breaking a bone. These astronauts would need food and water and have to deal with wastes (urine and feces) during the trip there, the time on Mars, and during the trip back.[10] Mars seems to be an unlikely place for the intermediate Heaven.

The next best place for the intermediate Heaven might be one of Jupiter's moons, even farther away than Mars. Jupiter has an elliptical orbit around the sun so its distance from earth varies from 365 to 601 million miles at different times of the year. At its closest to earth, light would travel for forty-three minutes to reach Jupiter from earth.[11] NASA's spacecraft Juno was launched in 2011 and reached Jupiter in 2016.[12] Messages from earth to Juno take forty-eight minutes showing how far away Jupiter is. Conditions on Jupiter are not considered life-supporting as the entire planet is gaseous. But in future flights, life will be searched for on Europa, one of Jupiter's fifty moons, because of the abundance of water there, and maybe a salty ocean. Europa is one of nine watery worlds in our solar system in addition to earth. Any life out there might at best be microbial in nature but would be significant just the same.[13]

The spacecraft Cassini was launched in 2004 to finally make contact with Saturn seven years later.[14] After this amazing journey of over a dozen years and after sending back much data of Saturn and its rings and moons, it crashed into the planet's surface and fell silent in Sept. 2017. The crash actually occurred eighty-three minutes earlier because it took that long for the radio signals to reach the earth. Ocean worlds were revealed on the moons Enceladus and Titan, raising the possibility of life. Could these planets or moons harbor all the souls of past humans now deceased? Very unlikely!

According to Popular Sci magazine,[15] our galaxy "brims with billions of planets, but even the closest would take hundreds of life-times to reach with current technology." If distance is not a limiting factor, then perhaps another earth-like planet orbiting another star (a sun) could be housing life forms or residents of the Intermediate Heaven. The first planet orbiting a sun-like star was discovered in 1995 by two astrobiologists, M. Mayor and D. Queloz, of the Univ. of Geneva, but its surface temp was estimated to be 2000 degrees and its orbit time around its sun was only four days. More earth-like planets were subsequently discovered, now numbering nearly 2,000, and more are being analyzed.[16] Over 1000 of these so-called "Goldilocks planets" (also called exoplanets) have been discovered that are not too hot and not too cold and may have water and carbon, essentials for life as we understand it. One earth-sized planet has been discovered orbiting a star in the Alpha Centauri star system, twenty-five trillion miles away.[17] Proxima B is earth's nearest exoplanet, 4.2 light years away.[18] The Kepler space probe, launched in 2009, discovered many exoplanets and completed that searching mission in 2012. Astronomers in Belgium have discovered seven earth-like planets orbiting a single star, Trappist-1, which is only thirty-nine light-years away in the constellation Aquarius.[19] At least two of these planets are in the habitable zone, near the star but not too near, providing the possibility of water and maybe life. While the search for life outside of our earth is of pure scientific interest, the likelihood of any one planet outside of our solar system housing the Intermediate Heaven or any life forms seems low, but the odds are not zero.[20]

The idea of an intermediate Heaven is essentially theoretical and comes from a few biblical passages and is expanded upon by Alcorn.[5] Evidence for an intermediate Heaven is scanty. Yet we commonly think of deceased people as "above us" looking down on us or "on the other side" and being able to see us.[21]

The immensity of the universe is discussed in Astronomy magazine[22] and its time scale is diagrammed in *Time*.[23] Astronomers are confident that the universe is 13.8 billion years old and the earth and solar system are 4.6

billion years old. We know that light travels 186,000 miles per second and a light year is the distance light travels in one year, which is 6 trillion miles. The part of the universe that we can see is 93 billion light years across. There are 400 billion stars scattered across the bright disc of our Milky Way Galaxy, which is 150,000 light years across. There are a hundred billion more galaxies spread across the vast cosmos. The universe is enormous and getting larger as it expands.[24] The Baryon Oscillation Spectroscopic Survey mapped 1.2 million galaxies in an effort to understand how dark energy accelerates the expansion of the universe. The region is 650 cubic light-years in volume. The data will "check Einstein's general theory of relativity."[25] Estimates of the size of the portion of the universe that we can see with present instruments puts that size at 93 billion light years across. Yes, our Milky Way galaxy is large but there are millions and perhaps billions more galaxies across the vast cosmos.

To further study galaxies beyond our Milky Way scientists are planning on having a massive telescope built on Hawaii's tallest mountain, Mauna Kea. The view from the top of this mountain will reveal fundamental information about the universe just after the Big Bang. The idea is that the earliest matter to coalesce after the Big Bang is the furthest out there. But wait a minute, says a group of kupuna, or church elders, who believe such construction would disrupt their religious worship; they consider the land holy and a realm of gods. The kupuna are demonstrating and blocking the road to the summit.[26] Perhaps the kupuna could be convinced that such a telescope would put them closer to their gods and they would thus have a more positive attitude about the telescope.

To gain fundamental information of the origin of the universe a European Ariane 5 rocket was launched in 2021 carrying the James Webb Space telescope. The James Webb telescope will detect the infrared spectrum and thus go beyond the Hubble telescope's capability which detected ultraviolet and visible light spectrums. The Hubble could look back 13.4 billion years, just 400 million years after the Big Bang. The James Webb will look back to 13.6 billion years, when the first galaxies formed and thus it will get closer to the actual origin of the universe, its "babyhood" so to speak.[27]

When considering life beyond the earth, a review of life on the earth might be useful, especially the uniqueness of the earth to harbor life.[28]Many things can be listed that make life possible on earth; here are ten:

1. The earth recycles carbon. Carbon makes the earth warm enough to support life; now industrialization is increasing the carbon (as carbon dioxide), so the earth is warming
2. The earth's ozone layer protects us from harmful rays
3. The moon stabilizes our axial wobble
4. The earth's magnetic field protects us from the sun's ionizing radiation
5. The earth's variable surfaces support many life forms
6. The earth is just the right distance from the sun
7. The earth's sun is a stable, long-lasting star
8. There are giant planets in our solar system that protect the earth
9. The sun protects us from galactic debris
10. Our solar system's galactic path protects the earth from hazards[28]

Is it no wonder the search for extra-terrestrial life has so far been negative? Just what is the chance, the probability, of life beyond earth? In 1961 an astronomy meeting was organized by Frank Drake, a young radio astronomer, to consider that question, and thus began SETI, the Search for Extra Terrestrial Intelligence. The idea was that another intelligent society out there would have developed radio communication and the nature of that transmission received here on earth would indicate intelligence. Drake scribbled an equation, the Drake Equation, on the blackboard to begin discussion. The equation started out with the rate of sun-like star formation in our Milky Way galaxy multiplied by the fraction of those stars having orbiting planets, multiplied by the number of life-friendly planets in such systems (those hospitable to life), multiplied by the fraction of those that might develop technology to emit radio signals we could detect, multiplied by the average time they might survive long enough for us to detect their signals. A difficulty with the Drake equation is that the only number known is the rate of formation of sun-like stars. None of the other numbers are known.[29] We can conclude that to find life out there, beyond earth, will be very unlikely, even if it is out there. But equally unlikely would be that a God created a vast world of universes with thousands of planets and created life only on one, our earth.

How could life on earth have begun and could life on other planets have begun in the same way? In 2018 an amateur meteorite searcher/collector found a meteorite on a frozen lake in Hamburg, Michigan two days after it landed. The meteorite, seen by hundreds the night it landed, was brought to the attention of a museum, and was ultimately analyzed by twenty-nine scientists of twenty-four institutions. Isotope dating determined its age to be 4.5 billion years and over 2,000 organic compounds were present within it, many heavy and complex. These results were published in the Meteoritics and Planetary Science journal. Because the discoverer recovered the meteorite quickly, the likelihood of organic compound contamination from the lake was negligible. The presence of large organic compounds supports the on-going theory that life on earth began from one or more of such meteorite contributions. Life on other planets may have begun in a similar fashion.[30]

Bart D. Ehrman[31] reviews ideas about when the resurrection will occur. When will God end life on earth and begin life in Heaven? Jesus thought that resurrection was imminent, an apocalyptic view, and likely would occur during his lifetime. He said, "Verily I say unto you that there be some of those standing here which will not taste death until they see the kingdom of God come with power." (Mark 9:1). But of course it didn't happen. Others after Jesus, for example the apostle Paul, also predicted that the resurrection was imminent. Here we are 2,000 years later and it still has not occurred but be assured pastors and priests are reminding parishioners that it is imminent.[31] The general thinking was that God would reward the faithful by accepting them into Heaven for eternal joy but destroy all evil and punish the wicked by putting them into complete darkness, a pit of fire, under continuous torture by various means, or death without a funeral.[31] Paul thought that Jesus would return soon and all the righteous, whether alive or already in their graves, would be resurrected and given an immortal, spiritual body, and their mortal bodies would be destroyed.[31]

The French philosopher August Comte, in 1835, said that the composition of the stars would never be known.[32] He wrote, "we understand the possibility of determining their shapes, their distances, their sizes, and their movements whereas we will never know their composition, their mineralogical structure nor the nature of any organized beings that might live on their surface." If Comte only knew what would be learned about stars and the universe he would be amazed. Now in 2021 we know that the universe is much larger and stranger than 19th century astronomers could have imagined.

Our Milky Way galaxy is only one of millions of galaxies. Cosmic history can be traced back to a fraction of a second after the Big Bang and today the universe is still expanding. A relatively new idea is that perhaps more Big Bangs have formed many universes (multiverses). Persistent astronomical studies have led to discoveries of dark matter, dark energy, black holes, neutron stars, supernovae, pulsars, quasars, and gravitational waves. Stars like our sun generate their energy (light, heat, radiation) via atomic fusion which is the coming together of hydrogen atoms to form helium with the release of much energy (think hydrogen bomb). Fusion of more and more atoms of heavier elements resulted in the formation of all the elements of the periodic table including carbon, nitrogen, oxygen, phosphorous, calcium and iron. Dark energy and dark matter cannot be seen but can be predicted by phenomena in the universe and are consistent with Einstein's relativity theory. Stars also die. When a lightweight star dies it forms a white dwarf. When a heavier star dies it sheds huge amounts of mass and explodes forming a supernova with a neutron star at its center. Super dense stars called pulsars can merge and when they do gold can be formed. A pulsar is a highly magnetized rotating neutron star whose electromagnetic radiation can be detected when the beam of radiation from one of its poles points toward earth. A quasar is a distant galaxy that emits fluctuating radiations with a black hole at its center.[33] Now read Genesis 1:1, "In the beginning God created the Heaven and the earth." Then read Genesis 1:16, "And God made two great lights; the greater light to rule the day and the lesser light to rule the night. He made the stars too." And verse 17, "And God set them in the firmament of the Heaven to give light upon the earth." The writer of Genesis knew very little about astronomy.

A twenty-first century view of creation can be garnered from thoughts of Andrew Fabian, a pioneering x-ray astronomer, and even gain an understanding of astronomical terms such as *event horizon, singularity,* and *worm holes.* Fabian says that all galaxies have black holes at their centers. In the early universe, galaxy formation began with dark matter. Because dark matter does not collide with ordinary matter, it could form clumps, forming galaxies, and at some point, black holes formed, which then had profound effects on formation of new stars. Cycles of star formation, starts and stops, may happen many times during the evolution of a galaxy. Larger x-ray telescopes will be necessary to look at more and more distant galaxies to find clues as to how these cycles get set up. He says there is much more dark matter in the universe than there is ordinary matter. Studies are continuing of the Perseus cluster, the brightest X-ray emitting galaxy cluster in the sky.[34]

The 2020 Nobel prize in physics (think of astrophysics) was shared by three investigators of black holes: Sir Roger Penrose, Reinhard Genzel, and Andrea Ghez. Penrose's contribution was innovative mathematical techniques to prove that the formation of black holes is a consequence of Einstein's general theory of relativity; hence black holes can truly exist.[35] If the creation story of Genesis was being written today, what would be said about galaxies and black holes?[20]

Does science have any notion when the universe will end? According to astrophysicist Katie Mack,[36] the end will be billions of years from now. And how will the universe end? Mack says there are five most likely ways, each related to dark energy, which she names:

1. Big Crunch; the Big Bang caused the initial expansion of the universe. The universe is still expanding. Gravity, even though a weak force but perhaps with help from dark energy, will finally in billions of years, stop the expansion and then everything will reverse and come together in a crunch.
2. Heat Death; here heat is not warmth but is a physics term referring to a disordered motion of matter and energy, meaning a big increase in entropy. This disorder destroys the earth.
3. Big Rip; in this scene dark energy will violently and inescapably destroy the universe and rip everything apart.
4. Vacuum Decay; the set of laws that governs the physical world, called the Higgs Field, undergoes disorder and molecules are broken apart and cannot reform. Everything is screwed up.
5. Bounce; the universe is contracting on itself but before completely contracted matter changes to energy and another Big Bang begins.

If these ideas of the end of the universe are anywhere near to being true, religious and non-religious people do not need to panic with regard to the end of life because each of the above scenes will be billions of years from now. No mention of Heaven is anywhere in Katie Mack's book. Could Heaven be in another universe, more stable than the universe we reside in? Is God in control of these "end of everything" possibilities?

NOTES

1a   *The Arizona Republic*, December 25, 2017, 14A.

1b   Wikipedia website, "List of best-selling books, accessed January 2021, https://en.wikipedia.org/wiki/List_of_best-selling_books.

2   Wayne Jackson, "When Was the Book of Revelation Written?," Christian Courier website, accessed April 2021, www.christiancourier.com/articles/1552.

3a   Wikipedia website, "Flat Earth," accessed March 2021, https://en.wikipedia.org/wiki/Flat_Earth.

3b   Wikipedia website, "Spherical Earth," accessed May 2023, https://en.wikipedia.org/wiki/Spherical_Earth.

4   Hannah Marcus, "Galileo's Lessons for Living Through a Plague," *Scientific American*, August, 2020, 32-35.

5   Randy Alcorn, *Heaven: A Comprehensive Guide to Everything the Bible Says About Our Eternal Home* (Illinois: Tyndale Momentum, 2004.)

6   Wikipedia website, "Isaac Beeckman, last edited April 28, 2023, https://en.wikipedia.org/wiki/Isaac_Beeckman.

7   Wikipedia website, "Antoine Lavoisier," last edited May 19, 2023, https://en.wikipedia.org/wiki/Antoine_Lavoisier.

8   Reader's Digest Association, *Reader's Digest ABCs of the Bible* (New York, Readers Digest Association, 1991) 42.

9   Katie Nodjimbadem, "Next Stop Mars," *Smithsonian Magazine*, May 2016, 72-73.

10   Joel Achenbach, "Elon Musk wants to go to Mars," *National Geographic*, November 2016, 41-61.

11   Doyle Rice, "Humanity to get closest look ever at Jupiter's Giant Red Spot," *USA Today*, July 5, 2017.

12   Bill Andrews, "How Juno Met Jupiter," *Discover Magazine*, January/February 2017, 73.

13   Corey S. Powell, "Europa or Bust," *Popular Science,* September 2015, 60-65.

14   Marcia Dunn, "7 Earth-Size Worlds Found Orbiting Star; The Planets Could Hold Life," *Detroit Free Press*, September 16, 2017, 2A.

15   R. Feltman, "The Longest haul," *Popular Science*, Summer 2018, 14-16.

16   Michael Lemonick, "The Hunt for Life Beyond Earth," *National Geographic*, July 2014, 26-45.

17   Steve Nadis, "Breakthrough to the Stars," *Discover magazine*, December 2016, 92.

18   *Popular Science*, January/February 2017, 24.

19   Jeffrey Kluger, "Searching for Life on the Newly Discovered Earthlike Planets," *Time*, March 13, 2017.

20 Martin Rees, "Our Place in the Universe," *Scientific American*, September 1, 2020, 58-64.

21 Elin Hilderbrand, *Golden Girl* (New York: Little, Brown and Company, 2021).

22 David J. Eicher, "How Immense is the universe?," *Astronomy*, December 2015, 20-23.

23 *Time*, January 17/January 24, 2022, 10.

24 Sophie Bushwick, "This is Your Universe," *Popular Science*, January/February 2017

25 C.J. Conselice, "Our trillion-galaxy universe," *Discover*, May 2018, 60-65..

26 Caleb Jones and Jennifer Since Kelleher, "Telescopes foes roped together, block road," *Detroit Free Press*, July 16, 2019, 11A.

27 J. Kluger, "What can the James Webb Space Telescope tell us about our universe," *Time*, January 17/January 24, 2022, 10.

28 Our Planet website, "Things that make Life on Earth Possible," accessed March 2021. https://ourplnt.com/life-on-earth-possible/.

29 Michael Lemonick, "The Hunt for Life Beyond Earth," *National Geographic*, July 2014, 26-45.

30 Rachael Zisk, "Pristine 'fireball' meteorite contains extraterrestrial organic compounds," *Popular Science* online, October 29, 2020, https://www.popsci.com/story/space/fireball-meteorite-organic-compounds-michigan/ www.popsci.com/story/space/fireball-meteorite-organiccomponents-michigan.

31 Bart D. Ehrman, *Heaven and Hell, A History of the Afterlife* (New York: Simon & Schuster, 2020).

32 Michel Bourdeau, "Auguste Comte," The Stanford Encyclopedia of Philosophy online, revised January 27, 2022, https://plato.stanford.edu/entries/comte/.

33 Martin Rees, "Our Place in the Universe," *Scientific American*, September 1, 2020, 58-64; Wikipedia search online, accessed May 2023, https://en.wikipedia.org/w/index.php?fulltext=1&search=Pulsars.quasars&title=Special%3ASearch&ns0=1.

34 Big Questions from Andrew Fabian, *Scientific American*, September 2020, 1A, 1B.

35 Nicola Davis "Scientists capture image of black hole emitting high-energy jets," published April 7, https://www.theguardian.com/science/2020/apr/07/scientists-capture-image-of-black-hole-emitting-high-energy-jets online, 2020.

36 Katie Mack, *The End of Everything: (Astrophysically Speaking)* (New York: Scribner, 2020.)

34

ENVIRONMENT
OF HEAVEN

IN CHAPTER 33 the possible places are discussed as to where Heaven could be located after the second coming of Jesus and life on the present earth is over, at the resurrection. One of these places is the present earth, to which God will give a "face lift." Proponents of this face lift call the result the "new earth." A new earth being made from the present earth seems to be a good idea. People are familiar with the present earth and could be comfortable to continue here after God's modifications.[1] Another interesting situation is to consider, especially as we do more and more damage to the present earth (see below), is that God will have resurrected humans somewhere else but animals and plants will remain here on earth so there will be a "world without us."[2] Buildings, sky scrapers, bridges, railroads, highways, and subway systems, would all breakdown and eventually deteriorate. "Plastic, bronze sculptures, radio waves and some man-made molecules may be our most lasting gifts to the earth." Microbes and fungi will continue to live here. Plants, even weeds and jungles, would take over. Animals would once again roam the earth and live and reproduce in a "survival of the fittest" environment.[2] Alternatively, the new earth would have resurrected humans but have little or no non-human life of any kind. God would begin Heaven sort of from scratch. It would make sense that God would then provide Heaven with plants and animals, invertebrates and vertebrates, perhaps even pets.[1]

Pollution is an issue with which God must be quite concerned. A USA city in the Midwest had a crisis in 2017; lead was leaching out of pipes into the drinking water. Children and adults were showing rashes and illnesses that ultimately were linked to the lead in their drinking water. Candidates for the presidency (election of 2020) were each visiting that city and interacting with the mayor, city health officials, and citizens. Why? Perhaps these candidates wanted to emphasize their concern for environmental issues, which was an issue in the election.[3] Note that Canada also has had issues with lead in the drinking water and levels equal to or higher than those in the city mentioned above.[4] There are three challenges here for God. 1. How to diagnose health issues in deceased children or adults due to exposure to lead or other pollutants. 2. How to correct the subsequent health issues (lower IQ, attention deficit disorder, brain, and kidney damage). 3. How to be sure the drinking water in Heaven is free of lead and other pollutants.

PFAS (polyfluoroalkyls), known as "forever chemicals," are being found in tap water supplies of dozens of major USA cities, including Washington D.C., Philadelphia, Miami, and Louisville, at levels potentially toxic, and at somewhat lower levels in Las Vegas, New York City, Sacramento, and Seattle. PFAS are also found in bottled water, and in fish and foods. These are human-made chemicals that are associated with many industries and may pose health problems to anyone coming into contact with them. They were used at air bases for firefighting. They degrade only very slowly (thousands of years) in the environment which is why they are called "forever" chemicals. PFAS are in popcorn bags, outdoor clothing, tents, and on the non-stick surfaces of pots and pans. PFAS have been linked to cancer, liver, thyroid and pancreas ailments, adverse effects on the hormone and immune systems, high cholesterol, low birth weights, and negative effects on growth, learning, and behavior of infants and children. A child health specialist said that avoiding all exposure to these ubiquitous compounds is probably impossible. The environmental protection agency has taken steps in detecting and cutting down on PFAS.[5]

There are many additional chemicals that humans have added to the environment with potential toxic properties. Some of these are in our most beautiful rivers and lakes. The North Branch of the Au Sable River in N. Michigan is a wonderful trout stream with some excellent fly hatches that attract fly fishers from all over. In 2018 a dramatic decrease in trout numbers was noted by anglers and confirmed by biologists using electro-shocking methods. One of many explanations for the decrease that was considered was chemical contamination. To this end, the river water was tested for organic chemicals. Eight legacy pesticides were detected (used on lawns, golf courses, wood preservation), one polybrominated diphenyl ether (many uses), nine polycyclic aromatic hydrocarbons (coal tar, petroleum, and exhaust), some currently used pesticides, and other organic compounds. Further investigations will help to determine if any of these are the cause of the declines in trout numbers.[6] Other hazardous chemicals found in the sediments of 71 rivers that feed into the Great Lakes are PAHs (poly-cyclic aromatic hydrocarbons), which are primarily the result of dust from coal-tar sealed roads, driveways, and parking lots. These potentially toxic chemicals eventually get into the Great Lakes, a source of drinking water and recreation for millions of people, and habitat for millions of vertebrate and invertebrate animals.[7] Will there be coal-tar sealed driveways, parking lots, and roads in Heaven?

Clean water is the subject of an entire issue of Popular Science magazine[8a] and deals with water in medicine, energy requirements to obtain water, exploration for water, and likely future conflicts in the world centered on water availability. Road salt entering fresh water systems is an issue as well.[8b] Will God insure that the water in Heaven for drinking, washing, and recreation is free of pesticides, herbicides, and other harmful chemicals? Where will that clean fresh water be found? Is God going to be a chemist? Is He going to figure out desalination methods and get fresh water from our oceans? Is He going to clean our oceans of plastics and other wastes?

Beginning with the Industrial Age, humans have added carbon dioxide (CO_2) to the air in quantities sufficient to cause the atmosphere to act as a greenhouse resulting in climate change. CO_2 levels have reached 415 parts per million and are the highest in human history, going back 800,000 years and more. Modern humans did not evolve until 300,000 years ago.[9] The result of this greenhouse effect has been to warm the temperature of the air; the warming is linked to melting of the ice at the poles, increased ocean water levels, severe storms, heavy rainfall, droughts, tornadoes and damage from the strong winds, and adverse effects on farms and forests with an increase in wildfires.[10]

In the USA thousands of deaths occur annually due to chronic wildfire smoke exposure, a situation that in Sept. 2020, was the worst ever due to a record number and large size of wildfires in Calif and Oregon.[11] Much carbon dioxide is being released by these USA fires but also as many fires burn in the Amazon forests causing somewhat of a worldwide panic. The Amazon is estimated to produce nearly 25% of the earth's oxygen and the fires are damaging the earth's atmosphere.[12] Fires in Australia where the temperature is over 100 are burning millions of acres, killing millions of those animals unique to Australia, and creating health hazardous smoke filled air that has taken 28 lives in 3 months.[13] The ice covering Greenland is melting at a record pace due to warm temperatures; 12.5 billion tons of ice were lost to the ocean on one single day.[14] By 2100 the estimate is that Greenland's melting ice will increase the world's ocean level by anywhere from 2 to 13 inches.[15] Glaciers are melting throughout the world and when completely gone that shortage of water will affect urban water supplies, agriculture, and ecotourism. United Nations Secretary General Antonio Guterres said data from the World Meteorological Organization indicate that July 2019, was the warmest July in earth's history and followed the warmest June in history. The decade that ended with the year 2019 was the warmest in human history.[16] For several days in a row, temperatures reached record highs, near 120 degrees F in Australia, and that heat was accompanied by drought and brush fires.[17] Finally, on this topic of global warming, National Geographic, Sept. 2019, had an article on the warming of the Arctic. The tundra is thawing and that will speed up warming of the planet, not a rosy picture. Also, the efforts of an Ohio State University graduate student in geography to document and understand climate changes are explained in the Ohio State University Arts and Sciences News magazine and in National Geographic magazine.[18] Climate change is real and the earth is warming. Is God paying attention?

Increasingly, youth around the world are becoming concerned about the environment, thanks in large part to Greta Thunberg, a sixteen-year-old high school student in Sweden. Greta was Time's person of the year in 2019 and the cover title with her picture was "The Power of Youth." Greta stirred up interest and much support to fight climate change when she stood before leaders of the countries of the United Nations and stated, "How Dare You?" meaning how can nations ignore climate change and continue policies that further increase CO2 in the atmosphere? Greta has met with the Secretary General of the United Nations as well as the pope and presidents of NATO countries and has galvanized support to fight climate change. She led over seven million climate strikers across the globe in Sept. 2019 and "Thunberg has become the biggest voice on the biggest issue facing the planet."[19] She has support from teens throughout the world and that raises a question about Heaven. Will God insure that there are young people in Heaven to call attention to issues that older people do not recognize or are ignoring? Sadly, the president of the USA in 2020, a writer for the Detroit Free Press, and a well-known musician, have "bullied" her and even suggested that Greta is "brain washed!" But her response was outstanding when she said, "It's not about what people call me. It's not about left or right. It's all about scientific facts...and that we are not aware of the situation and unless we start to focus everything on this situation, our targets will soon be out of reach."

Climate change was an issue in the 2020 presidential election as could be noted from listening to the democratic candidate debates and from reading newspapers. One newspaper writer said, "the fires in Australia and the Amazon are only some of the many telltale signs of climate disruption and are but a few of Mother Nature's urgent wake-up calls" and "we need to phase out fossil fuels on a rapid time-table, starting now." But, the President (in 2020) did not support or sign any meaningful climate legislation. This newspaper writer proposed seven new laws to curb use of fossil fuels that the democratic candidate chosen to run in the next (2020) presidential election should enact. These laws center on power plants, buildings, transportation (cars, trucks, trains, and planes), innovation relevant to climate change, and farms.[20] The current president, 2022, is trying to do all of these things and congress is only somewhat cooperating.

With billions and billions of people on the new earth after the second coming of Christ, will pollution be a thing of the past? Will global warming be non-existent? Will God provide for a Heaven with lowered CO2 levels, clean air and water, no trash, no plastic waste, no food discarded, no landfills, and weather conditions that are not extreme? Will we have summer, fall, winter and spring seasons? Will fish, whales, birds, butterflies, and dragon flies migrate?[21] Where will food come from? Will there be farms? Will there be grocery stores? Maybe the "glorified bodies" of Heaven residents will not need food or water. But according to Alcorn[1] there will be activities in Heaven, like dancing and singing, and those activities will require energy and thus food. The billions of people in Heaven will not be content to just worship God and Jesus all day every day. Will they?

The air quality in the USA and the world based on particulate pollution has worsened since 2016 according to the National Bureau of Economic Research. Several factors are major contributors: more wildfires, more economic growth, more motor vehicles, and less enforcement of the Clean Air Act.[22] Thousands of deaths each year are attributed to air pollution and almost half of USA people breathe polluted air. Pollution in the forms of smog (ground level ozone) and soot (particulate material) contribute to lung cancer, asthma, heart damage, and developmental and reproductive harm.[23] But of the ten worst polluted cities in the world, none are in the USA while seven are in India, the worst being New Delhi, a city of eighteen million people and 8.8 million motor vehicles. Breathing the air in New Delhi for a day in Nov. 2019, was as bad as a person smoking forty-four cigarettes for a day. People are wearing masks to escape at least some of the pollution. Imagine the health problems and early deaths related to such high pollution. The United Nations reported that over seven million people worldwide die prematurely each year from health problems related to air pollution.[24]

There is little room for optimism here on earth. But what about in Heaven? One view is that the present earth will be transformed into a "new earth," which will be Heaven. There will be music and sound, and both require air. There will be rivers and lakes and thus water will be present.[1] Will the air, water, and land be cleaned of pollution and pesticides?[25] Will there be protected areas where people can get away from worshiping God at least for a short time? The USA has eighty-four million acres within 419 natl. park sites, including Yellowstone Natl. Park, the first natl. park, established by President Grant in 1822. Wrangell-St. Elias in Alaska is the largest natl. park at eight million acres. The Great Smoky Mountains Park is the most visited, with eleven million visitors in 2017.[26] Russia has the most land considered "protected," a total of 209 million hectares (522 million acres), more than one-fourth of the total land mass of Russia.[27] Certainly God will have a relatively easy time incorporating Russia into the new Heaven.

The worst "environmental injustice" areas in the USA were identified in one mid-western state. Not surprisingly, the highest scores, those with the highest amount of exposure to citizens of air and water pollution, heavy motor vehicle traffic, and exposure to contaminated sites, were in high population density cities/areas where the poor, less educated and those with limited English language skills reside and are vulnerable to what are considered as environmental injustices. These people want to survive, they want longevity, they want good health.[28a] Graduate students who are conducting the study point out that the critical areas can now be identified and prioritized for resources and enforcement. This attitude should apply to Heaven as well. Will God insure everyone has the same opportunity for good health in Heaven? If everyone's environment is the same, there will be a step-up for those in bad environments on earth now and a step down for those in good environments now. God will have to adjust attitudes too.

Climate change is particularly harmful to child health worldwide.[28a,28b] Over 90% of the world's 2.2 billion children are breathing unsafe air as defined by the World Health Organization. The lifetime risk of these children is high for developing asthma, pneumonia, and COPD (chronic obstructive pulmonary disease). By 2050 70% of earth's population will be living in cities, where the air is dirtiest. The average temperature in cities will also be higher due to global warming and will further cause health issues such as kidney and respiratory disease. In India, where only 4% of the homes have air conditioning, 35% of the 1.3 billion population are fourteen or younger, leading to many of the above-mentioned health issues.[28a]

Worldwide rising temperatures and droughts are having adverse effects on crop yields of rice, maize, and wheat, while at the same time rising ocean temperatures are decreasing the yield of fish, important to the diet of 3.2 billion people, leading to under nutrition from which children suffer the most.[28b] Note from above chapters that the population of Heaven will be much higher than the nine billion projected on earth in 2050. Clean air, clean water, nutritious food, and dealing with human solid and liquid waste products will be major challenges in Heaven.

How will Heaven residents get around? Will there be motor vehicles? If they will have physical bodies[1] then they will physically move from place to place. Keep in mind there will be billions and billions of Heaven residents, breathing in oxygen and breathing out carbon dioxide. There will have to be plants to take in carbon dioxide and produce oxygen by photosynthesis.

What about animals? Will there be insects and other invertebrates and a diversity of plants, fungi and microbes in Heaven? If there will be fruit trees then bees will be essential for pollination. The importance of invertebrate animals, like bees, butterflies, ants, spiders, and beetles is recognized more and more by environmentalists today.[29] Prof. Douglas Tallamy, an entomologist at the Univ. of Delaware, quoted E.O. Wilson who said, "The truth is that we need invertebrates but they don't need us. If human beings were to disappear tomorrow, the natural world would go on...But if invertebrates were to disappear, it is doubtful that the human species could last more than a few months." Consider that scientists estimate there are 1.2 million arthropod species (insects, spiders, crustaceans) on the earth. There are 3,000 species of damsel flies and many more species of beetles. Insects were on the earth, having colonized land, 400,000,000 years ago, 200 million years before the first dinosaurs appeared. But insect populations are decreasing rapidly, and scientists are trying to determine the cause(s).[30] How many of these insect and other invertebrate species will be in Heaven and in what numbers?

Among the vertebrates, how many of the thousands of species of the fishes, amphibians, lizards, birds, and mammals will be in Heaven? How many of the 28,000 fish species? There are 5,500 species of mammals alive today and ninety-six species have recently gone extinct (examples of mammals are whales, bats, mice, deer, kangaroos, bears, apes, humans).[31] Next consider the bulk of flowering plants and with them the physical structure of the majority of forests and other terrestrial habitats of the world. Plants anchor the ecosystems of the earth and hundreds have already gone extinct and more are threatened.[32] There are 100,000 known species of fungi on the earth. Will these all be in Heaven?[33] Another of E.O. Wilson's quotes is, "I would say that for the sake of human progress, the best thing we could possibly do would be to diminish, to the point of eliminating, religious faiths, but certainly not eliminating the natural yearnings of our species nor the asking of great questions."[34]

There are many kinds of domestic animals, including dogs, cats, gerbils, parrots, horses, cows, goats, and pigs. Which of the five common types of cows will be in Heaven?[35] Will all the animals and plants on the earth today be represented in Heaven? There are an estimated eight million plant and animal species on the earth and one million of these face extinction today because of human activity. One study suggests that if we stick to the

Paris Agreement to combat climate change, we may lose fewer than one
million species but if the earth continues to warm, we may lose up to one-
third of all species by 2070.[36] What would Jesus say about this devastating
loss of biodiversity? Didn't God create all species? Were they not all saved
in Noah's ark? Now humans are killing them off. Human activity has
"severely altered" 66% of ocean and 75% of land environments. We are
also losing our ice environment and ice-free summers are predicted for the
Arctic by 2050. Three quarters of our crops depend on animal pollination;
will bees, butterflies and bats be in Heaven to pollinate crops? Scientists say
climate change and species loss can be corrected by major changes in human
activities such as investments in forests and green energy, overhaul of inter-
national trade, and changes in our individual behavior (such as eating less
meat and using better farming practices). Research is underway to engineer
corn so that it will fix nitrogen, like legumes do at present (clover, peas,
beans). But then if we grow more corn, we can make more alcohol. Maybe
God will remove addiction genes from the genomes of Heaven inhabitants
to decrease addictions such as alcoholism.[37]

Teams of scientists from the United Nations Intergovernmental Panel
on Climate Change examined the farthest corners of the earth, highest
mountains to deepest oceans, and found evidence of climate change even in
these remote regions. The Panel predicted that weather extremes and floods
will be more numerous and oceans will become less able to sustain fish and
other life; a dire prediction for sure. What is needed is a low-emissions goal
and even then, managing the impacts of climate change will be challenging
and expensive.[38]

To fight climate change and loss of biodiversity many celebrities have
joined billionaires and philanthropists to provide grants and educational
funds for this fight.[39] Levels of the greenhouse gas CO_2 are the highest in
human history, 415 parts per million, the highest in 800,000 years. Not
until the Industrial Revolution did CO_2 levels surpass even 300 ppm.
Needless to say, efforts to bring that 415 ppm down are essential. But how?
Swiss scientists say tree planting is the best solution and humans need to
plant trees in every available space; there is enough available space on earth
to cover 3.5 million sq. miles with a trillion new trees, an area the size of the
USA. India is also expressing a positive view of tree planting and has had
two plantings in their northern state of Uttar Pradesh. The first planting in

2016 was 50 million tree saplings and the second in 2019 was 220 million; each planting was in a single day.[40] Jed Daley, the President and CEO of the non-profit, American Forests, is advocating for federal funding to plant sixteen billion new trees in the USA by 2050, including 400 million in urban areas. Daley says "creating healthy forests is a moral imperative." These plantings will help to mitigate climate change.[41] The six countries with the most room for new trees are Russia, USA, Canada, Australia, Brazil, and China.[42] Every planted tree will help but the situation can look dismal. On June 2, 2020, the Global Forest Watch revealed satellite data showing that many soccer-field size areas of tropical rain forest are lost every day. Nearly a third of the loss is tropical primary forests, areas important to carbon storage and biodiversity.[43] Perhaps governments can fund tree plantings on all available lands. Will Heaven have an abundance of trees? Will global warming be a thing of the past? Will there be biodiversity?

Are there going to be farms in Heaven? Where will food come from? In one mid-western state, agricultural activity ranked the top 5 foods as dairy (milk and milk products), corn, soybeans, cattle/calves (beef) and hogs (pork). Chickens are probably #6 and turkeys a close #7. Farmers are under stress due to bad weather (too little or two much rain: early or late frosts), diseases, low prices for their goods (dairy etc.), cheap imports, tariffs, fewer pollinators, insect pests, and high feed costs.[44] Chemicals have been added, intentionally and unintentionally, to our water and food. We now have over 500 more chemicals in our bodies that are not part of our biology than we had in 1940. Some of these are herbicides, insecticides, fungicides, fertilizers, and plant growth regulators. While they may have beneficial effects in helping to provide food for cattle and people, they can have harmful effects too in being carcinogenic (cancer-causing) or may interfere with normal body functions such as endocrine (hormone) systems. Reading the labels on packaged foods can be scary.[45] Will God insure the environment of Heaven is free of harmful chemicals? How will he clean up the harmful chemicals that are presently in our environment? Will there be crop pests in Heaven?

Will God insure human life in Heaven is environmentally friendly?[46] According to Ethan Brown, founder of Beyond Meat, if we want to solve climate issues we have to move away from livestock, which require huge amounts of water and plants for food. So why not give up meat? Meat contains amino acids, lipids, minerals like iron and calcium, vitamins, and water. Plants such as peas and beans contain the same components. Producing a plant-based burger results in 90% fewer greenhouse-gas emissions than producing a beef burger and the plant burger is as tasty and nutritionally complete as a beef burger.[47] A global shift on earth from meat to plant-based diets would cut as much as eight billion tons of greenhouse gasses per year, which is more than the entire vehicle emissions of the USA in one year.[48] Maybe God will have a Heaven in which everyone is vegan, including our pets. Even then, humans and animals will generate waste (fecal and urine) so there will have to be disposal systems.

Alternatively, meat can be grown in laboratories. Cells can be taken from a fish, chicken or cow and increased to the billions in dishes in the laboratory after which the cells are processed for texture and taste. The result is chicken or hamburger with the same texture that tastes and looks like the real thing.[49]

Let's think about cows again. Can Heaven get along without cow's milk? Sure, it would be advantageous to not have to raise crops to feed dairy or beef cows. There are plant-based milks including almond, soy, rice, coconut, hemp, oat, and flax. Nutritional comparisons vary but none live up to cow's milk, especially for newborn children. Many of these have added sugars, some have higher fat content than whole cow's milk. All can be fortified with calcium and vitamin D. Certainly these plant-based milks would be good for people with lactose intolerance (lactose is the sugar in cow's milk).[50] These plants would have to be raised somewhere in Heaven; farms would be required. The glorified bodies people will have in Heaven will still require good nutrition, will they not, even if fashioned like the body of Jesus? After all, Jesus ate (Philippians 3:21). There is much speculation about what a "glorified" body will be like, including having wings and be able to fly![51] Flying would require huge amounts of energy, would it not? And strong and well-developed breast muscles! Would arms become wings in Heaven or would wings be separate appendages with separate muscles to power them?

So, what about pets? Will people have homes wherein they can keep pet fish, birds, lizards, dogs, cats, and pigs? Will they have horses? In the USA, 68% of families have one or more dogs. The American Kennel Club now recognizes 196 breeds of dogs, with a new one, the Belgian Laekenois, recently accepted.[52] These pets will require food and thus agriculture is a must in Heaven. Will there be farmers? Will there be farms with all the required farm machinery? Even a vegan Heaven will require farm products (wheat, oats, barley, peas, beans, fruits, onions, cabbage).

How will people move about in Heaven? Will there be public transportation? Automobiles? Planes? Will fuel be available? Will there be air and water pollution?

We are finally learning to recycle but we have a long way to go. We know that 80 percent of items buried in landfills could have been recycled.[53] But our oceans and freshwater lakes are already filled with trash much of which is plastics. One net off the coast of Hawaii revealed 2,459 plastic particles, most the size of a grain of sand but some easily recognized such as a discarded fishing net and bottle caps. Twenty-six different organisms and seventeen different types of plastic items were identified in that scoop. Eight million tons of plastics wash into our oceans each year. Less than 15% of plastic world-wide is recycled; the rest ends up in landfills or in the oceans. Estimates indicate there will be more plastic in the oceans by weight than fish by 2050.[54] Fish provide important protein to nearly three billion people worldwide. Baby fish are mistaking plastics for their food. If the first meals of baby fish are plastics, calories and nutrition will be sorely lacking. Fish stocks are already falling due to over-fishing, pollution, and climate change. Four of ten humans rely on the ocean for food. Plastic waste will further exacerbate the loss.[55,56] Only 9% of plastic waste is recycled in the USA and some point out that we have a "disjointed" recycling system.[57] The central govt of India is asking all states to end the use of single-use plastics by 2022. India generates thirty-three million pounds of plastic waste every day, only 60% of which is collected and recycled. China has banned single use plastics and non-degradable bags are banned. Malaysia is sending over 4,000 tons of plastic waste back to the countries of origin.[58] If the present earth is going to be the new earth (Heaven), God's first job will be to clean up the environment, and that will be a major task. He will need many angels with rakes and scoops.

Finland is actively pursuing a no waste, carbon circular economy and seemingly being successful.[59]

Will there be plastics in Heaven? If so, maybe God will make them biodegradable. Finnish researchers have made progress in making a plastic substitute using wood pulp and laboratory made spider silk.[60] This potential plastic of the future will biodegrade, unlike present plastics, which are rapidly filling landfills, lakes, and oceans, and have been found even in Antarctica.[61]

Food waste is a major problem worldwide. Decomposition of food waste contributes 8% of annual green-house gas emissions. Also, 25% of agricultural land goes to produce food that ultimately goes uneaten. In the USA we discard 40% of the food we produce. Food is wasted in harvesting, packaging, transporting, in groceries, in refrigerators, and at the table in homes, schools, and restaurants. Will this waste of food occur in Heaven? Will there be landfills to which wasted food is transported?[62] People are going to eat in Heaven and the many, many billions, perhaps mostly adults, will need a lot of food. Will there be babies requiring breast milk or formula?

Will Heaven be a world without waste? Such a world is the vision of a major part of National Geographic magazine, Mar. 2020, in the article, "The End of Trash." It is the vision of a "circular economy" wherein resources are used sparingly, and materials are endlessly recycled, often put to other uses than the original. Businesses and environmentalists are inspired similarly. Dow is one company "on board" and very much into the circular economy, developing sustainable packaging with low environmental impact, using recycled plastics to pave roads and build schools and more, giving plastics new lives and keeping them out of the environment. Companies in Italy are reusing clothing to make fashionable new clothing. Trash in Copenhagen, Denmark, is burned under efficient conditions resulting in a minimum of pollution to provide energy for homes, and none goes to landfills. Every year on the earth 100 billion tons of raw material are transformed into products. Long lasting materials like vehicles and infrastructure makes up 25%, reused resources like foods make up 10%, the remaining 65% is discarded or disposed of into the environment (like carbon dioxide) or becomes trash. Can we visualize Heaven to be a place of pure happiness with unlimited resources where everyone sits around and praises God?

Will there be seasons? Will there be weather? The sun is very much the main influence on weather as the earth rotates on its axis every 24 hrs. and goes from day to night and the earth revolves around the sun every 365 days (every year). The tilt of the earth on its axis is also influential as the sun's rays are more direct on North America and Europe in the months of May, June, July, and August and provide more heat, thus giving us summer, the main growing season. Because of this tilt the days are longer than nights in the summer months and days are shorter than nights in winter months. The heat of the sun is largely responsible for evaporation and cloud formation. Rain comes from clouds. The sun warms the air differentially which causes winds and storms. But the Bible says that in Heaven there will be no sun. Isaiah 60:19 says, "The sun shall be no more thy light by day, neither shall the moon give light unto thee, but the lord shall be an everlasting light..." Revelation 21:23 says, "And the city (Heaven) had no need of the sun, neither of the moon, to shine in it, for the glory of God did lighten it and the lamb (Jesus) is the light thereof." Revelation 22:5 says, "And there shall be no night there, and no need for a candle, neither the sun, for the Lord God giveth them light, and they shall reign forever." Note that the book of Isaiah was written between 740-680 BCE; the book of Revelation was written about 96 CE, both before the sun's nuclear energy was recognized in the 1930s (see below). We can ask if the entire earth, all sides and ends, will receive equal light amounts and continuously, where will God be positioned? Will he be wrapped around the earth? How will he generate light?

Might God make the new earth flat, as it once was believed to be? He then would not have to provide light all the way around but only from above. By changing his position slightly, he could provide seasonal changes in light amounts on different parts of the flat earth. He could make the surface equivalent in area to the present earth which is 510 million square kilometers of which 30% is land and 70% ocean. That is much larger than Heaven as described in Revelation 21:16. All this area and more would be needed if initially everyone who has died plus the presently living all go to Heaven. That would be over 100 billion people! See Chapter 33.

Genesis 1:26 states, And God said, "let us make man in our image after our likeness." And verse 1:27 says, so God created mankind in his own image, in the image of God he created them, male and female created he them. If these verses say that God looks like a person, then how is he going to generate more light than the sun and have that light continuously bathe the spherical earth from all directions. Perhaps the Apostle John, the writer of Rev. 22:5, was a believer in a flat earth and thus could visualize God above the surface, the firmament, sending continuous light down upon it.

Given that all life on earth, plants and animals, are adapted to day/
night and to seasonal changes in light quantity and temperatures, there will
be much adjusting to do. And what will God do with our sun which will
no longer be needed? Will he send it out into the universe?

The sun's ultraviolet B rays are important to provide vitamin D. These
rays stimulate the chemical reaction wherein ergosterol in the skin converts
to vitamin D. Vitamin D is important to strong bones and teeth and to
other health aspects of our bodies. Without sunlight foods would have to
be the source of vitamin D; these would be salmon and some other fish,
beef liver, soy products, cheese, and egg yolks.[63] Vitamin D fortified milk
might not be available in Heaven. Of course, God or Jesus could perform
a miracle every day and feed everyone in Heaven from a few fish as Jesus
does in Matthew 14:13-21, feeding thousands. Consider that Isaiah 60,
verse 19, says, "the sun will no more be the light of day; the lord will be your
everlasting light." Most important is to ask whether the light God provides
just from his presence will be sufficient for growing crops; will it stimulate
photosynthesis and thus plant growth? Also, will the light God provides
have the ultraviolet B rays needed for human skin to make vitamin D (see
Chapter 35). Will God's light provide heat as our present sun does?

Recognition that the sun's energy, both light and thermal, comes from
nuclear fusion, is credited to Hans Bethe, in the 1930s.[64] Hydrogen atoms
fuse to form helium with some loss of mass that is converted to much
energy. This nuclear fusion occurs in the core of the sun. If God is going
to provide more light than the sun (see Bible verses above) where is that
light going to come from? Nuclear fusion within the body of God? How
will it be possible to approach God intimately, to have God wrap his arms
around you?

Where will people live? In private houses? In public housing? God will
be faced with a plethora of challenges.

NOTES

1   Randy Alcorn, *Heaven: A Comprehensive Guide to Everything the Bible Says
     About Our Eternal Home* (Illinois: Tyndale Momentum, 2004.)
2   Alan Weisman, *The World Without Us* (New York: St. Martin's Press, 2007.)

3   Detroit Free Press, July 15, 2019, p. 1A.

4   Josh Sanburn, "Toxic Legacy," *Time*, April 22, 2019, 35-37..

5   Keith Matheny, "PFAS contamination is Michigan's biggest environmental crisis in 40 years," *Detroit Free Press*, April 25, 2019, 1A.

6   Bryan Burroughs, "Conservation Tippets: North Branch Au Sable - Case of the Missing Trout," *Michigan Trout Magazine*, Summer, 2018, 14.

7   K. Matheny, "Great Lakes contaminant source: your driveway," *Detroit Free Press*, July 10, 2020, 1A.

8a The Water Issue, *Popular Science*, June, 2014.

8b Rick Fowler, "The Effect of Road Salt on Rivers and Steams," *Mackinac Journal*, June 2023, 14-15.

9   *Detroit Free Press*, May 14, 2019, 11A.

10 GlobalGiving (website), "10 Climate Change Facts That Everyone Should Know," published April 19, 2019, https://www.globalgiving.org/learn/climate-change-facts.

11 Detroit Free Press, January 16, 2020; p. 13A; NBC News, September 12, 2020.

12 *NBC Nightly News*, August 23, 2019, https://www.nbcnews.com/nightly-news/video/staggering-number-of-fires-ravaging-amazon-rainforest-66915397642.

13 Detroit Free Press, January 16, 2020.

14 Pat Brennan, "Study: 2019 Sees Record Loss of Greenland Ice," *NASA* online, August 20, 2020, https://climate.nasa.gov/news/3010/study-2019-sees-record-loss-of-greenland-ice/#:~:text=Greenland%20set%20a%20new%20record,in%20the%20previous%20two%20years.

15 NSIDC, "Greenland Ice Sheet Today," National Snow & Ice Data Center online, accessed May 2023, https://nsidc.org/greenland-today/.

16 David Rising, "Hit by heat wave, Greenland sees massive ice melt," *Detroit Free Press*, August 2, 2019, 11A.

17 *Detroit Free Press*, December 14, 2019, 11A.

18 Jeff Grabmeier, "Science coverage of climate change can change minds - briefly," *Ohio State News* online, published June 20, 2022, https://news.osu.edu/science-coverage-of-climate-change-can-change-minds--briefly/.

19 E. Falsenthal, "The Choice," *Time*, December 23-30, 2019, 48-69.

20 *Detroit Free Press*, January 17, 2020, 15A.

21 S. Shalaway, "Swarms of Dragonflies," *Straitsland Resorter*, September 26, 2019, 7.

22 *Detroit Free Press*, November 2, 2019, 13A; *Time*, November 18, 2019, 9.

23 American Lung Association report summary, *Detroit Free Press*, April 23, 2020, 13A.

24 CNN website, "The perfect storm fueling New Delhi's deadly pollution,", updated November 14, 2019, https://www.cnn.com/2019/11/04/india/delh i-smog-pollution-explainer-intl/index.html.

25 N.T. Wright cited in *Time*, January 27, 2020, 24.

26 Wikipedia website, "List of national parks of the United States," last updated May 16, 2023, https://en.wikipedia.org/wiki/List_of_national_parks_of_ the_United_States.

27 statista website, "Proportion of land area covered by forest in Russia from 2005 to 2020," accessed May 2023, https://www.statista.com/statistics/435976/ forest-area-as-percentage-of-land-area-russia/.

28a K. Matheny, Michigan's worst environmental injustice areas are identified, *Detroit Free Press*, July 26, 2019, 4A.

28b "How Climate Change is Clobbering Kid's Health," *Time*, November 25, 2019, 17.

29 J. Adler, "Wild Man," *Smithsonian Magazine*, April 2020, 80-94.

30 Elizabeth Kolbert, "Where Have All The Insects Gone?," *National Geographic*, May 2020, 40-65; D. Quammen, "When Life Got Complicated," *National Geographic*, March 2018, 90-107.

31 Wikipedia website, "Fish," accessed January 2020, https://en.wikipedia.org/ wiki/Fish; Wikipedia website, "Mammal," accessed January 2020, https:// en.wikipedia.org/wiki/Mammal.

32 Michael Greshko, "Weakening Life's Green Foundation," *National Geographic*, October 2019; 32.

33 wise geek website "Clear Answers for Common Questions,", accessed February 2020, https://www.wisegeek.com/mushrooms-and-other-edible-fungi.htm; J. Adler, Wild Man, *Smithsonian Magazine*, April 2020, 80-92.

34 AZ Quotes, E.O. Wilson, 2010.

35 Wikipedia website, "List of cattle breeds," accessed December 2019, https:// en.wikipedia.org/wiki/List_of_cattle_breeds.

36 *Detroit Free Press*, February 15, 2020, 13.

37 *Discover* magazine, November 2019, 26-33; 49-53; *Detroit Free Press*, April 24, 2020, 3A.

38 Janet Wilson and Doyle Rice, "Climate panel sees dire future for planet/ people," *Detroit Free Press*, September 26, 2019, 14A.

39 LeafScore website, "10 Celebrities Leading the Fight Against Climate Change," accessed May 2023, https://www.leafscore.com/blog/eco-friendl y-celebrities-battling-climate-change/.

40 *Detroit Free Press*, August 11, 2019, 2A.

41 Michael Blanding, "Speaking for the trees," *Brown Alumni Monthly*, January/ February 2020, 49.

42 *Detroit Free Press*, July 6, 2019, 13A.

43 *Time*, June 15, 2020, 9.

44 Sarah Bowman, "'Most expensive crop in decades': Farmers face higher stakes than ever with inflation," IndyStar. Online, published September 30, 2022, https://www.indystar.com/in-depth/news/environ-ment/2022/09/30/stakes-higher-than-ever-for-farmers-as-they-feel-squ eeze-of-inflation/69520689007/.

45 K. Martin, "Food Safety; Chemicals on our Table," *Cheboygan Daily Tribune*, February 13, 2019.

46 Eco Friendly Habits (website), "How to Be More Eco-Friendly: 105 Ways to Live an Environmentally Conscious Lifesytle," accessed April 2020, https://www.ecofriendlyhabits.com/how-to-be-eco-friendly/.

47 Alice Park, "8 questions for Ethan Brown," *Time* online, June 17, 2019, 68, https://time.com/5601980/beyond-meat-ceo-ethan-brown-interview/.

48 Abigail Abrams, "How Eating Less Meat Could Help Protect the Planet From Climate Change," *Time* online, August 26, 2019, 1, https://time.com/5648082/un-climate-report-less-meat/.

49 Terence Chea, "Fresh from the lab: Startups make meat that avoids slaughter," AP News online, accessed May 2023, https://apnews.com/ar-ticle/california-health-us-news-ap-top-news-environment-9fb57e95ec494 66e96c7bba3ac4b5d60#.

50 Healthessentials, *Cleveland Clinic* online, accessed May 2023, https://health.clevelandclinic.org.

51 eBible website, "Do people earn wings in heaven?," posted June 10, 2020, https://ebible.com/questions/21622-do-people-earn-wings-in-heaven.

52 J. Peltz, "American Kennel Club adds a breed of dog," *Cheboygan Daily Tribune*, July 2, 2020.

53 *Detroit Free Press*, June 25, 2019, 4A; *Northern Express Weekly*, October 21, 2019.

54 Rehman Asad Getty, "A whopping 91 percent of plastic isn't recycled," *National Geographic*, May, 2019; "Images of plastic water," *Time*, May 20, 2020, 42.

55 L. Parker, "Little Pieces, Big Problem," *National Geographic*, May 27, 2019, 42-55.

56 A. Baker, "Turn the Tide" *Time*, July 20/July 27, 2020, 44-55.

57 Editors, "What can be done about plastic pollution on a global scale?," *Scientific American*, June, 2019, 8.

58 Claire Groden, "Report: Plastic Pollution in the Ocean Is Reaching Crisis Levels," *Time* online, October 1, 2015, https://time.com/4058503/repor t-plastic-pollution-in-the-ocean-is-reaching-crisis-levels/.

59   Barry, E., "Closing the Circle," *Time*, February 14-21, 2022, 64-71.

60   Finnish American Reporter, October 2019, 2.

61   *BBC News* website, "Microplastics found in fresh Antarctic snow," published June 9, 2022, https://www.bbc.com/news/science-environment-61739159.

62   *Time*, October 21-28, 118.

63   Wikipedia website, "Vitamin D," accessed December 2019, https://en.wikipedia.org/wiki/Vitamin_D.

64   LPPFusion website, "Brief History of Fusion Power," accessed January 2020, http://www.lppfusion.com/technology/brief-history-of-fusion-power/.

35

VITAMIN REQUIREMENTS IN HEAVEN

THERE HAS BEEN much suffering and many deaths in the past from vitamin deficiencies and even today in some parts of the world people suffer from these deficiencies.[1] There are at least a dozen different vitamin deficiency diseases each of which must be a challenge to God in Heaven. It seems that God did very little to save all the souls of people dying from these deficiencies and he allowed the search for vitamins and cures for the deficiencies to go on for decades while people of all ages around the world suffered and died and still are suffering and dying in the poorest nations.

RICKETS

This is a disorder that results in softening and malformation of bones in children due to deficiency in Vitamin D. In bones discovered and examined in archeological digs, children in Egypt and other countries where sun was prevalent rarely exhibited rickets but in Norway and other low sunlight areas of the world the bones of children showed a higher frequency of rickets. That was a puzzle until it was found that rickets could be prevented or treated with sunlight, but it was not known why sunlight cured the condition. Now we know that UV light changes the ergosterol of the skin to vitamin D and it is the vitamin D that is essential for healthy bones.[2a] Several passages in the Bible tell us that there will be no need for the sun or moon in Heaven because God's light will be brighter than both. Whether the sun will still be present is not clear. Alcorn[2b] says that both the sun and moon will be present but neither will be needed. Rev. 21:23 says, "The city (new Jerusalem) does not need the sun or the moon to shine upon it for the glory of God gives it light." And Rev. 22:5 says, "There will be no more night. They will not need the light of a lamp or light of the sun, for the Lord God will give them light." And Isaiah 60:19 says, "The sun will no more be your light by day…your sun will never set again." Hopefully the light provided by God will have the necessary wavelengths to convert ergosterol in the skin to vitamin D but if so, will exposure cause more sun burning and skin cancer?

PELLAGRA

Vitamin B3 deficiency is a terrible disease. If a person's diet is deficient in vitamin B3 (niacin), the disease seen is pellagra. The symptoms are diarrhea, skin rashes, hallucinations, paranoia, tremors, and depression. The mortality rate in America's south due to pellagra was as high as 40% in the early 1900s. The disease was not understood, was very scary and some hospitals refused to treat patients with pellagra. Atlanta and other cities established pellagrasoriums to house those suffering vitamin B3 deficiency. The cure, if it had been understood, was a balanced diet providing foods with B3. A diet of mostly corn, common in the south, led to the deficiency. In 2017-18, pellagra was found in hamsters in French corn farm fields, again due to lack of B3 in the corn diet of the hamsters. The health of these hamsters could be improved with vegetables or B3 supplements thus providing the first clues that pellagra in hamsters was related to diet.[3a]

The historical search for the cause and cure of pellagra is well-documented.[3b] Pellagra affected over three million people and more than 100,000 died of pellagra in the American south between 1900 and 1940. The disease would progress through what were called the four Ds: dermatitis, diarrhea, dementia, and death. The disease was first described/identified in 1735 by a Dr. Casal, who called it *mal de la rosa* (the disease of the red rash). The disease was seen in Europe and N. Africa but seldom in the USA. What had changed? The change was the improved diet (more leafy greens) of southerners which had become largely corn-based and thus deficient in vitamin B3. South Carolina alone had 30,000 cases in 1912. Did God diagnose pellagra caused deaths? Will there be pellagra in Heaven?

SCURVY

Sailors died of scurvy in large numbers on expeditions such as those of Vasco da Gama in 1497 sailing around the Cape of Good Hope and of Magellan in 1519 navigating around the globe. One hundred sixty began the former trip and 100 died of scurvy. In the latter trip, three ships began with 250 men and only one ship returned with just eighteen men, over 200 dying of scurvy. One terrible scurvy outbreak was seen during the expedition of Jacques Cartier, in the 15th century, to the new world. His three ships became locked in ice in an inlet (now Canada) and of 110 sailors, all but three got scurvy, Cartier being one of the three. One suspects that as captain he had a more balanced diet. Many of Cartier's men were saved from dying by drinking a tea made by Native Americans from the bark of a tree, likely providing vitamin C.

Scurvy killed nearly two million sailors between Columbus's 1492 transatlantic trip and the 1850 invention of the steam engine. Captains counted on a 50% death rate of his sailors on any major voyage with bodies thrown into the sea three to four at a time every day. Deaths from scurvy numbered more than the total from shipwrecks, storms, combat, and all other diseases combined.

People rushing for gold, as in the Klondike gold rush, suffered from Vitamin C deficiency which often led to scurvy, called "Arctic Leprosy." One of the more famous of the gold "rushers" was Jack London, author of "Call of the Wild," the book that began his writing career. Jack spent only a single winter in the Yukon sharing a small cabin with three others, braving 70 below zero temperatures, and living on sourdough bread, beans, and bacon. Most everyone suffered from scurvy and Jack became so ill he had to return to Dawson City, where he found a lemon which relieved his symptoms, and from there he returned to California but required months to get well before he could continue his writing career.[4]

During the American Civil War, thousands suffered from scurvy and confederate prisons had a death rate from scurvy of 25%. Scurvy is an absolutely devastating disease. If a person's diet is deficient in Vitamin C, which chemically is ascorbic acid, symptoms begin within one to three months. First one sees loss of appetite and then weight loss, fatigue, irritability, and lethargy. Note that alcoholics can exhibit these symptoms. Additionally, there occur anemia, myalgia (pain), edema (small red spots under the skin), gum swelling and then breakdown, loss of teeth, poor wound healing, shortness of breath, and weakness. Death follows in the severe cases. Vitamin C is necessary for collagen synthesis, a protein of connective tissues, and is necessary for a healthy immune system, for iron and copper absorption, for dopamine and norepinephrine synthesis, and for neurotransmission. It is not surprising the symptoms of deficiency are so terrible.

Finding the cause of and cure for scurvy was a difficult task and many wrong paths were followed. Finally, a Surgeon, Dr. Lind, in 1746, tested various treatments on British sailors suffering from scurvy. Only limes and lemons cured scurvy in sailors. Still, it was not until 1795 that the British govt. adopted Lind's suggested cure, i.e., citrus fruits. When that role of citrus became recognized, British sailors subsequently took along limes and or lemons on long voyages, and thus became known as "limeys." Even now in modern times scurvy can still be seen in the elderly, the poor, those institutionalized, the home bound, and in alcoholics.[5]

BERIBERI

In 1814 J. Ridley, a British army surgeon, traveled to Ceylon (now Sri Lanka) to take care of troops suffering from a strange illness. Their legs and arms swelled and exhibited numbness, they lost appetite, felt extreme pressure in their rib cage, and finally lost their voices, suffocated, and died. Every day five to eight soldiers would die. The illness was blamed on such candidates as bad water, damp air, and toxins in the diet. Ridley's "treatments" did no good and he himself became ill and went back to England but after getting good food at home, his good health returned. Ridley reasoned that the cause of this illness was due to a deficient diet and further studies showed that he was correct. The disease became known as Beriberi and the cause was lack of the B1 vitamin, available in yeast, grains, nuts, and meats. Still, it took 60 years for the British Isles to recognize that foods contained micronutrients, i.e., vitamins and minerals, and without them various illnesses were exhibited. The term "vitamin" did not appear in print until 1912 and additional vitamins were not identified until 1920.[6]

In the 1800s while people were suffering from vitamin deficiencies, they were also suffering from diseases that were carried by bacteria and viruses. Note that Robert Koch showed that a bacteria caused cholera in 1876 and in the next 25 years bacteria were shown to cause diphtheria, typhoid, syphilis, pneumonia, and bubonic plague. The germ theory was "an enduring distraction" and led physicians searching for cures for vitamin deficiencies to look for germs. Of course there were the ideas of bad water, bad soil, toxins in the diet, and damp air as possible causes. The difficult concept to accept with vitamins was that it was the "absence" of something that was causing the disease.[5]

In addition to pellagra, scurvy, and Beriberi, caused by deficiencies in vitamins B3, C and B1 respectively, seven additional vitamins are in the top 10 most frequently seen deficiency diseases. Biotin deficiency and B7, rickets and vitamin D, ariboflavinosis and B2, bleeding and vitamin K, hypocobalaminemia and B12, paraesthesia and B5, nightblindness and vitamin A. Each of these vitamins has importance to good health and deficiencies lead to characteristic symptoms of adverse effects on health or even death. For example, vitamin A deficiency leads to nearly a half million deaths worldwide even today.[7] All the vitamins plus the minerals, like iron, copper, magnesium, etc., together number twenty-six in total. Deficiencies can occur with each, and more than one at a time if the diet is poor. Also, if the diet of an expectant mother is poor, the fetus will be adversely affected. Vitamins are required in very small amounts and thus are called micronutrients. For example, pregnant women are recommended to take a daily folate supplement, vitamin B9, of 240 micrograms, the weight of two grains of salt.

These vitamin deficiency diseases raise questions about how God might diagnose and deal with them in Heaven. Consider that Hippocrates documented scurvy in 1550 so people have been dying from vitamin deficiencies for centuries. Are all these people who died of vitamin deficiencies in

Heaven? Did God give each soul a healthy body? God has to recognize that a person may die of other causes but at the same time be suffering from a vitamin deficiency. God could know each case and the extent of the deficiency and have a record of each so that when a person died with the disease, he would know the situation. It would seem very difficult to do an assessment of a body after cremating, embalming, burial, and de-composition. Perhaps the soul carries with it the health status of the body, even vitamin deficiencies. Pellagra and scurvy cases were and still are seen worldwide, among different nationalities, genetic backgrounds, and ages, adding to the challenges. The Bible says that everyone will be healthy and happy in Heaven, free of devastating diseases. Does that include those caused by vitamin deficiencies? Presumably, in Heaven there will not be such problems, but it will be a challenge because of the need to provide a balanced diet to the billions of residents.

NOTES

1   Wikipedia website, "Vitamin deficiency," last edited May 12, 2023, https://en.wikipedia.org/wiki/Vitamin_deficiency.

2a H.E. Sigerist, *A History of Medicine* (New York: Oxford University Press, 1951), 35.

2b Randy Alcorn, *Heaven: A Comprehensive Guide to Everything the Bible Says About Our Eternal Home* (Illinois: Tyndale Momentum, 2004.)

3a Ben Crair, "Cereal Killers," *Smithsonian Magazine*, March 2018, 23-26.

3b Kristin B. Rattini, "Pellagra," *Discover* online, July 18, 2018, https://www.discovermagazine.com/health/the-american-souths-deadly-diet.

4   R. Grant, "Jack London in the Wild," *Smithsonian Magazine*, November 2019, 28-41.

5   healthline website, "7 Nutrient Deficiencies That Are Incredibly Common," published on May 21, 2019, https://www.healthline.com/nutrition/7-common-nutrient-deficiencies.

6   Catherine Price, "Death by Deficiency." In *Vitamania, Our Quest for Nutritional Perfection*, (New York: Penguin Press, 2015.) 27-46.

7   NOOR Natural Wellness website, "Vitamin Deficiency - Four Common Diseases Caused by Vitamin Deficiency," published October 23, 2016, www.noorvitamins.com/health-blog/vitamin-deficiency-diseases.

36

FOOD AND WATER
IN HEAVEN

WILL THERE BE an abundance of food and water in Heaven for the multitudes? Perhaps with Jesus being there in Heaven food may be provided by magic. The Bible says Jesus has that capacity. As Jesus was traveling through Galilee, visiting synagogues, preaching, healing people, and even controlling the wind and weather, he provided food for multitudes. His disciples told him the multitudes to whom he was preaching had no food and asked if they should go and buy bread. Jesus asked how much food was available and it was five loaves of bread and two fishes. Jesus commanded everyone to sit on the green grass and he took the bread and fish and looked up to Heaven, blessed it, and broke up the loaves and gave them to his disciples to set before those seated, and divided the fishes similarly. "And they did all eat and were filled. And they took twelve baskets full of the fragments and of the fishes (leftovers). And those that did eat of the loaves and fish were about five thousand men." (Mark 6:34-44) Alternatively, Albus Dumbledore, Headmaster of Hogwarts School of Witchcraft and Wizardry, could be recruited to magically provide food as he did for Harry Potter and the other students at his Hogwarts's school.[1] If food could be provided by magic there would be no hunger on earth, assuming no storage or distribution problems.

If we assume that all of the 107 billion people who have already died and the eight billion people alive today (total of 114.5 billion), all go to Heaven, the density of people in Heaven will be high. Alternatively, if we estimate that 25% will either be in Heaven already or will go to Heaven, then Heaven will have nearly thirty billion people, still a high density. Perhaps entry into Heaven will be severely limited. The maximum carrying capacity of the earth in numbers of humans is believed to be roughly nine billion, a figure predicted to be reached in the 2020s. Many on the earth now, eight billion, are already suffering from food, water, and energy shortages, and many cities are over-crowded and the air and water are polluted. If Heaven has thirty billion people, disposal of human wastes will be a major undertaking. Will there still be trash?[2]

To get an idea of what problems will be caused by that high a population density, one can look at China, a country with one-fifth of the world's population and only one-tenth of its farmland. Nearly 60% of China's population lives in cities; 40% on farms with 90% of the farms only 2.5 acres each. China's diet is more and more resembling the Western diet, as in USA diet, with more meat and dairy. That means China is raising more and more cattle, goats, pigs, and chickens to provide the meat and milk products. China has some industrialized farms now, like those in the USA. For example, one farm of 600 acres has eight huge barns with 2,880 milking cows (Holsteins) in each barn. Along with calves and pregnant cows the total animals is 40,000. Now, one in three dairy farms holds over 200 cows. Yes, much waste is produced and there is a persistent odor of manure. Bio-gas digesters are used by some companies to turn manure into energy. Some is turned into organic fertilizer as well. One chicken farm has three million hens producing 2.4 million eggs per day; one worker along with robots can tend to 170,000 chickens. Agriculture is the largest polluter of water in China. China also raises crabs and crayfish and various species of fish. China's food industry is continually evolving.[3]

China clearly recognizes the dire need for more food for its people. China also recognizes the importance of seeds for growing crops. Of the country's fifty-six ethnic groups, forty-one have their unique myths about the creation of seeds. The Dong ethnic group believes that a compassionate deity bestowed seeds onto the people (mortals). The Wa ethnic group thinks seeds were spat out of the mouth of a world-devouring snake after it was slain by God of Heaven. One innovation being used successfully by China is to send seeds into space, far enough above the atmosphere and the protective ozone layer to allow cosmic rays to bombard them rigorously, causing mutagenesis at a much faster rate than on earth, and thus resulting in modification of the genes, both good and bad. The seeds are then brought back to earth and planted, hoping for the good mutations to result in faster growth, more and larger vegetables and fruit, better adaptation to climate change, and other beneficial traits. A relatively recent finding is with the big red robe peppercorns, a highly valued spice in China, which normally has sharp thorns along the stems making it difficult to harvest. Some of its seeds, after being in space, gave rise to peppercorns devoid of the thorns. Further studies of the seeds and thornless plants are underway. China has already released over 200 such modified plants to the public and more are in development.[4] Perhaps Heaven's farmers will have an abundance of these super seeds to help grow enough food for Heaven's billions of residents.

Imagine at the second coming of Jesus all life on earth ends and everyone ends up being individually evaluated for life in Heaven or hell. Is the earth prepared to be turned into a Heaven? Where else could Heaven be? It seems that an atmosphere will be necessary to protect life from cosmic rays. When people refer to their deceased family or friends as being in Heaven, are they out there being bombarded by cosmic rays? If not "out there" then where? Is the soul immune to this bombardment?

One view is that Heaven is going to be right here on our present earth, which will become the "new" earth.[5] If that is the case, the amount of land area will not change. Where will the food and water come from to feed the multitudes in Heaven? How many industrialized farms will be needed? God might modify the bodies of people in Heaven so that metabolism is slower and more efficient and thus the need for food would not be so great. But God created humans in his image and it seems unlikely humans would be different in bodily physiology in Heaven than on earth. However, if growth and maturity are set rigidly at age 33, the prime of life, an active lifestyle would be expected and thus much food energy would be needed. If babies and children are going to be growing up and maturing in Heaven, energy and nutrition from food will be necessary.

A study done by the Center for Disease Control (CDC) found that people who were food insecure, those without reliable access to a "sufficient quantity of affordable, nutritious food," spent more money on health care than people who were food secure. The state with the highest level of food insecurity had a rate of 17% insecurity while the state with the lowest was 7.8%. Thus, food insecurity results in overall poorer health and these people will be going to Heaven in poorer health. God will have to diagnose the many health problems that are related to lack of nutritious foods. And God will hopefully ensure that there will be no food insecurity in Heaven.

Eating, it seems, is going be a necessary behavior in Heaven. The USA had 406 million acres of cropland in 2007 much of which went to providing food for livestock – the US slaughters 10 billion animals every year for food. God might provide only a vegetarian meal plan for everyone and thus eliminate the need for huge dairy, beef, pig, chicken, and turkey farms. Thus, the grains needed to maintain these farms would not be necessary and all of that farming would not be needed. Avoiding the huge amounts of manure produced from cattle or poultry would be a good thing in Heaven. Grains, vegetables, and fruits would go directly to the people in Heaven. To provide fiber and the essential amino acids for making proteins of the body, lentils, beans, quinoa, nuts, and whole wheat will have to be grown. Citrus fruits will be needed to provide vitamin C and fiber. Apparently, there will be fish eaten in Heaven that could be caught from the oceans, lakes, or rivers. But considering that the oceans are already over-fished it is not reasonable to expect that even more fish than now will be provided for the billions of people in Heaven.

God could provide more tillable land for growing crops but that would require regulating rainfall, increasing the fertility of soils that humans have depleted through the ages, and regulating climate so that the growing season is longer. How God would do these things would require major modifications of the earth's orbit, the tilt of the earth's axis, the energy production of the sun, and consistency in the earth's atmosphere (fewer greenhouse gasses etc.). With the present climate change continuing, more and more seacoast land is going to be underwater by the time Heaven is established here on earth.

In 2007 the US had about 406 million acres of land involved in growing crops. Much of that was for growing food for livestock. This amount of farmland was barely sufficient to feed 375 million US citizens. Many still go hungry.

Will the farms be mechanized? Will there be tractors, combines, and other modern equipment? Fuel will be needed to power the equipment. Will there be farm animals? Perhaps God will have everyone living like the Amish, each with a piece of land to grow their own food, or perhaps there will be communal farms. Without farm animals such as horses, oxen, and mules, the effort to till and plant the fields would fall on the shoulders of the people. Many in China are living like this.

Heaven is going to continue forever and ever. The balance between people and the land must be established in such a way by God that this continuation in Heaven is maintained.

Every year, almost three trillion pounds of food, nearly a third of all the food produced on earth, never reaches our plates. Why not? Because we waste so much. There is loss all along the way from the farm to our plate: picking and sorting; storage and shipping; during juice production; canning and baking; discarded at wholesalers and markets; uneaten and discarded at home; a total of 53% lost and wasted.[6] Imagine the waste in Heaven with thirty billion people. Will God magically produce food in Heaven? Will bodies in Heaven need fewer nutrients? And be more efficient in use of food? Will there be food-borne diseases?

What about drinks? Fresh water will be a must and our fresh water supplies are dwindling due to pollution and climate change (see Chap. 34) What about our favorite drinks, like coffee? Will there be coffee for breakfast and for mid-morning and mid-afternoon breaks? Fifty-two million pounds of coffee are consumed world-wide each day. Most of the world's coffee comes from SE Asia, Brazil, and Central America. Estimates are that half of that coffee growing land may be lost by 2050.[7] The same issues can be raised about tea, soft drinks, and alcoholic beverages. Maybe Heaven residents will have only water to drink. What a pity!

NOTES

1   J.K. Rowling, *Harry Potter and the Philosopher's Stone* (New York: Scholastic, 1998.)

2   R. Kunze, "The End of Trash," *National Geographic*, March., 2020, 42-71.

3   Tracie McMillan, "Feeding China," *National Geographic*, February 2018, 82-107.

4   Zhang Zhihao "Crops bred in space produce heavenly results," *China Daily* online, updated November 13, 2020, https://www.chinadaily.com.cn/a/202011/13/WS5faddbf8a31024ad0ba93d27_2.html.

5   Randy Alcorn, *Heaven: A Comprehensive Guide to Everything the Bible Says About Our Eternal Home* (Illinois: Tyndale Momentum, 2004.)

6   Elizabeth Royte, "Waste Not, Want Not," *National Geographic*, March, 2016, 30-55.

7   Kelsey Nowakowski, "A Climate for Coffee," *National Geographic*, September 2015, 12-13.

37

HAPPINESS

WILL EVERYONE BE happy in Heaven? Happiness is not universally found in all countries of the world. Finland, Denmark, Costa Rica, and Singapore have the highest rate of happiness among their citizens. The factors associated with happiness are a sense of purpose, low stress level, sense of security, and knowing how to maximize joy. These factors come about by having good health, friends and family, a balance of work and leisure activities, plenty of sleep, a healthy diet, a good home, and sufficient income.[1] Will all Heaven residents eat the same foods and the same amount of food? Alcorn[2] says that Heaven residents will have exceptional senses and will hear better, see better, and taste better. People might even be able to sense ultraviolet and infrared light. We will have excellent health and strength and not feel arrogance nor insecurity. Lots of wishful thinking here. God will be challenged to make Heaven a happy place.

NOTES

1 The World's Happiest Places, *National Geographic*, November, 2017, 32-59.
2 Randy Alcorn, *Heaven: A Comprehensive Guide to Everything the Bible Says About Our Eternal Home* (Illinois: Tyndale Momentum, 2004.)

Printed in the United States
by Baker & Taylor Publisher Services